Francis Rattenbury and British Columbia

FRANCIS RATTENBURY AND BRITISH COLUMBIA:

Architecture and Challenge in the Imperial Age

Anthony A. Barrett &
Rhodri Windsor Liscombe

University of British Columbia Press
Vancouver
1983

Francis Rattenbury and British Columbia
Architecture and Challenge in the Imperial Age
© The University of British Columbia Press 1983

This book has been published with the help of grants from the Canadian Federation for the Humanities using funds provided by the Social Sciences and Research Council of Canada, the British Columbia Heritage Trust, and the Canada Council.

ISBN 0-7748-0178-6

This book is printed on acid-free paper.
Printed in Canada

Canadian Cataloguing in Publication Data

Barrett, Anthony A., 1941–
  Francis Rattenbury and British Columbia

Includes index.
Bibliography: p.
ISBN 0-7748-0178-6

1. Rattenbury, Francis Mawson, 1867–1935.
2. Architects - Canada - Biography.
3. Architecture, Modern - British Columbia.
4. Architecture, British Columbia.
I. Liscombe, R. W., 1946– II. Title.

NA749.R3B37 1983   720'.92'4   C83-091407-2

To Doreen Barrett & Philippa Windsor Liscombe

CONTENTS

PREFACE

The decision to undertake a study of the life and work of Francis Mawson Rattenbury was prompted by the inherent interest of the subject, and by the absence of a detailed analysis of his professional career. Yet, the very nature of the project presented us with two major problems. The first was that whichever standard format we might choose for the book – an architectural monograph or a straightforward biography – the result would undoubtedly be less than satisfactory. Rattenbury arrived in Vancouver in 1892, on the eve of dramatic changes in British Columbia, and his participation in the history of the province until his departure in 1930 depended not only on his talent as an architect, but also on his enthusiastic response to the challenge presented by the development of the interior and the north. His architectural career, commercial ventures, land investments, private life, and personality were all so closely interwoven that to confine our study to any one facet would have been to present an incomplete, and even misleading, picture. Accordingly, we decided to combine architecture and biography, so as to make our account as comprehensive as possible. On the other hand, we have deliberately provided no more than a brief review of the circumstances surrounding his murder in Bournemouth, because the 'Rattenbury case' is chiefly significant in the context of English social and legal history and has been extensively treated.

The second problem seemed, for a time, to be insurmountable—namely, the apparent loss of his entire private correspondence. It is dangerous to rely on newspaper articles and personal reminiscences in the case of a controversial man like Rattenbury, whose success aroused envy and whose public and private conduct caused offence in Victoria. In the late 1970's, fortunately, it was discovered that a batch of the letters written to his relatives in England from 1893 to 1931 had survived. This correspondence was generously placed at our disposal by his family, and, recently, we were also given the opportunity to consult a smaller collection acquired by the Victoria City Archives in 1983. The new material has served to amplify the relatively limited archival records and to correct some, at least, of the misleading information originating from the press reports and local traditions.

The discovery of these letters initially suggested consideration of an annotated edition. That scheme was soon discarded because there is a chronological imbalance in the letters, with most dating from the early years of the century, and because much of the information relates to trivial family matters, fascinating as anecdotes of the domestic context in which Rattenbury worked, but hardly meriting publication in full. Nevertheless, some passages from the letters have deserved extensive quotation; the original text has not been emended except that, for the sake of clarity, we have, where necessary, regularized Rattenbury's somewhat informal punctuation.

Rattenbury was so prominent in the life of the province that it might seem as though an estimate of his personality and character should be an easy matter. Not so. Despite his extrovert and flamboyant manner, Rattenbury often masked his innermost feelings, even from his family. Since our intention has been to concentrate primarily on his accomplishments—and his failures—we have restricted ourselves to conveying the striking and salient features of his personality, inasmuch as these affected his career. In doing so, we have attempted to present the evidence objectively, aware that personal correspondence, if viewed uncritically, can itself be misleading. If Rattenbury emerges in a more favourable light than hitherto, then that is what the primary evidence has indicated.

The completion of this book would not have been possible without the valuable and much appreciated assistance of a number of individuals and institutions: we wish to thank the staffs of the Provincial Archives of British Columbia, the Victoria City Archives, the Vancouver City Archives, the University of British Columbia Library, the Vancouver

Public Library, the Bournemouth Public Library, the Bodleian Library, Oxford. We must also note our debt, for their personal help, to Penelope Seedhouse of the Victoria City Archives, to David Chamberlin of the Provincial Archives, Professor Dale McIntosh of the University of Victoria, Jennifer F. Heron of the Yukon Archives, Mrs. A. Retallack of the White Pass and Yukon Route, Mary Denys, Principal of Havergal College, Toronto, Brian Kelly, of British Columbia Hydro, Omer Lavallée and David Jones of the Canadian Pacific Corporate Archives, W.R. Mathews of Canadian Pacific Hotels (Toronto), Ted Balderson, General Manager of the Empress Hotel, Trevor J.D. Powell of the Saskatchewan Archives, Glen T. Wright of the Public Archives of Canada, Alison Habkirk of the Nanaimo Planning Department, the Archivists of the Canadian National Railway and Bank of Montreal, Sir Michael Havers, Mr. Raymond Massey, J. Watts, K.C. Mackenzie, and Peter Shankland.

We wish further to thank those people who graciously allowed us to visit their homes, Mr. and Mrs. B. Bowes, Mr. and Mrs. R. Driscoll, Mr. and Mrs. J. Edwards, Mr. and Mrs. J.M. Mears and Miss Vera Easton in Victoria, and Mrs. Antonia Landstein in Bournemouth. Ainslie Helmcken permitted us to examine recently acquired and as yet uncatalogued material at the Victoria City archives and shared with us his memories of Francis Rattenbury. Robert G. Hill, author of the forthcoming *Biographical Dictionary of Architects in Canada 1800–1950*, guided us to a number of references that we might otherwise have missed. Geoff Castle, of the Provincial Archives, has given most generously of his time and energies in locating archival material for us, as well as providing information on previously unknown Rattenbury commissions. Particular gratitude is owed to relatives of Francis and Alma Rattenbury, to H.R.H. Dolling, Mrs. Daphne Kingham, Bert Harbottle and Betty Brown, for their recollections and use of family papers; to Mrs. Katharine Bentley Beauman, for making available her material on the early history of the Rattenbury family. We wish to acknowledge the aid of the late Frank Rattenbury and Keith Miller Jones, respectively eldest son and nephew of the architect, both of whom died during the course of this project. A special debt must be recorded to both Rattenbury's second son and stepson, John Rattenbury and Christopher Compton Pakenham, who entrusted us with much of the primary material that forms the basis of this book. We have both been fortunate in having the support of our own families. Doreen Barrett has carefully read the proofs. Philippa Windsor

Liscombe gave invaluable help through her own researches and by refining the evolving text. Dr. Jane Fredeman, of the University of British Columbia Press, has provided excellent counsel since the inception of the project, while Brian Scrivener has dealt efficiently and cheerfully with the practical problems of putting the manuscript to press.

*Francis Rattenbury
and British Columbia*

Intro 1. James Bay, Victoria c.1908–1909, showing (right to left) the Legislative Buildings, the first C.P.R. Steamship Office and the Empress Hotel.

INTRODUCTION

Has it ever been your good fortune, gentle reader, to enter the harbor of Victoria, British Columbia, on a summer's afternoon or evening? If so, you will recall a scene of memorable loveliness. In the foreground a fleet of pleasure boats riding at anchor in James Bay; on the left the large business blocks of the commercial section of the city; directly in front of you the majestic Empress Hotel of the Canadian Pacific Railway system; on the right the imposing legislative buildings of the government of the province; and the whole picture is framed by a massive stone causeway, beyond which lie beautiful green lawns dotted with flowers and shrubbery. [1]

Francis Mawson Rattenbury (1867–1935) was born in the year in which Canada began her history as a self-governing dominion. He emigrated to British Columbia as a young architect in 1892 and was to make the provincial capital, Victoria, his home for almost forty years. He left in 1930, the year in which the imperial conference at London began the negotiations that would culminate in the Statute of Westminster and Canada's effective independence. During that time Rattenbury participated directly in the economic development of western Canada and, more importantly, designed a series of buildings for the chief government and commercial institutions which, besides signifying the growing consequence of British Columbia (a member of the Canadian confederation since 1871), lent dignity and character to its major centres. He was the architect of a number of the most familiar landmarks of the province, of which the Legislative Buildings, 1893–98, and the Empress Hotel, 1904–8, both in Victoria (Fig.1.1), and the Vancouver Courthouse, 1906–11 (Fig.6.2), are the most celebrated. Addressing the Royal Institute of British Architects on the subject of "Architecture in Canada" in January 1924, Percy Nobbs, then professor of design at McGill University (and later president of the Royal Architectural Institute of Canada) included Rattenbury's Legislative Buildings and Empress Hotel among his illustrations of the best work in the Dominion.[2]

Rattenbury had won the international competition for the Legislative Buildings within a year of his arrival in British Columbia. Armed with higher technical and aesthetic standards than most of the architects who had preceded him to the province, he also had the good sense to adjust his style to prevailing fashions, looking mainly to Britain and the eastern United States as the centres of taste, while at the same time promoting the use of local materials.[3] For such reasons, as F.W. Howay, the historian of the province, commented, the C.P.R. quickly enlisted "the genius of this new light in the architectural world, and deluged him with work," so that during the first decade of this century almost all the hotels in their Pacific Division were designed or renovated by Rattenbury. He had already earned the unofficial position of architect in British Columbia to the Bank of Montreal, which, in company with the C.P.R., exerted a fundamental influence on the development of the province. Thus, he dominated the profession in the province until his temporary retirement from active practice in 1918, eclipsing earlier British immigrant architects such as John Teague (1836–1902), Thomas Hooper (1858–1935), and a fellow Yorkshireman, Thomas Charles Sorby (1836–1924). Where they had been forced to tailor their work to suit the limited budgets and small town attitudes of their private and corporate patrons, Rattenbury benefited from the expansionist policies that boosted the growth of the British Columbia economy from the 1890's. The change is highlighted by the difference in cost, and hence scale and ornamental efffect, between the two hotels the C.P.R. commissioned in 1887 and 1903: Sorby's modest Hotel Vancouver (Fig.1.2) and Rattenbury's impressive Empress Hotel. The comparison also underlines Rattenbury's greater talent, which aroused resentment in many of his rivals, whose jealousy spawned some of the hostile insinuations that persist to the present day. Only his friend, Samuel Maclure (1860–1929), gained a comparable fame, and then chiefly in the field of domestic design. By contrast, Rattenbury's renown depended upon a much broader practice, ranging from large-scale official buildings to small houses and displaying a wider vocabulary of styles. He set the pattern, or patterns, given the number of styles he used, for institutional architecture in British Columbia before the First World War. Thus his courthouses at Nanaimo and Vancouver, for example, were copied respectively by J.J. Honeyman at Rossland and by Honeyman in partnership with G.D. Curtis at Revelstoke. Moreover, he evolved a Neo-Tudor domestic style quite as early as had Maclure, both men seeking to celebrate the imperial connection with Britain. Rattenbury, no less than Maclure or R. Mackay Fripp (whose domestic practice flourished in Edwardian Vancouver), popularized the imitation of recent British domestic design and thus contributed to what Eastern Canadian architects saw as the "distinctness of type about British Columbia building."[4]

Rattenbury did more than manipulate a succession of styles. If parts of his earlier buildings in the province exhibit a kind of stylistic indigestion, those he designed from the second half of the 1890's, while still synthesizing a variety of sources, achieve an increasingly harmonious and appropriate aesthetic effect. These changes reflect a maturing of his ability to design and parallel a gradual consolidation of the Classical elements in his architecture. Nor was he content to be a passive exponent of current stylistic fashions. He reinterpreted the so-called Château mode, which, just before his arrival, had come to be considered the Canadian national style by virtue of its mixture of English and French mediaeval and Renaissance features. In place of the irregular, or Picturesque composition favoured by predecessors such as Bruce Price, architect of the Château Frontenac Hotel in Quebec City, 1892–93 (Fig.1.3), Rattenbury developed a more symmetrical rendering, epitomized by the Empress, which was emulated by most of its later adherents. Equally distinctive was his more austere version of the renewed spate of Classicism in European and American architecture at the turn of the century, culminating in one of the last of his designs to be constructed in the province, the second C.P.R. Steamship Terminal 1924–25. Neatly composed, elegantly proportioned, and nicely ornamented, it is a pleasing variation on the Classical temple theme (Figs.8.6–7).

Nevertheless, Rattenbury's talents as an architect should not be inflated. He was not endowed with outstanding powers of originality either in the use of stylistic sources or in planning. Nor was he an intellectual architect in the sense of pursuing a theoretical approach to design. Indeed, he seldom commented on such aspects of his profession, and when he did, he invariably supported a conservative, traditional attitude. His sense of scale, if grander and more worthy of the destiny of the province than that of any of his contemporaries, was not *truly* monumental—the ensemble of buildings he placed around the Inner Harbour of Victoria having been partly overshadowed by more recent, less inspired, development. Taken as a whole, his architecture did not match the sophistication of composition, plan, and decoration created by the best of the next generation of Canadian architects, such as Sproatt and Rolph of Toronto, the brothers E. and W.S. Maxwell of Montreal or the Somervell-Putnam and McCarter-Nairne partnerships of Vancouver. Admittedly, they did have the benefit of the greater prosperity and generally higher aesthetic expectations that prevailed in Canada from the second decade of the century.[5]

Rattenbury's achievements were considerable, yet his contribution to the architecture of western Canada has received relatively little attention. A major reason for this oversight undoubtedly stems from a disproportionate concern with the more controversial episodes of his life in Victoria, culminating in his divorce and remarriage in 1925, and with the tragic circumstances that surrounded his murder in Bournemouth, England, in 1935. This has resulted in a neglect of his professional accomplishments and a preoccupation with what has been perceived as his personal failings. Thus, while Howay admired what he called Rattenbury's "great energy and determination," later commentators have tended to interpret these same characteristics negatively, seeing him as over-ambitious and even devious, given to arrogance, ill-temper, and meanness. However, an objective appraisal of the remaining private and public documents suggests that his personality was a good deal less stereotyped.

Rattenbury was certainly ambitious, but in the sense that he saw his career as a series of challenges to be met with determination. "The greatest game in life," he wrote to his daughter Mary in 1920, "is to set out to do something, strive against all difficulties, and win." He was not ambitious to the extent of seeking to thwart professional colleagues unfairly nor of pursuing personal vendettas; on the contrary, his colleagues admired him enough to elect him president of the British Columbia Architectural Association in 1911 and honorary president a year later.[6] Nor was he unwilling to acknowledge the talents of competing architects. In a letter written in 1901, bearing the letterhead of the Château Frontenac Hotel in Quebec City, he praised its design, continuing with apparently genuine modesty, "It was built by Bruce Price, who went in for the Hotel Vancouver, but if I had realized what he could do, I would never have dreamed of competing against him." The Hotel Vancouver was, in fact,

Intro 2. T.C. Sorby, first C.P.R. Hotel, Vancouver, 1887–1888.

Intro 3. B. Price, Château Frontenac Hotel, Quebec City, 1892–1893.

but one of a series of commissions that Rattenbury won in anonymous competitions, discounting the popular view that his architectural success depended primarily upon favour. Equally unfounded, as his correspondence proves, is the persistent rumour that he stole the design for the British Columbia Legislative Buildings from his architect uncle and refused to pay him a share of the fees.

Similarly, Rattenbury's undoubted parsimony should not be overestimated. Throughout a relatively prosperous career he showed a marked reluctance to spend even trifling sums. Yet this frugality was often something of a pose, one that Yorkshiremen have traditionally liked to assume: "I see that I have inadvertently drifted on to a second sheet," he could write in 1900 to his mother, to whom he was consistently generous, "I am of a frugal nature and do not like wasting good paper." In the same vein he would write from London in 1919 to his daughter, to whom he was equally generous, that gloves in England were so expensive that she would have to paint her hands. Such banter with one's own family might not be thought especially revealing. But it is apparent that his own employees were not afraid to tease him about his legendary stinginess, as when in 1920 George Wood, manager of Rattenbury's land company, ended a letter with the remark that Mrs. Wilmot from the office would have sent her regards but she knew that he would complain about the cost of the paper. When faced with cases of real need, Rattenbury dropped this humorous façade as, for example, in the case of those of his fellow immigrants who had fallen on hard times. They are no more than names today, men like Tom Townsley of Leeds, who sought him out when "shattered in health and without a dollar," or Mr. Borrison, who was "completely broke" and whose family had come "completely to grief." Rattenbury gave money to Townsley and found a job for Borrison, planting trees in the grounds of his home in Oak Bay.

Rattenbury's temper was likewise the subject of much family humour. Writing to his sister in June 1900, he observed wryly of his infant son, "He never cries when he hurts himself, but if he does not get all he wants, how he howls! I cannot imagine where he gets his 'devil of a temper.' Not from me, I am sure." If this testiness caused friction in his dealings with politicians and officials, it does not seem to have seriously affected his relations with friends and colleagues. Hayter Reed, manager-in-chief of the C.P.R. hotels, for instance, recorded that he found Rattenbury "a charming man to work with."[7]

Nevertheless, Rattenbury did suffer from serious shortcomings. He was frequently impatient and invariably scornful of potential or real adversaries. "Nobody went in except duffers," he wrote scathingly on 16 August 1901, with reference to the commission for rebuilding Cary Castle, the lieutenant-governor's official residence, only to modify this opinion once it had been granted to him. Much later, on 17 May 1928, he explained the denial of his appeal against the levying of taxes by the British Columbia government on his northern properties on the grounds that "the local judges are political appointees." Such pronouncements reveal a chronic inability to acknowledge the truth when it threatened to confound his current enthusiasm or opinion. Indeed, his most striking failing was this capacity for self-deception. There may perhaps be something engaging in the youthful, if unrealistic, boast proudly made to his mother about his Yukon shipping company, that the leading newspapers of the world "all contain views of our steamers." But this trait persisted through middle life, involving him in costly land speculation and ruinous lawsuits against the government. Even in his old age, after shrewdly dealing with men at the centre of power, he was capable of believing implicitly in the smooth patter of a London music publisher, writing excitedly to his sister that his second wife, a moderately successful writer of popular songs, stood "in the centre of London [musical] life." In fact, beyond the field of his professional experience, Rattenbury's judgment, especially of people, was often poor. He seems to have assessed his acquaintances more by their social geniality than by their intrinsic qualities. Many were to desert him or even to join his detractors when he broke the rigid conventions of life in Victoria by his marital infidelity.

While opinions may be divided on Rattenbury's personal conduct and architectural accomplishments, there can be no denying that he was a man of initiative and of highly diverse interests. Shortly after arriving in British Columbia, he became involved in a scheme to market prefabricated houses, presumably for fellow immigrants intent upon settling the interior of the province, though the only order appears to have come from the Canary Islands. More dramatic, and successful for a while, was the provision of an efficient transport system to the Yukon goldfields in 1898–1900. Rattenbury's faith in the future of the Canadian Northwest remained undiminished despite the virtual collapse of his venture when gold was found in Alaska in 1899. In 1906 he acquired property in Edmonton at the outset of its development and interests in a local brewery. Apart from comparable land and business speculations in Victoria, including the ownership of a profitable decorating firm, he committed the bulk of his capital to the purchase of land abutting the proposed Grand Trunk Pacific line in the Bulkley and Nass Valleys and along the Nechako

River. Beyond the hope of gain, he seems to have been genuinely concerned to encourage agricultural settlement in that region. Regrettably, his drive and vision were not matched by sound business judgement, and in contrast with his sustained architectural success, his entrepreneurial activities invariably involved him in major financial losses.

Rattenbury was indeed a notable representative of those enterprising young professionals who emigrated to distant and unfamiliar lands in the late nineteenth century, not merely for the prospect of wealth but also for the challenge of forging a new society. The vigour and confidence of the Imperial Age pervade the letters he wrote to his relatives and are embodied in his architecture and schemes for land development. The significance of Rattenbury's contribution to the heritage of British Columbia — and Canada — was, in the words of a commentator on the architecture of Victoria's Inner Harbour, "an object lesson in the miraculous evolution of the West."[8]

One

BACKGROUND
1867–1892

On 1 June 1903, Francis Rattenbury wrote to his mother from the Canadian Pacific Railway hotel that he had lately enlarged at Field, set high in the Rocky Mountains. In his letter he mentioned that a certain F. Morton Rattenbury of Prince Edward Island had recently brought him a book, "descriptive of the foundation of 'Okehampton,' Devonshire." The "Rattenburys seem to have played a great part in it in the days of Henry VIII and Charles I. There were many Johns, a Francis, Catherine and others. They were Mayors often, and entertained at their house Charles I on two occasions. They had coats of arms which are now on plate. They gave to the church still in existence. I will send on the book; it will interest the Gov'nor. I did not know the Rats were such an old and very respectable family, nearly always leaders."

The book was undoubtedly Wright's new edition of W.B. Bridge's *Some Account of the Barony and Town of Okehampton*, published in 1889, and, while there is no evidence to indicate that Rattenbury was a serious student of history, he did have a romantic appreciation of the subject and a strong sense of the continuity of tradition, an attitude that he displayed in his architecture. This book may have stimulated him to delve into his ancient links with Okehampton, and his decision to quit British Columbia in 1929 was determined, in part, by the desire to have his second son, John, christened in its parish church.

The recorded history of the Okehampton Rattenburys began in the late fifteenth century when a Bavarian lady, who cannot now be identified, came from her home town of Ratenburg to England to be married into the powerful Courtenay family, which held the earldom of Devon. She was escorted on her journey by a leading citizen of the town, Johannes von Ratenburg. So charmed was he by Devon, that instead of returning to his native Bavaria, he anglicized his name and settled in the vicinity of Okehampton.[1] Nothing is known of the subsequent history either of Johannes or of his immediate descendants until one James Rattenbury was listed in a charter signed by Henry VII, recognizing the privileges of certain burghers of Okehampton. In 1620 a visitation of Devon was conducted, and the diary of John Rattenbury, the incumbent mayor of Okehampton under Charles I, has survived.[2] Information from these sources, amplified by entries in the parish registers, reveals that by then the family had become firmly established in the area. Apart from serving as mayor, John Rattenbury was appointed coroner of the County of Devon and enjoyed the confidence of King Charles, who stayed with him in 1644 "on returning from Tavistock." Other members of the family held public offices in the town, though not all prospered; for instance in 1688, Edward Rattenbury is reported to have "drowned going home to his house in a poole beyond Beare Bridge." More fortunate was Hester Rattenbury, granddaughter of Robert Rattenbury, another mayor of the borough. According to Wright's account, Hester, "after a protracted illness, lay to all appearances, dead" until "the person engaged in performing the last offices, remarking the want of that change which betokens actual death, thought of holding a looking-glass over her mouth." Restored by bleeding, she presented a flagon bearing "her name and family arms" and lived to be buried on 14 October 1770. Quite different was the John Rattenbury, born in 1778 at Beer, Devon, who made a living as a privateer and smuggler before retiring in 1836 on a pension of one shilling a week provided by Lord Rolle. His reminiscences were published as the *Memoirs of a Smuggler based on the Diaries of John Rattenbury, commonly called The Rob Roy of the West*. The diary states that one of this John's sons was charged at the Exeter Assizes after a fracas with the local excise officers.

The northern branch of the family was established at the beginning of the nineteenth century when Henry Rattenbury (1783–1825), a builder and contractor of Tavistock, moved to Manchester, taking his son, John (1806–1879) (Fig.1.1). On his father's death, John resolved to enter the Methodist ministry and pursued his vocation with an extraordinary de-

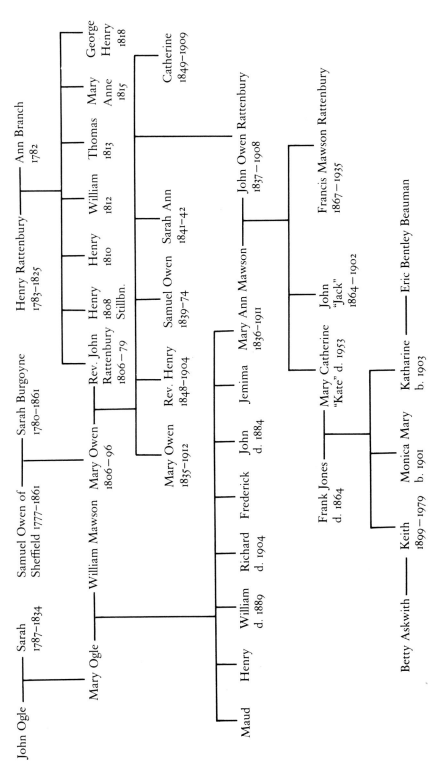

1.1 Rattenbury family tree.

votion, even to the extent of ignoring current fashion and shaving his upper lip clean the better to project his voice.[3] He was eventually elected president of the Wesleyan Conference. One of his sons, Henry (1848–1904), also became a Methodist minister, as did two of his grandsons, John Ernest (1870–1963) and Harold Burgoyne (1878–1961), the latter also serving as president. "The Rattenbury family," Harold's obituarist wrote in *The Times* of London on 28 December 1961, "is one of a series of notable Methodist ministerial dynasties."

The Reverend John Rattenbury spent much of his life on circuit, carrying God's Word through the squalid manufacturing towns of the West Riding of Yorkshire, with a determination and passion for improvement to be inherited by Francis Rattenbury, his grandson. The woollen industry flourished there in the nineteenth century, largely as a result of the almost total monopoly commanded by the Yorkshire mills in imperial trade. While this brought great prosperity to the mill owners, the rapid industrialization of the countryside and the overcrowding of the cities inevitably caused widespread disease and poverty. In these circumstances the life of a circuit minister, who was obliged to uproot himself every few years and move from one dismal town to another, was hard and challenging. He was fortunate to find a compatible wife, who was able to share his mission and the adversities it entailed, in Mary Owen (1806–1896), the only child of Samuel Owen (1777–1840), a prosperous coal merchant and a prominent member of the Methodist congregation in his home town of Sheffield (Fig.1.2). They had six children, one of whom, Sarah Ann, died at birth. By contrast with their third son, Henry, who entered the ministry, their two other sons were restless, even feckless by temperament. Samuel Owen (1839–1874), according to the family Bible, "ran away from home," and no details of his later life have survived, while John Owen (1837–1908), the father of the architect, went to sea.[4] Young John, however, soon returned to Yorkshire, where, no doubt to the satisfaction of his parents, he married Mary Ann Mawson, a member of a prominent Yorkshire family. The Mawsons had made their fortune in the woollen industry, but they had other interests. Mary's father owned a printing firm in Leeds, and two of her brothers, William and Richard, were highly successful architects in Bradford.[5]

John and Mary were wed in 1862 in Leeds, and, for a while, he endeavoured to settle down to the routine of a career in business. The couple took up residence in the respectable Leeds suburb of Headingly where John worked first for the Mawson woollen firm and then, briefly, for an insurance company. By the early 1870's he decided to devote him-

1.2 John and Sarah Ogle, Rattenbury's great-grandparents on his mother's side.

1.3 Kate and her husband Frank Jones in the 1930's.

1.4 Lockwood and Mawson, Saltaire, Yorkshire, from 1858, showing the alpaca mill.

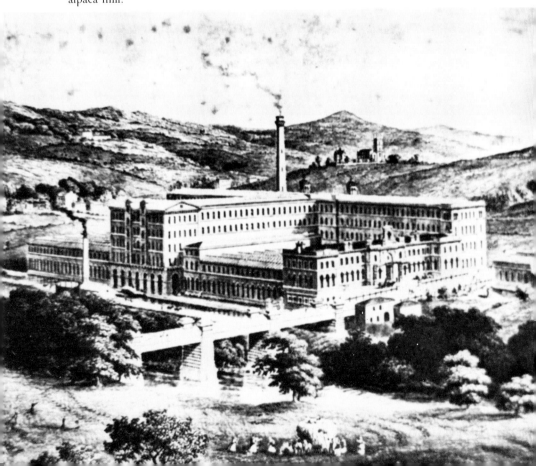

1.5 Lockwood and Mawson, St. George's Hall, Bradford, 1851–1853.

1.6 Lockwood and Mawson,
The Wool Exchange, Bradford,
1864–67.

1.7 Lockwood and Mawson, Town Hall, Bradford, 1873–1875.

1.8 C. Broderick, Town Hall, Leeds, 1853–1858.

self to painting. This did not shock his relatives as much as might be expected, for in nineteenth-century England the artistic profession had become socially acceptable and financially viable. Moreover, his two surviving sisters, Mary Owen (1835–1912) and Catherine (1849–1909), were talented artists. John was a genial character who is still remembered by his granddaughter, Mrs. Katharine Beauman, as a "quiet man" whom "we usually saw sitting behind an easel surrounded by oil paints and brushes." Although he sold the occasional canvas locally, real success eluded him. He was forced to copy the paintings of the popular artists of the day and became the butt of family teasing. The general impression of John is that he was a somewhat inconsequential figure, and Rattenbury's attitude towards his father, as evidenced by a postscript added to a letter written to his mother some time in 1900, while good-humoured, seems to verge on the patronizing:

> What are you painting now, daddy? Grapes? It used to be dogs, then deer, then Italian scenes and sea-pieces, then birds' nests and eggs and then grapes and an apple, I believe. You ought to go in now for the Dutch school and paint "Welsh rarebit," as they used to be a specialty of yours, or when particularly bobbish and inclined to be a gay dog, a "buck rabbit," or perhaps a boiled onion and roast potato would make a touching subject.

By contrast, Mary was much admired by her architect son. She was a woman of strong will, on whom responsibility for the family devolved. Yet her authority was tempered by a lively sense of humour, and she seems to have inspired both the respect and affection of all who knew her.

John and Mary Rattenbury had three children, Mary Catherine (Kate) (Fig.1.3), who died in 1953, after having been a history teacher at Leeds Girls' High School, John, "Jack", (1864–1902), who entered the merchant navy, and Francis Mawson, born in Leeds on 11 October 1867. Theirs was a closely knit family, and Francis apparently enjoyed a happy childhood. In later life, he reminisced to his mother, "It does not seem long since I was hanging up my stocking. I never remember you once filling it, though I used to try and keep awake."[6] He was also to recall pleasant family holidays in the Lake District, as well as his earliest independent adventure when, at the age of thirteen, he pedalled his first bicycle to Lincoln.[7] He was educated at Leeds Grammar school and, despite the fact that he was reputed to have been involved in frequent scraps with his fellow pupils, the surviving report cards indicate that his academic record and behaviour were exemplary. Thereafter he enrolled as a student at the Yorkshire College, an institution which offered vocational training in various aspects of the woollen industry. But he chose not to enter the tex-

tile trade and, doubtless under the influence of his uncles, decide
become an architect. Referring in a 1901 letter to his choice of career, ..
complimented his mother for nurturing his artistic talent. Apparently,
in December 1884, he had amused himself by drawing a number of
Christmas cards which his mother brought to the attention of his uncles:
"It does not seem long since I made those Christmas cards which led to me
going to Uncle's office. For me that was a lucky thing."[8]

William and Richard Mawson were by then partners in one of the leading architectural practices in Yorkshire. In 1849 William had formed a
partnership with H.F. Lockwood, and they were joined a few years later
by Richard. The reputation of the firm was to be founded on the commission to design the ideal manufacturing town of Saltaire (Fig.1.4),
awarded in 1858 by the progressive and liberal-minded industrialist, Sir
Titus Salt.[9] Over the ensuing twenty years they superintended the erection of the alpaca mill (the structure and machinery being the work of the
celebrated engineer, Sir William Fairbairn), nearly nine hundred workers'
houses, two churches, a school, and the Saltaire Institute. They also
designed many of the important civic buildings in the chief towns of the
West Riding of Yorkshire, Harrogate, Keighley, and, particularly, Bradford, where they were responsible for St. George's Hall, 1851, the Exchange, 1864–67, and the Town Hall, 1873, ranging in style from the
Classical to the Venetian and Flemish Gothic (Figs.1.5–7). Their effective
use of historical sources and efficient planning fulfilled the traditionalism
and prosaic requirements of the Victorian middle class, and thus brought
commissions from further afield, as, for example, a branch of Barclay's
Bank in Boston, Lincolnshire, 1853,[10] the Clock Tower in Airmyn, 1865,
the Victoria Chambers in Leeds, 1870, and the Wakefield Building
Society office at Wakefield, 1879.

Rattenbury began his architectural career in 1885, by which time the
firm had been renamed Mawson and Mawson (later Mawson and Hudson), since Lockwood, perhaps the most talented of the partners, had
moved to London in 1874.[11] During his period of training, he continued
to live with his parents in Leeds, travelling each morning to Bradford by
the 8.32 train.[12] Already he was beginning to exercise the frugality that
became a lifelong trait. He preferred to save the money allowed by his
mother for lunches, so that his family was constantly amazed by the vora-
cious appetite that he displayed at the evening meal. Conversely, his
bachelor uncles lived in great style, driving about in their phaeton and
attending parties at the houses of the local notables, including Tranby
Croft, a favourite haunt of the Prince of Wales.

Under the supervision of his uncles, Rattenbury received a solid training, centred on a largely commercial and institutional practice. He would have gained experience in utilitarian planning, structural design, and, of equal importance, the manipulation of a number of historical styles, chief among which were the Italianate (or Renaissance) and the Classical. Victorians and Edwardians generally believed that the progress of modern industrial society was most appropriately celebrated in the architectural reflection of its historical origins in the Classical, Mediaeval, and Renaissance cultures.[13] This notion was no less prevalent in such developing "outposts" of civilization as British Columbia, as Rattenbury was to find to his advantage.

The humane and orderly plan of Saltaire, and the architectural richness and substance of the Yorkshire towns in which he lived and worked (Fig.1.8) were to inspire his endeavours to improve the urban landscape of western Canada. More specifically, the firm's eclecticism implanted a flexible approach to design in Rattenbury, who, once in British Columbia, confronted a wide variety of environments, as well as of commissions. He was evidently also encouraged to keep abreast of recent popular trends in architecture, most notably the "Queen Anne" style (Fig. 1.9). This had been fashioned by Richard Norman Shaw from the late Mediaeval and early Renaissance architecture of seventeenth-century Britain and Holland and was appreciated on both sides of the Atlantic because it allowed greater artistic freedom than the preceding Greek and Gothic Revivals. The Queen Anne style, with its varied outline and gables, was to prove especially appropriate to British Columbia and to Vancouver Island in particular, where the climate is similar to that of Britain.[14] Equally suitable was the related Arts and Crafts style, distinguished by more simply composed vernacular motifs and more convenient plans. Another highly important transatlantic development was the adaptation of French Romanesque architecture pioneered by Henry Hobson Richardson, an American architect whose work was admired by British critics and regularly illustrated in the British professional journals.[15] The Richardsonian Romanesque obviously impressed the young Rattenbury, who, in his first major Canadian design (for the British Columbia Legislative Buildings), imitated something of its bold composition of broad three-dimensional forms, powerful arched openings, and strongly patterned masonry (Fig.1.10).

Rattenbury's awareness of current English fashion, as well as his own architectural promise, are apparent in his "Design for a Public Day School," for which he won the Soane Medallion in 1890. This prestigious award was organized under the auspices of the Royal Institute of British

1.9 R. N. Shaw, Leyswood, Surrey, 1868, the pioneering example of the Queen Anne Style.

1.10 H. H. Richardson, Allegheny County Courthouse, Pittsburgh, 1884–1888, the epitome of 'Richardsonian Romanesque.'

91. Allegheny County Courthou Pittsburgh. Plan, 1884-88.

Architects, and was made to students and articled architects after a national competition. Rattenbury's plans were published in *The British Architect*, together with a fine perspective view of the façade, signed "F. Mawson Rattenbury, Invt." (Figs.1.11–12)[16] Despite the reduction in size of the incidental figures (intended to enhance the scale of his design), the drawing is accomplished for a twenty-two year old student. The irregular external composition creates a picturesque effect that is reinforced by the pleasing diversity of the ornamental features. The least effective part is, perhaps, the bell-turret, even if its mixture of complex form and intricate detailing echoed contemporary English taste. In a short description printed in *The British Architect* on 4 April, Rattenbury commented that the design was based "on the type of the old Elizabethan Grammar Schools." The Elizabethan character (and the new importance of the state-funded school in the late nineteenth-century British society) was to be denoted by the textured "ashlar wallstones and red tiles for the roof," while the ceiling of the assembly hall, to the left of the entrance and above a gymnasium, was "to be of oak with enriched plaster panels." However, he was at pains to emphasize that his "dignified and picturesque structure" was arranged on simple lines, affording "ample light and air to every part of the building." His concern for the functional aspects of architecture was further evident in the placing of the lecture theatre on the ground floor, with its general entrance reached from the lower landing of the main staircase "in order that it should be easily accessible for the public on the occasion of popular lectures." Similarly, the master's rooms and library were separated off in the lower gabled section on the left side, neatly fitted in adjacent to the lavatories (conveniently close to the covered playground). Another instance of his already intelligent planning was the situating of the kitchen and laboratory "on the upper floors, so that no odours from them should permeate through the class rooms." He had also "carefully worked out" the heating and ventilation system, detailed in a separate report accompanying his design.

The composition of the Soane Medallion school, comprising a lower block linked by a staircase tower to a cross-axial gabled projection, is echoed in the Queen Anne style Town Hall, built at Cleckheaton, near Bradford in 1891 (Fig.1.13).[17] Rattenbury was later to refer to the Cleckheaton design as his own, and the fact that it was attributed not to him but to Mawson and Hudson at the 1891 Royal Academy Exhibition might be explained by the junior position he then occupied in the firm. The town hall exhibits many details characteristic of Rattenbury. In several of his British Columbia buildings, he was to refine its Queen Anne style and embody versions of its compositional features. The Cleckheaton tower, topped by an arcaded octagonal lantern and dome, reappears on the Legislative Buildings in Victoria, while the asymmetrical arrangement of the tower and projection prefigure a recurrent motif on his houses and later hotel designs. The curved "Dutch" gable on the projection to the right of the tower reappears on the Nelson Courthouse, 1903–1909. The dominance of the tower, in deliberate contrast to the falling ground on one side of the building, foreshadows his striving after grand scale and exploitation of site. The underlying practicality of his mature work is also anticipated in the concentration of decoration on the main front, the compact plan, and the ample windows on the longer side (providing light for the Council Chamber).

In the spring of 1892, Rattenbury decided to leave his native Yorkshire, realizing that his prospects for independent success within Mawson and Hudson were limited. The local economy was less buoyant and the firm had passed its zenith, William Mawson having died in 1889 (though Richard remained professionally active until his death in 1904). But why did he choose British Columbia? The Rattenbury family had no known personal connections with Canada, unless one counts the three miserable months that John Rattenbury the smuggler endured at St. John's, Newfoundland, curing cod. F. Morton Rattenbury of Prince Edward Island – or the "pork packer," as Francis dubbed him – was undoubtedly related, but unknown to him until he received the Okehampton book in 1903.[18] So there was no one to greet him when he first reached Canada. "Here I am at the old Windsor again," he later mused in a letter written to his mother from this celebrated Montreal hotel in 1905, "It recalls many memories. I came here first some twelve years ago when I first landed in Canada and when I knew no-one."[19]

His decision to emigrate to British Columbia was probably inspired by reports in the British press of the burgeoning economy of the province. This had been spurred by the arrival of the Canadian Pacific Railway tracks at Vancouver in 1887 and the award to the company in 1889 by the British government of a £60,000 subsidy for the movement of mail from the Pacific dominions and Far Eastern colonies to Britain. Rattenbury must have concluded, correctly, that the growth of development in the lower mainland would produce a spate of public and commercial buildings and that the consequent creation of a prosperous capitalist class held out the prospect of valuable domestic commissions. Also, the potential

THE
SOANE MEDALLION
DESIGN FOR A
PUBLIC DAY SCHOOL

1.11 Elevation of Rattenbury's design for a Public Day School, 1890.

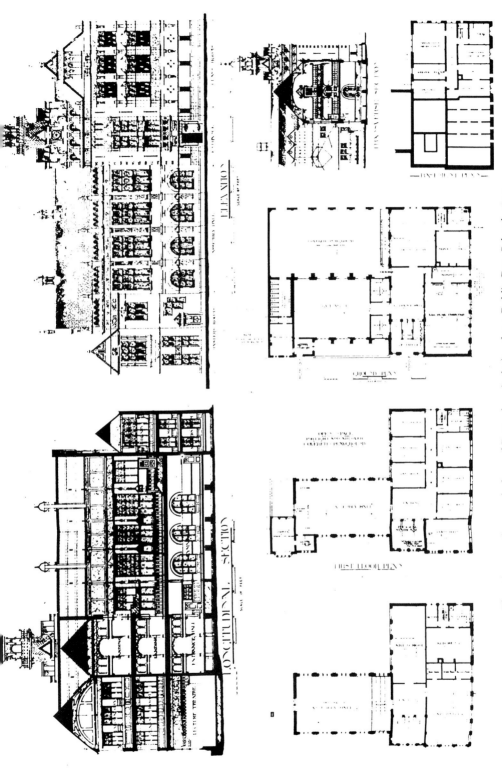

1.12 Elevation, sections and plans of Rattenbury's design for a Public Day School, 1890.

1.13 Town Hall, Cleckheaton, Yorkshire, 1891.

1.16 Rattenbury at the time of his arrival in Canada.

1.15 E. Hughes, Technical School, Huddersfield, 1881–1884.

1.14 Vancouver, showing the harbour front, C.P.R. railway tracks and Burrard Inlet, c.1892.

of the former British colony had been remarked by a number of authors, including W. G. Blaikie, a distinguished Presbyterian whose books would probably have been read by an educated Nonconformist family like the Rattenburys. Blaikie's *Summer Suns in the Far West*, an account of a journey through North America published in 1890, contained a description of Vancouver that could well have excited the young man's ambition:

> Its site was unmitigated forest in 1885, and in June 1886 every building that had been erected was burned to the ground. The city is literally only three years old. And though I have been used to the sight of cities of rapid growth, I must say that Vancouver beats them all. It is already a city of long streets, big blocks, handsome churches, and elegant villas. The Vancouver Hotel, built by the Canadian Pacific Railway, is as commodious and handsome a house as you could desire. Many persons connected with that railway have bought lots and built blocks in Vancouver, of course with the object of booming the place. And now the price of land is simply ridiculous. I was told of a couple of building stances that had been sold lately for thirty-two thousand dollars. Whether this boom will last is doubtful; but the town seems to grow apace meanwhile.

Precisely how and when the twenty-four year old Francis Rattenbury reached Vancouver is unknown (later press reports state that the transatlantic voyage was preceded by a study tour of Europe), but it seems that he travelled across Canada on the C.P.R. transcontinental express in the spring of 1892. Thus he would have had some preparation for the tremendous changes in scale and cultural environment in which he would find himself. His correspondence tells of the excitement he experienced in steaming through the glorious mountain ranges of the west, the outer fringes of which skirted the bustling frontier town of some 14,000 people that was to be his first Canadian home.[20] But the letters do not record his initial impressions upon disembarking onto the planked C.P.R. Vancouver station, perched above the shores of Burrard Inlet and below the still haphazard collection of mainly wooden two- and three-storey buildings, thrusting out from the original 1860 Granville townsite (Fig.1. 14). Dotted among these clapboard structures were some brick and stone buildings, notably Thomas Sorby's simplified Château-style C.P.R. Hotel of 1887 at the corner of Georgia and Granville, the florid Italianate J. W. Horne Block on Water Street, and the more sophisticated Queen Anne style J. W. Browning House at the northwest intersection of Georgia and Burrard Streets. All of these he could have related to his

English background, for even the supposedly Canadian Château style had antecedents in Britain, one being the Technical School that had been erected 1881–84 in the Yorkshire manufacturing town of Huddersfield, complete with the steeply pitched roof and the contrast between large forms and more delicate tracery decoration of the Châteaux in the Loire valley (Fig.1.15).

This kinship with his former milieu, together with the evident scarcity of professional architects and such signs of ebullient growth as the British Columbia Electric Railway line, probably fired rather than diminished his enthusiasm. Certainly, in contemporary photographs, his strongly modelled features radiate an air of self-confidence and determination. Tall and possessed of a good physique, he wore a heavy moustache in the fashion of that period, said, like his hair, to have been of a reddish brown hue. He was clearly bent upon establishing himself as a leading architect and thereby participating in the realization of the "splendid destiny" of British Columbia (Fig.1.16).

Two

EARLY SUCCESS
1892–1898

Throughout his career Francis Rattenbury was keenly aware of the importance of public relations and characteristically advertised his arrival in Vancouver, which, despite the impression that he might have gained from his readings in Britain, was then in the throes of an economic depression that persisted until 1896. "Mr. Francis Rattenbury," the *Vancouver Daily World* announced on 5 July, 1892 had "opened an office in the New Holland Block, Cordova Street," after "ten years erecting all classes of buildings in conjunction with the well-known firm of Lockwood and Mawson of Bradford." Understandably, Rattenbury did not dissuade the newspaper from embroidering the precise nature of his experience, for while some people might just have heard of Lockwood and Mawson, scarcely any would know of the firm under its new name of Mawson and Hudson. He was, in any case, justified in declaring his superior qualifications, since Vancouver, even six years after the great fire of 1886, was little more than a bustling frontier town with few architects as yet.[1]

The announcement might have brought Rattenbury some clients. The Toronto based *Contract Record* for 20 August stated that he was "preparing plans for a building on Hastings St., Vancouver, for Messrs Roursay Bros & Co."; later, on 26 November, the same publication noted that "Mr. Rattenbur[sic] was working on plans for a "large 3 storey brick and stone block at the corner of Oppenheimer Street and Westminster Avenue" for a gentleman named Davis.[2] There is no evidence to confirm whether either building was erected, any more than that he was responsible for the design of the Gustav A. Roedde house at 1415 Barclay Street.[3] This last attribution rests largely upon the fact that Roedde had previously rented accommodation at 50 Cordova Street, not far distant from the Holland Block. Equally inconclusive are the main design features of the actual house, which may not have been begun until 1893. While the omission of a basement follows English precedent, the bay windows and octagonal towers are, like the ship-lap siding and bracketted verandah, typical of current North American domestic design.

The bulk of Rattenbury's earnings during his first months in Vancouver could, indeed, have come from the completion of commissions in Bradford gained through Mawson and Hudson. The end pages of the March 1893 *Canadian Architect and Builder* contain illustrations of two boldly rendered drawings, signed "F. M. Rattenbury, Architect, Vancouver, B.C."[4] The first is entitled "Shops and Offices, Chapel Lane, Bradford, Eng." and the second "Residence for C.J. Holtanz M.R.C.S., Undercliffe, near Bradford, Eng." (Figs.2.1–2).The Holtanz house, designed for a local surgeon, is in a rustic Queen Anne style, given a picturesque profile by the dominant, asymmetrically composed Tudor and Dutch gables. These, and the compact arrangement of rooms around the central stair-hall, as shown in the sketch plan, were adapted by Rattenbury for various of his British Columbia buildings. By contrast, the broad and more elegantly detailed Château-style corner tower of the commercial building suggests that it was conceived after Rattenbury had seen Bruce Price's C.P.R. Château Frontenac in Quebec, begun in 1892. This more eclectic design, thrusting French, Dutch, and British motifs together in an uneasy, if eye-catching, ensemble, also contained several features he was to employ in later commissions in the province. The most noteworthy are the Châteauesque candle-snuffer roof, steeply pitched gables and polygonal Scottish "Bartizan" or battlemented turret. It is quite likely that his uncle gave him these two commissions to provide a solid financial base while he established an office in Vancouver. That Rattenbury maintained his British contacts is indicated by an entry in the *Contract Record* for 23 February announcing that he would prepare plans for a three-storey brick and stone building, 50 by 120 feet, at the corner of Cambie and Water Streets in Vancouver, for "an English client."

The first real opportunity Rattenbury had to display his talents came about a year after his arrival, in the competition for the Legislative

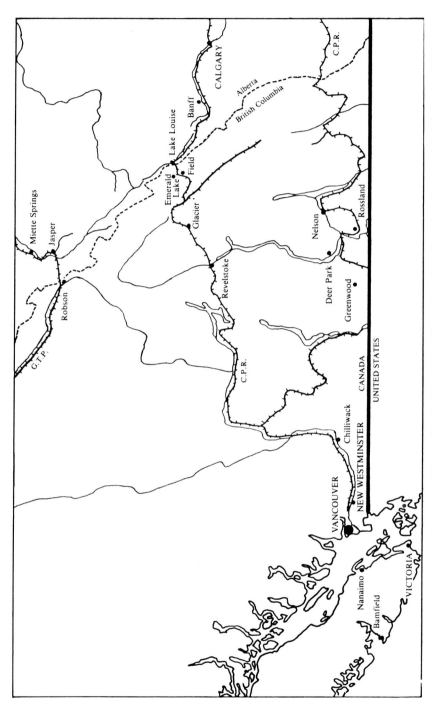

Map 1. Southern B.C. and southwestern Alberta, showing locations of Rattenbury's projected or completed buildings. For Prince Rupert, see Map 3.

Buildings, gazetted in the same issue of the *Vancouver Daily World* that had carried his advertisement. The members of the Legislative Assembly were loathe to continue the conduct of public affairs in the gimcrack "Birdcages," a series of buildings thrown up on the site of the present legislative precinct to the eccentric designs of H.O. Tiedemann. The functional deficiencies of Tiedemann's brick and half-timbered structures, erected in the autumn of 1859, are well known. Worse than the total lack of temperature control was their paltry appearance, to be berated in the *Colonist* of 16 March 1893, as giving the impression of a "sordid, narrow-minded and uncultivated State or Province." Conscious of the dignity of the westernmost province of the Dominion, the premier, Theodore Davie (another English immigrant), and his cabinet voted a budget of $600,000 for a new, more worthy, symbol of British Columbia. Thus in July 1892, the chief commissioner of lands and works called for designs, not only from local architects, but also from those in the rest of Canada and the United States.

The precise instructions dispatched to the competitors do not survive, but obviously the Davie administration sought a visually impressive as well as a functional building. To ensure a fair and informed decision, the chief commissioner employed two practising architects as judges. Closeted in the Rocabella Guest House in Victoria, A.G. Taylor of Montreal and W.S. Curry of Toronto (president of the Toronto Association of Architects) studied the sixty-seven sets of elevations, plans, and details submitted to the government, from which they were to select a short list of five. None was signed, each being identified by a motto or adjectival phrase. Rattenbury signed himself "A B.C. Architect," but the appeal to local pride would hardly have weighed heavily with the easterners; indeed, in their formal report on the outcome of the preliminary competition, published in the 15 December issue of the *Canadian Architect and Builder*, 1892, they gave Rattenbury's *nom de plume* as "A.B.C. Architect."[5]

The real reason for the inclusion of Rattenbury among the five finalists lay in the successful union of grandeur and practicality in his scheme. His perspective elevation, with inset ground floor plan, depicts a magnificent and orderly complex, patently superior to the other submissions that have survived (Fig. 2.3).[6] The extended principal façade, planned to be over 300 feet long, satisfied the general wish for a "handsome" building, while the strongly defined cross-axial plan promised to be "commodious," to use the term employed by the *Colonist* on 16 March 1893 in describing the design. Dominating the composition is a stately central dome, 42 feet in diameter, raised upon a tall octagonal drum above the hub of corridors linking the executive offices with the entrance hall, Legislative Assembly, and lieutenant-governor's quarters. The ornamental features, and particularly the turrets, clearly define the various sections of the building and combine to create a graduated movement to the gilded statue of Captain Vancouver atop the lantern on the dome. Adding variety, the turrets progress from versions that project strongly and have circular domes on the outer pavilions, to the thinner ones with octagonal lanterns framing the gabled side bays of the main building, then on to the single but yet higher turrets guarding the ceremonial entrance and base of the dome. The ascending movement of the turrets across the façade is sustained by the square pilasters and colonnades along the first floor and the repeated arched windows on the second. The sense of elevation is enhanced by the transition in window shape from the rectangular openings on the ground and first floors through the semi-circular headed rectangles on the second to the circular forms of the attic.

On 11 November Rattenbury received the welcome information that this design had been short-listed. Thereupon he began to prepare a more detailed set of drawings and an estimate. These were submitted to the Davie cabinet under the patriotic citation "For our Queen and Province." In these, Rattenbury's clever blend of European and North American references was more apparent (Fig.2.6). The Romanesque style of the massive arched ceremonial entrance, the rough cut masonry and the stumpy columns of the drum of the dome inject a sufficiently medieval note to allude to the Neo-Gothic Parliaments at Westminster and Ottawa. Also, by modelling the dome and lantern upon the ones Brunelleschi had erected on the Florence cathedral in the fifteenth century and by introducing other motifs from the Italian Renaissance, like the round-headed windows, Rattenbury clearly differentiated the Victoria Legislative Buildings from the customarily Neo-Classical federal and state capitols of the United States.[7] However, the choice of the Italianate, and more so the Romanesque, placed it in the mainstream of North American architecture. Both styles were clumsily manifested in two quite recent Victoria buildings, the Bank of British Columbia of 1886 on Government Street and the coal magnate Robert Dunsmuir's ostentatious mansion, Craigdarroch Castle, of 1888–89. And, while he was working on the second set of drawings, A.M. Muir's plainer Victoria Board of Trade Building was being completed in the Renaissance style. The most popular of the two architectural fashions was the Romanesque, particularly associated with H.H. Richardson, and adopted by Bruce

Price for the C.P.R.'s Windsor Station at Montreal, 1888–89 (Fig.2.4), through which Rattenbury had passed. Nor can it have been without significance for Rattenbury that the "loyal" aldermen of Toronto had only recently in 1890 selected E. J. Lennox's Neo-Romanesque scheme for their city hall.

Some of the cabinet members would have appreciated Rattenbury's symbolism. A few might have recognized his references to two well-publicized and representative British institutional buildings of the period: Sir Alfred Waterhouse's Romanesque-faced and Classically planned Natural History Museum, South Kensington, London, begun in 1876, and T.E. Colcutt's nearby Imperial Institute, 1887–93, also symmetrical in plan but Northern Renaissance in style (Fig.2.5).[8] All would have welcomed its arrival on the existing architectural scene of Victoria, since their quarters would, at last, relegate the City Hall, designed in 1878 in the Italianate style by John Teague, to its proper, inferior, consequence. None could have detected the deficiencies of his design: on paper the Legislative Buildings appear considerably more monumental in scale than in reality, and the relation between the side wings and central section less awkward. Nor could they have anticipated how flat and even brittle the exterior would appear under certain light conditions.

On 15 March 1893, W. S. Gore, deputy chief commissioner of lands and works, wired "Accept Congratulations. Come to Victoria by tomorrow's boat if possible." An elated Rattenbury took up lodgings in Victoria's most expensive hotel, the recently completed Driard House; later, for economy's sake he moved into a boarding house on Menzies Street. There he began to trace the working drawings, expending most effort on the structural details and interior (Figs.2.7–11). The floor plans show a logical arrangement of accommodation through the double "T" shaped plan of the main building, beginning at the grandiose ceremonial entrance. Behind its triumphal arch-like opening, a staircase ascends to the Waiting Hall and Rotunda, the latter ringed by piers and arches that carry the Roman theme into the interior. On either side of the Rotunda are vaulted corridors leading to the chief offices controlled by parliament and also staircases leading to the lieutenant-governor's apartments and committee rooms, while the Printing Office and busier Land Registry Office were placed in the east and west pavilions.[9] Beyond the Waiting Hall and Rotunda, intended as the place of meeting for politicians, civil servants, and public, rises the Legislative Assembly, of two storeys and the most lavishly decorated part of the building.

The Assembly (the restoration of which began in 1972) is typical of the institutional Queen Anne style, ornamental rather than splendid. Above all, and of great appeal to the local press when opened, the Legislative Assembly sports an architectural *pot-pourri* of Classical, Renaissance, and even Baroque features—from the bastardized Ionic capitals on the members' wooden desks and columns dividing off the public galleries, to the handsome Jacobean screen and Speaker's chair and the frigid-looking Nereids supporting the frames of the circular windows below the glazed ceiling.

The specific functionalism of the plan and the direct correspondence between the composition of the façade and the interior should have long quashed the persistent rumours that Rattenbury plagiarized it from an alternative Classically styled design for the Bradford Town Hall, prepared by Lockwood and Mawson in 1873,[10] a notion that is, in any case, belied by the fact that Richard Mawson remained on such close and affectionate terms with his nephew.[11] Obviously Rattenbury was influenced by their work, particularly by the centralized composition of Bradford Town Hall, and the octagonal shape of the glass and iron dome surmounting the centre of their Bradford Covered Market (1872–77) (Fig. 2.13–14).[12] Rattenbury may have set such speculations in train by frequently alluding to his connection with Lockwood and Mawson, as in an interview he gave to the *Vancouver Daily World* on 18 March 1893.[13]

Within a month of that interview Rattenbury had completed the working drawings.[14] Before the contract could be signed, he had to compile a detailed specification of the work; this was distributed with blueprints of the working drawings on 30 May to the prospective contractors. A letter he later wrote on 1 December 1893, to the chief commissioner (by this time F. G. Vernon) indicates that he followed the traditional practice of dividing the specification into various trades: masonry, joinery, metalwork (and fireproofing), slating, plasterwork, and painting.[15] In May he believed that his design could be erected for less than the $600,000 budget voted by Parliament, but the task of estimating construction costs was fraught with difficulties, particularly since such a major commission tended to exhaust the local supply of labour and building materials, hence inflating prices. As it turned out, the lowest bid, submitted by R. Nichols of Tacoma (having "doubtful references"), in conjunction with six other contractors, was $617,574. The next lowest, amounting to $661,612, represented a combination of the tender sent in by the Victoria builder Frederick Adams and the one for the slating, plasterwork, and fireproofing offered by R. Drake, then of Washington State. Even this discrepancy was not extraordinary, though

SHOPS AND OFFICES, CHAPEL LANE, BRADFORD, ENG.

F. M. RATTENBURY, ARCHITECT, VANCOUVER, B.C.

2.1 Design for a commercial building, Bradford, c.1893.

RESIDENCE FOR C. J. HOLTANZ, M.R.C.S., UNDERCLIFFE, NEAR BRADFORD, ENG.

F. M. RATTENBURY, ARCHITECT, VANCOUVER, B.C.

2.2 Design for C. J. Holtanz House, Undercliffe, near Bradford, c.1893.

2.3 Elevation and block plan entered in the first stage of the 1892 competition for the Legislative Buildings, Victoria.

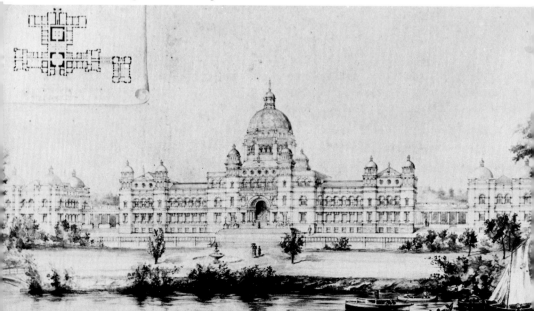

2.4 B. Price, C.P.R. Windsor Station, Montreal, 1888–1889, showing later additions.

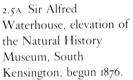

2.5A Sir Alfred Waterhouse, elevation of the Natural History Museum, South Kensington, begun 1876.

2.5B T. E. Colcutt, Imperial Institute, South Kensington, 1887–1893.

ACCEPTED COMPETITIVE DESIGN FOR PROPOSED NEW GOVERNMENT BUILDINGS AT VICTORIA, B.C.
F. M. RATTENBURY, Architect, Victoria, B.C.

2.6 Elevation and plan entered in the second stage of the Legislative Buildings competition.

2.7 Ground floor plan, as originally built, Legislative Buildings, Victoria, 1893.

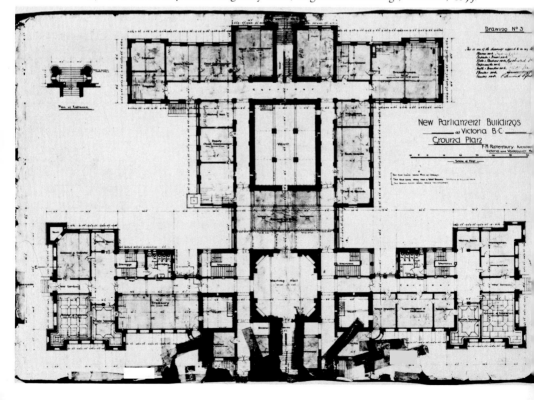

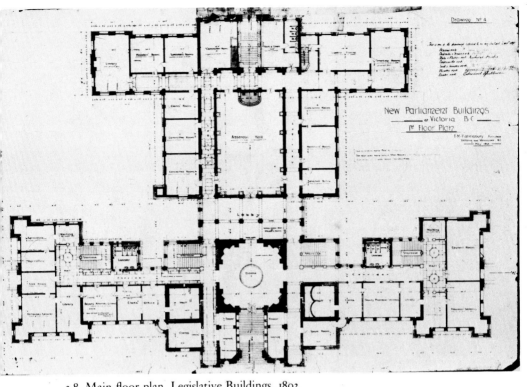

2.8 Main floor plan, Legislative Buildings, 1893.

2.9 Upper floor plan, Legislative Buildings, 1893.

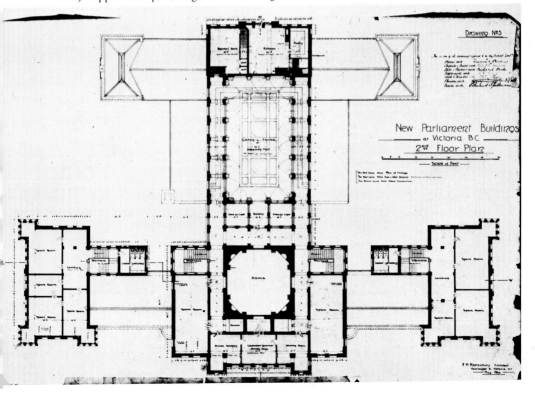

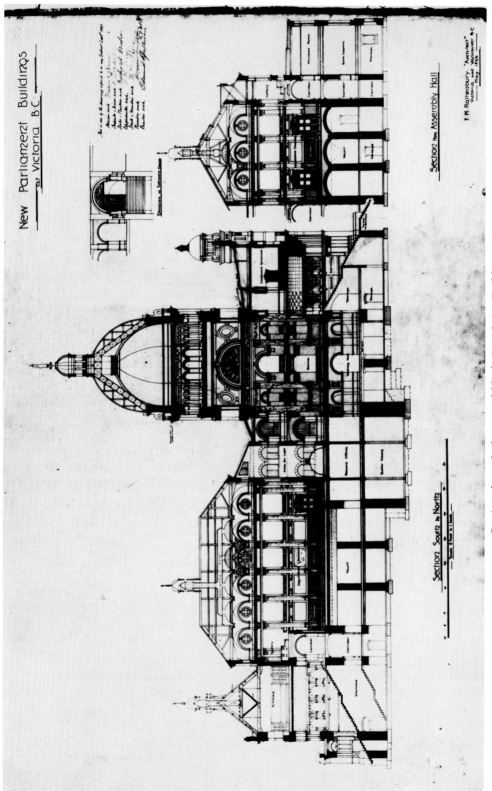

2.10 Section through the central block, Legislative Buildings, 1893.

New Parliament Buildings
at Victoria B.C.

F.M. Rattenbury "Architect"
Victoria, from Vancouver B.C.
May 1893

South Elevation
—Scale ½ Feet—

Section

2.11 Elevation and section of the south block of the Legislative Buildings (before the addition of the Parliamentary Library), 1893.

2.12 Legislative Assembly, Legislative Buildings, 1893–1898, after restoration.

2.13 Lockwood and Mawson, Covered Market, Bradford, 1872–1877.

2.14 Covered Market, Bradford, interior.

2.15 Sketch of dome structure, Legislative Buildings, Victoria, 1894.

2.16 Section and details of the Rotunda and dome as built, Legislative Buildings, 1893.

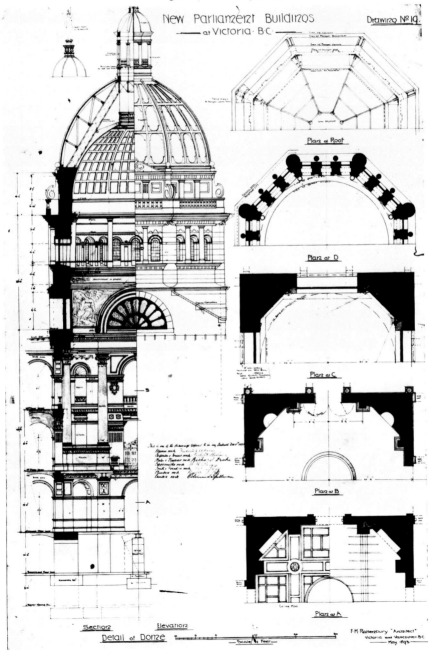

New Parliament Buildings
— at Victoria · B·C —

Drawing Nº 19

Plan of Roof

Plan at D

Plan at C

Plan at B

Plan at A

Section   Elevation
Detail of Dome

Scale 4 Feet

F.M Rattenbury "Architect"
Victoria and Vancouver. B.C
— May. 1893 —

2.17 Courthouse, Nanaimo, B.C., 1895–1896.

2.18 Courthouse, Chilliwack, B.C., 1894.

2.19 E. H. Fisher, first Courthouse, Nanaimo, 1887.

2.20 South (rear) block of the Legislative Buildings, Victoria, nearing completion c.1897.

2.21 W. H. Williams, Bank of British Columbia, Government Street, Victoria, 1886; beyond are S. Maclure's Temple Building, 1893, and Rattenbury's B.C. Electric Company Offices, 1904–7.

2.22 Bank of Montreal, Government Street, Victoria, 1896.

2.23 Main (north) façade of the Legislative Buildings nearing completion c.1897, with H. O. Tiedemann's "Birdcages" in the foreground.

2.24 Florence Rattenbury as a young woman.

May 1897.

2.25 Early sketch for a house, 1897.

2.26 British Columbia Electric Railway Company, Vancouver, 1897.

2.27 The Legislative Buildings on their completion in 1898, with James Bay in the foreground.

Rattenbury was being excessively optimistic when he blithely informed Vernon on 1 December that the expenditure could be held to $550,000 by reductions in the quality and quantity of materials. In truth, he hoped to encourage the politicians to proceed, knowing that the commission would boost the depressed economy and appease a powerful Victoria lobby concerned by the adverse effect upon the local trade of the increasing industrial and resource development on the mainland. For these reasons the government was eventually prepared to condone an increase of almost $400,000 over the original budget.[16]

The government also heeded Rattenbury's suggestion that it would be preferable to employ a local tradesman, especially since he might be persuaded to reduce his bid. Once selected, Frederick Adams did, in fact, agree to match the figure submitted by Nichols — possibly indicating that his original estimate was somewhat inflated — partly by securing lower tenders from sub-contractors such as Bishop and Sherborne, the carpenters; the contracts agreed in 1893 amounted to $567,986.[17] Surprisingly for an experienced tradesman who had worked previously in Quebec and Ontario, Adams inadvisedly agreed to a fixed-price contract, which was to be the ultimate cause of his bankruptcy and withdrawal from the commission in December 1894. Nevertheless, as 1893 drew to a close, Rattenbury and Adams seem to have been contented men, corresponding on letterhead notepaper that boasted their success: Rattenbury's carried a large depiction of the main front of the Legislative Buildings. The Public Accounts printed in the B.C. Sessional Papers show that he received $3,179.90 before the New Year, consisting of 5 per cent commission ($2,817.30) on the contract for laying the foundations and the early stages of the construction, and a similar fee ($362.50) on the first delivery of brick.[18]

This congenial state would not continue. Early in 1894 Rattenbury rejected a large shipment of stone from the Koksilah quarry in favour of a more expensive type from a second site on Haddington Island, opposite Alert Bay on the northeast coast of Vancouver Island. It has been suggested that he was at fault in having selected the Koksilah stone only to find that it was too dark, and then in covering his error by claiming that it was of poor quality.[19] There may be some truth in this, since most of the disputed shipment was considered good enough to be used later by John Teague for an addition to the Jubilee Hospital. At the same time, however, the correspondence between Adams, Rattenbury, and the chief commissioner of lands and works, preserved at the Provincial Archives, partially confirms the architect's claims about the inferior quality of the

Koksilah stone.[20] For example, one document dated March 1895 concerning the case brought by the government of B.C. against the defunct Koksilah Quarry Company includes the admission by a Mr. Lubbe that much of the stone was of poor quality because it had been cut in midwinter. There is also a letter written by Adams to Lubbe on 22 February 1894 complaining that some of the stone was split. Nonetheless, had he been better disposed towards Adams, Rattenbury could have attempted to win government approval for a revision in the contract. Instead, he derided him and, doubtless wielding economic arguments in his favour, marshalled the chief officials on his side. The unfortunate Adams could not absorb the losses suffered on the Koksilah stone, nor the extra costs of other changes ordered by Rattenbury, and forfeited the contract to Messrs. McGregor and Jeeves (although the Public Accounts continue to record payments for the major contracting work to Adams' "executors"). Adams' tragic death by drowning, on the night of 22 March 1895, closed that unsavoury episode.

Rattenbury did not allude to the Adams affair in the long letter that he sent to his uncle Richard Mawson on 25 August 1894 (the earliest of his private letters to have survived). On the contrary, it exudes a sense of self-satisfied achievement, praising the scenery and climate and his own success:

> We have some lovely places here for boating, both along the shore, where the scenery is rugged, with bays and inlets penetrating in at all points and with magnificent scenery in the distance, and then we have an arm of the sea, or inlet, called the Gorge [still a familiar Victoria beauty spot], resembling somewhat the Thames and about six miles long. I bought a Peterboro Canoe early in the summer,[21] and have done a good deal of boating and swimming and this, with long walks, have made the summer like one long holiday. I also have a charming place to live in, near the sea and with a beautiful shady garden, where we often spend an afternoon in hammocks. This does not sound much like business, but the Parliament Buildings are going along so smoothly and all the details being made out. I have not much to do; I have several other buildings which are to be started immediately, including a stone Court House at Nanaimo, which was postponed until after the elections were over,[22] and the drawings of which are completed, and two larger residences at Vancouver, which I obtained last week, and which will cost together about $20,000. I have also completed a Court House at Chilliwack, which has turned out a success.
>
> I could have obtained a good deal more work at Vancouver, but I was tired of journeying backwards and forwards during the summer and wanted to have a rest, so I refused it. Now winter is coming on through, I shall go in again for solid work, so that I can take it easily again next

summer. I could never imagine a country with so many inducements as this has for lotus-eating, and I think it just as wise to enjoy life whilst I have the opportunity and desire, especially as I have been as fortunate as my most sanguine expectations, having carried on works in the last two years involving an expenditure of over $800,000. I have steadily invested my money in the safest securities I could find, now and then putting $100 in a speculation, just on the chance. One of these there is every possibility will turn out magnificently, but of course I don't reckon on it. If it does – good; if not, I don't lose much.

Only then did he respond to his uncle's inquiries about the construction of the dome of the Legislative Buildings.

> Regarding . . . the Iron Work of the Dome . . . I looked carefully into it on getting your letter. Did you notice there was a curb all round the walls; this being bolted down would prevent spreading, would it not? The whole of the Ironwork is like a cage, the purlins of iron being tied as sketched, and would be in tension ½, the other side in compression.
> The Concrete fire-proofing is coming out splendidly, many of the spans having been loaded with materials and heavy weights of many tons since being put up, without sign of a fracture.

The rough sketch of the dome structure that he drew in the text of the letter is also delineated in working drawings 13 "Section East to West" and 19 "Detail of Dome" (Fig. 2.15–16). These show that the outer skin is supported by a wooden frame resting on eight steel truss girders (supplied by E.G. Prior) from which the ceiling of the rotunda is suspended. This system and the steel and concrete fireproofed floors show that Rattenbury was abreast of the structural technology of his period.[23]

As for the other commissions mentioned in the letter, the wood frame and shingled Queen Anne style courthouse at Chilliwack survived from 1894 until 1951, when it was destroyed by fire (Fig. 2.18).[24] The courtroom and offices were raised up a floor, partly to accommodate the cells below, but partly also, given the positively grandiloquent proportions of the staircase, to signify the importance of the law in the development of such new communities. Rattenbury had been trained in an age that revered historical symbolism, and it is likely that he also intended an allusion to the ancient origins of the legal system in the Classical arch, ornamental triglyphs and Venetian Renaissance triple windows. Nor were the decorative motifs drawn only from the Classical tradition, since the projected entrance was capped by a quasi-mediaeval turreted gable. In ornament the courthouse was European, but in its gaunt profile and use of wood it was wholly North American.

No trace survives of the Vancouver houses, and it is possible that they were abandoned, perhaps as a result of the poor economic conditions then prevailing in the city. Happily, the Nanaimo Courthouse was built, between 1895 and 1896; its cost was some $28,000, well within the appropriation of $35,000 (Fig.2.17).[25] Like the rising Legislative Buildings in Victoria, this concrete, granite and sandstone structure replaced a wooden building, E.H. Fisher's crude "Gothick" frame courthouse of 1887 (Fig.2.19), and represented the increasing consequence of the town. With a population of more than 5,000, Nanaimo had become the busiest port in the province, following the completion of the Esquimalt and Nanaimo Railway in 1886. Yet it was not the relative grandeur of the building that appealed to the inhabitants, but rather its practicality, to judge from a comment in the Nanaimo *Free Press* of 10 September 1895, that the courthouse was "composite in character, the element of convenience having been taken into consideration by the architect." Within the walls, an area of 66 by 64 feet, he had arranged the accommodation nicely, placing the various government offices on the ground floor with the court above, itself served by a separate staircase at the rear.[26]

In the design of the façade, Rattenbury reworked some of the major themes of the Legislative Buildings, such as the grand arched entrance reached by steps, the projecting corner turrets, the Richardsonian Romanesque semi-circular banded windows, and the variegated rusticated masonry. The insertion of the colonnade and of the slit openings over the entrance, and the joining of the side windows by a tall enclosing arch, tell of his continued study of Richardson's architecture. A new element is the steeply pitched roofs on the square turrets, which were obviously inspired by the rising popularity in Canada of the Château style.[27] Typically, Rattenbury handled this motif with greater conviction and panache than had Sorby or Teague, whose Hotel Vancouver and Driard House also had pitched roofs.

A year later Rattenbury won the competition for the Victoria branch of the Bank of Montreal with a more full-blooded Château style design. Although he was following the example set by the branches recently completed in Vancouver and Calgary, the reason for this success lay in his bold exploitation of the style. The characteristic steeply pitched roof dominates the Government Street front, while the slightly projected oriel window above the original corner entrance helps to integrate the side façade, itself ornamented by two peaked gables (Fig.2.22). Almost certainly, he took his cue for the diagonal entrance bay from the nearby Italianate Bank of British Columbia (Fig.2.21) built in 1886 on a comparable corner site to the designs of W.H. Williams of Portland, Oregon. But Rattenbury won greater critical acclaim, in the *Colonist* at least, for having "sought, with great success, to combine a picturesque outline with massive solidity, relieved by carving and moulding work, the façade, on Government Street being particularly impressive."[28]

Rattenbury again used a steel and concrete flooring system to fireproof the vault in the basement and the banking hall on the main floor (the upper floor had office-space and accommodation for the manager). The *Colonist* was more impressed with the aesthetic quality of "the magnificent new chamber," in which no "garish or gaudy work" offended the eyes. "The walls are panelled in various shades of brown Tennessee marble," the article continued, supplying a valuable contemporary description of the original arrangement (before its unfortunate modernization) with

> six massive columns dividing the room into bays. The woodwork is of rich walnut enriched by carving. . . . The floors are in ceramic mosaic with an elaborate border of delicate and beautifully blended colouring very pleasing to the eye. The counter front is marble, supporting a hand-forged wrought-iron grille: this screen is pronounced by several architects to be the finest piece of metal work in the province. The fine effect of the room is increased by the deeply coffered and richly panelled plaster work on the walls and ceiling. The quaint glazed windows are a special feature, as are the fine chandeliers of wrought-iron and bluish milk glass very similar to those in the Parliament Buildings.

Obviously, Rattenbury studied the visual effects to be obtained in his works with considerable care. That the bank directors were well pleased is proved by the series of commissions he was later awarded for branches in the interior of the province.

In the meantime, construction continued on the Legislative Buildings, the complex being roofed by the autumn of 1897. "I like to hear that they are so busy at the Office," he was to comment with mock-smugness in a letter to his mother on 14 November 1900. "It is pleasant to hear that people have to work and pleasanter still to be lazy oneself and see others work hard. It used to be such a great enjoyment to me when we were building the Parliament Buildings, to take it easy in the cool shade and watch a couple of hundred men pounding away for dear life at the hard stone" (Fig.2.20). But all was not the peace and harmony he implied. While he could take comfort from an additional $31,107.09 in fees paid since 1893, Rattenbury was confronted by a government worried by increases in costs and officials who demanded changes in his internal plan.

The first major disagreement came in November 1895, when the newly appointed chief commissioner, G. B. Martin, challenged him to comply with his claim of 1 December 1893, that at least $44,000 could be saved by omitting the monumental marble and stained glass from the "Domical Hall" and "Legislative Hall." In reply, Martin received a letter dated 13 November arguing persuasively for the retention of the materials and particularly the marble:

> The grandeur of the whole scheme would be absolutely ruined, should the culminating feature, "The Legislative Hall," be poor and commonplace, and it would be so if the Marble is omitted, for the whole character of the Hall depends on the rich and massive marble columns and we cannot in any adequate way replace these with any cheaper imitation material. No future expenditure, however large, could in any way compensate for the omission, and the amount, in comparison to the cost and character of the buildings, is comparatively small, considering the marvellous improvement it would effect.[29]

This affords confirmation of Rattenbury's interest in appropriate architectural character and was quite justified, the Rotunda and Legislative Hall being the finest features of the Parliament Buildings. Fortunately, Martin saw the validity of his plea, and allowed him a relatively free rein up to the spring of 1897. Then the government interfered once again, demanding that the east pavilion, formerly destined to house the Land Registry, be transformed into a museum with the mining bureau laboratories in the basement. Rattenbury responded on 8 April with two indignant letters. In one of them he let his anger course through his more cogent objections, seven in number: the laboratory would create noxious smells; access to it was inadequate; the Bureau of Mines would be dispersed; the east pavilion was unsuitable for a museum, especially in the matter of lighting; the sanitary facilities were wanting; the taxidermist's office would have to be placed in cramped rooms under the Treasury, and, lastly, the caretaker's quarters would have to be omitted.[30] Instead, he proposed leaving the land registry office in the east pavilion, placing the mining bureau laboratories above the offices of the department and creating a separate brick museum, the whole process to cost about $12,000 to $15,000. In the other note, a more cautious alternative (it is certainly less abrasive), he again objected to the museum proposal, but then suggested that the mining bureau as a whole be accommodated in one of the old "Birdcages," which were still standing either side of his Legislative Buildings (Fig.2.23).[31]

What seems to have specially angered Rattenbury was the questioning of his professional judgment, as is made clear in one paragraph in the first letter, "I speak strongly, because I feel strongly in this matter, and I must clear myself from all appearance of concurring in the suggested arrangement, for should I do so my reputation as an Architect will inevitably suffer." He regarded Martin's interference as an impertinence; confident in his own abilities, he yet lacked the humour and tact to coax the commissioner away from a patently misguided scheme. In fact, rather than concur, he preferred to relinquish the museum work to another architect. Apparently he chided the commissioner a third time, which prompted the following entry into the minutes of the Executive Council for 19 May: "It was decided to reply that his statements were quite inaccurate and that his letter of May 18 was highly intemperate and that the most charitable course was to permit him to withdraw it [the letter is absent from the Archive] as it had been intimated that he was desirous to do so." So, with time for reflection, Rattenbury had enough sense to give ground, though only when Martin partially recanted by admitting that the proposal concerning the mining bureau laboratories should be reconsidered. Nevertheless, Martin pressed ahead with ordering fittings for the museum and gained his colleagues' approval to relocate the library on the main floor. When Rattenbury learned of these covert manoeuvres he expressed his indignation to the chief commissioner and dramatically offered his resignation: "Believe me, much as I would regret to sever my connection with the Parliament Buildings especially after having for so many years exerted every faculty and made such painstaking endeavours to carry out the works to as perfect and satisfactory a conclusion as possible, still, I am ready to resign my position as Architect of the Buildings, a position no longer tolerable, if not accompanied by confidence, and so afford you the opportunity of obtaining other professional advice and assistance." Although some of the changes proposed by Martin were effected, the museum being initally placed in the east pavilion, Rattenbury was the final victor. The Bureau of Mines was located in one of the "Birdcages" left standing behind the new parliament, and in 1911 he was commissioned to add a new library behind the Legislative Assembly and also to design a new, separate museum. Though his new museum was not built, the disputed accommodation in the Parliament reverted to its original purpose upon completion of the Library.

Later, in the fall of 1897, when faced with the opposition of Dr. Pope, superintendent of education, to the removal of a partition wall in his office, communicated to him by W. S. Gore, Martin's deputy, Rattenbury adopted a more crafty approach. Profiting from the knowledge gained by his recent experience he presented the commissioner with a *fait accompli* – the contract for the removal of the partition had already been let.[32] Rattenbury also informed Gore that he lacked the necessary professional qualifications to make alterations in the plan, conveniently ignoring Gore's training as a civil engineer and experience as surveyor general of British Columbia.[33] When Martin entered the fray on Gore's behalf, Rattenbury treated him like a recalcitrant junior, writing on 14 November that he had heard from E. C. Howell, superintendent of works (who carved the columns in the Legislative Hall), that Howell

> was imperatively ordered by you and Colonel Baker to make certain alterations... according to your instructions. Knowing that they were acting without professional advice, and feeling convinced that you did not realize you were making a serious blunder in having the alterations made in the manner insisted upon by Colonel Baker, I had previously instructed Mr. Howell not to make any change in the contract work except with my sanction. As Mr. Howell, in my agreement with the Government, is expressly stated to be under my orders, I was very much surprised to hear of the Government giving orders to him direct. I consequently asked Mr. Howell to produce them. He informs me however that altho' the work has been carried out... you refuse to issue the order to him in writing.

There was more in that ironical vein, including another remonstrance about the museum and library episodes. Moreover, a month later he felled Martin with bureaucratic logic about his [i.e., Martin's] refusal to pay the contractor (Drake) who was laying the sidewalk, because the task had not been sanctioned by the works department. In a crisply worded letter to Martin dated 26 December he wrote:

> As regards this sidewalk... it was ordered by me, at the request of yourself and Mr. Turner, the premier. Of course, however, if you desire me not to take any instruction from you, unless in writing, I am quite prepared not to do so. But if you will permit me to remind you that on a previous occasion on which you issued orders, which you insisted should be carried out, you refused to give those orders in writing, and I wrote to you about the matter... with no avail.... There certainly seems to be a little confusion in these various mandates.

This was surely a brilliant example of verbal enfilading!

Rattenbury had by then mounted a last sally against the government. On 18 December he wrote to the *Colonist* to lament the government's decision to chop down the trees in the vicinity of the Legislative Buildings, revealing an innate appreciation of the Picturesque:

> It is so rarely that an architect is fortunate enough to have the opportunity of erecting a large building amongst the delicate tracery of woodland

scenery. And the peeps of high masses of masonry through the trees gives so distinctive a charm, so different to what one can usually see, that words fail me to express my grief at seeing this charm disappear.

I had no voice in the matter or I would have saved at least some of these trees; but, Sir, it is not yet too late to save the magnificent poplars at the corner of James Bay bridge, standing out in bold relief against the sky, acting as a foil to the outline of the dome and giving distance and perspective to the whole building. If they are cut down, the loss will, I feel sure, be realized when too late.

Alas, his pleas were in vain.

Despite the almost constant clashes of will between Rattenbury and government bureaucrats, the work went ahead, the east wing being finished on 19 September 1896 and the Legislative Assembly in use by 1897. Perhaps to counteract the continual stress he faced during the later stages of the commission, Rattenbury sought relaxation in female company. Young, handsome and successful, he must have been attractive to women and have enjoyed their attentions. He may also have yearned to have a more permanent home now that he was well established at Victoria. But his choice of partner is less easy to explain. Florence Eleanor Nunn was the daughter of George Elphinstone Nunn, a former captain in the Indian Army who had been attracted to British Columbia in the 1860's by the discovery of gold in the Fraser Valley. Nunn abandoned his family and died shortly afterwards. His wife then left her young children with friends in Victoria and departed for Oregon. Florence was brought up in a quiet boarding house in Victoria by Mrs. E. Howard and grew to be a shy and somewhat priggish young lady. Short and rather plump, she was plain in appearance, with a square shaped face and a stocky jaw (Fig. 2.24). She had little money, but liked to give the impression that she came from a distinguished family. Her father, she claimed, was a descendant of the Elphinstones, a family that had played a leading role in the history and government of British India.

Exactly when the two met cannot now be determined, but it may have been as early as May 1897. This is the date scribbled on the only casual sketch of his to have survived from the period, drawn on a scrap of paper and found among his private letters (Fig. 2.25). It depicts a Queen Anne style house, set against what appears to be the mountains of the Olympic peninsula, with two figures in the foreground. A man in a sailing boat—a familiar Rattenbury motif—waves to the girl in the verandah, and it is tempting to assume that the figures represent Rattenbury and his future bride, and the house his initial conception of their future home.[34] If it was drawn for Florence, then it suggests that Rattenbury was seeking an ideal of romantic domesticity. Thus he may have welcomed her reserve and placidity as holding out the promise of calm companionship as an antidote to his busy professional life, for, even as he courted her, he seems to have received yet another commission, the combined office and depot building of the British Columbia Electric Railway Company at Carrall and Hastings Streets in Vancouver.[35] He probably received it from the company's president Frank Barnard (later knighted when lieutenant-governor of the province), brother of Rattenbury's close friend Harry Barnard, who was to serve as mayor of Victoria from 1904 to 1906. Constructed of brick at a cost of some $10,000 and designed in a suitably plain commercial Renaissance style, it borrowed the unifying arched openings and angled corner entrance of the Victoria Bank of Montreal (Fig. 2.26). The building was completed on 2 September 1898, eight months after Rattenbury's responsibilities for the Legislative Buildings ceased.

The official opening of what the *Victoria Times* called "A Marble Palace" had taken place on 10 February 1898, presided over by Lieutenant-Governor T. R. McInnes, to the accompaniment of military parades, choirs, and a fireworks display. Rattenbury must have been more than satisfied by local reaction. He had, as their reporter put it, succeeded in "blending into one design the Romanesque, Classic and Gothic, not a jumble by any means, but an adaptation and modulation to the general effect in a masterly and artistic whole, pleasing to the eye yet not sacrificing the utilitarian purposes which public departments demanded. . . . The beauty of the structure calls forth the admiration of everyone who has seen it, while the perfection of the work and the thoroughness in which details have been carried out is a surprise to visitors. In general design and in choice of the stone for the buildings the good taste and judgement displayed has been decidedly happy, the result being a harmonious picture delightful to the eye." (Fig. 2.27).[36] An even greater accolade came in 1901 when, during a visit to Canada, the future King George V singled out Rattenbury's Legislative Buildings and the Ottawa Parliament Building (Fuller and Jones, 1861–66), as the two finest examples of architecture in the Dominion.[37]

Three

NORTHERN CHALLENGE
1898–1900

Rattenbury was absent from the festivities that marked the opening of the Legislative Buildings in February, 1898. In the first week of the month he and Wellington J. Dowler, clerk to the City of Victoria, boarded the eastbound transcontinental express. They booked passage aboard the *Lucania*, then the largest liner in service on the Atlantic—though not sufficiently stable to prevent Rattenbury from suffering seasickness. It appears that the two had already formed a partnership in pursuit of a scheme to profit from the most frenetic speculation in the history of Victoria, the Yukon Gold Rush. This brief but colourful period began the year before with the discovery of gold in Bonanza Creek, one of the feeder streams of the Klondike River. Because the Klondike lay within Canadian territory, prospectors crossing the border from Alaska were obliged to pay Canadian duty on their equipment, unless they outfitted themselves in a Canadian city. Victoria merchants were quick to exploit the new commercial opportunities; Tapran Adney, who was despatched by *Harper's Weekly* to report from the Klondike, commented on 15 August 1897: "The streets of leisurely Victoria are thronged with strange men, and there is an earnest look on their faces and firmness in their step.... Klondike! magic word, that is possessing men so that they think and talk of nothing else."[1]

Armed with the bulk of the $40,826.07 he had earned from the Legislative Buildings, and daily confronted by reports and advertisements in

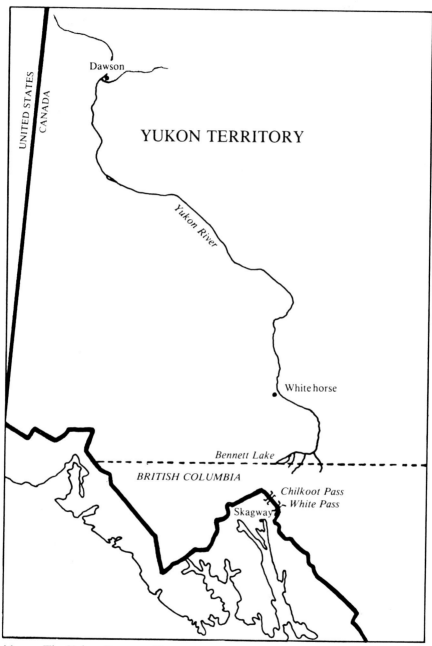

Map 2. The Yukon Route to Dawson.

the local newspapers boosting the gold fever, Rattenbury realized that great financial returns lay in providing transportation to the goldfields. He would have known that most of the prospectors travelled there by combination of sea, land, and inland waters, starting from a southern port along the Pacific coast and sailing to Skagway at the head of the Lynn Canal. The demand for berths on ships moving north was tremendous, as is illustrated by a contemporary description of conditions aboard the steamer *Amur*, operated by the Klondyke Mining Trading and Transportation Company between Victoria and Skagway.[2] The vessel was "a floating bedlam, pandemonium let loose, the Black Hole of Calcutta in an Arctic setting," being "less than a thousand tons burden, with accommodations for about sixty cabin and one hundred steerage passengers. She actually had aboard more than five hundred passengers and nearly that many dogs." But the real problems began at Skagway. From there the prospector had to traverse the coast mountains over the White Pass, or the even more fearsome Chilkoot Pass, to Lake Bennett, at the headwaters of the Yukon river system, from which he could, in theory, continue all the way down to Dawson, apart from a portage at the treacherous White Horse Rapids. Yet scarce as berths up the coast might be, proper transportation by steamboat on the upper Yukon was almost nonexistent. Making an intelligent analysis of contemporary reports, Rattenbury appreciated both the importance of the waterway and the pressing need for steamboats, at least four months before Sam Steele, commander of the North West Mounted Police in the Yukon, reported on the flotilla of canoes and make-shift light boats that began the journey in 1897: "On May 29, the lake being free of ice, the wonderful exodus of boats began. I went up the hill behind the office to see the start, and at one time counted over 800 boats under sail on the 11½ miles of Lake Bennett."[3]

Thus Rattenbury, probably inspired by the numerous advertisements for small locally built boats in the *Colonist*, ordered three prefabricated steam vessels (possibly from the Albion Iron Works, which manufactured ships at its yard on Store Street), either late in 1897 or early in 1898. It appears that by February he and Dowler (there is no hint of another backer at this stage) required additional funds and decided to seek financial support on the London market. The details of their stay in England have evaded discovery, but it is clear that they were successful. No doubt showing the plans of their sturdy vessels and selected newspaper reports to potential backers, Rattenbury and Dowler were able to persuade a number of individuals that their investment would yield handsome dividends from the shipping of passengers and freight to Dawson City. The Bennett Lake and Klondyke Navigation Company (B.L.K.N.C) was floated, as the list of incorporated companies in the 1900 *Henderson's Gazetter* records, with a capital of £75,000 (sterling) in £1 shares and with head offices at 23 Leadenhall Street, London. The local press misprinted the company's capital as $75,000 (dollars) and compounded the error by suggesting that Rattenbury had raised the money in Victoria. Apparently he never corrected the report, perhaps wishing to play up to local pride.

After Rattenbury's return to Victoria the three steamers were completed, duly named after Florrie, *Ora, Flora,* and *Nora,* and shipped in sections to Skagway (Fig. 3.1). From there the packing cases were hauled, by the longer route, over the White Pass to Lake Bennett. At the lake the sections were reassembled at a mill that had been constructed in great secrecy on the water's edge. This procedure, and the northern operations of the company, was entrusted to a native of the Yukon, Otto Partridge. He was assisted by Rattenbury's brother, Jack, formerly a captain in the merchant navy.

Early in May Rattenbury's enterprise was rewarded with a particularly valuable freight contract from Patrick Burns, the genial western Canadian "cattle baron." Dawson City, at the confluence of the Yukon and Klondike rivers, was at the centre of the gold mining activity and had grown in a single year from a collection of shacks to a town of 30,000 individuals, who were willing (or obliged) to pay horrendous prices for imported provisions. Burns, who was to become a close friend of Rattenbury, engaged the B.L.K.N.C. to deliver a large and valuable consignment of cattle to Dawson. According to a report in the *Colonist* of 15 May 1898, the cattle were to be driven along the Dalton Trail to Five Fingers and there loaded upon the steamboats and carried to Dawson for $40,000.[4] Besides that profitable exercise, the vessels were in full service by June, when newspapers in the Lower Mainland were carrying the proud notice, "Steamer *Flora* leaves Bennett every day for Whitehorse, connecting with steamers *Ora* and *Nora* for Dawson city."[5]

A reference in the *Contract Record* of 11 May 1898 (p.3) suggests that Rattenbury might also have had a stake in another of the routes to the goldfields. He was reported as calling for tenders for a sixty-room hotel 140 miles up the Stikine at Glenora, British Columbia (also known as Telegraph Creek and operated as a trading post by the Cassiar Central Railway of Victoria). There is no proof of its construction—the contemporary B.C. Directories provide no information beyond the existence of a hotel – but the commission in any case indicates that Rattenbury had not entirely abandoned his architectural practice.

With the company, he thought, securely established, Rattenbury married Florrie in a quiet service at Christ Church Cathedral in Victoria on 18 June. The relatively modest ceremony, given his extrovert, even flamboyant personality, and the birth of their first child some seven months later, might imply that the marriage was hastened, or even necessitated by Florrie's condition. He subsequently came to regret the match, and a lack of ardour at its very outset is suggested by his combining their honeymoon with a tour of the company's Yukon facilities, accompanied by a Victoria friend, Mrs. Temple Hall.[6] Even in the naming of the steamers after Florrie he simply followed the convention established by another shipping line, the Arctic Commercial Company, which named its vessels after the wives of the directors.

Whatever Rattenbury might have felt towards Florrie at this time, he was, not unnaturally, inclined to take a positive view of his experiences. "Here we are at Bennett," he wrote in a letter to an employee, T. E. Potts, printed in the *Colonist* on 9 July 1898, "over the Chilkoot Pass, having arrived last evening at six o'clock." Since they had not left Dyea until after four o'clock on Friday, "we did pretty well to get here by Saturday, but really there are no difficulties on the trail." They had "simply strolled along, and actually did not know that we had come to the dreaded part of the Pass, until we were told that we were over the summit. You can judge by this how ridiculous and exaggerated the accounts we have read of it must have been." Having scorned the perils of the Chilkoot trail, so vividly described by journalists like Tapran Adney – and it can be supposed that Rattenbury hoped that Potts would transmit these favourable impressions to potential customers – he stressed the success of the steamers. They were looked upon as "splendid craft" and "a great surprise to everyone, doing the 120 miles to White Horse against the wind in under ten hours." After complimenting his employees on their achievement, he went on to commend the amenities of the area. "The scenery on Bennett is superb, and tomorrow we are all intending going for a trip down the Lake 25 miles to our mill camp. The climate is delightful, cool and fresh. I have not yet seen one single mosquito. . . . We are all in capital health and spirits, and shall probably stay here about a fortnight, taking the run down to Dawson and back in the meantime."[7]

However, by the time that he had returned to Skagway, Rattenbury's attitude was markedly different. In a private letter to Otto Partridge (there was no likelihood of publication in this instance) he confided:

Of all men I was the most miserable. I tried riding, the trails were too rough. I tried walking, it was just as bad. Some stretches of the trail were so nauseating, owing to the carcases of dead donkeys, mules and horses that it overcame me. I could simply not stand it. In the higher latitudes the mosquitoes were scarce, thanks to a breeze blowing. How on earth the packers managed it is past my comprehension. Asking them how they could put up with it day after day, they said, "Oh, we thrive on it. It saves us a meal once in a while." I could not see anything to joke about. Of the two evils, mosquitoes on the Mclintlock, or the Skagway trail, I could make no choice. I must have taken a fever for several days until nearing Victoria. I was sick, which was something new to me. Carry on up there! I can now understand how so many men died on those putrid trails, and know what you have to contend with. I'll remember you. Everything is in your hands.[8]

Reminiscing some time after 1935, Partridge testified to the misery that Rattenbury suffered on his return to Bennett aboard the *Flora*. If Rattenbury had not seen a single mosquito on the outward journey, as he claimed in the *Colonist* letter, on the return trip he had oil and greases "rubbed into his swollen body to soothe the sores." Partridge's employer "had had enough of the North and realized what the (as he termed them) poor devils had to suffer to get to their destinations and he realized the price many had paid in hardship and suffering to have 'Ora' 'Nora' and 'Flora' running on schedule. He knew now what the staff had to put up with on the boats, with smudges constantly going to keep off the plagued mosquitoes." Rattenbury, he believed, "was touched at last, as he sat nursing his head, hands, and legs, swollen and poisoned."

Rattenbury, nevertheless, had committed himself to the certain notion that travel in the Yukon was a pleasant experience. Once returned to Victoria, he seems to have succeeded in banishing all recollection of the hardships from his mind. In a letter to his mother on 24 August, the self-congratulatory enthusiasm, so noticeable in the *Colonist*, reappears, reflected by the very notepaper, with its high-sounding letterhead "Bennett Lake and Klondyke Navigation Company Limited. Cable address: Rattenbury."

We are home again after a lovely trip to the Yukon and back. We spent over a month at Bennett and down the Lakes, but never had time to go into Dawson. Jack went in and some others, and wrote up to us, but we were too busy on the upper lakes, and though within 2 days of Dawson it would take 5 to come back, 4 on the steamer the whole while. Much though I would have liked to see Dawson, I was too busy. It seems strange how out of dozens of companies that made preparations for running boats to

Dawson they all made mistakes and failed, whilst we have succeeded so far beyond our expectations. The steamers are making regular trips now into Dawson and it is a perfectly easy matter for a lady to leave Victoria and go in alone, as Miss Flora Shaw, the lady Editor of the London Times did, going in by our boats; we met her at Bennett.[9] She stayed with us and when at Dawson stayed with our people. It only takes nine days now from Victoria to Dawson, 4 on the steamer up, 1 on the trail, and three to four on our steamer down the river.

So Yukon travel is revolutionized and has lost its terrors, in summer at least. We have done a good business and have taken in a lot of freight and brought out a lot of passengers, who were simply astounded at the ease and speed that they could travel with, when they expected so long and difficult a journey. The country up here is lovely in summer, as lovely and with as beautiful a climate as anywhere.

When Rattenbury referred to Florrie, he did so in terms that were complimentary, but hardly affectionate or romantic. She "stood the trip easily. Coming out we chose a long way and rode 50 miles, 25 each day on horseback; it was rather tiresome but interesting." After digressing into another enthusiastic report on his company—"The Paris Figaro, London Sketch and other papers will all contain views of our steamers shortly.... They are household words in this part of the world"—he returned to Florrie, noting that she had a "marvellously good temper—a jolly good thing for me, for as you know mine is rather short, especially when rushed with work. So we pull along well together." Rattenbury's mother might have hoped at this point for more information on her new daughter-in law, but her son was obviously far more interested in telling her about his own ambitious plans, and particularly of a further expansion on his northern operations.

> You will see by the newspaper we sent you, that we are organizing a scheme to open up a winter route and if we can get it finished by the time winter sets in it cannot fail to be a big success. We shall carry the mails in this way and gradually establish trading posts.
>
> A London company has also asked us to take charge for them of running a steamer the "Amur" from Victoria to Skagway at so much a month salary. So I seem to have got into a general shipping business.

Information on both these projects has survived. On 12 August it was announced in the press that the B.L.K.N.C. would take over the Klondyke Mining Trading and Transportation Company. This placed the management of that "floating bedlam," the *Amur*, under Rattenbury's control and enabled him to move into the K.M.T.C.'s old offices at 39

Government Street, Victoria.[10] He further devised a scheme for a series of way stations from Skagway to Dawson, each with a company agent to provide food and shelter, which would maintain a line of communication to Dawson during the winter months. As originally conceived, the system was to be under the aegis of the B.L.K.N.C., but the plan was changed, and on 19 August the *Colonist* reported that Rattenbury had "promoted and incorporated commercial interests, being known as the Arctic Express Company." The press reports create the impression that Rattenbury was the original founder of the A.E.C., and he seems to have done nothing to alter that impression. In fact the A.E.C. was an American company, and *Henderson's Gazetteer* indicates that its head office remained in Seattle. Rattenbury's decision to amalgamate with it for the purposes of organizing winter travel was not without shrewdness, since the company had already obtained a four-year contract at $80,000 to carry the U.S. mail to Dawson.

Yet Rattenbury's confidence proved to be unfounded, and his expectations that the shipping company would impress international celebrities like Flora Shaw unwarranted. Indeed, Miss Shaw adopted a distinctly patronizing tone, writing in the London *Times* on 10 September 1898, "Already a service of small river steamboats has been placed on the waterways which flow from the north-eastern base of the coast mountains for nearly 600 miles to Dawson. The accommodation which is offered on these boats is, of course, extremely bad, but their existence represents a plucky and successful pioneer attempt to navigate by steam a river declared at first by apparently competent authorities to be navigable by only small hand craft."

If Rattenbury's enterprise could have prospered without international acclaim, it could not survive without passengers and freight. By 1899 the Klondike gold rush was collapsing, because the more recently arrived prospectors discovered that all the promising stakes had been claimed, and richer lodes were being discovered at Nome in Alaska. Where the cabins of the *Amur* had been filled to capacity, and beyond, during the height of the Klondike boom in 1897, she carried only ten passengers from Victoria to Skagway in August 1898, the month Rattenbury assumed control. By the end of September, the company was offering reduced rates to Skagway. Business also declined on the upper Yukon, and in 1899 Rattenbury found himself competing with another forty-six boats plying the river for an ever dwindling supply of passengers and freight.[11]

On 9 April 1899, the *Colonist* reported that Rattenbury had decided to sever "his connection with the Bennett Lake and Klondyke Navigation

Company steamship line, an experienced man in Mr. H. Flocton having taken hold of this latter enterprise as manager." He was, in fact, summoned to Montreal by the directors to give an account of the problems facing the company, and the anxiety that he felt was later acknowledged to his mother in a letter written from the Windsor Hotel on 2 March 1905. After recalling that he stayed at the Windsor on first arriving in Canada, he went on "I was here in 1899 when one of my Yukon adventures was looking disastrous and I was endeavouring to save it, with considerable success as it turned out, although it was an anxious time and I remember pacing the marble floor of the big Rotunda, backwards and forwards, backwards and forwards, for several days." Though Rattenbury wrote of his "considerable success," perhaps trying to convince himself as well as his mother, the whole sequence of events must have been a crushing disappointment. It is not known whether he learned of the humiliating end of the boats. They were eventually dismantled and converted into barges.[12]

The Arctic Express Company continued to operate for several years with Rattenbury as its Canadian agent.[13] The difficulties of winter travel had been seriously underestimated and, despite the company's advertising claim of "Prompt delivery of parcels and letters guaranteed," they were unable to maintain the mail service to Dawson without the aid of the Mounties. Sam Steele, commanding the Yukon detachment, recorded that in 1898 he "arranged that for the remainder of the winter men and dogs should be relieved every thirty miles, the distance separating our posts. The mail was to be kept going and coming, night and day, the changes of men and dogs to be made in 20 minutes. All attempts made by others during the winter to send out mails were failures. The Arctic Express Company's agent started one off on December 8, but the effort had to be given up at our Stewart River post, where Corporal Greene took charge of it and sent it on with his dog train."[14] After 1899 the mail to Dawson City was severely reduced; even if the company had been able to operate efficiently, its profits would have been minimal.

The uncharitable might view Rattenbury's northern enterprise as an act of folly, a display of arrogance on the part of a man who insisted on meddling in an area of which he was totally ignorant. But this would be unfair. While the B.L.K.N.C. was a commercial failure, it was not without symbolic importance. The Klondike region lay within Canadian borders, but the gold rush had remained essentially an American phenomenon. Most of the prospectors, and the commercial businesses set up to cater for them, were American, so that British Columbians were proud of the fact that a citizen of Victoria, not an American, had introduced safe and reliable navigation on the upper Yukon and contributed to better communications between the outposts of the Empire.[15] Besides this, Rattenbury's knowledge of northern Canada seems to have been highly regarded by those of his contemporaries who were in the best position to judge. "I have just had Colonel Perry, the Commanding Officer of the North-West Mounted Police, and the boss-man in the Klondyke, staying with me," he wrote on 4 May 1900, "He is fairly young and a good chap." Aylesworth Bowen Perry, an Ontario man and head of his graduating class at the Royal Military College at Kingston, was one of the most distinguished officers to serve with the N.W.M.P. He was appointed superintendent at the early age of twenty-five as a result of his services during the 1885 Riel rebellion, represented the Mounties in London in 1887 during Victoria's Jubilee celebrations, and eventually reached the rank of commissioner. In September 1899 Perry replaced Sam Steele (who was transferred from the Yukon to the Northwest Territories), assuming official command in the Yukon on 1 August 1900. It is surely significant that Perry, who was to bear the responsibility for good order in the Yukon, seems to have considered Rattenbury among those who ought to be consulted before he assumed his new post.

All the same, the next surviving letter, written on 4 November 1899, to his sister Kate, indicates that in the space of a year Rattenbury had undergone a profound change. The bitter lesson of his Yukon adventures aside, he now had new responsibilities, for on 14 January 1899, his wife had born him a son, Francis Burgoyne, nicknamed "Snooka," to whom, whatever his subsequent public image, Rattenbury was an affectionate and even overindulgent father.[16] Temporarily unnerved by the virtual collapse of his northern venture, he seems to have assumed the different role of the English gentleman-farmer, pottering about in the bucolic surroundings of his home in Oak Bay and pretending that the business of earning money was an unwelcome distraction: "Somehow the mornings creep on, dodging around the garden, in the woods, and along the beach, sometimes potting away at the ducks, so that before one can tear oneself away it is about 1.0 P.M.; then I get away down town after a little tiffin. Is not that a shocking way to go to 'biz'?" Still, he was concerned with events in the Transvaal, where the British Army was faring badly against the Boers, and, more significantly, he was engaged upon architecture: "Although I have a lot of buildings going on I have got through much of my work so am not busy. If the buildings were in Town I should most probably put in some time going to see them, but they are nearly all out of Town. So I am taking advantage of the opportunity to have a quiet good old rest, and it is rather jolly. After a few hours at the office I call in at the club for half an hour, and catch the 7.0 car home, in time for dinner at 8." Rattenbury's architectural practice was, in fact, very healthy at this point, but his commissions were of a routine nature. Essentially, he was bored. Flocton had "just come down from the north," an unwelcome reminder of Rattenbury's failure, even if he might have derived a perverse consolation from the fact that the new company did not seem to have performed well enough to satisfy the directors in London. "I am glad I am clean out of it," he claimed, adding: "Speculations are fun for a year, but when the misery is drawn out over several years it is hard to see the point of the joke. At the same time, it is a curious feeling to be without any little ventures, as they certainly add a zest and excitement to life unless one burns one's fingers." Bereft of a major challenge, Rattenbury jokingly pondered whether he was "vegetating into a farmer," and reported that he had added "three ducks to my stock, so now there are hens, ducks, pigeons, cat, dog, canary bird."

The scene of these rural pursuits was "Iechinihl," the house completed in Oak Bay soon after the birth of Snooka in January 1899. Rattenbury had chosen the site with care, writing in his letter of 24 August 1898 of his plan to take "a furnished house, a pretty place [on Rockland Avenue, owned by J. C. Galletly, manager of the Bank of Montreal], whilst I make up my mind where to build. I thought I had decided but am still hesitating." Iechinihl represented something of a departure from traditional architecture in Victoria (Fig. 3.2). It was smaller than mansions of the type built in the Queen Anne style for J. J. Flumerfeldt in 1896 by Rattenbury's contemporary Samuel Maclure.[17] On the other hand, it was larger in scale, if not in actual size, than the "Maclure Bungalow," having gables and two full stories rather than low roofs spreading over a single main story. The half-timbering and wooden verandahs also imported a more distinctly Tudor character, akin to Norman Shaw's smaller country houses (such as Merrist Wood, near Guildford, 1877 [Fig.3.3]), while the shingling echoes the related but more informal and wood-generated architecture of the United States.[18] Essentially an adaptation of the English cottage, it was probably most directly inspired by the more modest Arts and Crafts style domestic architecture that abounded in the suburbs of the cities of Yorkshire. The plan of Iechinihl, as for his later houses, is compact and practical.

The origin of the name is explained in a later letter (written on 30 May,

1900), which also included a description of the house's charming setting:

> We have at last found a name for the house IECHINIHL, pronounced softly, Eye-a-chineel. It is an Indian name, and has a story connected with it. In one part of our garden I have often noticed there was a good many clam shells and there is also a spring of fresh water. Mentioning this to an old timer, he told me that for centuries our particular garden has been an Indian camping ground and that they had a legend that formerly all men were dumb and looked at each other like owls. But one day on this very spot the good spirit conferred on them the gift of speech. The name means "The place where a good thing happened." (I. is "good" in Indian.) Rather an interesting story. The legend is still in existence amongst the Indians. The country here is just now looking its best. All the yellow broom is still in blossom, and now all the wild roses are as well, a dense mass of them around the house.

In his letter of 4 November 1899, Rattenbury mentioned to Kate that nearly all of his commissions were "out of Town." He was referring, in the main, to a series of lucrative commissions for buildings in the southern interior of the province, work that was begun as early as 24 August 1898. Although preoccupied with his shipping business, he wrote to his mother on that date that he was "still doing a little architectural work" and added, "I ought now to be off to Rossland to see my new Bank." The Rossland bank was one of three contracts awarded to him by the Bank of Montreal in the spring or summer of 1898 (the year is confirmed on a boldly rendered signed sketch of the Rossland design [Fig.3.4]). The Bank of Montreal, already well established in Victoria and Vancouver, was at this time actively involved in the rapid exploitation of the rich mineral deposits discovered in the Kootenays, a development given added impetus by the promotion of railway construction in the area by the Davie and Robson administrations.[19] A number of lucky strikes on the south slope of the Red Mountain had led to the creation of Rossland in 1892, not incorporated until 1897 but already known as the "Golden City." More important was Nelson, where the bounteous, if predominantly low grade lodes of gold, silver and copper ore, embedded in the nearby Toad Mountain, and the associated smelting operations and railroad construction, transformed it into the largest town in the interior. Here Rattenbury was also to erect a larger and more elegant branch. The third was built at New Westminster, possibly conceived before the others, to serve that well-established centre. It lay at the end of one of the land routes from Nelson and Rossland, a route that passed through Greenwood where Rattenbury designed the capacious Hotel Greenwood. Beneath the shade of its ornamented verandah, doubtless, lounged some, at least, of the local assembly of reportedly snobbish remittance men, a number of whom chose Greenwood as their watering place.[20] The wood frame, gabled hotel, more American in character than Rattenbury's previous work, was the product of the mining boom, for Greenwood, incorporated in 1897, boasted a number of mines with names evocative of the age of the prospector: "Mother Lode," "Old Ironsides," and "Knob Hill." Something of the excitement surrounding the emergence of these towns and the pride of their early inhabitants can be seen in a photograph of the Hotel Greenwood taken just before its completion late in 1899 or early in 1900 (Fig.3.5).

The importance of these projects for Rattenbury is made evident in the two pieces he obviously inspired in the *Colonist* of 9 April and 24 December 1899. According to the earlier article, this new spate of commissions and particularly those for the Bank of Montreal had finally decided him to sever his connection with the B.L.K.N.C. Although he was being coy about the real reasons behind the abandonment of his Yukon interests, there can be no denying that the "business block at New Westminster," "the large hotel at Greenwood," and "plans" for remodelling the courthouse at Victoria would indeed demand much concentrated work. Also, as the April article continued, the bank intended to "put up a very handsome and substantial building at Nelson and evidently have very great confidence in the progress of the province, as at the present time Mr. Rattenbury is acting as architect in the erection of three fine modern structures at Rossland, Nelson and New Westminster respectively" (Figs.3. 6–8). An appreciation of their significance to the growth of the interior appears in the next sentence, for the three branches were to be constructed of "fire-proof material" and "beautifully fitted up," in an area still pioneer in character with semi-temporary wooden buildings designed by contractors rather than architects. Each was welcomed as adding a sense of permanence and of aesthetic quality to their respective towns, even to the more sophisticated New Westminster. Its citizens, no less than those elsewhere, would have been only too aware of the ravages of fire, which just months earlier had consumed much of the former capital city, including the Bank of Montreal branch building. Indeed, the *Colonist* repeated the points for good measure in reference to the Nelson branch, "fifty feet square and three stories high, with fireproof floors. The banking chamber somewhat resembles the bank at Victoria but the outside appearance is in a totally different style, being of free renaissance design executed in rich deep buff pressed brick and terra cotta of very effective design."

The term "free renaissance" is an appropriate description for all three banks and reflects the residual influence of Lockwood and Mawson, who executed a number of buildings in that style (Fig.1.5). The Italian Renaissance palazzo was clearly the inspiration for the tripartite floor division of the Nelson and Rossland branches, comprising a basement, "piano nobile" the raised main floor containing the banking hall, and an upper storey; at New Westminster the rising ground of the site, at the intersection of Church and Columbia Streets, may have decided Rattenbury to confine the building to a main floor and basement. He also selected a variety of other Renaissance themes (arched openings, balustrades, pilasters, friezes, and domes) to ornament the banks and achieved a considerable difference in effect between them. More recent influences are also discernible. The central elliptical arch of the New Westminster branch, and the compressed staircase that it spanned, again recalled H. H. Richardson, specifically the Holy Trinity Church Rectory, Boston, 1873–77 (Fig.3.9). The combination of such an arch with thin rectangular windows framed by small pilasters was, too, a feature of the libraries Richardson had built in the eastern United States. In addition, the division of the front into three parts and the decorative frieze and attic suggest that Rattenbury was competing consciously with Maclure's Temple Building, Victoria, 1893 (Fig.3.10), itself probably influenced by the work of Louis Sullivan, a Chicago architect inspired by Richardson. The crisp definition of the ornamentation of the Nelson branch, however, suggest an awareness of the sophisticated and synthetic Classical style that had been brought to the United States from the Ecole des Beaux-Arts in Paris by a number of fashionable American architects, most notably C. F. McKim.[21] With its disciplined composition, and rich decoration, culled from Classical and Renaissance ornament, the so-called Beaux-Arts style had come to dominate institutional architecture in the United States following its adoption for most of the buildings at the famous World's Columbia Fair held in Chicago in 1893.[22] But the rich Classicism of the Nelson branch also has an inspiration from England, as illustrated by Lockwood and Mawson's Congregational Church, Saltaire (Fig.3.11).

Stylistic issues aside, Rattenbury's three stone and brick structures set a new standard for commercial development in the interior. As a photograph of the New Westminster bank preserved in the Vancouver Public Library confirms (Fig.3.8), even this lower structure was more impressive than the majority of adjacent buildings, partly as a result of Rattenbury's use of rustication (masonry blocks cut on a large scale) for the basement and partly from the more original ornamentation. It was later to earn a different distinction as the scene of the province's largest bank robbery when, in 1911, "Big John" McNamara and his confederates stole over a quarter of a million dollars.[23]

In the absence of the original documents from the Bank of Montreal archives it is not possible to reconstruct the precise chronology of the bank building programme. (When Rattenbury wrote on 24 August 1898 of going to see his "new bank" at Rossland he might well have been referring to the site alone.) Two details of the New Westminster design suggest that it was the first to be completed: the domes echoed those capping the Land Registry Office and Government Printing Office wings of the Legislative Buildings, and the building stood awkwardly on its site, with an uncomfortable break in the line of the basement. The inference receives some corroboration in a remark in a letter written on 13 April 1900: "I have just finished my buildings in Rossland and Nelson; the New Westminster ones are also complete." Assuming that New Westminster came first, then the next to be planned was probably Rossland, similarly erected on a corner site and having two distinct, though related façades. Again the transition between front and side is achieved by the repetition of the frieze, arched windows and the pilasters, though at Rossland the last are concentrated in two projections, so as to separate the side façade into three parts. The division looks back to the Government Street branch of the Bank of Montreal, where the two gables served the same purpose. While the diagonal corner entrance at Nelson also echoes that earlier work, it is the most accomplished of the three later banks and, to judge from the report in the April *Colonist*, his favourite. Being unrestricted by adjacent buildings, Rattenbury could place matching façades on either side of the entrance. Thus, the pattern of arched and rectangular openings, pilasters, frieze and balustrade flow onto either side, each part nicely controlled by the thin and slightly projected half-bays decorated with the Bank's initials and capped with ornamental pediments. The continuity between the three sections produces a more monumental effect, even from the oblique angle of the adjacent sidewalk.

The Bank of Montreal was not Rattenbury's only patron in this period. On 24 December 1899, the *Colonist* announced his return to Victoria from a "trip around Calgary and by the Crow's Nest Pass, after inspecting buildings which he has now in the course of construction, and making arrangements for several new buildings." He had travelled to Calgary to see Patrick Burns. Born in Kirkfield, Ontario, in 1855, Burns had moved west to Manitoba in 1878 to establish a highly successful business as a cattle dealer. He had then expanded into the Northwest Territories, Yukon, and Alberta (supplying Dawson with cattle in 1898, as noted earlier) and moved his headquarters to Calgary in 1890. In that year he incorporated his enterprises, now including a meat-packing business and a number of ranches, as P. Burns and Company Ltd. By the time he met Rattenbury, almost certainly in Vancouver where he had set up a branch office, his retail meat business extended throughout Western Canada to Yokohama in the Orient and Liverpool and London in Europe. The satisfactory execution of the Dawson contract decided Burns to engage Rattenbury's services in 1899 as architect for two cold storage depots, one built in Vancouver and the other at Nelson (and, possibly, a third in New Westminster and a fourth at Greenwood);[24] more importantly, he asked Rattenbury to design a mansion in Calgary for his prospective bride, Eileen Ellis. The two men were alike in many ways, ambitious and resourceful, although it must be said that in public, at least, Burns possessed the more easy going and equable character of the two. He succeeded in avoiding the personality conflicts that dogged Rattenbury's career, enjoying a happy marriage, numerous directorships, and elevation to the Canadian Senate, in the Liberal interest, before his death on 24 February 1937.

The cold storage depots at Nelson and Vancouver and the mansion are mentioned in a later letter to his mother (13 April 1900): "in a month the two cold storage buildings and a residence will also be completed, leaving only the Victoria Court House, also well on the way, and Pat Burns' larger house"—and are cited in the impressive list of Rattenbury's work published by the *Colonist* on 24 December 1899, in another article celebrating "the rapid development of the interior cities, all of which are doing considerable building." The list is set out in columns with the location and a brief description of each commission on the left and the estimated cost on the right. It begins with three unnamed buildings in New Westminster, one of which was certainly the bank and a second possibly the Brown Block, all three valued at $40,000 in total; this figure suggests that the Brown Block and the third building were relatively insignificant, to judge from the costs of the banks that appear later in the list. In Vancouver he had the Burns cold storage, $20,000, and a "block of stores" still not definitely identified, $15,000. Next came Calgary, with the "stone residence for P. Burns" at $25,000 and an office block, probably also for Burns, at $8,000. At Nelson there was the bank for $35,000 and the Burns cold storage for $15,000, while at Rossland the bank was estimated at $50,000 and a "projected hotel" at $75,000. This last might be the Hotel Strathcona, a large four-storey seven-bay frame structure with a broad three-storied verandah across the front, illustrated in *Henderson's Gazetteer* for 1904. The same figure of $75,000 is assigned to the hotel at Greenwood. There follows a "residence" at Deer Park, near Rossland,

3.2 Iechinihl, Oak Bay, as originally built, 1898–1899.

3.1 The *Nora* in service.

3.3 R. N. Shaw, Merrist Wood, near Guildford, Surrey, 1877.

F.M.Rattenbury. "Architect"
Victoria. B.C. 1898

3.4 Sketch for the Bank of Montreal, Rossland, B.C., 1898.

3.5 Hotel Greenwood, Greenwood, B.C., 1899.

3.6 Bank of Montreal, Rossland, B.C., 1899.

3.7 Bank of Montreal, Nelson, B.C., 1899.

3.8 Bank of Montreal, New Westminster, B.C., 1898–189

3.9 H. H. Richardson, Drawing for Rectory, Holy Trinity Church, Boston, 1873–1877.

3.10 S. Maclure, Temple Building, Victoria, 1893.

3.13 Rattenbury in his early 30's.

3.11 Lockwood and Mawson,
Congregational Church, Saltaire
(1858–1859).

3.12 E. V. Bodwell House, Victoria (extreme right), 1900–1901.

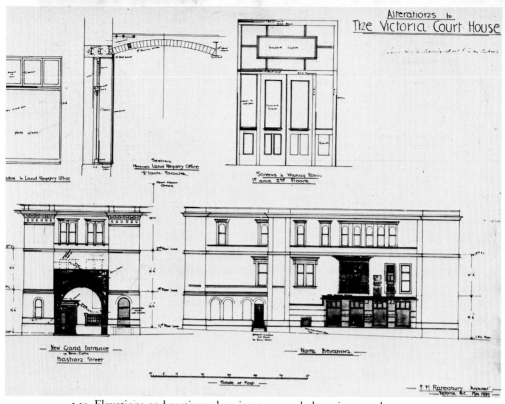

3.14 Elevations and sections showing proposed alterations to the
Courthouse, Victoria, 1899, executed 1900.

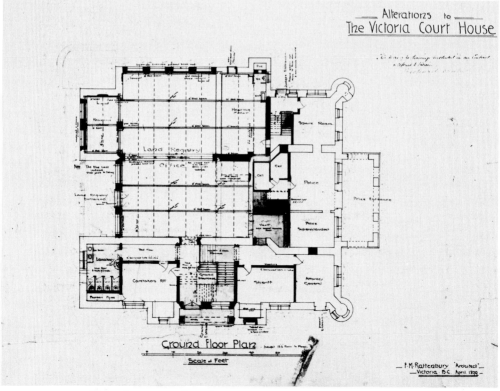

3.15 Plan of proposed alterations to Victoria Courthouse, 1899.

3.16 Patrick Burns Mansion, Calgary, 1901–1903.

valued at $10,000, a relatively large sum for a house. In view of the reference to "Pat Burns' larger house" in the April 13 letter to his mother it is just possible that the Deer Park house was built for his friend as a summer residence near the scenic Lower Arrow Lakes. The last two commissions listed are the Victoria Courthouse alterations, $25,000, and a "residence for E.V. Bodwell [a Victorial lawyer], $15,000."[25] The Bodwell house is also mentioned in the *Colonist* of 1 January 1900; it was built on Rockland Avenue and finished in 1901 (Fig. 3.12). Closer in style to current North American domestic architecture than Iechinihl, the front is enclosed by a verandah on the main floor level and surmounted by a broad gable which is more like a Classical pediment than a late medieval pitched roof. No less American are the simple rectangular plan of the house and the symmetrically placed cross-axial gabled roofs. The grand total of Rattenbury's commissions at the end of 1899 thus amounted to $345,000, yielding quite enough in fees to compensate for the debts incurred by his Yukon exploits.

On 26 March 1900, Rattenbury wrote on the notepaper of the Hotel Phair, at Nelson: "I am dodging through the mountains again – not a long trip this time, however, just to Nelson and back with a day off at Vancouver (a week's trip altogether). We are just completing the Bank at Nelson and also the Cold Storage." The trip, however, involved not only work. It coincided with news of the relief of Ladysmith, greeted with jubilation in Nelson, as in the rest of British Columbia.[26] Rattenbury clearly enjoyed the celebrations. It was "a tremendous day here. From 2 A.M. to midnight there was tremendous cheering, a constant fusillade of fireworks, processions, and so on, the whole town turning out and every building decorated. I never saw greater enthusiasm before. By all accounts good old stolid England seems to have turned topsy turvy as well." He claimed in his letter that he was anxious to "clear off" his work so as to have "a free and easy 'dolce far niente' this summer," but this hope perhaps masked a concern that he began to entertain at this time about his future career in British Columbia. He expressed this concern more openly in his next letter, on 13 April. While welcoming a slackening in his work and expressing the hope that he would not "get a lot more," he continued revealingly "when I am busy I always want to get the work done; but when done I feel compelled to rustle up some more, and so I go on." Perhaps doubting the prospects for further challenging commissions in the province, he mused, "I do not think I should care to anticipate always living here; I have notions of trying Rome or some continental city for a time, so as to have a complete change of life, surroundings and interests." This is but one instance of a number of extended trips to Britain and Europe that he contemplated but did not undertake, and even now he decided, "in any case I should keep this house, as I have always so far found that when away from Victoria one wants to get back very badly."

Perhaps closer acquaintance with Burns was also a factor, for on 4 May, 1900, he wrote to his mother from Victoria: "I almost imagine that towards the end of June I am going down to Mexico with Pat Burns, to look at a copper mine he has bought there. I shall feel greatly tempted to take a steamer to London from there, especially as Pat is going to do so, I think, but we shall see in a little time. Pat is coming to spend a few days with us on May 24 (Queen's birthday). For one thing, I shall have pretty well cleaned up all my work by then except his new house."

At that time Victoria did have its own special attractions, such as the Mafeking and Royal Birthday celebrations, "three or four days of it," he wrote on 30 May, including a "large procession of decorated waggons, some of them very beautiful, perhaps the best being a bus decorated with flowers so as to form a large nosegay, with bonny little girls all in white looking out of the window openings and singing." But, as he wrote to Kate on 22 June, "it seems rather a pity to spend the next few years in Victoria, charming as it is." Hard though it might be "to tear oneself away from here in glorious summer, still in the autumn I think I shall come to England and look around in the neighbourhood of London for a nice little place to make my headquarters, and if I find one, then send for the family and let my house in Victoria. It would be nice being able to run on to the Continent and spend a few weeks here and there."[27]

By July his restlessness had diminished, though not disappeared, as he completed the courthouse commission and became involved in the preliminary work on the Burns House. "Tempus 10.15 P.M. and a glorious full moon," began a letter to his mother on 10 July. "I have just been strolling in the garden and the air is fragrant with perfume and the moon on the water looks most romantic .... I have just returned from a trip to Vancouver, where I met Pat Burns and let the contract for his 'Manor House.' I always enjoy a trip to Vancouver, where I went to see a Baseball match between 8 Bloomers (girls) and the local team. Some of the Bloomers, about three of them, played splendidly. The rest ran and threw like girls. It now turns out that these three are boys in wigs etc. A bit of a sell, for they got big gates and are evidently making money. A regular Western scheme." But there is a forced jollity about his description of life in British Columbia, perhaps intended to conceal a conviction that life was beginning to pass him by: "I am going in for the quiet, gentlemanly game of croquet," he added, "as more becoming to my sedate age [a mere 32]" (Fig. 3.13).

The additions to the Victoria Courthouse were probably finished in those summer months, giving him another reason to postpone his ideas of travel outside Canada. Two sheets of drawings signed "F. M. Rattenbury 'Architect' Victoria B.C. April 1899" are preserved in the Provincial Archives, comprising a ground plan and elevations, with details of his additions in coloured washes (Fig. 3.14–15).[28] Externally, he introduced a new arched entrance onto Bastion Street and extra windows and a door on the north façade of H. O. Tiedmann's plain Renaissance styled courthouse (built in 1899 and noteworthy as the first instance of the use of concrete in the province).[29] The main purpose of Rattenbury's work was the insertion of new courtrooms and the provision of enlarged, fireproofed office space under the courts for the Land Registry Office, as well as the installation of an elevator. All this he achieved by opening up the major part of the ground floor, and by supporting the first storey on steel beams. Nonetheless, it must be admitted that the new arrangement of windows on the north façade was unsympathetic, and Rattenbury called the work "tedious" when writing to W. C. Wells on 21 January 1901 with a final account of $50,386.47.[30]

Meanwhile, in the summer of 1900 he had returned to Calgary, sending a brief account of his activities to his mother from the Alberta Hotel on 26 July: "Just a line from Calgary, 1,000 miles from Victoria, being on the other side of the mountains. I got a telegram from Burns asking me to come and left Victoria the same night. We are laying out the lines of his new house. Tomorrow I am going down to a large cattle ranch, to see the cattle loaded for shipment to England. Perhaps you may partake of them later." The sense of *ennui*, however, lingered: "I had a grand trip across the mountains – they always look magnificent – but I could not help contrasting the feelings with which I now gaze on them and the exciting interest I took in them on my first trip over, when they seemed so trapped in glamour and romance. It was almost saddening to feel," he added, perhaps reflecting also on his marriage, "that all enthusiasm had vanished and could not be reawakened."

The Burns house, or more properly, mansion, was not entirely finished until 1903, by which time the building had probably risen above the revised estimate of $30,000 he gave to his mother on 20 August 1901. Before its unfortunate demolition in 1956, the mansion stood on 4th Street South West between 12th and 13th Avenues. Photographs preserved at the Glenbow-Alberta Institute show how it formerly dominated its surroundings, even after the encroachment of undistinguished speculative buildings (Fig.3.16). The main façade comprised a one-storey, three-bay entrance flanked by two taller wings, remarkable for their battered or inward curving sides (a form he later used on a smaller scale for the pilasters framing the fireplaces in the 1901 Duff house) against one of which rose a broad buttressed tower. The irregularity imparted by the tower and the conservatory that extended from it was offset by the symmetry of the body of the mansion, centred about the pointed arch of the entrance porch and the gable above. On the rear façade the "E" formation of wings and central gable were shifted towards the tower so as to create a more regular composition. The fundamental influence was obviously Gothic architecture. Yet the entrance arch and square headed windows imitated Tudor domestic design, the tower was derived from an earlier stage of English medieval ecclesiastical design, and the steeply pitched roofs and gables reflected the French Gothicism inherent in the Château style. The chunky surface of the roughly cut masonry and such quasi-medieval features as the gargoyles and coat of arms on the tower were intended, no less than the size and costly materials of the structure, to symbolize Burns's position as a financial baron. These historical elements aside, the curved edges of the wings on the entrance façade suggest that Rattenbury was by now more sympathetic towards the growing appreciation of pure design or of the creation of aesthetic effect by shape rather than by the copying of historical ornament, promoted by the Arts and Crafts Movement. Perhaps those wings and their neatly turned tops were Rattenbury's response to Maclure's increasing interest in that inspiration. Still, as the mixture of sources in the design of the Burns mansion shows, Rattenbury was a conservative eclectic at heart.

The stone foundations of the mansion might have been laid out by 8 October 1900, when Rattenbury had written to his mother about another "castle" nearer at hand.

> Well, what shall I tell you about? I cannot talk business as I am not doing much, just finishing off old work. I may be asked to build "Cary Castle" the Lieutenant-Governor's Residence, which was burned down last summer. I am going up to the site tomorrow to advise the Government about it. On the other hand the other architects want a show and think I have had my share of government work, so are using all the political influence they can. I do not know how it will turn out and I cannot say that I care much.

Whether or not the last sentence was bluff, the award of the Castle Cary commission was to involve Rattenbury in the most bitter feud of his career. Therefore, it is ironic indeed that he should have ended the letter with the words, "I wish something exciting would happen so that I should have something to write to you about."

Four

RAILWAY HOTELS &
GOVERNMENT HOUSE
1900–1902

By the fall of 1899 Rattenbury believed that he had finally un-
burdened himself of the problems resulting from his Yukon enterprises,
confiding to his sister on 4 November that he was relieved to be
"clean out of it." But his relief proved to be premature. In the winter of
1900 he was served with a writ charging him with failure to pay all the
debts incurred by the company. The details of the case, or cases (it is not
clear whether one or a number of charges were brought against him), are,
unfortunately, lost, though the general outline can be gleaned from three
letters sent to his mother.

"Don't trouble your head about the lawsuit," he wrote on 14
November, "it is only about a matter of £400 or £500 that some fellows
are trying to get me to pay on a technicality. I don't think they have a
ghost of a chance, it is only a bluff. The details you would hardly com-
prehend, so it is not worth while going into them unless I explained
at great length. The only thing is the annoyance, although there is
something very interesting in law cases. I think I should have enjoyed
being a lawyer." Before 18 December he had been able to call the plaintiff
to testify under oath "and he made a mess of it, swearing false statements,
easily proved so by his own letters. So I expect I shall not hear much more
about the matter; I am almost dead sure to win now, anyway." On 1 July
1901, having won a favourable decision, he could afford to indicate the
true scale of the claim against him:

At last my lawsuits are settled. A fellow sued me for £3500 and it has been dragging on for 18 months. We got him under examination at last and the worthy gentleman got himself into a hole, swearing to statements that were false. I happen to have letters from him showing this (he would never have started this action but he thought I had lost the letters) now he is more than anxious to drop it, and offers me £300 to let the action stop and I have consented. The £300 will more than pay all my costs, so it is a successful termination. Of course, I was expected to win, but when at variance with a blackleg you never know what you will hit up against.

The experience sharpened Rattenbury's suspicious attitude towards his professional associates during the protracted negotiations that preceded the award of the Cary Castle commission. That controversy was to blight another period of considerable success between 1900 and 1903, when he did much work for the Canadian Pacific Railway.

Cary Castle, the rambling and uncomfortable official residence of the lieutenant-governor had burned down on 18 May 1899. The commission to design its replacement was clearly attractive, and Rattenbury proceeded to remove an impediment which he thought might prejudice his chances. Although he had received $42,544.51 in fees for the Legislative Buildings by the close of 1899, he was still owed $2,382.[1] The government was as loathe to settle this account in 1900 as it was to commence the rebuilding of the lieutenant-governor's residence, owing to the magnitude of the public debt, which had risen as high as $7,425,262 in 1898.[2] On 27 August 1900 Rattenbury detached himself from direct involvement in the unresolved claim by assigning to his wife, Florrie, "all his claims against the Government of British Columbia for services rendered as Architect of the Parliament Buildings of British Columbia."[3] On the same day he informed the recently appointed minister of lands and works, W. C. Wells, of his willingness to "lay before you, for your consideration some designs for the rebuilding of Government House." These, he suggested, would be appropriate for the site, and he was prepared to spare no pains to make the residence creditable to the government, adding obligingly, "If the Government desired, I would prepare a full set of plans and full sized details of every part, and the Government could engage another architect to carry out the work from the plans — as I myself am desirous of travelling abroad this winter."[4] Although he had contemplated various journeys earlier in the year, it seems that Rattenbury had learned the value of a more subtle approach in his communications with government officials and anticipated accusations of favouritism from the local architectural community. He went on to advise Wells on the failings of competitions — ironic, this, in view of his own triumph of 1893 — and, lastly, while declining to compete he offered "to render any assistance I may be able, in getting out the particulars or in assisting at the selection of a design should you desire me to do so."

As he suspected, other Victoria architects were anxious to secure the commission. Thomas Hooper, for one, solicited Wells on 28 August, supported by four members of the Legislative Assembly, "using all the political influence they can," as he worded it in his 8 October letter. Rattenbury's fears were realized on 31 October, 1900, when the government advertised a competition for designs for a new, plain residence, to be constructed of wood on a stone basement at a cost not exceeding $50,000, the entries to be submitted anonymously by 22 December.

The extent of Rattenbury's disappointment is difficult to gauge. Writing to his mother on 14 November, he initially referred to the competition for a much larger project, the C.P.R.'s new Hotel Vancouver: "I have sent in my plans in the Hotel Competition and we ought to hear the result in a week or so." Rather disingenuously, he continued, "I cannot say that I am anxious though. Of course one always likes to win, and I like competing, but I am not desirous of 13 or 14 months hard work again." Then came his account of the announcement of the Cary Castle competition: "The new Governor's residence is also a competition. The Government has told me that they regret it, but so much pressure has been brought to bear. On my saying that I did not think it worth-while competing, they begged me to do so. 'You know, Rattenbury, the feeling the Government have towards you,' the Attorney-General said." Rattenbury was unenthusiastic because, "it would be an awful nuisance carrying on a building at Victoria and one at Vancouver if I get them both," being "not too fond of the travelling on the water so constantly; I have had too much of it." His misgivings about the prospect of supervising two major commissions in different locations were warranted, and his thoughts were probably occupied less with Cary Castle than with the reconstruction of the C. P. R. Hotel.

Designed by Thomas Sorby and opened on 16 May 1887, the Hotel Vancouver had comprised a six-storey brick structure built in a simplified Château style at the intersection of Granville and Georgia Streets (Fig.1.2).[5] Despite the addition in 1893 of a block on the south side (along Granville Street), there were insufficient rooms to accommodate the increase in travellers. So, on 11 October 1900, Sir Thomas Shaughnessy, the president of the C. P. R., informed the *Province* of the company's intention to demolish Sorby's building and replace it with a new facility to contain 250 bedrooms and a ballroom. Clearly, it represented the most important commission in the province since the erection of the Legislative Buildings.

The Cary Castle episode taught Rattenbury to be cautious. "I have not yet heard the result of the Hotel Competition," he had informed his mother on 18 December 1900, "the architects of the East are pulling strings. Today, however, I got a telegram from the C. P. Railway Company asking for further information as to the cost of my design, which shows that the matter is not yet decided." Despite his anxiety over this commission, he was consoled by the award of two local contracts. "I have just got tenders in for a block of Offices [possibly the Scholefield Block in Victoria, since demolished] and have also made Plans for a Hospital up country [sadly unidentified], a fairly large building though not costly at all."

Neither contract had been decided by Christmas 1900, but this did not prevent Rattenbury from enjoying the celebrations, which appear to have lasted for a whole week. "Last night," he wrote to his mother on New Year's Day, "we had a Xmas tree and Snooks invited about a couple of dozen youngsters. They had a great time. – Santa Claus distributed the presents; then the parents came and we had supper." On New Year's Eve he attended "a Club dinner, a very jolly affair, there being a lot of rattling good singers amongst the fellows there. We really have one of the most sociable clubs here possible, a lot of good chaps. It adds a great deal to the attractions of the Town as a place to live in."[6] Whether as a result of the festivities or of his professional commitments, he was late in choosing a Christmas gift for his mother. Yet, when he did so, he showed a characteristic flair, writing to Kate on 3 January 1901, "I have been wondering what would be a good present for the mater, and it struck me that if an arrangement was made for a carriage and pair for two or three hours once a week it would be a good idea. If you think so too, you might ask Frank to arrange for this and let me know."

On 16 January 1901, the judges of the Cary Castle competition announced their decision in favour of the Vancouver partnership of Byrens and Sait.[7] This was applauded by the *Colonist*, which considered their design both aesthetically pleasing and economical, being estimated at $4,000 below the projected appropriation. In response, the editor was bombarded with a host of anonymous letters critical of the winning scheme. One, dated 18 January, and signed "Architect," charged that Byrens and Sait had failed to comply with the specification that most of the ground floor rooms be positioned so as to open on to the ballroom. Another, signed "A Citizen," questioned the accuracy of the architects' estimates and also the rectitude of appointing judges from the local professional circle who might recognize the draughtsmanship of the contestants. While such protests apparently caused Wells to consult Rattenbury that summer, it cannot be assumed that he was the author of the letters, since he was not the only disappointed competitor. Nor, as it transpired, was the Byrens and Sait design faultless.

More pleasing news reached Rattenbury from eastern Canada at about the same time—the award of the Hotel Vancouver commission. By early February at the latest he was in Montreal, staying once again at the Windsor Hotel. A scrap of a letter to his mother survives, providing enough information to establish the significance of the occasion (Fig.4.1.). On the front of the sheet are the fragmented phrases "organize their staff. . . ." "take charge of the operations. . . . in the meantime to learn." On the back (where the text was written vertically and is thus more legible), he reported, "They have been very good to me and Gen. Manager McNicoll told me to get some instructions re. the Co's regulations etc., for he said you will do lots of work for the Co. in the future. This was very satisfactory." Thus Rattenbury assumed the lucrative, if unofficial, position of architect to the C. P. R.'s Pacific Division.

Presumably to offer him the opportunity to inspect their most famous Canadian hotel, the directors sent him to Quebec City, to be entertained at the Château Frontenac, a building that impressed him as an:

> exquisite Hotel, a magnificent feudal castle built on the edge of the heights of Quebec overlooking the immense [St.] Lawrence river, the Citadel rising immediately close by. It is easy to imagine Wolfe's difficulty when he had to climb the precipitous Cliffs to where the Hotel stands.[8] The interior of the Hotel is a marvel, in quaint, old style—oak, tapestry and beautiful old hand painted walls. I never saw anything like it. It is rich, quaint and convenient, more like a huge old house with the rooms thrown into each other than a Hotel as generally pictured. I am now sitting in the Drawing Room, which is only separated from the corridor by a screen, with openings not doors, (that is, the Corridor and Room are open). I have just dined and the band is now playing. In another large octagon room are a huge assembly of Quebec Belles, who are just going to a private supper and I am waiting to see them pass along the corridor to the supper room. They are chattering away in English and French. It is a quaint old town, as quaint as I have seen and the Hotel is delightful.

Rattenbury left Montreal on 12 February, writing to his mother the day before, "I am off to the coast again in the morning—3,000 [miles]— Jerusalem. I have got all settled and am to push ahead the Hotel rapidly and also the mountain hotel [the Mount Stephen House at Field, apparently the first concrete result of Rattenbury's conversation with McNicoll in Montreal] . . . . I expect I shall be back in Victoria in 10 days as I shall have to stop off at Field and Vancouver."

Once in Vancouver on 19 February 1901, Rattenbury proudly told the *Province* that his "delicate late French hotel Château style" design had been preferred over submissions from "some of the leading architects in New York, Montreal and Toronto" and that it "would have few rivals in Canada. The Windsor at Montreal will be larger; the Frontenac at Quebec will be about the same size—and these are the only ones that are really in the same class." The scheme with which he secured the commission is almost certainly represented by the "Rough Outline Sketch of the Front Elevation" published in the same newspaper. On the 25th of that month he wrote to his mother, "I am sending you a Vancouver paper, 'The Province,' giving a sketch of the Hotel, but it is more conspicuous for what it left out than what is in. However, soon I shall have a sketch illustrated more like what the Hotel will be."

The *Province* sketch shows a broad seven-storey building dominated by two flanking towers surmounted, like the main block, by steeply pitched Château style roofs (Fig.4.2). These roofs enlarge the main feature of the Bank of Montreal in Victoria, from which he also took the oriel windows that rise through the four main floors of the towers and front. Apart from his own bank, Rattenbury was surely influenced by the example of Price's Château Frontenac and Edward Maxwell's boldly composed brick and stone C.P.R. station at the foot of Granville Street, constructed between 1897 and 1898 (Fig.4.3).[9] However, he translated the style into a more orderly form, which may have appealed to the highly efficient Van Horne (who continued to oversee the company's architecture even after he had retired as president in June 1899 in favour of Shaughnessy).[10] The corner towers, oriel windows, and the colonnade of thick Neo-Romanesque stone columns create a symmetrical composition gathered about the central curved Dutch style gable. The "New Hotel Vancouver," indeed, promised to be "Equal to any in Canada" as the headline in the *Province* boasted, and within the context of British Columbia hotels, "A Palace for the Public." No doubt he hoped that his hotel would be accepted into the international corpus of grand railway hotels, among the first of which had been Sir George Gilbert Scott's St. Pancras Station Hotel, London, begun in 1868, a year after Rattenbury's birth. His choice of the Château also had an international dimension. The style was synonymous with wealth and luxury, being favoured by leaders of fashion (and holders of railway stock) like the Astors and Vanderbilts, as epitomized by Biltmore, the mansion built for George W. Vanderbilt, 1889–1895, at Asheville, North Carolina, by R. M. Hunt.

Rattenbury estimated the cost at between $400,000 and $500,000 and was happy to assure the citizens that the company would award the contracts to local firms. He planned to erect the hotel in stages so that it could remain in operation, beginning with a "huge new wing" on the west side of the present structure containing eighty bedrooms. A temporary corridor was to connect this wing with the old dining-room while its replacement, measuring 100 by 60 feet and finely decorated, was fitted out. Next, the old addition on the southeast corner would be dismantled and "replaced in harmony with the western wing." Finally, Sorby's building was to be reconstructed as part of the centrepiece "of pressed brick with a light and airy effect carried out by terra cotta mouldings." Thus enlarged, the Hotel Vancouver would have 250 bedrooms at its disposal. "You may add," Rattenbury loftily stated, "that I am preparing plans for a $20,000 hotel at Field" which "will contain fifty rooms and will be on the Swiss Chalet order of architecture." He provided the Victoria *Colonist* with the same information two days later on his return from Vancouver, adding that the pitched roofs of the Vancouver Hotel were to be covered with British Columbia slate.

The return journey brought Rattenbury a reminder of some of the dramatic differences between his life in western Canada and in the safe predictability of Yorkshire. Writing to his mother on the 25th he provided a vivid account of his "exciting time returning:

> For a few miles the railway is dug out half way up huge precipitous mountains, which in the winter are deeply covered with snow. The day happening to be warm the snow began to slide, and an avalanche is no joke. They start two or three miles away overhead and travel 80 miles an hour, smashing huge trees into fragments and hurling huge rocks as big as a house before them. You just hear a murmur and before you can say "Jack Robinson" they are away below you. If you happen to be in their way, and they are often ¼ mile long, you are a gonner. I knew they were expected as we reached the Selkirk mountains and was consequently a little nervous, but when one came down a little way ahead I got more so, and the train waited whilst a gang of loco men and two huge snow ploughs were clearing away the track. Three more avalanches came down in various places, close by a Railway depot two years ago, trains and everything and 13 people were swept into nothingness. I honestly confess that after waiting 10 hours, when the train started again in the dark to skirt this 15 or 20 miles I was in a blue funk and so were all on the train, awaiting each

second, expecting to hear the coming roar of an avalanche. But needless to say we got through; at the same time, I think I shall be a little nervous of crossing the mountains for some time to come, especially in winter.

The task of making the working drawings for the hotel occupied much of Rattenbury's time over the ensuing weeks. "I had to go down to the office [in the Five Sisters Block at 28 Fort Street, designed by Sorby in 1891] to complete my Vancouver Hotel Plans, which, please the pigs, will be ready to send out on Monday," he notified his mother on 13 April 1901. Thereafter, he was free to work on a number of local projects, including an entry for the Victoria High School competition, as advertised in June by the city school board. While the board considered the anonymous submissions, he seems to have received new instructions about the hotel from the C. P. R. directors, perhaps before 12 June when he confided to her, "No, I do not think my Hotel will be up to the 'Grand' [in Leeds], although I have never been in the latter." Evidence of a change is clearer in another letter to her, written on 1 July. "I am going to Vancouver tonight with the new tenders and Plans for the Hotel, and also the tenders for the New Car Depot [for the B. C. Electric Railway and Light Company] that I am going to erect at Victoria [a plain brick building still standing on Pembroke Street].[11]

The revision in the hotel was necessitated by a reduction in the budget, to which he alluded in a "stave" to his mother, dated 20 August 1901, invaluable as a record of his commissions in that period.

I am so busy that I have to go down to the office in the morning before the dew is off the grass.... I have just finished the working plans for the new High School, and, to crown all, the Directors of the [Royal Jubilee] Hospital requested me yesterday to push ahead with largish additions to the Hospital. So now I have underway, and just beginning:

1. Hotel Vancouver   —to cost—$300.000= £60.000
2. Field Hotel   " $20.000 = £ 4.000
3. High School   " $30.000 = £ 6.000
4. Government House   " $60.000 = £12.000
5. Scholefield Block   " $20.000 = £ 4.000
6. Car Depot   " $15.000 = £ 3.000
7. Hospital Additions   " $20.000 = £ 4.000
8. Cable Station   " $25.000 = £ 5.000
9. Burns House   " $30.000 = £ 6.000

as well as several smaller things. A pretty big list of work for one year. At last I had to engage an assistant [John S. Pearce, listed in the Victoria directories as an architect with a room in the 5 Sisters Block until 1909] as I could not spare the time to run around, looking after contractors, etc. But as I make every plan and tracing and write every specification you can guess that I have to work a little bit. It never rains but it pours.

While Rattenbury revised the Vancouver Hotel drawings, the C.P.R. ordered him to proceed with the extension of their hotel at Field.[12] A plain rectangular wood frame building had been designed by Sorby in 1887 as one of the two regular dining stops in the mountainous section of the line where the weight of a dining car would have severely impeded the speed of the transcontinental trains (Fig.4.4). The other was at Glacier; for a time, smaller versions existed at Canmore and Yale. At these watering places, the expresses stopped for anything between twenty and fifty minutes, while the passengers ate off clean tablecloths armed with stiffly starched napkins, highly polished silverware and gleaming crockery, confronted by the glorious scenery abutting the Kicking Horse (Field) and Rogers Passes. The commission to expand Mount Stephen House signalled a new phase in the campaign, initiated by Van Horne and pursued by Shaughnessy, to complement the railway's carriage business with tourism. As early as 1889 they had published brochures like *The New Highway to the Orient* to advertise their mountain inns at Field, Glacier, Shuswap Lake, and Banff Springs (the Château Lake Louise, a surprisingly austere wooden building designed by Sorby, was not begun until 1899). In its description of Glacier House, the similarities with Alpine scenery were duly noted since the hotel stood at what was then the base of the Illecillewaet icefield "five hundred feet thick at its forefoot, and... said to exceed in area all the glaciers of Switzerland combined."[13] The best publicity came from independent writers like Lafcadio Hearne, whose account of the approach to the Kicking Horse Pass from the east, printed in the November 1890 issue of *Harper's New Monthly Magazine*, had especially pleased Van Horne. "The legions of spruce, always preserving the same savage independence of poise, perpendicular as masts, now climb six thousand feet above us—climb perhaps even higher, until the hems of the perpetual snows mass over them and hide them from sight. Far above their loftiest outposts, peaks are lifting glaciers to the sun. At Stephen we reached the loftiest point of the route; we are nearly five thousand three hundred feet above the sea—but we are still walled up to heaven."[14]

On the west side of Sorby's diminutive building, situated beneath the escarpment of the majestic Mount Stephen, "amidst marvellous scenery, glaciers, waterfalls, 1,220 feet drop," as Rattenbury described it, he added a large frame building. It was divided into two sections, the larger having four stories covered by a steeply pitched roof. Erected on a concrete base, the walls were sheathed with shingles and, at the upper level, with Tudor half-timbering (Fig.4.5). According to a report in the March 1902 issue of *The Railway and Shipping World*, the addition "transformed" the old building into a "small but first-class hotel," affording not merely fifty new bedrooms "with up-to-date plumbing" (some having "private sitting rooms en suite"), but also a "large and handsome hall and billiard-room, with heavy beams and panelled walls and ceiling, and a huge open fire-place for burning logs; there is also a smoking-room and a drawing-room commanding views of the Kicking Horse valley."[15] The public rooms seem to have been placed in the taller part, illustrated with the report.[16] The cost of the additions may be recorded in the C.P.R.'s *Contracts and Proposals* book, 1903-10, in which a retrospective entry for 22 October 1902 states that the contractor J.J. Disette had been paid $24,000 for "Alterations to Hotel" at Field.[17] The gabled projections, variety of windows, and half-timbering lent the whole complex more the character of an English manor house than of the Swiss chalet. Rattenbury had, in any event, shed the mantle of Price, whose Banff Springs Hotel retained more French and Scottish features.

While Mount Stephen House was being enlarged, Chief Commissioner Wells asked Rattenbury to examine the design submitted by Byrens and Sait for Cary Castle in order to determine whether the criticisms published in the Victoria press had been justified. On 14 August 1901 Rattenbury told Wells that he had met the architects to calculate the costs anew and discovered that to come within the government's budget their design would have to be altered radically. Nevertheless, he thought that "there should be no difficulty in building a very good and suitable residence for the sum of $50,000."[18] The implication of greater professional skill conveyed by that sentence, combined with the urgency of budgetary restraint, impressed Wells. He awarded Byrens and Sait the $250 premium but not the actual commission, despite their protests that Rattenbury's calculations were not correct.

On 16 August, two days after his interview with Wells, Rattenbury had run off one of his regular reports to his mother, in which he prefaced his account of the Cary Castle saga with a notice of his success in the high school competition. He had participated only "for fun, but it has come my way all the same. I seem to have been awfully lucky, as I have won every competition that I have been into. It is very funny, I made two designs and personally I liked the other twice as much as this one, and yet had I only sent in the one Design that I liked I should have been out of it."

This modesty is not altogether convincing, having the same studied diffidence that is evident in the account he gave of his current part in the Government House commission. Encumbered by Byrens and Sait's "absolutely riciculous" design "the Government asked me to give them an idea of what they could build for the money, and I made a plan, which tickled them immensely, and they asked me to build it. But I did not see how I could, for, as I told them, it would appear as if I had used my position as their confidential adviser to knife those other chaps, and then bag the work myself, and I was not going to put myself in that position." He expected that "they will give the work to another architect and appoint me as permanent Government architect, to generally keep an eye on buildings," adding "it was rather hard lines on me getting into such a position, as if another man had looked at the plans he would also have been compelled to reject them, and then I would have had a whooping fine 'Castle' to build."

Contemporary attitudes also coloured his response to a more dramatic and recent event in Oak Bay: "Just opposite our seaside 'maison' there is an island ¼ mile away and on it there were a number of Indian Rancheries built of huge logs and largely deserted. Tonight someone set them on fire and there has been a huge and glorious blaze, lighting up the whole country and reflected on the water. It was a magnificent spectacle." As was typical of his generation he took no interest in native Indian architecture. To him the conflagration was remarkable only as a "spectacle," whereas he had bemoaned the demolition of an historic part of Headingly, near Leeds, for a new housing development, in a letter to his sister Kate.[19]

Early in September 1901, Wells asked him to respond to Byrens and Sait's charge that his revised estimate had been deliberately distorted. On the 11th he assured Wells that his calculations were fair and cited the costs of his most recent domestic commission as a parallel.[20] This was the house he had just designed for Lyman P. Duff, a talented Q.C. (later to be appointed chief justice of Canada) who was to defend Rattenbury in 1904 when he was accused of malpractice in the Cary Castle commission. Erected at 1745 Rockland Avenue, it is more imposing than Iechinihl and dominated externally by a large Jacobean window which lights the fine hand-carved fir and cedar staircase (Figs.4.6A & B). The window, with stained glass, is set within a broad, shingled gable, curved on one side and flanked on the other by a battlemented projection enclosing the service stairs, washroom, and butler's pantry and, on the upper level, the children's bathroom. The interior is an equally attractive blend of the Queen Anne

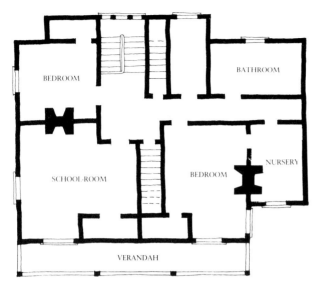

BLOCK PLAN, UPPER FLOOR, L.P. DUFF HOUSE

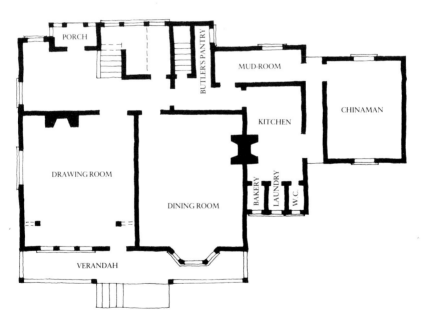

BLOCK PLAN, GROUND FLOOR, LYMAN P. DUFF HOUSE, VICTORIA, 1901

4.6A Block Plans, L. P Duff house, Victoria.

and Arts and Crafts styles. Beyond the lobby is a spacious entrance hall (approximately 14 feet deep by 24 feet wide), with a window seat facing towards a broad sliding door into the elegant and well lit drawing room. The drawing room is made to appear larger than its actual dimensions (22 by 20 feet), by two pilasters screening a wide window that opens onto the broad verandah spanning the back of the house. In the contiguous dining-room (22 by 15 feet) and hall, Rattenbury had, as he informed Wells, used a "good deal of hardwood panelling... and whilst I understand that Messrs Byrens and Sait had specified similar work in their design. I only estimated in my report to you for a simply finished Interior executed mainly in Cedar."

Rattenbury's letter may have been intended merely for the public record. Indeed, Wells had invited tenders for the commission as long before as 6 September, almost certainly based on the "Plan" which Rattenbury had mentioned to his mother. Aware that he might be accused of underhand dealings, Rattenbury persuaded Wells that he should collaborate with another architect on the execution of the commission. This solution had been agreed on or before 20 August 1901, when he explained to his mother, "Since I last wrote you the Government urgently requested me to make Plans for Government House... so I am doing it in conjunction with another architect, an arrangement I insisted upon for the reasons I gave in my last letter. However, I am responsible to the Government and so I am planning and designing the structure." Samuel Maclure had accepted the post, suggesting that he concurred with Rattenbury's criticism of the Byrens and Sait design. But before the building had progressed beyond the foundations, Maclure succumbed to a lengthy illness that virtually removed him from the scene. Thus, although the basement plan preserved at the Provincial Archives is signed, "S. Maclure Architect September 1901," the bulk of the commission should be attributed to Rattenbury; and upon its official opening in August 1903 he received full credit in the local newspapers.[21]

Maclure may have contributed to the internal layout, distinguished by an intelligent use of space, as in the positioning of the banqueting room on the same axis as the entrance with reception rooms on either side, but the exterior bore all the characteristics of Rattenbury's previous domestic architecture (Fig.4.7–9). The fieldstone walls of the entrance block were framed by a tall bay window capped by a gable which recalled both Iechinihl and the Duff house. The battlemented turret placed alongside the gable corresponded with the entrance to the Burns house in Calgary and Cleckheaton Town Hall. The combination of simple underlying

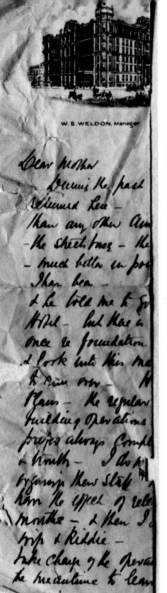

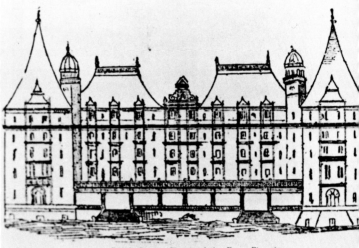

Canada.

Rough Outline Sketch of the Front Elevation.

4.2 Sketch design for the Hotel Vancouver, 1901.

4.1 Scrap of letter, about February 1901, from the Windsor Hotel, Montreal, reporting Rattenbury's appointment by the C.P.R.

4.3 E. Maxwell, second C.P.R. Station, Vancouver, 1897–1898, as decorated for the 1901 visit of the Duke and Duchess of York.

4.5 C.P.R. Mount Stephen at Field, with Sorby's original building on the extreme left and Rattenbury's two additions, 1901–1902, to its right.

4.4 T.C. Sorby, original C.P.R. Hotel at Field, B.C., 1887.

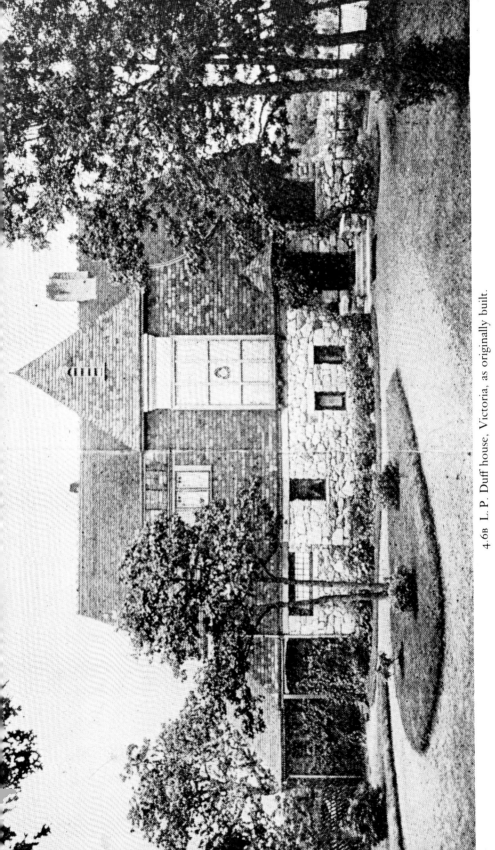

4.6B L. P. Duff house, Victoria, as originally built.

GOVERNMENT HOUSE - VICTORIA - B.C. CANADA

4.7 Rattenbury and Maclure, Cary Castle, Victoria, 1901–1903. Contemporary postcard.

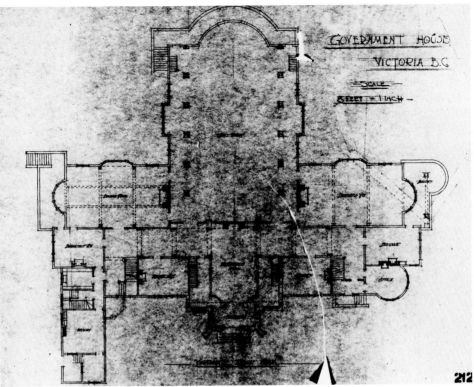

4.8 Main floor plan, Cary Castle, 1901, as executed.

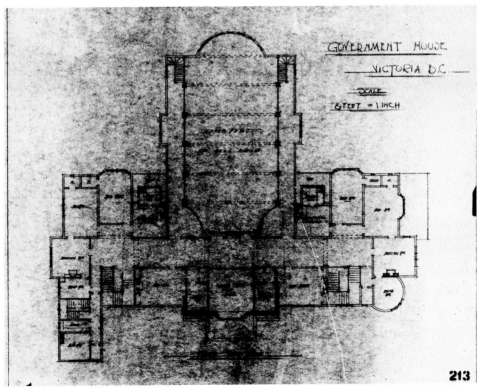

4.9 Upper floor plan, Cary Castle.

4.10 J. H. McGregor House, Victoria, c.1901–1902, photographed c.1905.

4.11 Third Victoria High School, *Victoria*, 1901–1902.

4.12 Cable Station, Bamfield, B.C., 1903, photographed shortly after its completion.

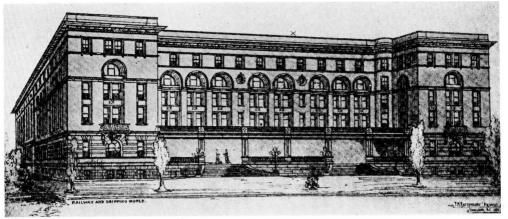

4.13 Revised design for the proposed C.P.R. Hotel Vancouver, 1902, as partly built 1902–1908.

4.14 C.P.R. Hotel, Vancouver, 1887–1908, showing T. C. Sorby's original hotel, and, on the right, Rattenbury's south wing.

4.15 Iechinihl, with Rattenbury's additions of 1903 on the extreme right.

form and picturesquely arranged projections, gables, and windows was foreign to Maclure's more symmetrical composition. (However, it is of interest that not long after working with Maclure on the design of Cary Castle, Rattenbury adopted a more symmetrical version of the Arts and Crafts style with the house commissioned by the surveyor and local bard, James Herrick McGregor, built on Mount Baker Avenue (later St. David) circa 1901–2 (Fig. 4.10).[22]) Only Rattenbury, with his strong sense of historical symbolism, could have been responsible for the rounded corner on the left side of the main front which would have reminded the lieutenant-governor's guests of the tower that had stood at the entrance of the former Cary Castle. "Baronial English," the description given by the *Colonist* in 1903, is perhaps the best term for Rattenbury's creation, which survived, with the addition in 1908 of a granite porte-cochère designed by him, until it was burned to the ground in 1957.[23]

The course of the construction of Government House turned out to be as irregular as the composition of its exterior. The problem partly derived from the sheer quantity of work that Rattenbury had undertaken in 1901. "For the next few weeks I shall be working," he continued in his 16 August letter, "as I have to get out all the drawings for the High School in the next seven days and at last the Hotel Vancouver is going to be started and this, with work on Government House, in addition to my other buildings, will keep me rushing. I wish the rush had come in the winter." Despite accusations of foul play, chiefly instigated by the losing architects, Maxwell Muir and Thomas Hooper, the school board maintained their decision to award the commission for the high school to Rattenbury. As he had remarked, Rattenbury felt that the board had selected the lesser of his two submissions, a utilitarian "H" plan brick and stone building in a bare-boned Neo-Gothic style. The plain walls, thin corner buttresses, and unadorned gables recalled the cheap Gothic Revival schools and churches erected from the early nineteenth century in his native England. There might have been a touch of wit in the two-by-two arrangement of the gables on each front, expressing both the internal division of the sexes and the double crocodile of students favoured by the school teachers of those times (Fig.4.11): Equally plain were the extensive brick additions he designed contemporaneously for the (Royal) Jubilee Hospital. At that time he refused to accept a fee from the Hospital Board, as he had a year before when invited to design a house for the Resident Medical Officer.[24] These acts of generosity were not appreciated by some of his colleagues, including Hooper and Muir, whose plans for the hospital additions had been rejected as less capacious and functional.

Rattenbury was bound to arouse envy, even antipathy, by his very success, which seemed to be manifest in every sphere. "I think I am going to design the Triumphal Arches for the Duke of York—the Minister of Finance asked me to do so, also to arrange the illuminations of the Parliament Buildings," he had written to his mother on 9 July, concerning the visit to Victoria of the future George V. This proved to be a momentous event. "Thirty thousand loyal citizens shouting a hearty British welcome, perfect weather and a beautifully decorated city—what more could be desired to make a reception for a Royal party a success," the *Colonist* declared on 2 October 1901. "Nothing was placed on the exterior of the [Parliament] building other than long strings of incandescent lights to outline the building in a blaze of light and vie with the general illumination of the city after nightfall." The same issue of the *Colonist* printed a photograph of Rattenbury's arches with an article headed "Graceful and Artistic Genius Apparels the City in Beauty and Splendour," containing a fulsome description of the vista that greeted the Royal couple as they approached the James Bay Bridge: "Arch after arch rose above the carriages as they drove along past the lines of spectators, which cheered the son of Britain's king. The arches were simple, built in skeleton form and with bunting of various colours draped between the sides of the simple frames," with "festooned strings of evergreens drooping from pole to pole along railings which divided the roadway from the pedestrian's domain." The arrangements for the visit, incidentally, show that Rattenbury could, if necessary, exercise tact. His uncle Richard had submitted a design for a triumphal arch for the occasion, which might have influenced Rattenbury's own abortive scheme for the Paardeburg Gate Memorial, announced in the *Contract Record* for 2 January 1901. This was to have commemorated the B.C. contingents that had fought in the Boer War and was estimated at the not inconsiderable sum of $25,000. Neither Rattenbury's nor Richard Mawson's design has survived, but both might have been rejected as too costly. However, when writing to his mother on 16 August, Rattenbury had attributed their decision, in his uncle's case at least, to the lack of suitable local craftsmen: "It was immensely admired and I think it will be erected if they can find anyone conversant with doing such work (it is all in evergreens and flowers)."[25]

A more lasting and significant achievement, mentioned in the 20 August letter, was the contract to design the cable station at Bamfield, on the southern arm of Barkley Sound on the west coast of Vancouver Island; it was to become the terminal of a system that reached across the Pacific to New Zealand and Australia, organized under the supervision of

Sir Sanford Fleming, the former engineer-in-chief to the C.P.R.[26] This monumental advance in imperial communications, energetically promoted by the C.P.R., entailed the laying of cable over 8,000 nautical miles at a cost of some $1,795,000. The nearest station was on Fanning Island in the South Pacific, 3,540 miles distant. Rattenbury surely derived great satisfaction from participating in this immense technological achievement, which linked Australia, New Zealand, and Canada with his native Britain.

He was instructed to provide an accommodation block containing the operating rooms for the equipment and quarters for the staff of up to twenty bachelor operators and Chinese servants, a house for the chief telegraphist, and a small structure for the cable terminal, situated below on the shore of the sound (Fig.4.12).[27] All were in the Queen Anne style and of frame construction covered with shingles. The accommodation block was fronted by a verandah ornamented with coupled Roman Doric wooden columns. These stood between side projections having arched windows which were topped by three gables. To one side, a tower joined the kitchen wing and the gallery leading to the chief telegraphist's house. Inside the main building were facilities for the operators, including a communal dining-room overlooking Barkley Sound, billiard room, library (with space for more than 3,000 volumes), and music room. The complex was finished just before the cable was opened officially on 1 November 1902 and remained in operation (with additions by other architects) until 1959. Unfortunately, the bachelor's quarters were demolished in 1965.

Some months before the station was opened, the C.P.R. sent Rattenbury to San Francisco, the booming metropolis of the Pacific seaboard, "on some business." Instead of disclosing the nature of his visit, Rattenbury chose to register his impressions of the city, in a letter to his mother of 24 February, written in the Pacific Union Club:

> It is raining here very hard unfortunately or I should have had a good time as the people are very hospitable. One multi-millionaire, an unassuming dear old chap, took me out driving all around the Parks and other places yesterday, behind a splendid team that travelled like lightening and yet which would slow up or stop at a word. He drove all the time with the reins absolutely loose, it was astonishing.
>
> San Francisco is a very bright attractive city, and very busy. The building going on here is astonishing. I almost feel tempted to come here and I could get hold of a lot of it, but I am afraid that the hold Victoria has got on me is too great, and in settling here I am afraid the prevailing desire

to make a million would get hold of me, and I should become a slave to it, as others are. No, I think quiet old Victoria, with its semi-country life suits me better, although had I come here originally I fancy I would have been an enthusiastic Yankee. They do things so astonishingly well here. This club is a splendid place and the service and everything about it is perfect. The Palace Hotel [built in 1875, it was seven stories high and contained eight hundred bedrooms][28] where I am staying is fitted up gorgeously and yet in good taste; even the sidewalks are marble. On their Park they spend £50,000 a year in maintenance. Think of it! a city much smaller than Leeds. I am expecting to enjoy the novelty of the climate at Los Angeles and the orange groves etc., although I shall not be sorry to see the Olympia mountains again and Iechineel [he varied the spelling in his letters] and its contents.

The visit was very probably connected with the revival of the Hotel Vancouver project, for the San Francisco Palace Hotel was in a Renaissance style, bearing some relation to the drastically revised Vancouver design accepted by the C.P.R. in the early weeks of 1902. That was described in the March 1902 issue of *The Railway and Shipping World* and illustrated in the April number; in February the journal had already announced that "a contract for the erection of a large addition. . . and the reconstruction of the original buildings except the northern wing" had been let to Messrs. Robertson and Hackett of Vancouver (Fig.4.13).[29] All that remained of the noble Château scheme was the façade compostion of the side pavilions, joined to the main block by towers (now semi-circular) and linked by a broad colonnaded verandah. Rattenbury probably took his cue for the Renaissance style arches that harmonize the façades of the "H" plan from those on the existing northern addition of the hotel. However, he manipulated that theme, like the other Italianate motifs, more impressively. Rattenbury's arches, divided into single and triple groups across the front, enclose the three main stories. On the side pavilions the composition of arches and windows recalls the Roman triumphal arch. The effect was appropriately elegant for a city hotel and reminiscent of the sophisticated revival of the Italian Renaissance "palazzo" that C. F. McKim had created for the celebrated Boston Public Library, 1888–95.

That Rattenbury was responsible for the revision is suggested by the first reference to the project in the March *Railway and Shipping World*, probably written by Rattenbury and valuable as a testimony to his functional planning. The estimated cost had again risen to $400,000. Behind the "classic Renaissance style" main front on Georgia Street "having ample chaste lines with delicate enrichments" would be "a fine arcaded corridor [leading] to a spacious rotunda, 50 by 60 ft., finished with a glass dome and tiled pavement, and elaborately decorated walls." Around the rotunda he envisaged the office, the "approaches" to the billiard room (the old dining-room in the original Sorby hotel), bar, and lavatories. On one side a "short and spacious corridor leads from the main entrance... to the grand central staircase," to "electric elevators" and the new dining room, 120 by 48 feet, "with large plate glass windows reaching to the floor," overlooking Georgia and Howe Streets. This would have no columns, "the superstructure being carried by large steel trusses and... finished with hardwood floor, panelled ceiling and oak panellings," creating "an exceedingly bright and cheerful" space. He wrote enthusiastically about the separate Ladies' entrance off Granville Street, communicating with a reading room and having direct access to the stairs and dining-room independent of the rotunda, and the many large well-lighted sample rooms for travellers in the basement. Mindful of the need for privacy, he planned only two staircases on the ground floor, others being "arranged at the main angles of the corridors on the [three] upper [bedroom] floors."[30] As for bedroom accommodation, guests would be able to choose between rooms 15 by 16 feet or 13 by 16 feet, half having attached bathrooms. They could sleep assured in the knowledge that the steel frame structure, clothed externally with "light grey pressed bricks with terra cotta trimmings" and internally with plaster on "steel lathes," was "practically fireproof." In addition, the interior was to be "divided into sections by fireproof walls, and fireproof doors are to be provided in the corridors, while balconies with iron ladders will be fitted at the end of each corridor." Finally, their comfort would be maintained by a "complete system of ventilating and of steam heating."

Construction of the western part of the new hotel had actually begun on 17 December, when the foundations were dug on the open plot adjoining Sorby's building.[31] By 4 November 1902 the *Colonist* could report that the roof was finished and the internal plastering about to be started. Most of the machinery was installed between the fall of 1903 and the summer of 1904, the fitting up of the interior being completed in the following year.[32] As it turned out, this was the only part of his design to be erected (Fig.4.14), apart from the refurbishing of the interiors in the older buildings, which included the redecoration of the dining room with Ionic columns and wood panelling, called "beautiful" in *Greater Vancouver Illustrated*, 1906. The decision to curtail the project a second time seems to have been reached before the end of 1902, either because the C.P.R. decided to reserve funds for a new hotel at Victoria, where land and labour prices were lower, or because the Hotel Vancouver became too busy to permit demolition.[33] Despite its ungainly appearance, the hotel, as reconstructed by Rattenbury, was very popular.[34] But he did not have the satisfaction of transforming it into a major architectural monument, as each of his complete schemes would have done. That task was to fall, in 1913, to F. Swales, whose more flamboyant Italian Renaissance style hotel stood until 1946. Even so, Rattenbury's second design heralded a change in company policy, resulting in their preference for the Renaissance and Academic Classical styles for metropolitan hotels, continued by E. and W. S. Maxwell in the Royal Alexandria at Winnipeg, 1904–1906, and the Palliser in Calgary, 1911–1914.

The demands of his practice kept Rattenbury in Victoria most evenings of the week. He preferred to entertain at his club, apparently being somewhat ashamed of his rather dull and unprepossessing wife. For her part, Florrie sought a greater financial independence, which she seems to have exercised injudiciously. At this stage Rattenbury tolerated her schemes with a jocular condescension, as revealed in a letter written to his mother on 22 October 1902: "She elected some time ago for an allowance to buy all her own necessaries. Now I find she was beguiled into getting jewellery at so much a month and her millinery bills consequently are mounting up. I am not supposed to know of the jewellery deal and she is trying to convince me that the allowance is too small and I ought to pay off outstandings and increase it. I ask for more information and to myself chuckle." There is, too, a stilted superficiality in the next comment: "We jog along in the same old way, quiet and jolly: the garden in the morning, business, the Club [the Union Club, to which he added a new wing at this time],[35] where there are some ripping good fellows and where I have some friends I think a great deal about, and usually a quiet evening at home with Snookie."

Professional, if not personal, problems loomed ahead and, although they belong, strictly speaking, to a later phase of his career, they can be addressed most conveniently at this juncture. No sooner had the outcry against the award of the Government House commission to him diminished, than he encountered fresh criticism for his conduct of its execution, the most damaging from George Jeeves, the government-appointed clerk of works. Jeeves was concerned about the number of alterations and improvements Rattenbury was making to the interior with the tacit encouragement of Sir Henri Joly de Lotbinière, the lieutenant-governor.[36] Lotbinière, not unnaturally, wanted the best quarters possible, and found a willing ally in the architect. Expensive fittings, including marble decorations, were ordered and inflated the cost of the building.[37] With Rattenbury's apparent connivance, the contractor, Richard Drake, refused to heed Jeeves's protest about these and other changes to the ornamentation. The result was that Drake submitted a final bill in 1903 for nearly $75,000, some $29,000 more than his contract. Wishing to defend his reputation as an honest citizen, Jeeves asked the recently elected premier, Richard McBride, to instigate an official investigation. Rattenbury's cavalier approach, or even, it was to be hinted, his malpractice, thus became the object of public scrutiny; (Maclure managed to evade the process despite the fact that he had received comparable fees). Unfortunately for Rattenbury, the board of arbitration appointed to examine the costs comprised William Dalton and two old rivals, Thomas Hooper and Maxwell Muir.

Earlier in the year both had again come into conflict with Rattenbury about the commission for a public library to be built in Victoria with a $50,000 donation from the steel baron-philanthropist, Andrew Carnegie. Rattenbury had indirectly questioned their professional ability in a letter to the *Colonist* printed on 20 April 1902. He criticized the petition they and other local architects had submitted to the council advocating the employment of one of their number and argued for a competition because it would offer "a fair field to all and no favour." He chose to ignore his earlier advice to the government and did not restrain his contempt for the signatories. "I am not advancing all this as any reason for entrusting the Carnegie library to me. I don't care tuppence about it, but you are adopting a principle which will cause trouble all the time." Not surprisingly, this elicited angry responses in the local press from some of the signatories. But their bluster was wasted. The council organized a competition, in which Rattenbury did not participate, and on 18 June Hooper was declared the winner with a modest academic Classical design.

Thus, in Rattenbury's eyes the very unfavourable Cary Castle report, sent by the board to Wells in December, could not have been unaffected by animosity. They recommended that Drake be paid an additional $19,500, not the $29,000 he had claimed and remarked on the irregular conduct of the commission. They were perturbed not merely by the want of proper process in the ordering of additional work and the casual accounting, but also by the expenditure of "some hundreds of dollars . . . paid out on the architect's orders for goods purchased by himself, the invoices for which we have not been able to see, but from evidence given by various witnesses all the goods charged to and paid for by the Government have not been used in the building."[38] In support of the second accusation, they cited the absence of marble specified to be used in the banqueting room and of one of the marble grates imported from England. Equally damning was the charge that he had ordered goods personally so as to receive the "consideration" habitually paid to contractors who placed sizeable orders.

Rattenbury's response was predictably indignant: "I emphatically deny the charges made," he asserted in a letter to the chief commissioner of lands and works, "and on my part, claim that they are slanders, maliciously and knowingly made by the arbitrators for the purpose of discrediting me in the eyes of the Government and the people of British Columbia."[39] Not without justification, he was incensed that one could be "virtually tried, condemned, and through your department, the verdict published before the world, without notice to him... and without any opportunity to defend himself." At the beginning of the second page, he warned that they were "misusing their temporary position as Arbitrators," and "attempting to use the privileges of Parliament in such a way to wreak their private malice upon me, without as they imagine, any personal responsibility on their part." Despite his rage, he managed one effective counterthrust against his accusers—the charge that they had drawn double the proper fee for their services on the board.

Thus Rattenbury might well have welcomed the presentation in the Legislative Assembly on 20 January 1904 of a petition signed by Hooper and Muir requesting the institution of a public enquiry. He engaged Lyman Duff to represent him before the resulting select committee, threatening action for defamation against the arbitrators. Significantly, when the committee began its hearings early in February, Dalton and Muir refused to testify. Moreover, Hooper proved to be a reluctant witness when questioned by the deputy attorney-general, appearing for the Department of Lands and Works, and emerged as an architect of less than perfect integrity when questioned by Duff. Indeed, he admitted that he could not be sure that Rattenbury had reaped improper financial advantage from the commission, although the select committee were to learn from F. C. Gamble, the chief engineer for the province, that such rumours had originated with Hooper. The committee also discovered that Rattenbury's assertion that the arbitrators had overcharged the government for their services was largely true, since of the fifty-six separate sessions that Hooper claimed to have attended, twenty-three were the continuation of meetings begun in the morning.

By contrast Rattenbury gave a good account of himself, offering plausible, if incomplete explanations for the errant marble and fireplace. The first, he said, had been delivered by mistake to Cary Castle instead of to Iechinihl (on the north side of which he had contemporaneously added a twin-gabled and half-timbered projection, to contain a new kitchen and dining room) (Fig. 4.15); the second, the fireplace, had been rejected in favour of a larger one of American design, the supplier of the original having failed to amend the bill as he had requested. As for the ordering of goods, he stated that he had notified the respective firms that the material was intended for Government House and that he never profited from any commission paid by dealers on goods ordered. Where such commissions were paid, he always allowed for them in bills that he sent to the government.

The disorderly state of Rattenbury's records and his unsystematic handling of the commission may have been the result of the large amount of business that he was carrying at the time: besides his other commissions, the *Contract Record* for 18 March and 21 October 1903 annnounced that he was calling tenders on a brick building in Victoria for the B.C. Land and Investment Agency and a house at Oak Bay for A.T. Howard. Thus it is quite likely that he failed to devote sufficient care and attention to the bookkeeping of any one particular project. Lack of adequate staff, or consultation of a qualified accountant, owing to his frugality, may have aggravated this situation. Two other personal factors possibly contributed, although neither were matters that Rattenbury would have mentioned before the select committee. Within months of his son's birth, it became apparent that he had a severe abnormality of the feet. While Rattenbury remained optimistic in correspondence with his relatives, he seems to have been fully aware that the disability might not be rectified. On 20 August 1901, for example, he wrote cheerfully, "Snooker's boots have at last arrived from England (eight months getting them – Good Old England – but better late then never), and I hope they will put him alright." The boots proved to be ineffectual and as a result of his visit there, Rattenbury was to send Florrie and his son to San Francisco in December 1902 so that the child could receive more advanced medical treatment.[40] "The house seems very quiet today without the little fellow," he confided to his mother on 7 December, two days after their departure. Then, on 26 January 1903, he told her about his son's operation, trying to be hopeful: "Snookie is apparently alright again, he has left the hospital several days ago." Both he and Florrie would have to stay "another two or three months as his feet are still in plaster of paris and this won't be taken off for several weeks, then he will have good-fitting boots." The separation was not beneficial to their marriage, for Florrie wrote, "once a week at most, quite a falling off from once a day," though he expected, "she will be enjoying it more, going out more, now that Snookie is out of the Hospital." And to dispel her thought that he was dispirited, and perhaps to reassure himself, he declared: "Why, I am having a bully time. I am looked after by Foy [his Chinese houseman] and the other joker as if I were a prince. They are wonderful servants. It was a little lonely at first and I missed the baby prattle, but I have got used to that knowing I shall soon hear it again."

The other personal anxiety that coincided with the construction of Government House concerned his brother Jack, for whom he retained great affection and a sense of fraternal responsibility. Used to his old role as naval officer, Jack had been unable to accept a life in which he had to receive rather than give orders and had quit his post with the B.L.K.N.C. to return to sea. Early in 1901 it seems that he had decided to settle in Hong Kong, where he had formed an attachment with a widowed mother of two sons. "I am expecting to hear from Jack if he is married or when he intends to be," Rattenbury wrote to his mother on 25 February 1901, continuing, "I suppose she must have money if they talk of sending the two boys to England to school as this would, I imagine, more than size Jack's pile." By 13 April the wedding had, apparently, taken place, and, for the first time, Rattenbury was distinctly cheerful about his brother's prospects. He had managed to secure the captaincy of a steamship plying between Malaya and China which he relinquished in favour of a position in Hong Kong some months later.[41] Then, when his future seemed assured, he succumbed to a fatal fever. On 7 December 1902 Rattenbury attempted to console his mother. "I got a letter last night from Kate, telling me that you had heard from Hong Kong.... Jack seemed to have endeared himself to a great many people, even in Victoria where he was only such a short time he had made a number of friends. We will have to try and make up for you, mother, as much as we can."

The members of the select committee would not have known of these private troubles, nor could they have taken them into account. In any case, purely on the evidence presented to them they decided not to continue their investigation into a new session of the legislative assembly and reported that they were "convinced that Mr. F. M. Rattenbury, as Supervising Architect, thoroughly protected the interests of the Province, and that in all matters brought to its notice his conduct throughout has been honourable and satisfactory."

The wording of the report is decisive and unusually complimentary.

Immediately after its publication a dinner was held at the Union Club to celebrate Rattenbury's "Certificate of Character," to quote the words he was to use in a letter of 15 February 1904 to his mother, the first after "a very unpleasant three weeks," during which he had "been practically on trial." He enclosed the "Parliamentary report, which was adopted by the unanimous vote of the Legislature," and contained "a sweeping verdict in my favour." At the end of the letter he supplied a roll call of those attending the celebration which deserves quotation as a vivid tableau of one group of the influential Victoria establishment:

> H. Barnard, Mayor of Victoria. A young fellow, 35. A great friend.
> C. Holland. Manager of the largest Land business here – Galpins Cassells son in law & do
> Capt. Tallon. Minister of Finance.
> C. Fulton. President of the Executive Council
> S. Rogers. M. P. an old Cariboo miner, now wealthy.
> Maurice Hills. a lawyer, a clever Englishman, a member of the best London Clubs living here now and a friend.
> W. S. Oliver. Another friend, a lawyer. Lives close by me. I see a deal of him.
> W. Farrell of Vancouver. Director of the Telephone Company.
> F. Gamble. Chief Engineer of the Province, a jolly good fellow.
> Rather a respectable lot. We had a good time, some good speeches.

He then turned optimistically to the future, alluding to the chief commission on his books, the C.P.R.'s projected hotel in Victoria. "Now I am back at work again and I am very busy, a lot of things on hand, new houses, buildings and, as well, I am making the Plans for the big new Hotel."

Five

THE EMPRESS
1902–1905

That Rattenbury's work was highly regarded by the directors of the C.P.R. is evident from a letter sent to his mother on 2 October 1902: "Last week I was in Vancouver to meet with Sir William Van Horne, the father of the C.P.R., a great man. Fortunately we hit it off and he gave me a $100,000 building to build.... So I am chock full." Later, on 21 January 1903, the *Contract Record* announced that Rattenbury was "preparing plans" of a four-storey block to cost $60,000 for Sir William.

Sir William Van Horne (1834–1915) certainly merited Rattenbury's admiration. Beginning his working life as a telegraph operator in 1857, he rose eventually to the position of general manager of the C.P.R., and it was under his direction that the construction of the line to the west coast was completed. After serving as president of the company, he became, in 1899, chairman of the board of directors, and in this capacity met Rattenbury. Van Horne was a determined and ambitious entrepreneur, an "Empire Builder" in the old sense of the term, the kind of man Rattenbury most wished to emulate. Little wonder their meeting was so agreeable. Doubtless their discussion revolved around the western development of the company, which had acquired the Canadian Pacific Navigation Company in January 1901.[1] Captain J. W. Troup, creator of the C.P.R.'s highly profitable lake and river services, had been appointed manager of the newly purchased fleet, which was reconstituted as the

British Columbia Coast Service. Backed by Shaughnessy, Troup immediately placed orders for a number of new vessels, ranging from the "Princess" ferries (named after one of the oldest C.P.N. ships) to coastal cargo ships and, in 1911, to two liners, the elegant *Empress of India* and *Empress of Russia.*

The programme of expansion, well established by 1902, was eventually to cost more than $5,000,000. Given such a large investment and the company's policy of improving its tourist facilities, the decision to enlarge rather than rebuild the Hotel Vancouver made the construction of a new hotel in Victoria a strong possibility. The prospect of improved communication between Victoria and Vancouver, and the absence of any serious rival for the increased tourist traffic that could result, induced the owners of the Hotel Dallas in Victoria to engage Rattenbury early in 1902 to renovate their property close to the city's ramshackle Outer Wharf. The work seems to have been confined to the interior and was completed by May 1902. However, even as he was engaged on the remodelling, the decision to build a version of his first Hotel Vancouver design in Victoria may already have been made.

Rattenbury was to be preoccupied with hotel designs over the next two years. "I have just received a telegram to go to Vancouver tonight," he informed his mother on 7 December 1902, "and I expect I shall have to go into the mountains, not a very pleasant time of the year for the trip." Although the itinerary is not specified, he was to visit the scenic resorts, particularly Mount Stephen House, to check progress on a second addition and to view the Glacier Hotel in preparation for a new extension. The growth of the Glacier commission especially was to force him to cancel a hoped-for trip to England and instead to embark on a strict routine. Thus, on 12 March 1903, he was "plugging away trying to get all my plans made, contracts let and everything in order so as to get on easy street before summer, glorious summer." To maintain his stamina he had "been taking a course of physical culture which consists of sleeping with windows wide open all weathers, on getting up 10 minutes of muscular exercises, eating less, drinking a gallon of cold water during the day and I walk to town (3½ miles and back), the result is very effective. It is a great fad at present in America and you really do get your muscles into shape." He returned to the mountain hotels in the early summer, writing on 1 June 1903 from Mount Stephen House, "Just a line from the mountains. I have been up to Calgary, stayed the day with P. Burns, the house looks charming. Now I am going to each of the mountain Hotels, which are all to be completed in a few days ready for the tourist season. It is a jolly trip, as the weather is charming. We rode along one valley on a freight train this morning, seated on the top of a freight wagon." Two weeks later, ensconced in the Union Club, he reminisced, "I had to stay up there ten days, and had some beautiful drives through the country to the various chalets, which will all by now be doing business."[2]

The full extent of Rattenbury's work on the resort hotels is difficult to reconstruct because the C.P.R. records are incomplete. This is intriguingly highlighted by the announcement in the 4 June 1902 issue of the *Contract Record* that Rattenbury would "prepare plans" for a "first class hotel" to be built by the railway at a cost of $50,000 on the beautiful shores of Okanagan Lake at Summerland, B.C. Nothing came of that commission. Instead, the company apparently asked him to design their new but smaller hotel at Revelstoke (Fig.5.1).[3] Of frame construction with ship-lap siding, its double pitch (or gambrel) roof and dormer windows are not typical of Rattenbury's style. But the division of the façade into three parts linked by the continuous entablature running below the eave, and the overall clarity, relate to his architecture in a Classical vein. Another explanation could be that he supervised the construction of plans supplied by the headquarters office in Montreal, as appears to have happened with the contemporaneous extension of the Banff Springs Hotel. In the June issue of *The Railway and Shipping World*, the company announced that a contract for $100,000 had been awarded to J. A. Tompkins of Brockville, Ontario, to add a large wing designed by Hutchinson and Wood of Montreal.[4] Rattenbury, it will be recalled, had written of Van Horne's giving him "a $100,000 building to build," which might have referred to this hotel commission rather than to the [$60,000] building on Granville Street. The wing contained ninety-four bedrooms, thirty-eight "with bathrooms adjoining," and was erected sixty feet west of the original Price hotel "in order to guard against fire." Joined by a low split-level passageway, it was built of steel and wood, shingled externally and lined with Douglas fir (Fig.5.2).[5] The new accommodation soon proved to be inadequate, since the number of guests increased from 3,890 to 9,684 between 1902 and 1904. Also, it seems likely that Rattenbury had some part in the construction on the west end of the large symmetrical six-storey addition finished in 1904, and an even further extension in 1905.

Rattenbury probably acted in a similar supervisory capacity for the company's new small chalet at Emerald Lake (Fig.5.3), six miles from Field. From plans "prepared in the Co.'s office at Montreal," according to another report in *The Railway and Shipping World* of June 1902, a hewn-timber structure "on the lines of a Swiss chalet" had recently been completed, housing a dining room and fourteen bedrooms. Rattenbury's contemporary association with the hotel is indicated by the reference, in the index of hotel drawings in the C.P.R. archives, to a "Plan of Guides Cottage, Kitchen and Cool Room. Location of Buildings," signed "Rattenbury" and dated "January 1904."[6]

Beneath the Emerald Lake entry is a brief report headed "Improvements at Field" stating that "$40,000 or $50,000" would be spent during the year "in improving the station buildings, and in laying out pavilions and other places for the entertainment of tourists." This figure probably includes the cost of constructing a separate bedroom wing, illustrated in photographs of the Mount Stephen House taken in 1905 and clearly designed by Rattenbury (Fig.5.4). Built on concrete foundations, this wood-frame wing had an asymmetrical tower with a conical pitched roof and verandahs at each end from which guests could view the stunning scenery. The design followed the essentially English Arts and Crafts style he had introduced in his earlier additions. Thus enlarged, the Mount Stephen thrived as the second largest resort hotel in the C.P.R.'s western chain; the buildings remained in use until the 1950's, latterly as a youth hostel.[7]

The stamp of Rattenbury's style is equally clear on the shingled Arts and Crafts style wing built alongside the renovated second chalet hotel at Lake Louise (Fig.5.5). The narrow end of this wing, facing the stupendous glacier hovering above the neck of the Lake, was squeezed up to a steeply pitched roof between two lower polygonal towers capped by "candle-snuffer" roofs. Below was a broad verandah raised one floor high. An entry in the *Contracts and Proposals* book, records the completion of the bulk of its construction, including a payment of $31,288 to J. Kernaghan on 21 November 1902.

On 9 January and 18 May, W. E. Vanstone and the Hinton Electrical Company respectively received $3,020 and $1,000 for installing a steam-heating plant and electrical lighting.[8] Here again, Rattenbury continued to be responsible for further additions as shown by the fact that on 16 August 1905 he wrote to Hayter Reed recommending "at Lake Louise that Plan No. I showing the addition on the hill should be first gone on with as there would be less difficulty in the foundations, and the rooms obtain a better view."[9] From 1906 W. S. Painter designed alterations to this wing as part of a new extension programme[10] (Fig.5.6); both Rattenbury's and Painter's addition burned down in 1924.

Rattenbury continued his August 1905 letter to Reed by proposing the creation of a further twenty-one room addition "AT GLACIER," the most fully documented of his hotel commissions.[11] Throughout his business correspondence with Reed during the summer of 1902 he had referred to the creation of a new wing above Sorby's original small frame hotel. Its bracketted window sills and lintels and projected eaves had caused many visitors to think of Swiss architecture. Among these had been Mrs. Arthur Spragge, who, in her essay "Our Wild Westland," called it " a very artistic building of the Swiss chalet type," continuing, "the view from the verandah and the windows of the little hotel, which contains fourteen bedrooms and a very large dining room, was of fairy-like beauty."[12] In response to a letter of 24 June in which Rattenbury mentioned "another large addition for 'Glacier' in the mountains, ordered yesterday by telephone," Richard Mawson had sent him some "Swiss Hotel pamphlets," which "were exceedingly interesting to me naturally," as he was to assure his mother on 19 August. Nevertheless, the pamphlets arrived too late to be of use, since he had written to her on 25 June, "struggling away designing another addition to 'Glacier Hotel' in the mountains—a big new wing is only just being completed but still another was ordered the other day by telegram. It is a unique place and I am trying to get a quaint, unique design" which would be "about twice as big as the Queen's Hotel, Leeds."

On the rising ground behind Sorby's "chalet," Rattenbury had already built or enlarged a new two-storey frame wing with an unusual triple-gabled section elevated above the three central bays and projected forward on curved brackets (Fig. 5.7–8).[13] The $32,660 paid to A. Holland on 29 December 1902 for "Hotel Additions" may be the account for this wing.[14] It was fronted by a wide verandah and contained only bedrooms. The guests descended to the public rooms in the original building by a semi-enclosed octagonal timber staircase topped by a covered viewing platform. The second wing, erected above and parallel to the first, was designed in a picturesque Tudor style more akin to his Mount Stephen addition, but shingled and separated into two parts to follow the grade of the site (Fig. 5.9–10). At the intersection of the two levels stood a conically roofed staircase tower and a battlemented projection with Tudor arches enclosing steps between the verandahs. Equally distinctive were the gables with curved inner frames. This motif was favoured by American architects influenced by the Arts and Crafts movement, such as the San Franciscan Lewis Polk, who, for instance, used it on a double house, 1013 Vallejo (1892), which Rattenbury could have seen during his visit to the city.[15]

The start of work on the second addition to this oasis of comfort 4,100

5.1 C.P.R. Hotel, Revelstoke, B.C., c.1902.

5.2 B. Price and Hutchinson & Wood, C.P.R. Banff Springs Hotel, Banff, Alberta, with additions supervised by Rattenbury on the right, 1902–1904.

5.3 C.P.R. Chalet, Emerald Lake, Alberta, 1902.

5.4 C.P.R. Mount Stephen Hotel, Field, rear façade of Rattenbury's second addition, 1902.

5.5 C.P.R. Hotel, Lake Louise, Alberta, as enlarged by Rattenbury, 1902, with T. C. Sorby's original chalet enclosed by verandahs on the right.

5.6 C.P.R. Hotel, Lake Louise, showing Rattenbury's wing, as altered by W. S. Painter in 1906.

5.7 T. C. Sorby, C.P.R. Glacier House Hotel, Glacier, B.C., 1888.

5.8 C.P.R. Glacier House Hotel, showing, on the left, the extensions built by Rattenbury, 1902–1905, above T. C. Sorby's original chalet hotel, lower right.

5.9 C.P.R. Glacier House Hotel, with Rattenbury's additions terminated by the observation tower.

5.10 (inset) C.P.R. Glacier House Hotel; staircase between Rattenbury's later additions.

5.11 Sketch elevations of proposed C.P.R. Hotel, Victoria, 1903.

5.12 "Proposed Canada Western Hotel."

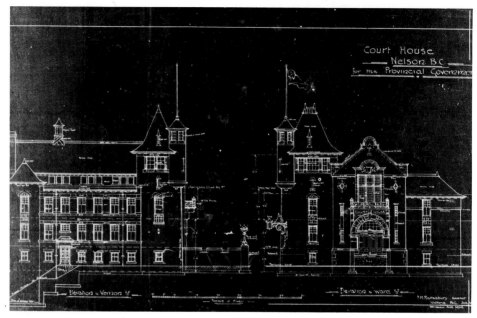

5.13 Elevations for Courthouse, Nelson, B.C., designed in 1903 and revised in 1906.

5.15 E. Cormier, Supreme Court of Canada, Ottawa, 1938–1939.

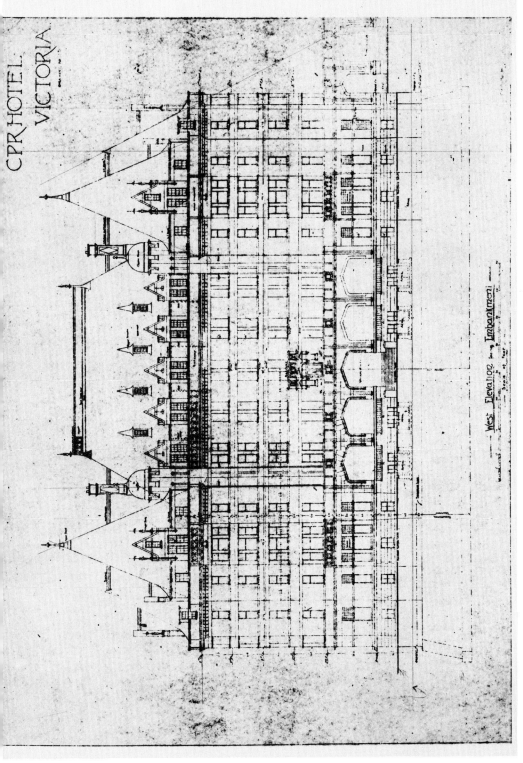

5.14 Elevation of the main façade of the Empress Hotel, Victoria, 1904, as built, 1904–1908.

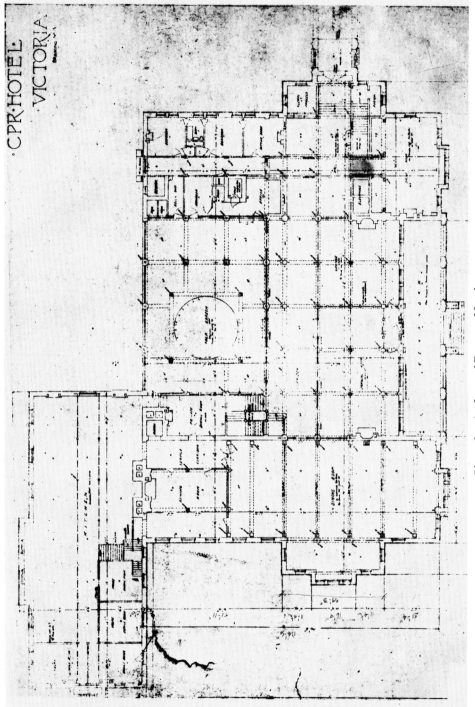

5.17 Plan of main floor of Empress Hotel, 1904.

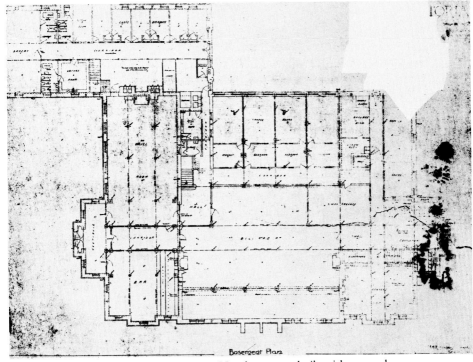

5.16 Plan of basement of Empress Hotel, 1904, as built with some changes, 1906–1908.

5.18 Plan of the first floor of Empress Hotel, 1904.

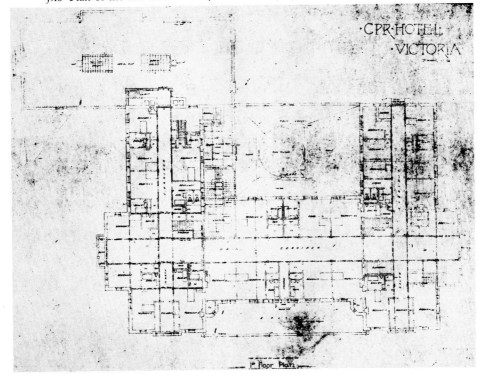

5.19 Dining room of Empress Hotel, as originally completed in 1908.

5.21 Reading room of Empress Hotel, as originally completed.

5.20 Hall and public lounge of Empress Hotel as originally completed.

5.22 Palm room of Empress Hotel, as originally completed.

5.23A First C.P.R. Steamship Office, Victoria, 1904.

5.23B Detail, C.P.R. Steamship Office.

5.24 Dr. C. N. Cobbett House, Victoria, 1905.

5.25 Mrs. Henry Clay House, Victoria, 1904.

5.26 Oak Bay Hotel, Victoria, 1904–1905.

5.27 G. Kirk House, Victoria, 1904, with later addition at upper left.

5.28 B.C. Electric Railway Company Office, Victoria, 1904, 1906–1907.

5.29 Law Chambers Building, Victoria, 1905, possibly designed by Rattenbury.

5.30 Judge Lampman House, Victoria, commissioned 1905, built 1907–1908.

feet high in the Selkirk Mountains — watched over by Mount Sir Donald —
may be recorded in another letter to his mother dated 4 August. He had
been "rather busy, letting contracts for some houses and an addition to a
Hospital and making plans for some buildings for the Mountain Hotels.
One of the mountain hotels seemed to delight the Manager of the
C.P.R. [D. McNicoll] who was here lately. He said it was the most
charming country Hotel he had ever seen; it again has an exquisite site,
which is really its chief charm, although I did not take the trouble to point
this out to him. One of the other hotels is really a much better thing
[Mount Stephen House?] although it did not strike his fancy as much,
simply because the site was not as good." There is no record of the cost of
the second Glacier wing or its contractor, but in a letter written on 9
November 1903 to I. G. Ogden (third vice-president, with responsibility
for the Pacific Division), Shaughnessy approved the expenditure of $2,100
for a new water supply and additional fire protection.[16]

These commissions pale into insignificance when compared with
another he had described to his mother while staying at the Mount
Stephen on 1 June 1903: "I suppose you got the sketches for the proposed
Hotel at Victoria. It is going to be a whopper if it goes on, and I think it
will go on alright. It will make a decided attraction to Victoria, as we
really have wanted a first class Hotel. The thing will keep me busy though
for a year or two, just when I anticipated a lazy time." Among the drawings may have been the "Sketch for Proposed C.P.R. Hotel, James Bay
Causeway," published in the *Colonist* on 23 May 1903 (Fig. 5.11). The drawing shows an aggrandized version of the unexecuted Hotel Vancouver
scheme, rising from a broad terrace covering what was then the polluted
tidal mud flats at the head of James Bay and intended to be the pivotal
point of a picturesque cityscape. The sketch embraced part of the Legislative Buildings and a projected Neo-Gothic College in Douglas Gardens
on the right[17] and the proposed Anglican Cathedral (for which
J. M. C. Keith had won an international competition in 1891), Hooper's
Carnegie Library, and the recently completed Dominion Customs
building on the left. By adjusting the relative scale of the various structures — Rattenbury was too accomplished a draughtsman to have created
the effect by default — he rendered the hotel as magnificent as the
Parliament Buildings while yet not eclipsing the much smaller buildings
to its left. In fact, the sketch was a clever piece of visual propaganda
intended to persuade the taxpayers of Victoria to accept the scheme, for if
it were implemented, they could look forward to the prospect of two
new adornments to their city: the romantic Château hotel and a greatly

improved Inner Harbour. By presenting such an enticing image, Rattenbury realized the council's policy, endorsed by a recent plebiscite, to replace the extant James Bay Bridge with a causeway (designed by the city engineer, C. E. Topp) and also put the considerable required expenditure in a proper perspective.

The sketch cannot be dated with certainty. Rattenbury might have begun it immediately after his meeting with Van Horne in October 1902 or in the weeks following the receipt by the Victoria City Council of a letter Shaughnessy sent to them on 19 January 1903.[18] In it, and no doubt to gain an advantage in future bargaining, the C.P.R. president had declared that the company "could not see their way to accepting the proposal" to build a hotel on Douglas Gardens adjacent to the Legislative Assembly.[19] Yet within four months Shaughnessy was prepared to commit the C.P.R. to erecting one "to cost not less than $300,000," provided, as he informed the *Colonist* on 23 May, the council would "supply the site and exempt us from taxation and give us free water for 20 years." Fortified by Shaughnessy's undertaking and inspired by Rattenbury's sketch, a committee of representatives from the Victoria council, board of trade, and tourist association agreed on 25 May to present Shaughnessy with three counterproposals. The first scheme envisaged the construction of the hotel on the Douglas Gardens site, the transformation of the reclaimed part of James Bay into a public garden, and the exemption of taxes for twenty-five years (subject to a plebiscite). The problem with this plan was that the hotel would stand too close to the Legislative Buildings for their mutual visual advantage, and the arrangement would leave an architectural hiatus between these buildings and the developments on Humboldt Street. Nor was the second proposal very inspiring, since it envisaged merely the purchase and expansion of the Driard Hotel, John Teague's rather stilted Romanesque structure of 1892 at 1151 Broad Street. By far the most inviting proposition, from the standpoint of both Rattenbury and the company, was the third, namely the gift of the reclaimed James Bay flats as the site for the construction of a first class hotel, as envisaged in Rattenbury's sketch.

Thus, it appears that Rattenbury manoeuvred himself into the position of reconciling the interests of his fellow citizens with those of the company. The idea of a grand hotel on James Bay had long preoccupied the city council, as is evident in the 1891 publication *Victoria Illustrated*. On page 30 appeared an engraving of a large five-storey building with a Châteauesque roof bearing the caption "Proposed Canada Western Hotel" (Fig.5.12). This may have been designed by Thomas Sorby, but it lacked the consistent ornamentation and impressive scale of Rattenbury's scheme. Rattenbury also enjoyed the close friendship of Harry Barnard, one of the guests at his "Certificate of Character" dinner. Barnard, son of Francis Barnard, who had operated the Barnard Express to the Cariboo during the gold rush of the 1860's, was committed to the construction of a major hotel in Victoria. In 1902, to ensure that the necessary inducements would be offered to the C.P.R., he secured election as alderman (and then, in 1904, as mayor for a two-year term). Throughout the spring and summer of 1903, he campaigned vigorously for public acceptance of the tax exemption, aided by other local worthies, including the mayor, A. F. McCandless. Their advocacy and the successful passage through the provincial legislature of a bill supporting the construction of a hotel, helped to persuade the taxpayers to endorse the motion presented before council on 24 August, "for the creation of a tourist hotel at James Bay and to grant certain lands and exemptions in consideration thereof."[20]

Wisely, the company did not proceed until the taxpayers had ratified the agreement. While Barnard and the councillors canvassed support, Rattenbury waited in Victoria to be called to Montreal to discuss the detailed specifications for the hotel. "I am half-expecting that I shall have to go to Montreal again in two or three weeks, over the big hotel proposed for Victoria," he wrote to his mother on 14 June, "I don't fancy the trip much in the middle of the summer. I much prefer basking on the shores of the Pacific ocean at Oak Bay surrounded by myriads of flowers and with a nice cooling drink within reach and Snookie's prattle to keep me awake." Ten days later he informed his uncle of the situation, "I am expecting to go to Montreal shortly about the big hotel (it will cost about £150,000) that the CPR are going to put up in Victoria. I have the sketchplans all out. There is some ratification of their agreement to be passed by the people first, then the building is to be rushed. If I go to Montreal I am going to try to run over to England. I was expecting a peaceful and lazy summer, as all my buildings are about completed, all at the same time, but this big hotel and another large addition for 'Glacier' . . . will keep me occupied for some time." But he clearly did not think the situation in Victoria (or in England) a very encouraging one for architects, and in this letter he inserted one of his very rare political statements, adding advice for a prospective immigrant. "What a doleful outlook for architects in the old Country with the socialistic tendencies you describe.[21] I was lucky I came out when I did. No wonder young Hudson [presumably, the son of his uncle's partner] whom I just remember as a wee boy, wants to branch out, and if he has any get up at all he need not have any fear of trying America. He could certainly without any trouble make a living in any City in the States and so much more, as he is able to seize the opportunity always offering. In Victoria, which is only a small village (20,000) there are naturally few chances, and there are many architects, some very clever ones, already. They come here and love the place so much that they prefer to stay, even on the smallest inducement. I luckily got three good clients, the Government, the C.P.R. and the Bank of Montreal, but only the slightest local work. There is not much." The situation described in this discouraging report helps to explain the intense rivalry and sometimes bitter relations between the architects already established in Victoria.

The next day, 25 June 1903, he was asked to meet McNicoll in Vancouver to discuss the preliminary work for the Victoria hotel, as noted in a letter despatched to his mother that evening. Even without the hotel he had a full schedule, spending at least five hours each day in his office and undertaking "a little thinking at home." One result of these ruminations was a well-timed investment in land that may have contributed to his later decision to engage in this type of speculation on a much larger scale, if with a less fortunate outcome. "You will see enclosed a small momento of a little investment in Timber lands that turned out trumps. I put in £200 and drew out £800 without any risk. So if you can make use of a little more, let me know; it is burning a hole in my pocket." On a more mundane level he was beginning to notice unwelcome signs of middle age, "Do you know I am getting a wee thin in a little spot at the back of my head! Can you recommend anything? What about 'Thatcho'? Getting on to forty and poor Snooks has not got a playmate nor seems likely."[22] When he next wrote to his mother, on 6 July, the hotel was still "not yet quite decided," but he found distraction in the purchase of a new mechanical wonder: "I bought a gramophone the other day and Snooks is delighted with it. He thinks it is a little man shut up in the box who sings, and tonight he asked if the little man had a cold, he sang so funnily."

On 4 August, he was able to tell her that the company had finally reached an agreement with the city. "I think the hotel will go on soon. The agreement between the city and the C.P.R. has been approved of. Very soon the people will vote on it and I don't think there is any doubt that they will be overwhelmingly in favour of it and then I expect I will start in with the plans. It will be a very big thing, nearly as large as the Parliament Buildings and adjoining them." In essence the council had agreed to prepare the site and exempt taxes and water rates for fifteen, not twenty, years. Thus on the 19th of the month he could report that he was coming closer to his goal. "I have to go to Vancouver next week to meet the general manager of the C.P.R. and talk over Hotels, I expect the new Victoria Hotel, as this matter is quickly coming to the tapis—£150,000 they are now proposing to spend, quite a little sum." However, the taxpayers had yet to vote when he wrote to his mother on 4 September from the Union Club in Victoria. "We are getting close to the time when the big Hotel question will be decided. I view it with mixed feelings. It is a big enough building to make me want it, but it means several years of work and I am getting to like plenty of play and less work." He had just returned from yet another inspection tour of the mountain hotels, "I fancy I wrote you last week from the mountains, where I was again inspecting the Mountain Hotels, which are now all finished. In fact nearly all my buildings are about finished and I am in the midst of the uncongenial work of setting up the Accs [accounts], a business I dislike except my own Ac."

Surprisingly, he omitted mention in these letters of one important project for which tenders were advertised in the *Colonist* on 7 August. This was the Nelson Courthouse, to be built of local Salmo marble, which had been commissioned in 1902 by the provincial government. He had been working upon it on 23 January 1903, the day on which he told his mother of "designing a marble Court House" (Fig.5.13). After viewing the designs with Rattenbury on 7 August, a reporter from the *Colonist* complimented the internal plan, especially in the "vitally important matters of light and ventilation," and described the façade as being "after the graceful Renaissance type" with a "very picturesque appearance most pleasing to the eye in its chaste proportions and air of strengh." With its pitched roof corner tower, gable, late medieval and early Northern Renaissance windows and detailing, the scheme reflected his current interest in the Château style.[23] Construction was deferred in the fall, following the election of Richard McBride as premier in the spring of 1903 and the imposition of a rigid policy of budgetary restraint. Not until September 1906 were the tenders readvertised, and the design is best analysed in the context of other commissions Rattenbury completed in that year.

Fortunately for him, the financial austerity of the McBride government did not deter the Victoria taxpayers, who, on 15 September 1903, ratified the city council's latest offer to the C.P.R. A delighted Mayor McCandless, representing the whole council, immediately telegraphed Shaughnessy: "Bylaw carried by over twenty to one—only eighty-six against—greatest satisfaction over result." An equally satisified Shaughnessy replied on the next day: "The good will indicated by the vote is a source of gratification to all of us here. We shall commence work on the plans immediately."[24] Similar telegrams passed between David R. Ker, chairman of the Brackman Ker Milling company and a future associate of Rattenbury and of Shaughnessy. On the 16th Rattenbury, too, telegraphed Shaughnessy: "I have sketch plans completed, shall I come to Montreal with them next week as proposed?" Shaughnessy delayed this visit, hoping himself to travel to Victoria within the week. When that did not happen, Rattenbury, keen to seal the commission, wired on the 19th to ask whether he should proceed to Montreal "with sketch plans and all particulars for Hotel as you suggested." On the following day he received the welcome message that he was to "get down here about the first of November." Part of Rattenbury's anxiety may have derived from the knowledge that the New York architect A. B. Jennings, designer of the large Romanesque-cum-Château Hotel Denny in Seattle had communicated with R. Marpole, the C.P.R. superintendent in Victoria, offering to furnish plans for the hotel that would incorporate his patent fireproof structural system.[25] Interestingly, a note written by the general manager, D. McNicoll on 23 October, to acknowledge the receipt of Jennings' proposal, advised Marpole to instruct the company's engineer to check Rattenbury's ongoing Hotel Vancouver work "as Rattenbury otherwise would be sure to run the expense up for incidentals." Adding to Rattenbury's concern was a failure in the retaining wall of the causeway across James Bay, reported to McNicoll on 8 November by Marpole.[26]

The 15th found Rattenbury back at the Windsor Hotel in Montreal, where, he told his mother, he had been waiting a week "to get instructions from Sir Thomas Shaughnessy, who has been away. But on his return today he heard of his father's death and had to go away again. So I have to stay another week until his return." Rattenbury made the best of his opportunities while in the east, travelling down to Boston and other cities "to see what they have been doing in the hotel line."

When he finally met Shaughnessy, Hayter Reed was on hand to advise upon Rattenbury's proposed internal plan.[27] The instructions he received are, unfortunately, not mentioned in the interview he gave to the *Colonist* on 1 December 1903 (on his return from Montreal), but one must have been the division of the commission into three stages: (a) the main block, to be followed by (b) the north, and then (c) the south, wing. He seems to have shown the reporter a worked up version of his May sketch, in which the dominant corner towers may have already been broadened to their present form. The arrangement had first appeared in his competition design for the Hotel Vancouver, which also showed two octagonal domed turrets abutting the towers, ornamented with flat bay windows and linked across the front by an arcaded verandah. But the Victoria hotel, even at this penultimate stage in its development, was more compactly designed, as reflected by the substitution of the Neo-Tudor arcade for the verandah of the Vancouver hotel.[28]

As he pointed out in the *Colonist*, his Victoria hotel would pioneer a new interpretation of the Château style, "to a certain extent. . . suggestive of the much admired Château Frontenac" but "more symmetrical in appearance than the well-known Quebec hotel." Where its architect, Price, had been inspired by the broken skyline and late medieval character of celebrated examples like the Château de Jaligny, Rattenbury chose to adapt their underlying composition of enframing towers and more classically designed windows (Fig.5.14).[29] He was offering a reformed C.P.R. style, an orderly structure, as much Scottish Baronial as French Château, entered through English Tudor cloisters, guarded at each side by what he called "snuffer turrets of the baronial style," and chastely ornamented—for the quatrefoil tracery work on the balconies and their piers are equally sharply drawn.[30] Only in the interior was he prepared to indulge in such architectural whimsy as an "Old English Style" panelled hall, a Chinese glass roofed palace-garden, a grand dining room with "carvings and frescoes," a "Marie Antoinette" style oval ladies saloon, and a Queen Anne style reading room with an Inglenook imitated from the one in the Tourraine Hotel in Boston.

Externally, Rattenbury's classical reinterpretation of the Château style established a pattern for its later development in Canada; (interestingly, H. J. Hardenbergh's more massive Châteauesque Plaza Hotel, erected almost contemporaneously, 1906–1907, on the south side of Central Park in New York, also had a strictly balanced composition). Rattenbury's influence was most immediately apparent in Ross and MacFarlane's Château Laurier, Ottawa (1908–1912), and Fort Garry Hotel, Winnipeg (1911–1913), both commissioned by the Grand Trunk Pacific Railway and distinguished by symmetrical corner towers and flat façades. The final phase of this development can be seen in Ernest Cormier's Supreme Court Building, Ottawa (1938–1939), (Fig.5.15),[31] completed, ironically, ten years after W. S. Painter's Humboldt Street wing had spoiled the symmetry of Rattenbury's Empress.

Rattenbury sent a copy of the 1 December *Colonist* article to Shaughnessy.[32] In his covering letter, he outlined the council's endeavours to improve the site by reinforcing the causeway and, at Rattenbury's request, by improving the drainage. To underline the concern he had expressed in November that the site be properly prepared, he also enclosed a second cutting from that day's *Colonist.*[33] Headed, "Architect Rattenbury Advises City Council to Proceed with Greater Expedition," the report printed the full text of the letter to the council, in which he estimated that at least another five feet of infilling was required, as well as better provision for drainage. He then warned the councillors that work on the hotel could not proceed until these processes were completed, continuing: "While the method that will be adopted for the foundations is not yet definitely settled, and cannot be until the ground consolidates and tests are made, it is probable that piles will be driven in about twenty feet deep over the site to be built upon, then withdrawn and the holes filled up with packed gravel or concrete." The problem of adequate foundations continued to nag Rattenbury over the ensuing year and was ultimately to be solved by a more complex system than the one he envisaged in his letter.

Armed with Hayter Reed's suggestions, Rattenbury started to make the detailed drawings in December, writing on the 27th: "I am rushing off my drawings for the Hotel Victoria, but I don't think we shall start building for a year, owing to the foundations." Consequently they "had a quiet Xmas," enlivened only by an accident with the Christmas tree, when Snooka "pulled the whole show down over him." New domestic responsibilities were soon to be added to the demands of his office: "Florrie's shadow gets larger; I don't think she will be travelling this spring. We tell Snookie he is going to have a brother called Nicolas, one of the old names." However, perhaps because he was then commuting across the Strait of Georgia between Victoria and Vancouver on hotel business, much of his letter concerned the "fearful shipwreck" of the steamer *Chatham*, echoing in some ways the alarm that he had felt during the avalanche on his return from Montreal in 1901. The vessel had gone down "within sight of our house and many were drowned, including several I know. Poor Galletly [manager of the Bank of Montreal in Victoria] lost his wife and only daughter. The whole thing was so tragic that it engrossed the city for a long time."

At this time Rattenbury was also expecting to collaborate with the company engineers on the design of the foundations, noting in a letter of 29 February 1904, "We have to go down 100 feet for a foundation, 15 feet in stone, then piles I expect. This will cost a lot of money, £20,000, I expect, before we are through with it." The problem was complicated by the fact that the concrete and stone causeway had, by now, bulged "some 8 inches."[34] Eventually, in July, Shaughnessy instructed Sir William Whyte, vice-president of the C.P.R., based in Winnipeg, to entrust the problem to the best foundation engineers then available, the celebrated Chicago firm of E. C. and R. M. Shankland, who recommended the use of wooden piles and planking covered by concrete.[35] But as February passed Rattenbury remained "hard at work finishing off the Hotel Victoria plans. It will be a fine picturesque building and as it is close to the Parliament Buildings I shall be well represented in that quarter of the Town." Nevertheless, he had time to contemplate buying a car. "I wrote off today to England re. an 'automobile,'" he told his mother on 9 March, "Somehow I seem to prefer an English one to an American one. I saw a cut in 'Country Life' of what seemed a really handsome and simple little one, so I thought I would have a shot at the sport. We have beautiful roads round here for driving and automobiling."[36]

Not until 5 May 1904 could he telegraph Shaughnessy: "Will mail plans of hotel tomorrow (5.16–18).[37] Nor were these yet complete, as he admitted in a letter to Shaughnessy two days later: "I am forwarding by same mail the Working Plans of the Hotel Victoria, arranged as determined upon at Montreal – am including the valuable suggestions of Mr. Hayter Reed." He also regretted that the constraint imposed by the $350,000 budget had forced him to limit the projected fireproof construction to that part of the building above the kitchen. He could have had little time to ponder their reception in Montreal, because on the 13th he wrote excitedly to his mother, "I sent a cable yesterday 'May arrived safely.' I hope you got it alright, as the last one I sent you never seemed to have reached you. Well, you have another grand-daughter, with huge blue eyes and a big crop of curly black hair – we were hoping for red! It also has a powerful pair of lungs and knows how to use them and this makes Snookie quite jealous. Snookie was very amusing when he first saw the new arrival. His eyes opened wider and wider then he quietly walked up to it and gave it a kiss." Perhaps understandably, the Victoria hotel assumes a secondary place among these domestic matters. "We have not started the big hotel yet, they are buying some more ground so as to make the grounds larger. It will be a great improvement but it inevitably causes delay and I cannot get away until it is well underway."

Then, on the afternoon of 26 May 1904 he was handed what must have been a shattering telegram from Shaughnessy: "Plans very incomplete and proposed arrangement will require [a] good many alterations. Returning them to you with [Reed's] memorandum today."[38] Reed had finished his lengthy memorandum at the Château Frontenac the day before, sorry to appear to be "at variance" with Rattenbury "though possibly not really so, as he was a charming man to work with."[39] Reed's most significant criticisms concerned the absence of proper separation between the billiard room and bar in the basement, the placing of the drawing and dining rooms on the ground rather than the first floor (as at the Frontenac and Place Viger Hotels), the positioning of the private dining room too close to the kitchen, and the location of the baggage elevator away from the centre of the hotel. Among a host of lesser criticisms, he judged that the bathrooms were too large, the corridors on the third and fifth floors too wide, and the "Moorish" curved tops of the towers on the front too ornamented.

Upset, no doubt, at first, Rattenbury did not respond until 3 June, that day typing a diplomatic letter to Shaughnessy; his uncharacteristic tact reflected a genuine respect for Reed's expertise as much as a desire to retain the commission.[40] He stated that when he "went over the sketch plans with Mr. Reed" the previous November he had taken "careful notes" and "all of these, so far as I am aware, were incorporated in the working plans sent you." Nevertheless, he thought there would be "little difficulty" in accommodating the "Comparatively few additional suggestions now made by Mr. Reed." He wanted to confer with Reed in Montreal immediately, "but for the next ten days or so I am under Doctor's orders, and he will not let me travel" being "after my appendix." He would travel as soon as he was able, "meantime, to save delay, I have asked Mr. Pearce of my office, who has assisted me with the plans, and is very familiar with them, to come to Montreal and talk the matter over with Mr. Reed, and I think they will easily settle the various points together." But there was "one big change" with which he could not agree, namely the placing of the "Dining Room and Ladies Drawing Room on the floor over the Hall, as at the Château Frontenac." He claimed that Reed had not proposed that arrangement in November, and while it was "charming," the original placing "*also works out very well* and is similar to the arrangement of the '*Touraine*' at Boston, also the 'Portland' Oregon, Hotel, and the 'Angelus'—all most popular hotels, and combined Tourist and City Hotels, as Victoria will be." He disagreed with Reed that "the City people will use the Hall, and so make it unpleasant for ladies" since "at the above hotels... as in Victoria there is a lower floor where the Bar, Billiard Room and Grill Room are placed, and this is the lounging floor which the City people frequent." More telling, the change would entail "throwing all the present working plans aside (now that they are all complete) and beginning again with new sketch plans, just where we were last November." He won that point, for the final set of plans used by the contractors were those finished in March 1904, with some revisions. But he was asked to prepare at least two sets of specifications, the second detailing

a more complete set of fireproofing. His frustration (making him reluctant to see Reed again) is clear in two letters of the immediate period that
he wrote to is mother: "After getting in Tenders for the CPR Hotel, they
have decided to make a different arrangement, so I have it all to do over
again," he had complained on 1 June 1904. "Annoying in a way, as you
never like to do the same work twice, but a good thing in another way as
it is like getting another new work. It means, however, that actual
building operations will not begin this year." When he wrote on 10 June
the preparation of the new working drawings was in train:

> I ought to have gone to Montreal last week but as I knew I should have to
> come back at once I shirked it and sent my clerk 'Pearse.' When I go later
> to Montreal I want to come over to your side, but I must get the foun-
> dations started first. . . . My 'pièce de resistance' is still the Hotel plans. I
> have these about complete now, in pencil, but it will take nearly a month
> yet to have them all quite finished.[41] I am taking them rather leisurely, as
> the foundations will be quite a time before they are ready."

When he next wrote to her, on 4 July, he had regained some of his
enthusiasm, writing that he was "*Hard at work at the office . . .* making the
building larger and more elaborate. It will be a pretty place when all
complete and, situated in its 6 acres of grounds, quite a park." Given the
fact that the March 1904 plans continued to form the basis of the design,
Rattenbury's comments might refer to the difference between the original
scheme of December 1903 and the March 1904 drawings. On 1 December
he had told the *Colonist* that the whole hotel would contain 175 bedrooms,
whereas the central block alone in the March plans envisaged 173 bedrooms (excluding the four attached to the "Sample Rooms" in the basement for travelling salesmen).[42] Certainly the March 1904 plans
correspond essentially to the present layout of the original, centre section
of the hotel.[43] The main entrance lay through the porte-cochère facing
Douglas Garden and gave access to stairs to the basement and to the
elevator and reception areas. Beyond, was the main connecting corridor
with the ladies drawing room and public lounge on the left. It could also
be entered from the loggia along the front. To the right was the single-
storey Palm Garden. At the other end of the corridor, past stairs to the
first floor, stood the main dining room, the large dimensions of which (79
by 42 feet) were made possible by the structural system of steel columns
and beams used throughout the hotel. Immediately below the dining
room Rattenbury placed the grill room and bar. The rest of the basement
was given over to the needs of the male guest. A billiard room occupied
most of the centre front with a barber's shop and gentlemen's lavatory

below the south tower and porte-cochère. It was a commodious and functional plan, providing excellent public and private accommodation. Typifying Rattenbury's ingenuity were the provision of a wine lift in one of the "dummy columns" in the main dining room, a second private dining room on the first floor, and fire escapes running through all the balconies served by the corridors intersecting the upper floors.

While Rattenbury prepared the working drawings and specifications, the C.P.R. bought the property to the west of the reclaimed hotel site. All but one of the leases had been acquired by early June 1904, and the last property was expropriated by the council soon after and passed to the C.P.R. That achieved, the taxpayers had to approve the extension of the previously agreed exemptions. This they did on 7 July under the leadership of the determined Harry Barnard, and they did so no less handsomely than before—1,205 votes in favour and only 46 against. While Barnard wooed the voters, Rattenbury steeled himself to this last grinding task with the promise of a trip to Europe later that year. "I am saving up for my trip home; I shall come either at the end of September or December. The advantage of the latter date is that I could run over to Rome and Egypt and get some good weather. Will you go with me and have a chassez up the Pyramids?" Thus he wrote confidently to his mother on 4 July, but on 27 July, he added a slight note of caution. "I am looking forward to arranging my trip home—I hope to goodness nothing will crop up to prevent me." At that juncture he was "just finishing off the Hotel Plans, they all had to be remade owing to various changes being decided upon," continuing, "I have been designing the interior of the various rooms, some of which are to be very handsome, not elaborate but rich. I was designing the Dining room in a French (severe) Renaissance when I received from Uncle Richard a whole bunch of postcards with views of the French Touraine Châteaux. They were very useful to me as well as interesting. I should very much like to take that trip through the Touraine country in a motor car." Once again, his use of architectural terminology is loose. Photographs of the dining room as originally decorated show that it was as much late Tudor as French Renaissance (Fig.5.19), having blind arches around the walls similar in shape to those on the verandah, and a finely carved wooden beam ceiling resting on pilasters with rather bulbous brackets above their capitals—a feature repeated in the hall and palm room. If anything, the fairest description of the style of the dining room is "Old English," the term he had applied, equally loosely, to that of the hall (Fig.5.20) in December 1903. It is also an appropriate description of the decoration adopted for the reading room (Fig.5.21) with its late Tudor and Jacobean style plaster ceiling. His choice of the word "severe" has more merit, since the original interiors, though ornamented, were not ornate. Style aside, he was seeking to create a more open and attractive layout for the public rooms to contrast with the dark corridors and ubiquitous screens, which, he was to remark in an interview with the *Colonist* on 9 August 1905, had contributed to "that aloofness which has ever been the abomination of desolation" for strangers travelling in England. The decoration was, too, related to the structure. In the hall, the Ionic Order columns and decorated beams correspond with the structural system of steel columns and beams, as the similar columns and pilasters in the palm room formerly did. Before its glass roof collapsed in 1969, the palm room (Fig.5.22) was delightfully light and capacious, graced at its centre by a delicate oval-shaped low dome. The original bedrooms were more chaste, the chief ornament being the Ionic columns which supported the mantlepieces, diminutive echoes of the order adorning the public rooms.

The European holiday had to be abandoned, and by way of relaxation he set off on a hunting trip to Lake Cowichan on 30 August 1904, joining friends on a houseboat with whom he had "a pretty good time, swimming, loafing and camping out." At last, by 22 October, he could write to his mother, "We are calling for Tenders for the Big Hotel—the foundations are already being put in [these were completed by March 1905]." But there was no hope of a respite, for he had "a lot of work going on just now," which he proceeded to list:

> The Hotel Victoria
> Hotel Vancouver—part of the new additions
> Steamship Offices
> Office Block with 12 suites of offices and vaults
> Oak Bay Hotel
> Residence for G.A. Kirk
>   "   for Mrs. Clay
> Large stone Office Block for the B.C. Electric Railway

Small wonder that he reported on 14 November, "Lately I have been going down to the Office at nights, as I can do more than 8.30 to 11.20 P.M. than in a whole day. There are no interruptions and I have had lots of work to do."

The list of works included in the 22 October letter is further proof of his pre-eminent position among Victoria architects. The C.P.R. Steamship Office stood at 468 Belleville Street from 1904 to 1923, when it was replaced by another Rattenbury building (the present London Waxworks).[44] Rectangular in plan and of two and a half storeys, the first

Steamship Office was a grander version of the 1902 McGregor house, having an entrance porch projected from, rather than contained within, the overall shape (Fig.5.22–23 A and B). It also had a fieldstone basement, shingled ground floor, and half timbering, but somewhat flatter bay windows on either side of a broad window rising through the two floors to a squat gable. The composition apparently attracted the local physician, Dr. C. N. Cobbett, who commissioned Rattenbury in 1905 to build a similarly arranged but more Queen Anne styled house on an open site at 1040 Pemberton Road (Fig.5.24).

The design of the C.P.R. Office, and of the Oak Bay Hotel, also appealed to the editor of the Toronto based *Canadian Architect and Builder*, who included an illustrated article on them in the September 1906 issue. However, he betrayed a tinge of eastern envy of the more temperate Vancouver Island climate. The tall central gabled window of the C.P.R. Terminal was, he wrote "reminiscent of England; and it is it, more than anything else, that gives a sort of transitional character to the whole building. Its scale belongs to the many gabled type of building which is not our type. With our need [in eastern Canada] for simple roofs, and simple well-separated gables, we cannot very well have, as they do in England, a large building with a small scale." The unsympathetic, and regional, criticism applied better to the less concentrated composition of the Oak Bay Hotel. Then called "The Old Charming Inn," it was erected near Iechinihl, immediately overlooking the sea, in a style that reverted to the more picturesque, varied array of projected gables and dormers of his earlier houses and his additions to the C.P.R. hotels (Fig.5.26). The gables, with their shingled framing arches, like the verandah with its coupled columns, are more American than Tudor in character. The former, used already on the second addition at Glacier, recalled the work of Joseph Silsbee and even the early essays in the Arts and Crafts style of his pupil, Frank Lloyd Wright. Unfortunately, the hotel was demolished in 1962.[45]

The houses mentioned in the 22 October letter were both of frame construction, and commissioned respectively by Mrs. Robert Dunsmuir for her daughter, Elizabeth, and son-in-law, George Kirk (managing director of Turner Beeton and Co. Ltd., a wholesale dry goods firm), and by Janet Clay, widow of Henry Clay, who had owned a confectioner's shop in the Five Sisters Block, possibly frequented by Rattenbury. The Kirk residence, "Riffham," stands at 582 St. Charles and the smaller Clay House at 810 Linden Avenue. Where the Clay house (Fig.5.25) is in a neatly variegated Queen Anne style, the Kirk house (Fig.5.27) represents a further development of his disciplined Tudor style, anticipating the comparable, if more sophisticated, direction taken by Maclure in the Biggerstaff-Wilson house of 1905. It has an "L" shaped plan formed by the triangulated main body and a gabled projection next to the entrance, containing the drawing room and, above, the master bedroom.[46] The prominence of this projection is modified by the terrace and verandah, which cover all but one bay of the front, and by the continuous half-timbering of the upper floor. The side façade, to the right of the verandah, is composed symmetrically, with a square window at the centre of the ground floor, three equally spaced windows on the first floor, and a dormer in the middle of the roof. The interiors of both houses are compact but commodious. The main living rooms, almost twelve feet high, and the bedrooms are pivoted about the staircase halls, each with an inglenook. The floors are oak, and the finely wrought woodwork is simpler than in Maclure's houses.

The underlying movement of Rattenbury's style, and of conventional North American architecture of that period, towards a Classical conception of design was made manifest in the B.C. Electric Railway Company Office, located at 1016 Langley Street in Victoria (Fig.5.28). Although construction was delayed until 1906 (Rattenbury called for tenders in the 28 March issue of the *Contract Record*) and the walls were built of brick with stone facings rather than of stone alone, his original [1904] design appears to have been retained. It is a more concentrated and austere version of the Nelson Branch of the Bank of Montreal.[47] The entrance is canted and framed by pairs of pilasters supporting projected sections of the continuous cornice. On either side, further pilasters harmonize the unequal lengths of the two façades, both storeys of which are defined by a slight variation in the window design. On the ground floor the openings have arched pediments on stone brackets derived from Italian High Renaissance architecture. The upper ones are plain and rectangular in shape. The addition of an attic floor and of an extension to the west end about 1912, possibly by Rattenbury, have barely disturbed its original equilibrium.

Meanwhile in 1904, apart from building a conservatory on to his house, as noted in a letter to his sister dated 14 November, he laboured on the hotel. He had already dictated a full specification for it in September, but this had to be rewritten in November, largely to render the entire structure fireproof.[48] The task was tedious, detailing every aspect of building from the steel structure and installation of machinery to the plumbing and ornament; from the Haddington Island stone facing and Jervis Inlet slates to the Australian red bean and Flemish oak panelling.

The receipt of tenders bulked large even in the letter of condolence upon the death of Richard Mawson that he wrote to his mother on 29 January 1905.

> I was very glad to get Kate's letter to see that you were recovering from the shock and also your letter enclosing the sympathetic letters from George Perkins and Fred Beluens. What a great affection both of them seemed to have had for Uncle, but then everyone had who ever came into contact with him at all. I was rather hoping that you would send me a Bradford Observer giving an account of him, for he has been a great factor in Bradford's existence. We got the tenders in for the Hotel – £103,000, not including the foundations which are costing £20,000. The CPR are grumbling somewhat at the outlay and I am fearing. . . that they may send for me to go to Montreal to discuss some means of reducing the cost, a thing that I cannot see that they can do. I am hoping they will not do so, however, as it would put off my trip to England a month or two, as I should have to go to Montreal and then come back again, so as to let the contract before I could get away. However, I have written them very fully and I do not see what good I could do going to Montreal and told them so, so perhaps I can avoid it.

All to no avail, and on 2 March 1905 he wrote to her from the Windsor Hotel, reminiscing about previous stays and informing her that he had come "to settle the contract" for the hotel. The meetings with the officials of the company were sweetened by the prior payment of $5,694.75 as commission for the working drawings and specifications.[49] He was also able to secure a larger budget, boasting on 17 March to his mother, "Well, I let the contract for the Hotel today and it will be signed tomorrow – $565,000 – £120,000 – quite a nice building. It will really be a handsome place." The company records actually state that the contract was signed with Gribble, Skene and Barrett on the 25th for the sum of $465,000, the remainder, presumably, being for the foundations, machinery, and decoration.[50] The cost of construction may not have exceeded the contract price, since the total expenditure on the hotel, including the two wings added on the basis of Rattenbury's 1903 sketch under the supervision of W. S. Painter, amounted to some $1,600,000.

At last, in April, he was able to return to Britain, sailing on the newly commissioned *Celtic*, but he decided against going to Europe because of the exceptionally hot weather that summer.[51] In any event, his chief purpose might have been to acquaint his mother with her grandchildren. He devoted much of his stay in England to the study of hotel designs and was happy to tell the *Colonist*, shortly after his return at the beginning of

August 1905 that it had become more "humanized."[52] He was also intrigued by the growth in motor transport and impressed by the new methods of road construction, while a brief visit to Coney Island on his homeward journey via New York had excited his interest in building a public amusement centre at Victoria, an idea eventually to be realized on a miniature scale in the Crystal Garden (or Gardens). The generalized accounts of this trip published in the press can be filled out with retrospective passages in two letters written to his mother. In one, dated 24 October 1905, he described the installation of furniture shipped from England:

> the old oak table and two small oak chairs I bought in Brighouse [a town near Bradford] just fill in a niche, and beaten plaques which I have hung on the frieze add artistic feeling; these I bought in London. . . . The case of books and pictures is at the office. . . . When I have arranged these in my office it will take me back 15 years, to the old days when I travelled from Leeds to Bradford on the 8.32 every morning.

In the other, composed on 10 September, and one of the most remarkable letters in the correspondence, Rattenbury uncharacteristically, gave expression to his deepest feelings:

> I have been thinking a good deal of you tonight and it was strongly impressed upon me what a wonderful mother I have had. I suppose it will not turn your head to tell you what I thought, though as you know I am not of a demonstrative nature and whilst I think a lot I don't say much. But during my last visit to England I seemed to get to know you better than I ever did before. Perhaps having seen life I am better able to appreciate you. I suppose that is it.
>
> It was a constant marvel to me in England to hear you expressing your opinions and a delight to see the broad tolerant spirit with which you viewed people, apparently realizing their weaknesses, their efforts, and your knowledge that the good would eventually overcome the faults, and all the time doing it in a spirit of loving kindness. Day by day I learned my lessons from you and hope and know that I shall be a better man from what I learned. As I listened to you on every topic that came up I instinctively endeavoured to gather from you a truer view of life. I don't suppose you know how every utterance was noted. I knew it at the time and watched out for every word you said. But tonight I realized it more vividly and realized what a splendid thing a charitable, broad and loving view of your fellow creatures was. Don't think this is all "taffy," Mother, it is not. It is rather hard to write down, in plain words, one's thoughts and when you do it seems theatrical. I have sometimes thought that the gift of being entertaining and having tact was a great source of being believed, but I

know now that whilst these go a long way, still, that back of these there must be a great heart and a true ring. The gifts you have, we can't all have, but the loving nature I suppose we can get. I only hope that my youngsters will, in some small degree, have the same feeling for me that I have for my charming mother.

Most revealing of all is Rattenbury's final sentence, which implies that while he never hesitated to show his disapproval, even in public, he had much more difficulty in expressing affection: "I am going to post this at once, for if I do not my instinctive nature of self-repression will make me tear it up."

Perhaps to dispel the melancholy that clearly accompanied their parting, he quickly immersed himself in work. On 8 August 1905, the *Colonist* announced that the first courses of brick and stone of the hotel had been laid and that the steel pillars of the lower floor were in place. With his flair for arousing public interest, he contacted the editor eight days later and proposed that a competition be held to select a suitable name for the hotel. He favoured a "dignified and attractive" name which possessed "some historical associations." The exercise led to the choice of "The Empress," appropriate for its kinship with the company's Pacific, and later Atlantic, liners and the imperial title of the sovereign for whom the city had been named. Other commissions also required attention, beginning with yet more improvements to the mountain hotels. "Back home again from the mountains," he wrote to his mother on 31 August, "and full of work," which even included "a house at Philadelphia and one for Manitoba, the two latter owing to people travelling and passing our house. I also have a warehouse building." It is unfortunate that he did not describe the three new commissions in detail. While the houses are virtually impossible to trace, if actually executed, the warehouse might be Humber's Furniture Store, now the Law Chambers Building at 5 Bastion Square (Fig.5.29).[53] The synthetic Classical style of this building and its projected corner bays, sophisticated brickwork, window articulation, and emphatic continuous cornice relate to some of his earlier designs. Of particular interest is the form of the upper windows on the corner projections, rising through two storeys. These are capped by raked mouldings, part pediment and part gable, which are supported on thin brackets that extend below the elliptical arch of the opening in a manner that is comparable with the design of the windows on the tower of Cleckheaton Town Hall. The detailing is precise and integrates the two street façades with the projected corner bays, which act as the frontispiece of the building when viewed from Government Street.

In the midst of these successes Rattenbury still found time to better what he considered petty officialdom. Now it involved restrictions on the sale of game—for once his conservationist principles deserted him—described in a smug letter dated 12 October: "I had a nice little dinner party last week and a quiet one last evening: grouse, pheasant etc. They have passed a law here prohibiting the sale of game. You have to shoot it yourself or get it given to you, so I have engaged a man on monthly salary to take me out shooting and as I cannot go easily he fills in his spare time and I get the game. One way of driving a coach and four through the law."[54]

In the fall he received another commission. "I am just designing a nice house for a friend of mine recently made a judge—Lampman," he wrote on 31 October, "He is building close to us so I am trying to do something extra nice, as I shall see it often enough. I built him a smaller house two years ago."[55] Compared with the earlier Neo-Tudor house on Rockland Avenue (number 1771, since demolished), the second house at 1630 York Place is a mansion (Fig. 5.30), although this is partly the result of additions made by Maclure in 1924. As completed to Rattenbury's designs in 1908, it was "L" shape in plan with a lower sunroom at the intersection of the two gabled blocks. Lit by eight tall windows, the sunroom was covered by a roof with a deeper eave than he normally used, indicating, as indeed does the composition of the main wing, an awareness of current progressive American domestic architecture, and especially that of Wright. The main wing, fronted by two-storey windows lighting the drawing room and study and master bedroom and boudoir, commanded a fine view of Oak Bay across the terrace and magnificent garden. The subsidiary wing, running parallel with the hall and staircase alongside the sunroom, housed the dining room and service quarters. Once again the variety and practicality of the interiors belies the usual description of Rattenbury as a weak domestic designer.

The steady progress in building operations on the hotel and sundry other work for the C.P.R., including the design of the stately interiors of the newly commissioned *Princess Victoria*,[56] enabled Rattenbury to spend a pleasant Christmas season with his family. "Xmas day is over and Frank had a grand time," he wrote to his mother on Boxing Day, "Santa Claus bringing him a beautiful tree and lots of presents, including a railway train that ran on real tracks, with switches etc.... Babs also ("Mary," plain Mary, after all)[57] was in great form, dining with us, and when the plum pudding came on, very excited.... Tonight they have all gone off to "Cinderella." I did not go as I had a slight cold and am pretty cautious now, so have stayed in the last four days." He was fully recovered by

New Year's Eve, when he attended a boisterous party at the home of William Oliver, manager of the Bank of British North America. "I had to buy a new dress suit," he wrote on 6 January, "the evening became rowdy and I parted with my new dress coat (shreds) and nearly 40 — awful! It is not bad to become boys again, though, even for a night."[58]

By the 28th a more sedate Rattenbury was installed in the Alberta Hotel at Edmonton, embarked on yet another new phase in his career.

Six

FURTHER AFIELD
1906–1907

"I don't know whether you can find Edmonton on the map," Ratten-bury began a letter to his mother from the Alberta Hotel on 28 January 1906, "but it is about 300 miles north of Calgary. It is a beautiful place, with a magnificent river running through it and the country is wooded like an English park, and the weather is glorious beyond description —about two inches of snow but bright clear sunshine and you feel as warm as in summer, although it is just at freezing point."

The precise reason for Rattenbury's visit to Edmonton is unclear, but surely it was connected with the vigorous expansion of this new northern capital. According to the *Edmonton Journal*, he had arrived from Calgary with David Ker, a member of the Victoria hotel sub-committee for whom he was to design office blocks in 1907 and 1909.[1] As an indication of their confidence in the future of the city, they bought a lot at the corner of Second Street and Jasper Avenue for $60,000 within twenty-four hours of their arrival. On this site, according to a report in the *Victoria Times*, it was "their intention to commence at once, as soon as weather permits, the construction of a one storey brick block covering the entire lot."[2] The building, if erected, has not survived.

Although named capital of the newly created province in 1905, Edmonton had been incorporated as a city (with a population of 7,000) only a year earlier. Rattenbury was much impressed by its potential and flattered by the respect paid to his reputation as an architect, writing in his January letter:

> I wish I could live in two places at once, at Victoria and Edmonton. This is going to be a very big city and it is rushing ahead now, buildings of all kinds going on. If I stayed here I could get all kinds of work, in fact I have got a large hospital in the two days I have been here, but it is too far away from Victoria for me to really engage in work, unless I made up my mind to come up here. I find the Government are really anxious to engage me to build their new Parliament Buildings and the chances are they will. If they do, however, I will only make them the complete Plans and Designs and let them get some one else to look after the erection of the work. They say they have been looking over all kinds of buildings – nothing like the Parliament Buildings at Victoria, rather complimentary.

Later that year Rattenbury might have regretted his casual attitude towards the commission for the Alberta Legislative Building, since the government was to spend lavishly on its legislature. Possibly because Rattenbury would undertake only to supply the designs and was unwilling to supervise the actual construction, the cabinet eventually chose an American, A. M. Jeffers, as their architect.[3] Between the spring of 1907 and January 1912, Jeffers supervised the construction of his Beaux-Arts style legislature that was necessarily much larger than, if not aesthetically superior, to the Classical courthouse Rattenbury was to design for Vancouver shortly after his return from Edmonton.

In the interview he gave to the *Victoria Times* about his visit, Rattenbury attributed his enthusiasm for the city of Edmonton to the "effort of three of the most influential railway companies to obtain direct communication with that point at the earliest possible moment. Already the Canadian Northern had reached there on its way to the coast. The Grand Trunk Pacific was aiming in that direction as fast as the rails could be laid. Up to the present the Canadian Pacific Railway was not on the scene with a direct line, their communication being by a branch line via Calgary. The Canadian company did not intend being behind the others, however, as was evidenced by the announcement that they contemplated constructing another main line from Winnipeg to Edmonton."

The Canadian Northern had been developed from a modest 123-mile line from Gladstone to Winnipegosis, northwest of Winnipeg, built in 1895 by the energetic partnership of two Ontario entrepreneurs, William Mackenzie and Donald Mann.[4] Just a month before Rattenbury arrived in Edmonton, their company had carried its main line as far as Strathcona on the Edmonton River adjacent to the town, and it seems that one of the purposes of Rattenbury's visit was to make contact with the representatives of the company. This is implied by another passage in his letter of 28 January: "Yesterday I met Mackenzie, a man who is building and runs a new transcontinental line, a bigger system than the Midland Railway, but just a quiet unassuming man. Such is democracy at the start; at the finish it is much like any other community."⁵ Yet, so far as can be determined, any hope that he might have entertained for commissions came to nothing.

Rattenbury had a more advantageous meeting with A. St. Clair Blackett of Edmonton. From Blackett he bought Mary Tod Island, a five-acre property located in the waters of Oak Bay opposite Iechinihl and then inhabited by a sole Indian. The purchase, announced in the *Times* on 3 February, allayed a nagging fear of his that a house or even a fish-packing plant might be built on the island and spoil the view to be had from Iechinihl. No less delighted were Florrie and his son whose "principal ambition just now," he wrote to his mother on the 21st, "is to go over to our island and trap mink." Once spring arrived, he planned to row over and plant broom and flowers. Nor was this his only real-estate acquisition that year. On 28 April 1906 the *Colonist* reported that for $6,000 he had purchased forty-four acres of land on the western side of Shoal Bay from the Green Worlock Estate. This fulfilled a hope he had expressed in a letter written on 27 July 1904:

> I am looking out now for a Country place of 100 acres or so, in a lovely peninsula about 7 miles from Victoria. I want a scenic place, with good oak trees, fine view, lake or sea beach and a stream through it, part good land and part romantic, rocks etc. It seems a large order but they are to be got, and in a few years, when motor cars are more general here these places will be harder to get; already many people are beginning to awake to their desirability. I have one in view that is said to have a stream with sufficient water to run a small electric plant, so that I could light up the place by electricity as well as run fountains etc. Does that not make your mouth water? I should stock the place with game and then I could get good shooting at week-ends.

In February 1906, however, Rattenbury had other concerns, one being to defend himself to his mother, who apparently had expressed her disapproval of his New Year celebrations with Oliver. "I am sorry you did not approve of my New Year party," he wrote on 21 February, "'Honi soit qui mal y pense' you know. I never imagined you would put a construction of that kind on our innocent merriment." After relating a couple of domestic anecdotes, he added a final reassurance of his diligent conduct,

6.1 Sketch of design for Courthouse, Vancouver, 1906.

"I have almost finished my Competition Plans for the Court House. I am rather set up with them. It looks quite swagger, but I dare say there will be a swaggerer."[6] Alongside, in the margin of the letter, he drew a freehand sketch of a tripartite building, with a portico and dome at the centre, closely approximating the present Vancouver Courthouse (Fig. 6.1).[7]

The competition to replace W. S. Hofar's second Vancouver Courthouse of 1891 (the first was designed in 1888 by Sorby, and, interestingly, possessed an Ionic Order portico) had been announced some weeks before by the McBride government and made feasible by a reversal in the provincial finances. Between 1905 and 1910 unprecedented surpluses were amassed, so that public funds became available for its construction and also for the execution of Rattenbury's design (with minor alterations) for the Nelson Courthouse. The commission was awarded to Rattenbury at the beginning of August, the tenders being called for on the 24th, ten days before those for the Nelson Courthouse.[8] Coincidentally, on the last day of that month, the *Victoria Times* published the following announcement, "F. M. Rattenbury, of the city of Victoria, to be a Justice of the Peace in and for the province of British Columbia."

Rattenbury chose to imitate two features from Hofar's building : the central dome and the positioning of porticoes on each façade. But he handled these symbolic motifs with far greater refinement. When a drawing of the main elevation of his design appeared in the *Province* on 30 August, its style was, with reason, described as "pure classic." The design established a pattern for the larger courthouses built in the province prior to World War I and for institutional architecture in Vancouver, the most notable examples of which were the two branches of the Bank of Commerce, one erected at Hastings and Granville, by Darling and Pearson, 1906-8, and the second on Main Street, by V. D. Horsburgh, 1915.[9]

The Vancouver Courthouse is an excellent statement of the North American Beaux-Arts style, melding features from the ancient and modern Classical traditions (Fig.6.2). The main portico, on Georgia Street, imitates the Greek *in antis* type (the columns being framed by spur walls) but has a quasi-Roman Ionic Order. The order is reduced in scale and engaged into the walls of the flanking wings of the rectangular body (measuring 198 by 113 feet). The composition imitates the tripartite arrangement favoured by British architects of the Palladian school. Horizontally, each of the four façades is divided into three parts: on the main and rear fronts by the central Classical porticoes and balustraded corner projections, and on the side façades by the recession of the porticoes between wider projections (Figs.6.3-5). The inversion of the portico theme on the sides, heightened by the substitution of pilasters for columns, serves to create a movement around the building, so that the courthouse commands its open site upon the former "C. P. R. Park."[10] The unification of the ensemble is completed by the severely geometrical Neoclassical dome, raised on a square podium above the rotunda. The purity of these forms recalls the work of the nineteenth-century German K. F. Schinkel, whose linear Greek Revival style possibly inspired the chastely monumental main entrance. By contrast, the corner pavilions and side porticoes carry decorative motifs more worthy of seventeenth-century Baroque. Such an academic blend of Classical styles and the combination of incisive forms with carefully controlled but rich detailing indicate Rattenbury's appreciation of the architecture produced by the two most celebrated east coast firms of the period, McKim, Mead and White, and Carrere and Hastings (the latter were to design the Bank of Toronto, in Toronto, 1911-13, in a grandiose version of the style). If anything, Rattenbury's interpretation is simpler and more precise, though equally catholic in its sources.

A similar combination of judicious ornamentation and logical arrangement predominated on the interior, although Rattenbury had to revise his plans in April, 1907, to include an office for the registrar of the Supreme Court and additional space for the Land Registry Office and its all important vault.[11] The original layout can be reconstructed from the almost complete set of working drawings in the Provincial Archives (Fig. 6.6-11).[12] Beyond the fine entrance a short flight of steps led up to the hall and rotunda; on either side stairs descended to the ground floor, reached directly from the street level at the rear. The ground floor contained various government offices, chiefly the Land Registry Office and the Police Department, while the lower ground floor was reserved for the cells, heating equipment pumps for the ventilating and vacuum-cleaning systems, and the electric apparatus. From the entrance hall two further flights, supported on steel beams, ascended to the upper storey and a gallery around the upper part of the rotunda. At this level the four sides of the rotunda were decorated with tall pilasters enclosing columns and supporting a continuous entablature surmounted by large semi-circular windows, perhaps in emulation of the Roman triumphal arch and thus intended to symbolize the triumph of justice through the law (Fig.6.12). The canted sides of the rotunda, ornamented with thick drip mouldings, masked the structural steel footings of the octagonal drum and circular dome, both of which carried Roman motifs. Four semi-circular windows and a glazed aperture in the dome afforded ample light for this pivotal space. On either side, he provided dignified accommodation for the courts, and, as importantly, separate entrances for the public, the law officers, litigants, and prisoners.

The specification which Rattenbury drew up at this time displays his characteristic concern that only the finest materials be used: unflawed steel pillars and beams and Portland cement mixed to his satisfaction for the main structure, undamaged marble for the exterior, "Best Victoria common bricks" for the internal walls, "Best Douglas fir of the first quality," and "best Indiana quartered oak" for the courts, carefully laid Terrazzo mosaic floors with Tennessee marble slips for the corridors and first-rate copper for the clerestorey roofs.[13] It is little wonder that the final cost of the building greatly exceeded the $150,000 appropriation. Yet the increase was largely the result of the inflation that accompanied the post-1907 "boom," aggravated by the slow pace of construction. The builders, Messrs. McDonald, Wilson and Snider of Vancouver (owners of the Haddington Island quarry from which the stone for the upper walls was cut) failed to meet the 1 July 1909 deadline demanded in the specification and did not complete their contract until the spring of 1911.[14] Building operations, not commenced until December 1907, were, in any case, supervised by the Vancouver firm of architects, Dalton and Eveleigh. Over this period the population of Vancouver virtually doubled, reaching 100,000 by 1911, and there was a great increase in the amount of litigation, which rendered the accommodation inadequate before the courthouse was formally opened. That function was performed by Attorney-General Bowser, who had the grace to apologize for the lack of space on behalf of the tight-fisted government. In 1906, Rattenbury had proposed that in such an eventuality the government offices be moved to detached wings or to two-storey additions built onto the sides of the courthouse.[15] Rather than adopt either solution, the government commissioned Rattenbury's old foe, Thomas Hooper, to erect an extension on Hornby Street, which was linked to his temple of Justice by a somewhat disharmonious double colonnade.[16] Hooper compacted the quadruple portico composition of Rattenbury's more commanding and sophisticated structure. Both have been integrated into the new courthouse complex (1975–79), conceived by Arthur Erickson, who has transformed the old courthouse into the civic Art Gallery (opened in 1983).[17]

If the Vancouver Courthouse symbolized the Classical foundation of modern jurisprudence, the one designed in 1903 at Nelson represented its medieval development (Fig.6.13). Yet, though it appears as much a baronial hall as a seat of law, the relationship between the plan and external design is more exact (Figs.6.14-15). The basement, containing storerooms and the heating equipment, is surrounded by lower ground not unlike a moat and entered across a stone "drawbridge." The broad arched entrance portal is framed by thin windows apparently inspired by the slit windows of Norman castles and surmounted by a Jacobean oriel and curved gable. Beyond the entrance stands the staircase, and, on the ground floor, the County Court; the larger hammer-beam Assize Court (60 by 30 feet) occupies the two upper floors. To the left of the entrance, and housing the registrar and barristers' room (assigned to the police and library in the 1903 plans) and a court reporters' room in its three storeys, is a taller square tower with a projecting corner turret that seems at once Scottish and French, in company with the steeply pitched roof. The triple window under the cornice, however, reverts to the Richardsonian Romanesque of the Parliament Buildings, as do the entrance arch, small oval windows above, and rough-cut external walls faced in banded Salmo marble. The dramatic eclecticism of these components is moderated on the plainer right wing, accommodating the government offices, police, jury and witness rooms. But the medievalism of the main front is, nevertheless, continued in the composition of the remainder. The gabled entrance extends inwards to form a nave, as it were, of a church with clerestorey lighting for the Assize Court and its gallery; continuing the analogy of a church, the three-storey section behind the tower, containing further offices, corresponds to an aisle, while the pitched bay over the judges' chambers simulates a transept.

The Nelson Courthouse remains in use. It was built by a local contractor, W. G. Gilbert, who operated a marble quarry near Kaslo, on Kootenay Lake, and a brick kiln and sash-and-door factory in the town. Despite the fact that he was able to supply almost all the materials for the structure (concrete and brick walls faced externally with marble and wooden floors and roofs), the costs rose to $109,145.88. Completed in the fall of 1909 (notwithstanding the date incised on the stone course below the gable), its design influenced the courthouse that Honeyman and Curtis designed in 1908 for Kamloops.[18]

One type of case to be heard increasingly before the courts from the Edwardian era onwards was the traffic offence. After much hesitation, Rattenbury ordered his first car some time prior to 14 March 1906, when he wrote to his mother, "Well, do you know, I have ordered an automobile after all. I cabled to England for it, so it will not arrive for about six weeks, just in time for summer."[19] He delighted in this new machine and became an enthusiastic participant in rallies held in the Victoria area. Less enthusiastic was his reaction to the brief visit to Victoria by the Duke of Connaught on his return journey from Japan (where he had bestowed the Order of the Garter on the Emperor). "I am afraid I did not tell you much about the Prince," Rattenbury apologized to his mother on 16 April, "to tell the truth I did not think of it. He came here and a couple of fellows I know took him off fishing for two days, then he left. Whilst very loyal I do not think that we are much impressed by titles [according to his daughter, Mary, Rattenbury refused the offer of a title]. Living in England it would seem like heresy to consider them rather a farce, but in the Colonies where men are esteemed for what they do it seems natural to take them not quite seriously." This studied indifference, so much at variance with his response to the 1901 visit of the Duke of York, could reveal an acceptance of North American attitudes or, perhaps closer to the truth, chagrin in not having been invited to attend any of the official events organized for Connaught.[20]

Of far greater significance to him was the earthquake in San Francisco.[21]

> What an awful day they have had in San Francisco. I am looking forward anxiously for the morning papers to see if the disaster is as great as reported. Apparently the whole centre of the city is in ruins. There must be thousands who were rich this morning who are ruined tonight . . . they knew that they were living over the earthquake belt, they have often had

tremblings of the earth, and about 40 years ago they had a great earthquake, so much so that for years they built their costliest buildings of wood, buildings lined inside with ebony and marble. But recently they seem to have forgotten past experience and have been building stone and steel structures towering into the skies and now comes another earthquake and apparently down they have come or so damaged that it will be hard for a long time, I should think, to get people to occupy them. Even at the present time they are building an hotel there [probably the second St. Francis Hotel] to cost nearly two million pounds. I know of no hotel in England to compare to it. How they will get people into it now I don't know.

During the spring and summer, the workmen hired by the contractors (Gribble, Skene and Barrett) completed the fabric of the Empress. They hauled up the requisite steel, stone, timber, brick, and cement by main force, using lifting tackle suspended from sheer-legs placed at each corner of the building. By the end of July the great timbers of the roof, prepared on the ground, were raised and then assembled to enclose the sixth storey and to carry the boarding on which the 10" by 18" slates cut at Jervis Inlet were to be laid in the autumn. "I think it is going to look pretty fine," he forecast in a letter of 27 July. "How's this for swagger paper?" he asked in the same letter, which was written on illustrated notepaper then being distributed by the Tourist Association (led by Harry Barnard), partly on the strength of the hotel's progress. Under the heading, "Victoria, B.C., the City of Homes," are depictions of a selection of local residences, amongst which appear Iechinihl, Government House and Thomas Hooper's House.[22] "These are fair samples of dozens of houses here," he scribbled at the bottom, "and by no means the best of them. All these houses belong to friends of mine, except the top one – that belongs to the Architect [Hooper] who tried to down me when I was away, but he got pretty badly roasted." (Fig.6.16). A similar sheet in the correspondence shows a slightly different collection of houses. "The temperate summer and winter climate, unrivalled scenic attractions and healthy situation of Victoria make it the most desirable residential city on this continent for people of means who wish to live the rest of their lives in pleasure and comfort." However, it was Samuel Maclure who was to benefit most from such advertising, which succeeded in attracting a number of wealthy Britons and Canadians to Victoria.[23]

Rattenbury shared Barnard's desire that Victoria be developed as a superior residential and tourist city rather than be despoiled by industry or speculative building; their concern was well founded, as evinced by a report in the *Contract Record* for 20 October 1909 that Messrs. Arnoldi and Law of San Francisco had opened negotiations for building a large steel and iron plant at Victoria (subsequently abandoned). To preserve the natural beauty of the expanding Oak Bay area, he joined other residents, whose ranks were fortified by James Herrick McGregor, William Oliver, and Samuel Maclure, in founding the Oak Bay Improvements Association. Though they failed to persuade the City of Victoria to enlarge its boundaries to include Oak Bay, they successfully petitioned the provincial secretary for permission to establish a separate municipality. On 2 July the District of Oak Bay was officially incorporated. To all intents and purposes it was the Improvements Association under a new name, and the first reeve or chairman of the municipality was Oliver, Rattenbury serving as one of the councillors. At the inaugural meeting of the council, he was invited to design the municipal seal. Appropriately, instead of creating an heraldic device, he chose a favourite view, Mount Baker, named after the junior officer who had first glimpsed the peak some 120 years earlier from the foretop of H.M.S. *Endeavour* under the command of Captain Vancouver. The foreground is occupied by a lively sailing boat representing his own enduring pleasure in that particular activity (he was a member of the Royal Victoria Yacht Club).

Later that month he informed the *Colonist* of two forthcoming domestic commissions within the confines of the municipality. The first was a new house for the barrister J. O. Grahame, the second the addition of a porte-cochère to "Gisburne," a large house, on Rockland Avenue, which had the highly decorated millwork typical of San Francisco domestic design and belonged to J. B. Hobson.[24] The Grahame house was built over the next few months on a spacious site at 534 St. Charles Street (Fig.6.18–20), in a handsome Tudor style that Rattenbury and Maclure developed to counteract the influence of American west coast architecture as represented by "Gisburne." Of frame construction, it comprises a broad rectangular two-and-a-half storey block, containing the main accommodation, and a thinner single-storey rear wing (a second floor was added in 1956) for the kitchen and quarters for a Chinese servant. The longer garden façade is flanked by two square bay windows lighting the drawing and dining rooms and larger bedrooms. The composition of these bays, repeated in different guises around the house, reflects in miniature the arrangement of the towers on the Empress, and, though producing a more complicated pattern of planes and angles than attempted on the comparably scaled McGregor house, it also reinforces the underlying regularity of the design. Here again the floor divisions are clearly stated by the choice of materials: fieldstone basement, shingled ground floor and half-timbered upper level. The orderly composition and simplified decoration continue into the interior, where the spacious rooms revolve around the broad stair hall, entered from the side of the house.

As winter approached, the pace of work on the Empress slowed because of the City Council's delay in landscaping the grounds. The original plan had envisaged the creation of tennis courts, lawns, and shrubberies, but there was no likelihood of its being realized by the following summer, when the C.P.R. hoped to open the hotel. Indeed, a further seven feet of infill remained to be laid before the gardens could be planted. Rattenbury, espousing the cause of his employers in a letter addressed to the editor of the *Colonist* (and published on 3 November), berated the councillors for the absence of "some sign of the preliminary measures being taken . . . to fulfill their part of the contract." Then, quite unexpectedly on 5 December, the *Colonist* announced that he had resigned from the Empress commission. The paper reported that he was unwilling to change the location "of the office and the drawing room of the house" on the ground floor, as ordered by the company's chief architect, W. S. Painter, since compliance would necessitate a journey to Montreal which "pressure of business" prevented Rattenbury from undertaking. The Vancouver architect G. D. Curtis was appointed in his place and proceeded to Montreal immediately so that the schedule of work could be maintained.[25]

Rattenbury's explanation might be substantially true, especially since the question of the position of the rooms had been settled in his favour a year before. There is no mention of his resignation in the surviving C.P.R. records nor of any preceding clash with Painter. Certainly he did not lack for work, the *Colonist* noting on 6 December that he was "busy," and, on the 21st, that he was "engaged upon plans for a new hotel at Banff." Another, previously unnoticed, item on his books was a report on the design of the Vancouver Orpheum. On 18 December, the *Colonist* stated that Rattenbury "one of the best known authorities on the coast" had declared the theatre to be "entirely safe," an opinion endorsed by E. W. Houghton, architect to the Northwestern Theatrical Association.[26] Yet on 5 September, when replying to enquiries about the proposed Saskatchewan Legislative Buildings, Rattenbury had remarked that the "various large buildings . . . I am now erecting" were "close to completion at the same time." Thus Painter's intervention, following upon a succession of changes, might simply have been the culminating annoyance. All the same, it is difficult to imagine that his decision was not also affected by his pride, which appears to have kept him away from the delayed official opening of the Empress on 21 January 1908 (actual construction had ceased in 1907) (Figs.6.17A and B).[27] Had Rattenbury attended the ceremony he would have heard the unofficial poet laureate of the province, the loquacious Captain Clive Phillips-Wooley, liken the hotel to "Prince Charming" and claim that "Victoria waited for the kiss of love and now comes into her own."[28]

In retrospect, Rattenbury's resignation seems peculiarly ill-judged. He removed himself from the probability of receiving a number of lucrative C.P.R. commissions, beginning with the proposed new Banff Hotel, followed by the erection of the north and south wings of the Empress between 1909 and 1912 (the ballroom was added in 1914) and the rebuilding on a much larger scale of the Hotel Vancouver from 1913 (by Swales, with whom W.S. Painter not long afterwards established a partnership). But, at that time, he may have anticipated the patronage of the Grand Trunk Pacific Railway, which appeared poised to rival the success of the C.P.R. in the west. The G.T.P. was the western division of the thriving Grand Trunk Railway Company which had been incorporated in 1852–53 to serve the major cities of Upper and Lower Canada, with a connecting line to Portland, Maine. The company was essentially an amalgamation of existing lines with new systems constructed through private investment (mainly from the London money market) and publicly guaranteed funds. The expansion of the railway westwards was the vision of Charles Melville Hays, born in 1856 at Rock Island, Illinois. Having spent his early life working for American railway companies, Hays came to Canada in 1896 to be general manager of the Grand Trunk. In 1901 he had travelled to London to persuade the reluctant board of directors, chaired by Sir Charles Rivers Wilson, to invest in the western expansion of the company. Failing to raise sufficient funds, Hays engineered an agreement— mutually disadvantageous as it transpired—with the federal government. The Grand Trunk undertook to build a line from Winnipeg to the British Columbia coast with the name of Grand Trunk Pacific Railway; another section, to be known as the National Transcontinental, would be constructed by the Canadian government from Winnipeg to Moncton, New Brunswick, and leased (at uneconomical rates, since it duplicated existing lines) by the Grand Trunk Pacific on completion.

The agreement had been publicized in Montreal on 24 November 1902 and filed by the *Colonist* on the following day. Hays confidently declared that the line "would be of the most modern and up to date character, hav-

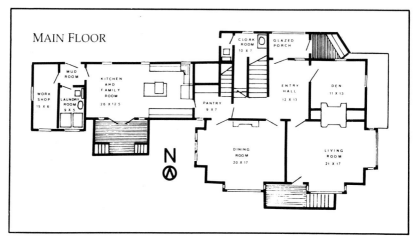

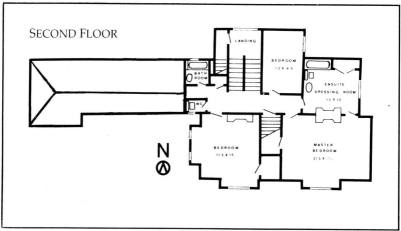

6.19 Ground and upper floor plan, J. O. Grahame house, substantially as designed by Rattenbury.

ing especially in view low grades, long tangents, steel bridges and heavy rails, as well as ample station facilities and equipment for the handling of both freight and passenger traffic. In fact the road will be of the highest standard in every respect." Nor would the G.T.P. confine itself to the west coast: "having reached the Pacific coast the company will undertake to establish a line of steamships to run to China, Japan and the Orient." When Rattenbury broke away from the C.P.R., there was no way of telling that the G.T.P. courted disaster. The crippling construction and running costs of the eastern line could not have been public knowledge in 1906; indeed, the magnitude of the company's indebtedness was not apparent until 1917 when it passed into government receivership, to be reconstituted as the Canadian National Railway. As late as 1914, the historian Howay had no qualms about quoting the following optimistic piece written in 1906, five months before Rattenbury resigned from the Empress commission, by the journalist C. Y. Warman:

> This, I believe, is to be a model line in every particular. It will profit by the mistakes of all existing lines and take advantage of every modern improvement. Nothing will be wasted, no opportunity for the reaping of legitimate reward for the men who furnish the capital will be neglected. The company will build, own and operate its own telegraphs, handle the express business, provide hotels and restaurants. It will have a line of steamers on the Atlantic and another on the Pacific and a fleet on the lakes.[29]

There is good reason to believe that Hays's gamble might have succeeded had he not been drowned in 1912 in the sinking of the *Titanic*, to be replaced by a much less shrewd business man, E.J. Chamberlain, and if the world economy had not been shattered by World War I.

To Rattenbury, who was easily captivated by visionary projects, it must have seemed in 1906 that the future lay with the G.T.P. Early in November he was commissioned by the company to build a hotel at their designated Pacific terminal at Prince Rupert. Though it was only a gabled frame building, three and a half storeys high and nine bays long with two short wings (a miniature version of the Empress in plan), the interior was spacious, and the large bedrooms were fitted with the latest conveniences (Fig.6.21).[30] Both Rattenbury and the company regarded it as temporary, even though it cost some $50,000 upon completion in the spring of 1907, to be replaced in a few years by a hotel on the grand scale when funds permitted.

And another enterprise beckoned. On 5 September 1906, Walter Scott, the premier of Saskatchewan, had visited Rattenbury while on a trip to Victoria and, evidently impressed by the Victoria Legislative Buildings, consulted him about the proposed Saskatchewan legislature and the best means of obtaining designs. On the very same day Rattenbury composed a letter to the premier advising against a competition and offering his own services, "In case the great honour of designing your new Parliament Buildings were entrusted to me, I am so situated at the present time.... That I could and would be delighted to come and live in Saskatchewan and study the conditions on the ground, and make the Plans and Models of the building there, and in consultation with you and your Ministers."[31]

Scott or, more truly, his colleagues, tactfully declined the offer, and on 1 November wrote to inform Rattenbury that a limited competition would be organized between him and a select group of other architects. Rattenbury, confident of success, affirmed his willingness to participate on the 5th, and, to underscore his wide professional experience, he proffered advice on the conduct of the competition. The prospect of receiving this valuable commission surely also influenced his decision to relinquish the Empress, and it was one that must have appeared specially attractive in the first week of 1907.

On 3 January Rattenbury was subjected to an uninvited attack upon his professional competence at a meeting of the trustees convened to discuss the best means of expanding the Victoria High School in the face of the rapid, and unforeseen, growth in enrolment.[32] Dr. Ernest Hall was infuriated to discover that Rattenbury had been approached by the trustees about preparing plans and, in a letter to the press, castigated the existing structure as "barn-like." Rattenbury foolishly and over-aggressively responded to the taunt. "It is too much, I suppose, to expect Dr. Ernest Hall to know what fair criticism is or what is not decent and honourable as between professional men," he asserted in a letter addressed to the *Victoria Times* and published on 5 January, "He cannot object to my saying that I consider him a pretty mean specimen of a man and by no means a credit to his profession. For my own part I would think, were I to entrust myself to his medical care I would be either qualified for New Westminster [presumably a reference to the provincial lunatic asylum] or was desirous of quickly terminating my existence." The letter is symptomatic of his habitual hasty anger in the face of criticism, however silly, as in this instance, and it redounded adversely upon him. He merely succeeded in drawing public attention to a design which, as he had confessed to his mother, was undistinguished, and in provoking a vote of censure from the trustees on 9 January, a factor in the abandonment of his scheme for an extension housing eight rooms.[33]

Perhaps to scotch his detractors, Rattenbury again mistakenly anticipated success by informing the *Colonist* on 23 January that he had entered the national competition for the Departmental and Justice Buildings at Ottawa, recently advertised by the dominion government.[34] The *Colonist* received the news enthusiastically, remarking that Rattenbury's participation in such an important competition reflected well upon the city and province and that his "friends" were "sure that for the designing of public buildings there are few in America who can surpass him." Unfortunately for Rattenbury, the three judges, from Ontario and

Quebec, did not place his Tudor Gothic scheme on the list of four prize-winners gazetted on 3 September.[35] His drawings have disappeared, but, to conform with the specifications, they must have shown two structures to be erected on the east side of Major Hill's Park in Ottawa. One of at least three storeys was intended for the Department of Justice, with accommodation for the Supreme and Exchequer Courts, the Railway Commission, a library, and a conference room. A second building, of five storeys above a basement, was to contain various federal departmental offices, and be linked to Parliament Hill by a footbridge "of monumental design." He would have known that the competition was "chiefly to be considered one of suggestion," in other words, that the government did not intend to proceed with construction at that time; he hoped instead to gain one of the premiums of $8,000 or $4,000, and to bring his name to the notice of a wider public. He might have fared better if he had based his design on a French rather than an English "phase of Gothic," to match the style of Fuller and Jones's Houses of Parliament.

Despite all these endeavours, Victoria remained his best source of commissions. As the *Colonist* reported on 3 January 1907, Judge Lampman had finally instructed Rattenbury to award the contract (to Noble Bros.) for his "elegant residence" to be built on Oak Bay for approximately $6,200. He had also been asked to prepare plans for "a handsome new dwelling for A.M. Coles," partner in a thriving real-estate firm with his brother-in-law Samuel Matson (who owned the land), to be situated off the Esquimalt Road on the outskirts of Victoria (now Wollaston Street; the house is number 851). The Coles house, which remains unaltered, was Rattenbury's most attractive rendering of the English Arts and Crafts style. Behind the picturesque façades, originally arranged with the main entrance on Dunsmuir Road, is a characteristically convenient plan, radiating from the entrance hall and staircase, both lit by large bay windows facing east and south. The drawing room and main bedroom (measuring approximately 22 by 15 feet) span the southwest front and communicate with the two-storey verandah. The two gables, repeating the forms used on his Glacier and Oak Bay Hotels, enclose a sitting room (16 by 14 feet) and the dining room (20 by 16 feet), with, above, two delightfully proportioned bedrooms (16 by 12 feet), in which the space beneath the pitched roofs was utilized for closets (Figs.6.22A&B-23). Perched on a rocky outcrop, the house formerly commanded a magnificent view towards the distant Inner Harbour.

Two months later, on 12 March 1907, the *Times* noted that he was "at work on plans for a new building to be erected by the Brackman-Ker

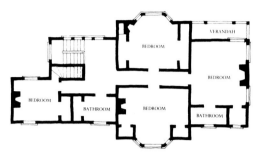

BLOCK PLAN. UPPER FLOOR A M. COLES HOUSE

BLOCK PLAN. GROUND FLOOR A M. COLES HOUSE, VICTORIA, 1907

6.23 Block Plans, A. M. Coles House.

Milling Company on the site of the old Methodist Church" at the corner of Broad and Pandora Streets. This utilitarian two-storey block, occupying the whole site and having pressed brick walls and a flat gravel roof, survives in commercial use. Then on 23 April the *Colonist* announced that he had been awarded the contract to design the new branch of the Merchants' Bank of Canada, to be built at the intersection of Douglas and Yates Streets. Rattenbury's two-storey Classically styled bank would replace an "accumulation of wooden huts" and become "undoubtedly the finest commercial block," being "probably the purest example of any one type of architecture in the city." Constructed of reinforced concrete faced with Newcastle Island limestone by the local contractors, Wood and McVickers, the bank, now operated by the Bank of Montreal, is an amalgam of elements derived from the Vancouver Courthouse, the Nelson Bank of Montreal, and the B.C. Electric Railway Company Office.[36]

6.2 Courthouse, Vancouver, 1906–1911.

COURT HOUSE
VANCOUVER   Nº 10

ELEVATION TO GEORGIA ST N.
Scale of Feet

F. M. Rattenbury Arc.
Victoria   B.C.
April 9

6.3 Elevation of main (Georgia Street) front, Vancouver Courthouse, drawn in 1907.

ELEVATION to ROBSON ST

6.4 Elevation of rear façade, Vancouver Courthouse, 1907.

EAST ELEVATION

6.5 Elevation of side façades, Vancouver Courthouse, 1907.

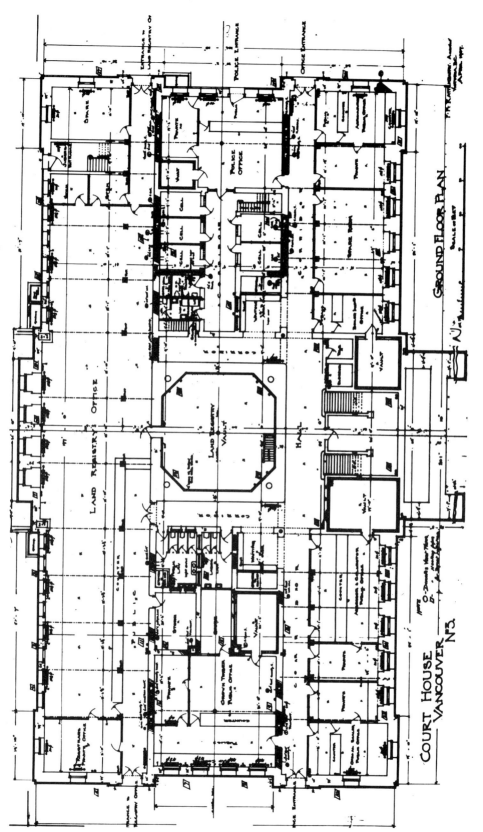

6.6 Plan of ground floor, Vancouver Courthouse, 1907, as originally built, 1907–1911.

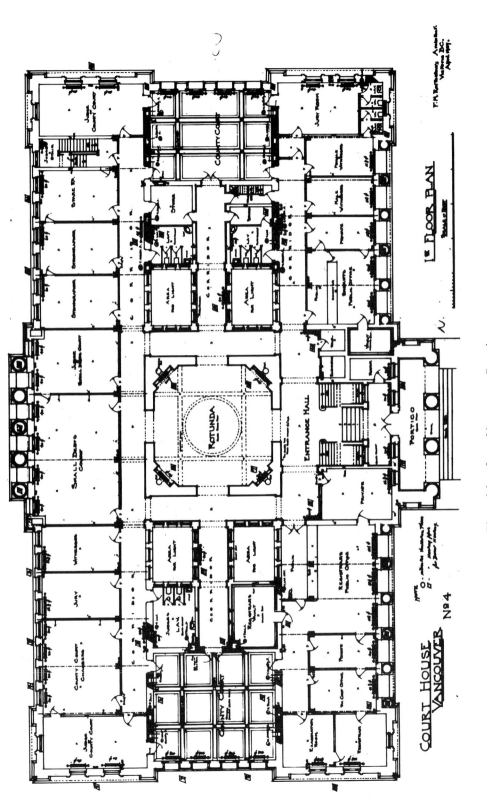

6.7 Plan of first floor, Vancouver Courthouse, 1907.

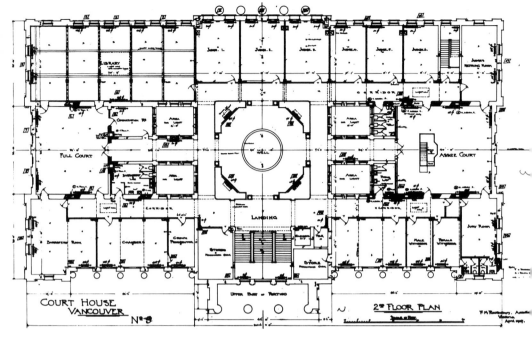

6.8 Plan of second floor, Vancouver Courthouse, 1907.

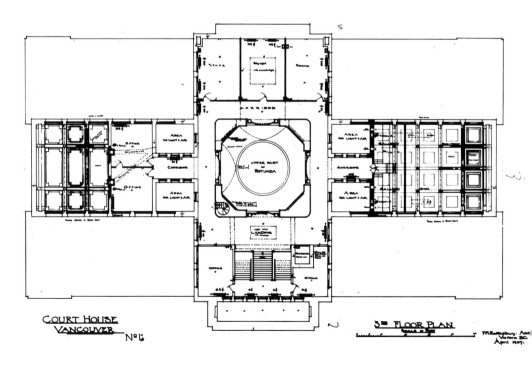

6.9 Plan of third floor, Vancouver Courthouse, 1907.

6.10 Longitudinal section, Vancouver Courthouse, 1907.

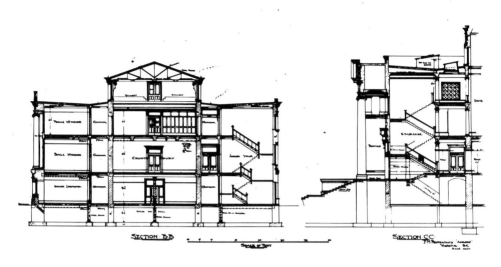

6.11 Transverse section, Vancouver Courthouse, 1907.

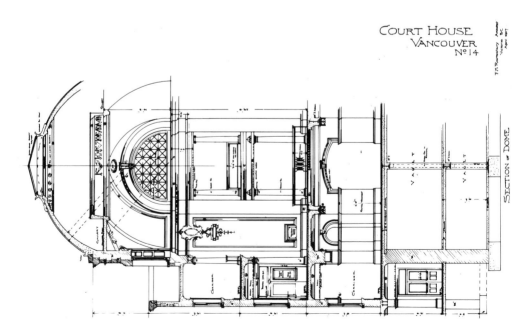

6.12 Elevation and details of the Rotunda and dome, Vancouver Courthouse, as originally completed, 1907.

6.13 Courthouse, Nelson, designed 1903, but with some revisions 1906–1909.

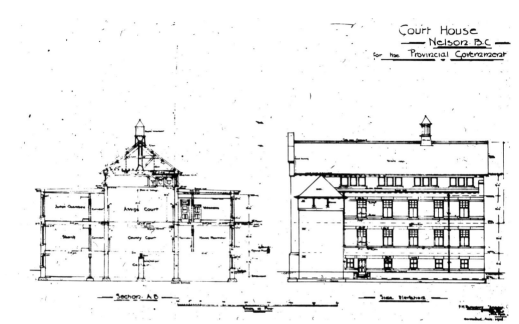

6.14 Elevation and section of Nelson Courthouse, originally drawn in 1903 and revised in 1906.

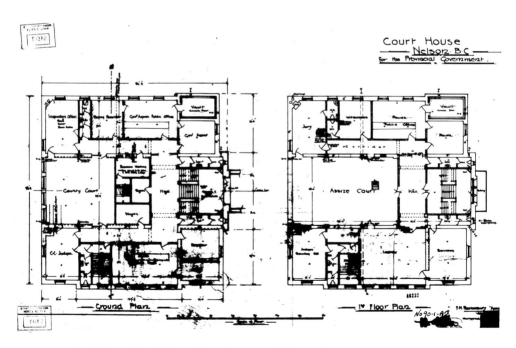

6.15 Floor plans, Nelson Courthouse, as built 1906–1909.

VICTORIA, B.C.
THE CITY OF HOMES

A SEASIDE RESORT
FOR HEALTH AND PLEASURE

NO HOT SUMMERS
NO HARD WINTERS

6.16 Promotional stationery, Victoria Tourist Assocation, about 1907, with notations by Rattenbury.

6.17A The Empress Hotel at the time of its opening in 1908.

6.17B The Empress Hotel, rear façade, as completed in 1907 before the landscaping of the grounds.

6.18 J. O. Grahame House, Victoria, 1906, side façade and office wing (the upper storey is a later addition).

6.20 J. O. Grahame House, entrance front.

6.21 Prince Rupert, B.C., showing G.T.P. Hotel, 1906–1907.

6.22A A. M. Coles House, Victoria, 1907, showing the original main entrance facing onto Dunsmuir Road.

6.22B A. M. Coles House, rear façade.

6.24 Merchant's Bank of Canada (now Bank of Montreal), Douglas St., Victoria, 1907.

6.25 Interior, Merchant's Bank of Canada.

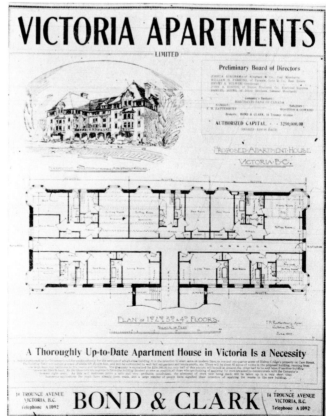

6.26 Sketch elevation and plan
for apartment building,
Victoria, 1907.

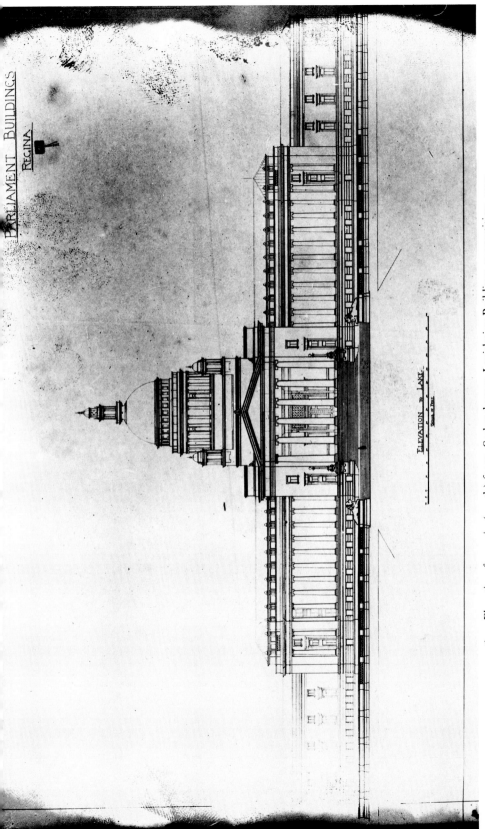

PARLIAMENT BUILDINGS
REGINA

ELEVATION to LAKE.
Scale of Feet

6.27 Elevation for main (north) front, Saskatchewan Legislative Buildings competition, 1907.

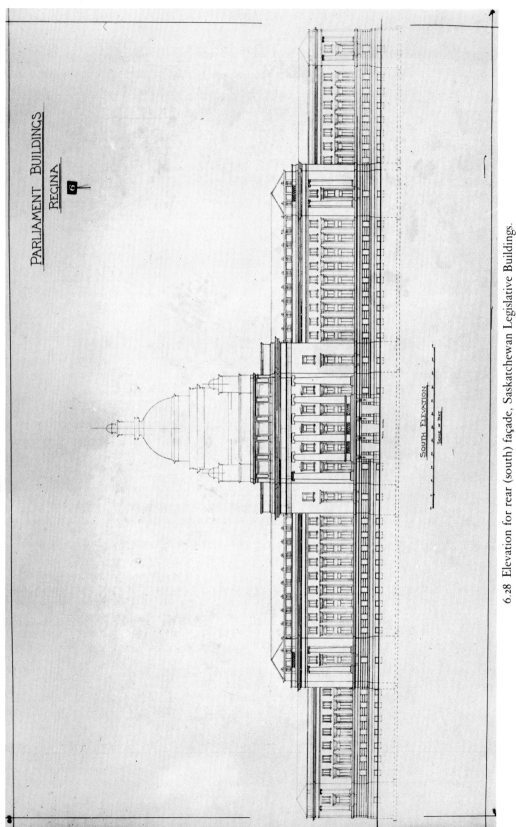

6.28 Elevation for rear (south) façade, Saskatchewan Legislative Buildings.

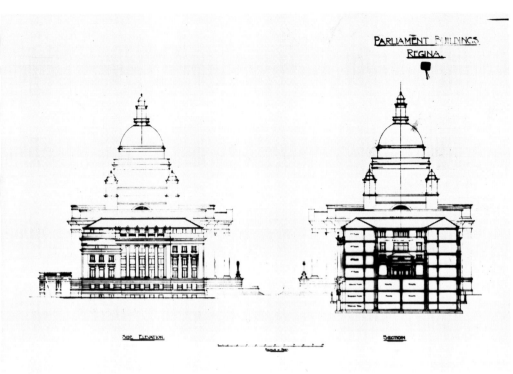

6.29 Elevation for side façade and transverse section, Saskatchewan Legislative Buildings.

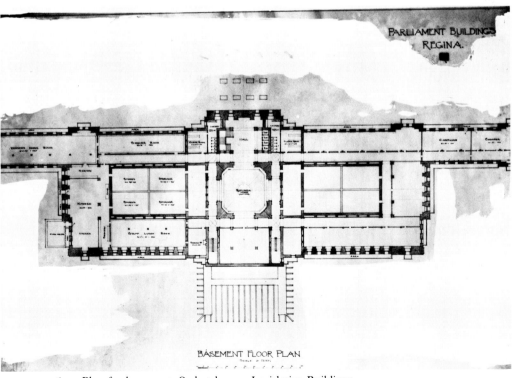

6.30 Plan for basement, Saskatchewan Legislative Buildings.

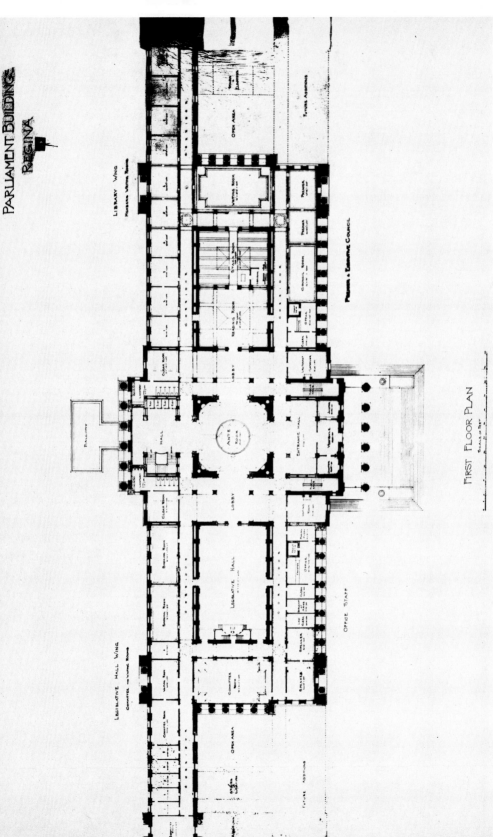

6.31 Plan for main floor, Saskatchewan Legislative Buildings.

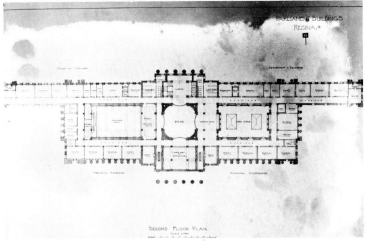

6.32 Plan for second floor, Saskatchewan Legislative Buildings.

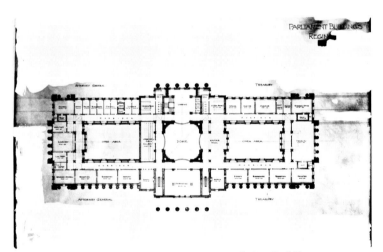

6.33 Plan for third floor, Saskatchewan Legislative Buildings.

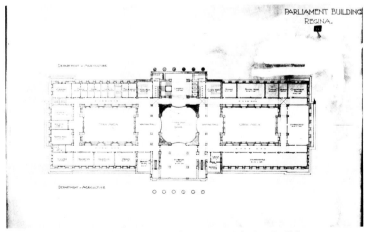

6.34 Plan for fourth floor, Saskatchewan Legislative Buildings.

6.35 McKim, Mead and White, Rhode Island State Capitol, Providence, 1895–1905.

6.36 E. and W. S. Maxwell, Saskatchewan Legislative Buildings, Regina, nearing completion in about 1913.

The raised and engaged Ionic columns, two on Yates Street and three on Douglas compare with the Vancouver Courthouse, while the corner entrance and the side projections, decorated with curved pediments and cartouches (here lions' heads and plaques), echo his earlier commercial buildings. The resulting ensemble is, arguably, Rattenbury's most accomplished building, being admirably scaled, inventively composed, and finely detailed (the editor of the *Contract Record* saw fit to include a photograph of the exterior in 1908: Fig.6.24). Unquestionably, it was among the most expensive, costing over $70,000 at a rate of 32¢ per square foot, as against 22¢ for the Legislative Buildings. A large proportion of the total costs was absorbed by the furnishing of the fireproof interior, which originally boasted marble floors, walls, and counters within the seventeen-foot high banking hall, set off by bronze grills in front of the tellers (Fig.6.25). The interior was subsequently modernized by the Bank of Montreal which in 1921 acquired this branch (and another that Rattenbury designed for Nanaimo in 1911–12); at that time the Douglas Street façade was extended.

The foundations of both the Victoria buildings were under way, when, on 23 June, Messrs. Bond and Clark of Trounce Avenue published a full-page advertisement under the banner, "Victoria Apartments Limited." The firm was acting for a group of Victoria merchants who were backed by the Merchants' Bank and had secured Rattenbury as architect.[37] The directors hoped to raise $125,000 through the sale of $100 shares in order to finance the building of a "high-class" apartment block covering about 120 square feet, containing some sixty-five suites "running from one large room and bathroom to five rooms and bathroom," and surrounded by "well laid out gardens tennis courts etc." on one and a quarter acres of Bishop Cridge's former property along Carr Street. Were this to prove popular, a second, similar building would be erected after the sale of further shares to the full extent of the company's permissable capitalization of $250,000. Two-thirds of the advertisement is taken up with a drawing signed by Rattenbury and dated June 1907, combining a "Perspective Sketch" of the main front and plans for the four floors of what seems to be the rear wing of the block (Fig.6.26). The façade is a compacted version of the Empress, though to be built of brick and wood, having two broad corner projections with central oriel windows, gabled dormers and pitched roofs which are linked by a balustraded Neo-Tudor arcade. The fourth storey is, apparently, half-timbered in the manner of the second addition to the Mount Stephen House. The Château theme of the exterior is echoed in the beamed ceilings of the drawing rooms of the economically planned suites, the larger of which were to have enjoyed bay windows. While it may have been true that "numerous applications for stock" had already been received, the scheme foundered in the sudden and sharp recession that assaulted the North American economy in the fall of 1907, which Rattenbury later lamented in a letter written to his sister Kate in 1908. As the advertisement proclaimed, "A Thoroughly Up-to-Date Apartment House in Victoria Is a Necessity," and Rattenbury's design would have established a high standard for a type of housing that only became popular in the city after his departure.

The recession did not impede the progress, albeit slow, of the competition for the Saskatchewan Legislative Buildings. On 12 August 1907, Scott formally asked Rattenbury to submit a design. Whether as the result of a delay in its receipt or indecision on his part, Rattenbury did not reply until 11 September, though the *Colonist* had, on 29 August, reported that he would compete against six other architects.[38] Sensing that he could no longer rely on winning the competition, he wrote again, on 31 October, asking Scott to join the two professional architects who had been appointed to judge the entries: Percy Nobbs, at this time McDonald Professor of Architecture at McGill University (the first institution in Canada to grant, from 1893, degrees in architecture) and Bertram Goodhue of New York. Rattenbury probably counted on the support of Scott, but, whether or not this confidence was well-placed, Scott suffered a breakdown in health which forced him to withdraw from the selection process. His place was taken by Frank Day, who was then president of the American Institute of Architects. Still, Rattenbury persevered and had completed his entry before 15 November, when Scott telephoned to inquire whether he would agree to an extension in the deadline as requested by a number of the other competitors. No doubt to prove his enthusiasm, Rattenbury replied that he had no need of any extension and sent his drawings with a brief explanatory letter five days later.

The design he entered for the Saskatchewan Legislative Assembly is grand in scale and dignified in effect, yet also simple in composition and restrained in decoration (Figs.6.27–34). In company with the majority of the other competitors, he chose the Classical style, although the Saskatchewan government had asked that the designs symbolize the British imperial tradition of the province; only Cass Gilbert submitted a Neo-Gothic scheme, which was the style most commonly associated with the British parliamentary tradition. However, Rattenbury and the remainder of the competitors may have judged that the Classically inspired Edwardian Baroque was the current mode of the Empire. This was a reasonable assumption, but Rattenbury avoided the lavish Neo-Baroque ornamentation and, to a lesser extent, the grandiloquent planning favoured by the late nineteenth-century British Classicists.[39] Instead, he emulated the sharply defined massing and detailing of the American Beaux-Arts. The compact cross-axial plan is derived from both schools of academic architecture. With its central and pivotal anteroom beneath the dome, the plan combines the condensed arrangement of the Vancouver Courthouse with the more extended "H" shaped layout of the central section of the Victoria Legislative Buildings, though it should be noted that Rattenbury envisaged the subsequent lengthening of the shorter rear wings. The external decoration resembles that of the courthouse, with similar "British" lions facing each other across the broad base of the triumphal staircase (apparently copied from the four designed for Trafalgar Square by Sir Edwin Landseer, the celebrated painter and favourite of Queen Victoria). Ionic columns are engaged along the wings fronting accommodation for the "Office Staff" and "Premier and Executive Council." The six columns of the central portico are larger, as at Vancouver, but freestanding. The order is repeated in the columns fronting the pavilions which, diminishing in scale, terminate the major and minor wings. Using the balustraded wall and banded rusticated basement as a platform, he conceived a nicely measured series of rising steps in the profile of the building to the four tall lanterns and great central rotunda. The lanterns, furthermore, echo the major features of the corner pavilions, having two columns framed by pilasters supporting thick entablatures, elements that reappear, further compressed, on the single lantern atop the dome. Between this triangle of comparable elements is the two-tiered drum of the dome, possessing a remarkable formal clarity. The lower peristyle of Ionic columns and the square openings in the upper tier had a precedent in a number of the more recent United States capitols, especially those of California, finished by 1878, and Arkansas, 1900-19.[40] The grouping of the lanterns around the tiered and colonnaded drum may also borrow from another of the American "Temples of Democracy," McKim, Mead and White's Rhode Island Capitol, Providence, 1895-1905 (Fig.6.35).

Admirable though it was, Rattenbury's design lacked the consistency and magnificence of the winning scheme entered by E. and W.S. Maxwell of Montreal and erected 1907-13 (Fig.6.36). Part of the explanation lies in the education William Maxwell had received at the fount of the contemporary academic Classical style, the Ecole des Beaux Arts in Paris. There Maxwell from 1899-1902 (in the Atelier Pascal) learned a highly analytical approach to planning and an intellectual appreciation of historical styles, which Rattenbury could not match. Indeed, Rattenbury suffered the fate of his own competitors in British Columbia by being bested by architects who represented the most recent cosmopolitan taste. It was not that his style was outdated, but rather that his interpretation of the style was too unsophisticated.

Whether or not Rattenbury appreciated the aesthetic significance of his defeat, the award of the commission to the Maxwells must have been a sore disappointment. Yet it is difficult to determine how long he was affected by these reverses. From the period between 1907 and 1909 only one letter survives, and as has already been observed, it is unwise to try to assess his frame of mind from contemporary press reports.[41] Addressed to Kate and her husband, Frank, on 5 January 1908, that letter is taken up with family news. He had been kept busy reading the *Arabian Nights* to Frank, except when called out on New Year's Day to rescue a teenager accidentally wounded when duck shooting on Mary Tod Island: "I rowed out to bring the boy in. In the meantime a gale had blown up and I had some fun getting in. I am not much of a hand with a boat and it was the roughest sea I was ever in. I generally lie snug when the ripples arise but it is a case of must. I hear tonight that it is touch and go whether the boy will get better." On wider issues, he confined himself to commenting on the 1907 collapse of the New York Stock Exchange: "I wish these financial panics would not arise. We are not suffering much here but it will make things dull, I expect, just as everything was going along rosily." Since he followed this remark with a reference to a recent large purchase of land in northern British Columbia adjacent to the probable course of the Grand Trunk Pacific line, it may be assumed that the crisis confirmed his view that the acquisition of real estate, rather than stocks and shares, represented the best protection against a comparable economic recession in Canada. Although construction of the line eastward from Prince Rupert was not to begin until the fall of 1908, the project had been initiated with the laying of the first section near Carberry, just over a hundred miles west of Winnipeg.[42]

Rattenbury had already acquired eleven thousand acres of the Nechako Valley in the north of the province in the hope of profiting from the agricultural and resource development that was expected to follow the completion of the G.T.P. line. Unfortunately, the exact date of the purchase cannot be determined; the newspaper reports of its subsequent sale in 1908 state that he bought the land "almost five years" earlier.[43] Even if the date is correct, it does not necessarily mean that Rattenbury had displayed special foresight or had access to privileged information to anticipate the course to be taken by the new railway.[44] A general survey of the feasible routes through northern B.C. had been undertaken by Sir Sandford Fleming in the 1870's on behalf of the C.P.R., and although the precise one chosen by the G.T.P. was not published until 1908, its likely course was predictable. Under the heading "Railway Enterprise," the 1903 *B.C. Yearbook*, for instance, conjectured that the construction of the G.T.P. line would "open up an entirely new district with considerable agricultural possibilities and mineral resources of great potentiality" and described the Nechako Valley as being "available for pastoral, if not agricultural purposes." He could also have read the glowing reports in the local papers of the region's potential, notably from the pen of Colonel E.S. Topping. A mine owner from Telkwa, he sent produce grown in the valley to fairs and also spoke throughout the province.[45] Passages from one speech, given in Victoria, were quoted in the *Colonist* on 6 April 1906, "The Bulkley Valley is the paradise of all the country I have seen. It is a country where the natural grass is so luxuriant that it grows as high as the armpits of a tall man.... Last summer the miners of the Bulkley Valley fairly lived on wild strawberries. The berries grew in such profusion that the ground was covered with them, they were as large as a man's thumb.... On the plains are grouse, pheasant and prairie chickens galore. We had birds during the season until we were thoroughly tired of them." The colonel acknowledged the absence of transport, but he declared, "I am sure I shall be amply repaid for my efforts when the G.T.P. builds through the valley."

Rattenbury's imagination seems to have been stirred anew by such statements since, in 1907, he began the process of purchasing what would eventually amount to over forty thousand acres of crown-granted land, committing, as he was to comment afterwards, the bulk of his earnings from the Legislative Buildings and the Empress commissions.[46] By then the route of the line had been settled, passing through what F.A. Talbot, writing in the 1911 volume of *United Empire*, would call "New British Columbia."[47] The track was to pierce the fastness of the Rocky Mountains through the Yellowhead Pass and then follow the course of the turbulent Fraser River to Fort George, where it headed west along the Nechako, a tributary of the Fraser. Talbot found the fertility of the Nechako Valley to be "amazing.... I met several settlers already in possession and they claimed that to exaggerate the possibilities of the land was a task almost beyond human endeavour. Everything grew in profusion, and the failure of crops was quite unknown. Amidst the poplars... the vetches grew to a height of about five feet, while the hay topped eight feet in many instances and averaged three tons to the acre." At Fort Fraser, the G.T.P. track would leave the Nechako Valley to traverse some 150 miles of rugged country until it reached the junction of the Morice and Bulkley Rivers. The route then ran the whole length of the Bulkley Valley, which spread, between four and six miles wide for the most part, to the meeting with the Skeena, where the line was to proceed southwest along the river into Prince Rupert. Talbot wrote that he had heard "wonderful stories" about the Bulkley Valley, "and certainly my investigations supported the descriptions I had heard.... I visited the McInnes ranch and pulled purple-top turnips measuring twenty-eight inches in circumference and weighing fifteen pounds apiece; plucked currants as large as marbles; and cut cabbages weighing fourteen pounds apiece.... The pioneers in the Bulkley Valley have had a stern up-hill fight, but one and all have made money, and now that the railway is approaching from the north the value of their land has reached remarkable figures." This disinterested account is significant as lending credence to the seemingly exaggerated claims made by the residents (and large landowners) in the B.C. press during the early 1900's. At that period, the newspapers carried numerous enthusiastic reports on the agricultural promise of the Bulkley Valley and of the massive mineral deposits, particularly of coal and copper near the settlement of Telkwa.[48] While it was conceded that prospectors and settlers faced enormous transport problems—loaded pack animals, for example, had to swim the Bulkley—most believed that with the advent of the railway, the area could yield phenomenal wealth.

Rattenbury's largest parcel of land was in the Bulkley Valley proper, where he acquired a series of lots on both sides of the river between Hazelton and Houston, with a concentration around Telkwa, amounting in total to 11,500 acres. Near Hazelton, west of the junction with the Skeena River, he acquired 6,714 acres. Despite the frequently repeated press accounts that he owned 40,000 acres in the Bulkley Valley, most of his land was scattered in a number of much more remote areas. In the Fort St. James area north of Vanderhoof he secured three holdings on Stuart Lake and on the Stuart River, totalling 6,760 acres, land to be described ten years later in government correspondence as "worthless." In fact, this last group does represent shrewd foresight on Rattenbury's part, lying as it does on the future course of the Pacific Great Eastern (later the British Columbia Railway). The G.T.P. envisaged the addition of a series of branch lines to serve the potentially rich agricultural areas not crossed by the survey for the main line. It was probably this policy that prompted Rattenbury to invest near Fort St. James and also in other areas, which,

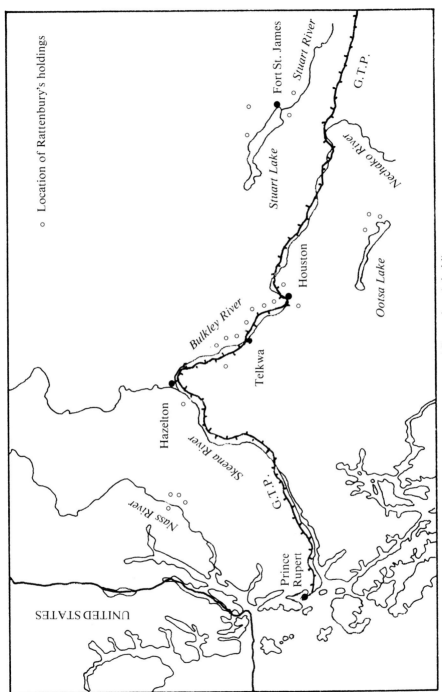

Map 3: The Skeena and Bulkley Valleys, showing the location of Rattenbury's holdings.

however, remained undeveloped, since the branch lines were never built. Southwest of the Nechako, near Ootsa Lake, he acquired 4,999 acres, much of which has since been submerged as a result of hydro-electric dam construction. All these acquisitions, costing $150,000 (£30,000) were completed by the end of 1907, as Rattenbury's 5 January (1908) letter to Kate and Frank shows:

> I have been busy paying for my big estate. Just to make sure, I had taken precautions so that I was not compelled to pay for two years. But I cannot abide owing money and this week have paid up in full – £30,000 – quite a lump to raise in a panic, so this year I did not buy any diamonds for my little finger. In five years though it will be worth five times as much, when the railway runs through, although I may not wait so long. I shall have lots of fun out of it anyway – it is a magnificent piece of land.

His investments had not ended, however. In 1908 he sold the Nechako Valley land he had obtained in 1903 for a reported sum of $100,000 to Trafford Huteson, who had travelled from England to act for American interests seeking to acquire large tracts of land for settlement.[49] There is no way of telling what the profit on the transaction might have been since the original purchase price is not known. But assuming that it was initially in the same range as the 1907 acquisitions, that is, about $5.00 an acre, Rattenbury would have gained about $45,000 (less taxes and interest). The bulk of this he seems to have invested in his final acquisition in the Nass Valley. The Nass (or Naas) River rises in a small lake amid the Skeena mountains and flows over 104 miles south into the Portland Canal, the enormous fiord that separates Alaska from British Columbia. In 1909 Rattenbury bought 10,301 acres south of Grease Harbour at a cost of between $40,000 and $50,000 and, in essence, exchanged his Nechako holdings for the Nass land.[50] Here also the branch line was never built, and to this day the Nass Valley has remained almost unpopulated.

In his 1908 letter to Kate and Frank, Rattenbury had quipped that even if his speculations yielded little profit he would have "lots of fun."[51] The rather forced humour of this phrase perhaps masked his own realization that he had dangerously committed the bulk of his funds to one investment, almost wholly dependent on the success of the G.T.P. Even so, in 1908 he could not have guessed the extent of the troubles this gamble would entail.

Seven

PROFESSIONAL MATURITY
1908–1914

The absence of any significant architectural commission at the beginning of 1908 indirectly benefited Rattenbury, for he was able to travel with a freedom that he had not previously enjoyed. That spring he returned to Britain, almost certainly because of the recent death of his father, bedridden for long periods during his last years. Rattenbury clearly wished to console his mother, then suffering from poor health.[1] He took her on a long motoring tour of the continent, a trip that seemed to renew his interest in town planning.

Rattenbury had always been an advocate of good planning, remembering Saltaire and its broad and pleasantly scaled streets surrounded by parks, and he wanted to conserve the unique natural advantages of Victoria, especially Oak Bay. For this reason he had eagerly supported Mayor Barnard's policy for developing Victoria as a tourist and retirement city. But when the demand for housing and development intensified from 1905, his sense of the urgent necessity of imposing planning controls increased. Twice in June 1908 he raised the issue in interviews with the *Victoria Times*. The first, published on 10 June, concentrated on his recent European tour and the enlightened laws governing development in cities such as Lucerne in Switzerland. Lucerne was an ideal tourist centre largely because the civic authorities exercised strict control, exemplified by their rejection of a proposal to increase the height of a hotel as it might be detrimental to the existing streetscape. "There was," he observed, "no question raised there as to the power of the municipality to control the situation." And the path of a street had been altered to preserve a fine tree: "Imagine a Victoria Council doing that!"[2] The second report, headed "Reservations for Parks and Playgrounds," was devoted to urban design. He complimented the efforts of John Burns to abolish tenement buildings in Britain, which were socially and psychologically injurious. Barely less odious than tenements were the "deadly straight" streets of the North American grid plan (he had, in December 1906, recommended that the corners of buildings on cross-streets be curved so as to afford better vision for drivers and thereby to reduce traffic accidents).[3] The streetscape should be more varied, he declared (implying an awareness of Camillo Sitte's writings on town planning, with their advocacy of irregular street layout) and interspersed with public parks. These were being created in Chicago to the plans of Daniel Burnham to relieve the monotony of the great straight thoroughfares, but "at enormous cost" because the city fathers had neglected to reserve suitable sites before development and before the consequent escalation in land values. Nearer home, the citizens of Vancouver, "who have been feverishly engaged in building and expanding in a material way, realize that they have no open space in the centre of their city and are now agitating to have the provincial government convey the old courthouse square, now of enormous value, to them for their purpose." What was required was "a board or bureau" to reserve such "open spaces," to banish uniformity and instill "some artistic taste" in the "treatment of streets and buildings." In this he was probably inspired by recent legislation in England which resulted in the Town Planning Act of 1909 and the establishment of committees to advise on the aesthetic quality of proposed developments. It was to prove a forlorn hope, as far as Victoria was concerned, going largely unheeded until the 1970's and the foundation of the Heritage Conservation Committee.

Only two documented architectural commissions are known from this period, possibly a consequence of the 1908 depression. In December 1908 Rattenbury invited tenders for a "substantial three storey" brick school house, to be erected for the Chinese Consolidated Benevolent Association in the centre of the Chinese quarter in Victoria.[4] In January 1909 he closed tenders "for the erection of a brick office building on Fort Street for Mr. D. R. Ker.[5] But these two projects may not represent his only architectural work, since there is a possibility that he had begun as early as December 1909 making preliminary proposals for the "large hotel" that the G.T.P. were planning to build in Victoria.[6]

7.1 T. C. Sorby, Five Sisters Block, Victoria, in which Rattenbury had an office.

Concern for his mother's declining health persuaded Rattenbury to return to England again in 1910, though scant information remains about that visit. "Here we are at home again," he told her after his return to Victoria on 1 November 1910:

I am having to write in pencil, for the house is so marvellously tidy that I cannot even find a stray pen around. We had rather a sensational arrival, for I found that three days before there had been a huge fire in Victoria sweeping out a large part of the city, and amongst the buildings destroyed was my office block [5 Sisters] (Fig.7.1) and nothing remains.[7] Fortunately all my goods and valuable papers were safely stored so I have lost only the sentimental goods and chattels, all my drawings that I have ever made – books, pictures and furniture, so I am homeless at present. However, it was fortunate that the fire occurred when I was away. Had I been at home I should have had many valuable documents destroyed and whilst, of course, I regret the things burned, still there is a sense of relief in being rid of a huge mass of stuff that I had accumulated. I am not sure whether to take another office or not; perhaps I will arrange to use another fellow's.[8]

Despite the humorous stoicism, he must have regretted the loss of the drawings. Rattenbury preferred not to dwell on his misfortune and seems to have been in buoyant spirits. In his next letter, on 16 November, he could not resist the temptation, one to which he often yielded, to crow about his skill as an entrepreneur: "yesterday I did a little business, rather sensational in a way. On going down to the city I had a piece of property offered to me. I bought it and resold it in half an hour."

The year 1911 opened happily for him: an entertaining football match between Victoria and California—"we lost by a fraction"—and the prospect of a further "Grand Tour": "I hardly seem to have unpacked when I shall be packing again. I have not decided on my plans yet but I expect I shall come direct to England and go to the continent afterwards, instead of sailing direct for the Mediterranean, and work backwards as I at first intended." Ten years before, he had written of taking up croquet as befitting a man of middle age, but now he was revelling in winter amusements, snowballing and skating with his son Frank. His standing among his professional colleagues was recognized by his election to the presidency of the British Columbia Architectural Association, and it was not surprising that fellow members of the Union Club invited him to chair a selection committee for the design of a new clubhouse in November 1910.[9] "I am interesting myself assisting at the selection of a new club that we are going to build. It will be a nice place," he commented on 10 January 1911, "although personally I like the old Club with all its associations." He and his fellow members were, in 1912, to choose an Italianate-style design by the San Francisco architect, L. P. Rixford. Somewhat ponderous, Rixford's club still stands at the corner of Gordon and Humboldt Streets. "But," he added, "we have to move with the times and Victoria is growing rapidly, even skyscrapers are now about to be erected [a ten-storey block, diminutive by international standards, was planned for Johnston Street in 1910]."[10] He closed with the wistful thought, "I like the old style best," probably regretting the standardized ornament of such functional buildings less than their obtrusive height. By no means unique in his conservative taste among members of the profession on both sides of the Atlantic, he sought compensation for the rising tide of utilitarian design in the reassuring peacefulness of his own garden, "The cold weather has brought a lot of pheasants and quail around the garden as we always put out grain for them. There is more delight in watching them than in bricks and mortar."

However, the old styles that Rattenbury cherished still retained their popularity in Victoria (as indeed elsewhere in America and Britain, where the Arts and Crafts and historicist styles continued to be in vogue well into the 1920's). In the spring of 1911, the McBride government voted funds for the extension of the Legislative Buildings, which would, of course, be expected to be in harmony with the "old style" of Rattenbury's original structure. The provincial administration had grown enormously since 1898 as a result of the development of the province and the great influx of immigrants over the intervening years. Rattenbury was the obvious man to undertake the task, and he was requested to provide accommodation for departmental offices and the Parliamentary Library, as well as new quarters for the Provincial Museum, the Government Printing Office, and a garage.

The earliest surviving drawings for the additions, a plan dated February and an elevation dated March 1911, show two wings running southwards to form courts on either side of the Legislative Assembly (Figs.7.2–3).[11] The new library is extended from the original south entrance, and has a Latin cross plan with a semi-circular front. Beyond the library, Rattenbury sketched in separate buildings for the museum and printing office. Where these last two, as well as the new office wings, echo the style of the original Legislative Buildings, the design of the library differs markedly, being composed of elements derived from French Renaissance architecture. Its curved façade, underpinned by a colonnade of banded Doric columns, ascends dramatically towards a gabled window and crowning Châteauesque roof. The upward movement is intensified by two corner towers, each capped by Atlas figures carrying globes.[12]

Within a month Rattenbury had altered that scheme, on the advice of Ethelbert O. S. Scholefield, provincial librarian and archivist. Scholefield was as meticulous and cautious as Rattenbury was anxious to proceed with the commission, and their differences in temperament were to lead to strained relations as the year progressed. Scholefield first proposed the change in a letter of 12 April [1911], basing his suggestions on the plans of various libraries in the United States sent to him through the American Library Association. "Perhaps they may help you in some particulars," he wrote, "although the buildings designed do not conform in shape to the one you propose to erect for the Provincial Library," and continued, "In my estimation the form of the Greek cross lends itself particularly to our requirements."[13] His estimation of Rattenbury at that stage was very high, and he informed Mrs. A. E. Ahern, editor of the journal *Public Libraries*, that the Provincial Library would be built to a budget of approximately "$350,000 with the assistance of the very able and energetic architect the Government has employed for the work." Rattenbury was initially prepared to accept Scholefield's advice because the librarian shared his exalted view of the commission, as he showed by writing on 18 April "we are practically building for all time." Then, six days later, Scholefield changed his mind about the basic plan. He had been "thinking very deeply about the new Library and I am afraid that alterations will have to be made to the plans which you showed me this morning. If the form of the "Greek Cross" is to be adhered to, it will be necessary to plan the interior very carefully, with especial regard to the administration of the Department. A Building of such shape is not easily adapted to library purposes. As the plans now are, I fear the rooms are too scattered." He wanted the whole of the second floor to be devoted to "library purposes," (since the great majority of books would be stored there), with the reading and reference rooms in the south and west wings, and the "charging desk" in the "centre of the rotunda, with automatic tubes leading directly to the stacks for the delivery of books." He also disagreed with Rattenbury's proposal for introducing statuary in the rotunda, preferring that provision be made for future expansion. Rattenbury, however, chose to reject most of these suggestions, no doubt believing that his revised layout was more functional. And, at this stage, he worked up a second set of plans, preserved at the Provincial Archives, together with a perspective of the south front (Fig.7.4–6).[14] The change is visibly recorded on another sheet signed "F. M. Rattenbury Archt. April 6 1911," combining an elevation of the original proposal for the Library with, on the left, a sketch plan tracing out the Greek Cross form (Fig.7.7).

The library was redesigned with a Greek Cross plan, one arm of which was occupied by the vestibule communicating with the Legislative Assembly. The main south façade of the library had also undergone a fundamental change in composition and style. The colonnade was three-sided rather than semi-circular and surmounted by a flat cornice, pierced at its centre by a pedimented circular window, and a lower pitched roof. The detailing was more distinctly Classical, particularly on the corner towers. These were decorated with niches containing statues of celebrated explorers of the Pacific Northwest and capped by arched pediments similar to the ones he had used on his earlier bank buildings.[15] The other major change could be seen in the museum and printing office.[16] Both had been considerably enlarged, giving a more complex plan, and extended further south, the museum almost touching the boundary of the parliamentary grounds.

At that stage Scholefield accepted Rattenbury's view, informing the architect on 26 May that he had shown the plans "to a committee of experts consisting of the ablest librarians in the profession. When I explained to them the position of affairs and why it is necessary to subordinate the new buildings to the old one, they readily agreed that the plan adopted is, in many respects, an excellent one. It is true that they suggested certain alterations and modifications, but these, if adopted, as they certainly ought to be, needed not disarrange your plans to any great extent."[17] Scholefield's courteous instructions might have served as a model for the conduct of official business, but his indecision through May and June over the final detailed plan to be adopted exasperated Rattenbury. Finally, on 19 June he asked Scholefield to state "in writing" how he would like "the interior of the new Provincial Library planned."[18] As before, Scholefield excused his slow response with words that must have gone some way towards mollifying Rattenbury, already dreaming of new towns rising in his northern lands, "as British Columbia advances in importance, wealth and population—and it is impossible to estimate even approximately at this time the grand destiny which the future holds for this great province—the membership of the Provincial Parliament [42 members at that time] will be largely increased." As Scholefield continued to propose different improvements throughout the summer,[19] Rattenbury became increasingly restive, to the extent that he lost patience and refused to entertain any further suggestions. On 25 July, Scholefield brought their disagreement before W. R. Ross, acting attorney-general. While he did concede that Rattenbury's plan represented a "compromise," he expressed dismay that it contained so few of the recommendations that he had submitted to the architect on 19 June. Instead of realizing that Rattenbury was wrestling with the practical issues of budget and building schedules,[20] Scholefield had further persuaded his minister, W. J. Bowser, to request "the Minister of Public Works by telephone in my presence, to tell the architect that he was to take instructions from me as to the internal arrangements." To Rattenbury this episode must have seemed disturbingly like a repetition of the later part of the Legislative Buildings commission. Still, if he had exercised more tact, he might have retained Scholefield's goodwill.

There the matter rested, Rattenbury returning with Florrie that summer to England. Part of a letter dated August 10 [1911] survives, recording their recent return to Victoria, "we arrived here safely last Friday, after a delightful trip." This is the last surviving letter to his mother, who died later that year. While her death could hardly have been unexpected—his previous letters contain many anxious enquiries about her health—it must have affected him profoundly, for he had lost his closest confidante. Thus, even the problems posed by the Provincial Libary could have come as a welcome distraction from his distress. In any case on this issue the government seems to have taken Rattenbury's side since the final remaining blueprints taken from the working drawings dated September 1913 to May 1914 conform quite closely with the April 1911 set (Fig.7.8).[21] The only concession he made was to replace the reading room (planned for the south wing) with stacks, and to remove the delivery desk to the south side of the rotunda. Actual work on the Provincial Library and extension of the Legislative Buildings did not begin until November 1911,[22] G. A. Fraser receiving the first instalment on his $8,500 contract to dig the foundations in February 1912.[23] While Fraser's men worked through the bad weather,[24] other workmen began assembling the wooden members of Rattenbury's picturesque, if bijou, Neo-Tudor Parliamentary Garage, built at the intersection of Belleville and Superior Streets (and still standing). The original blueprints are dated "January 1912." (Fig.7.9).[25]

Meantime in the fall of 1911, Rattenbury had been busy with a new building for St. Margaret's School and the first of a series of designs for the Grand Trunk Pacific. The two-storey school was built in 1911 at the junction of Fort and Fern Streets and was demolished in 1970. By contrast with the medieval "barn" of the Victoria High School, Rattenbury adopted a simplified domestic style. The three projections of the "E" plan inverted the usual Palladian tripartite composition, since the central entrance portico, sheltering two Doric columns *in antis* was lower than the side pavilions (Fig.7.11). The broad windows, and especially the embryo strip windows under the eaves of the wings once again suggest that he was aware of Wright's early neo-classical "Prairie" houses, probably through Maclure.[26]

However, such influential intimations of Modernism exerted no real sway over Rattenbury. Even less could he respond to the more radical European theories of contemporary design, for he admired simplicity rather than the uncompromising utilitarianism advocated by the most articulate and advanced theorist of that period, Hermann Muthesius, the pivotal member of the German group dedicated to the synthesis of fine and applied design, the "Deutsche Werkbund."[27] While Rattenbury accepted that ornament might be reduced for aesthetic or economic reasons, he could never have associated it with "crime," as did the contemporary Austrian architect, Adolf Loos, a leader of another progressive movement, the Viennese Secessionists. "In his travels in Italy, Switzerland and elsewhere," the *Victoria Times* had reported dutifully on 10 June 1908, "Mr. Rattenbury was struck by the simplicity manifested in the architecture. Utility characterizes every line and feature. Ornamentation is reserved for the great works undertaken and then nothing is spared." The diverse historical traditions of European architecture enshrined for

Rattenbury all the requisite types and forms of design, and he was content to adapt these rather than to seek an entirely new conception to suit the "Machine Age." A child of the Victorian era, he remained a conservative eclectic. This attitude is also apparent in the commission for a branch of the Merchants' Bank at Nanaimo, received in late 1911.[28] It was a smaller, if no less elegant version of his earlier "free Renaissance" commercial buildings, with his preferred corner entrance and arched openings harmonizing the uneven façades along Wallace and Albert Streets (Fig.7.10). Most of the ground floor was occupied by the banking hall, with a large reinforced concrete vault and a securities office, originally reached through the guard room behind the inner side entrance on Albert Street. The outer side entrance communicated with the furnace room in the basement and a series of offices on the upper floors. Besides providing good communication and ample lighting, Rattenbury secured the building against fire by means of a concrete and steel structure.

Similarly, when Rattenbury was invited by the G.T.P. to prepare designs for their projected chain of hotels and resorts, he developed schemes based on those Medieval, Renaissance, and Classical themes that he considered appropriate to the specifications of each commission: French Renaissance and English Jacobean for the larger hotels, the Swiss Chalet for the smaller resorts, Renaissance and Classical for the terminals, and an American vernacular for the mountain stations. He seems to have been awarded these commissions late in 1911, although there is good reason for assuming that Hays had informed him of his plans for a network of western hotels as early as 1906 (when he was asked to design their first Prince Rupert Hotel); it is significant that Rattenbury, according to the June article in the *Victoria Times*, had "visited every hotel of standing possible" on his 1908 European tour "in the hope of gaining further knowledge in that line of architecture to be used by him in the future."

The projected buildings that Rattenbury alone was asked to design represented an expenditure in excess of $3,000,000, probably more like $4,500,000, a huge investment which reflected Hays's determination that the new line be the best built and equipped on the North American continent. By 1911 the progress of the line eastwards from Prince Rupert and the prospect of the profitable shipment of grain from the northern Prairies to the Orient (and through the Panama Canal, constructed 1903–14) decided Hays to inform the shareholders at the annual meeting that the company "proposed to construct a chain of first-class modern hotels," beginning with one at Winnipeg and followed by others at Regina, Edmonton, "Jasper Park in the Rocky Mountains and at Prince

Rupert."[29] Had he been called upon to justify his choice of Rattenbury as architect of the western hotels, Hays could have pointed to his wide experience of hotel design and to his local reputation, as exemplified by his important role in organizing the competition for the Point Grey campus of the University of British Columbia.[30]

Hays's priorities apparently lay with the terminal hotels at Prince Rupert and Victoria. Rattenbury had virtually completed the plans for both hotels by 17 January 1912 when he informed the *Contract Record* that work would start "early in the spring" on the Victoria Hotel and implied that the Prince Rupert Hotel would go to contract immediately.[31] No further information on the Victoria proposal has been discovered, but the *Contract Record* contained a brief description of the Prince Rupert project: "Main building, 12 storeys; two wings, 9 storeys, steel, brick and terra-cotta, reinforced concrete floor slabs, fireproof construction." The projected cost was $1,000,000.

Hays's death in April 1912 did not cause the company to retrench. By the end of the year, when the track had been laid almost 200 miles east of Prince Rupert and nearly 1,200 west of Winnipeg, Rattenbury had submitted schemes for the two scenic hotels in the mountains of Alberta and B.C., the Château Miette at Miette Hot Springs and the Château Mount Robson, facing the celebrated mountain from which it took its name, and he continued working on new designs at least until the end of 1914, though apparently without payment.[32] E. J. Chamberlain, Hays's successor, referred to the expanded western hotel programme in his 1913 annual report, in the October issue of the *The Canadian Railway and Marine World*, describing them as "attractive resorts" of the "most modern architecture and equipment."[33] He further reported that the "excavation for a large hotel at the terminal at Prince Rupert was also recently commenced."

The absence of personal correspondence or reference to Rattenbury's work in the company records (now at the Public Archives in Ottawa) is to some extent compensated for by the survival of a large number of sketches and finished drawings of designs for the G.T.P. Some of the latter appear in an illustrated article entitled, "Grand Trunk Pacific Hotel Development in the West," published in the *Contract Record* on 30 July 1913, based upon material submitted to the editor by Rattenbury (Figs. 7.12–14).[34] The company had asked him to design "a system of hotels and hydropathic establishments to accommodate the extensive traffic which they expect to handle between Europe and the Orient." As a result of the faster progress of the construction of the line from Winnipeg westwards, the first hotel to be erected was "the Château Miette at Jasper

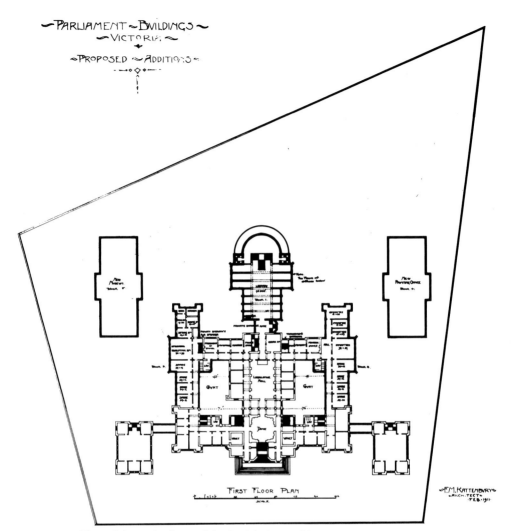

FIRST FLOOR PLAN
SCALE

F.M. RATTENBURY
ARCHITECT
FEB. 1911

7.2 Plan of the main floor of the Legislative Buildings, Victoria, showing Rattenbury's first design for the extension of the executive offices, the Parliamentary Library and the proposed Government printing offices and Provincial museum, 1911.

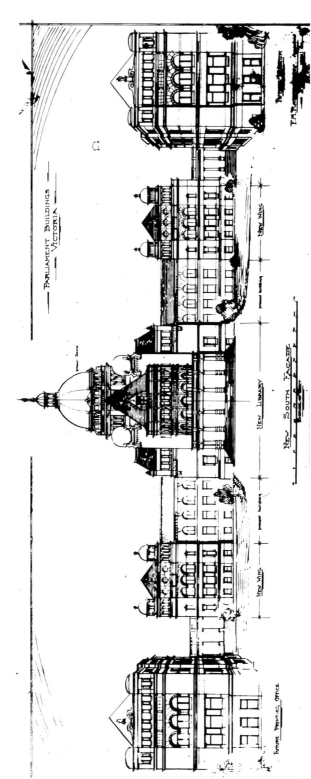

7.3 Elevation of first design for the Parliamentary Library and the proposed Government Printing Office and Provincial Museum, 1911.

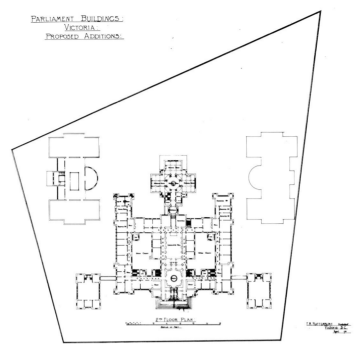

7.4 Plan of second floor of Legislative Buildings and proposed Parliamentary Library (conforming with Rattenbury's second design), 1911.

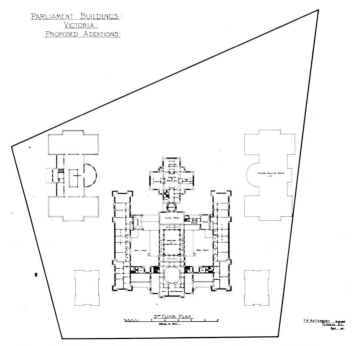

7.5 Plan of third floor of Legislative Buildings and proposed Parliamentary Library, 1911.

7.6 Elevation of second design for Parliamentary Library, and Government Printing Office and Provincial Museum, c.1911.

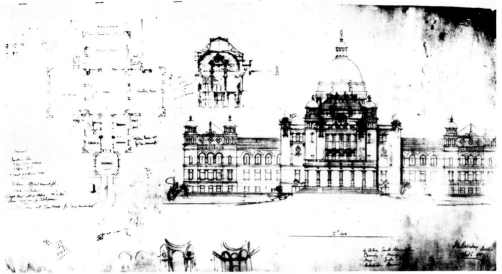

7.7 Elevation for first design for Parliamentary Library with sketch plan for second scheme, 1911.

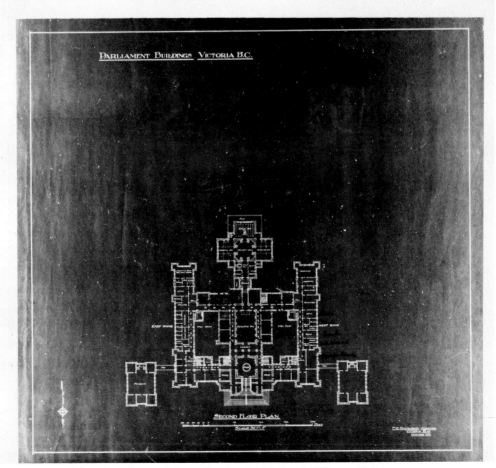

7.8 Blueprint of second floor plan for Legislative Buildings additions, 1913.

7.9 Parliamentary Garage, Victoria, 1912.

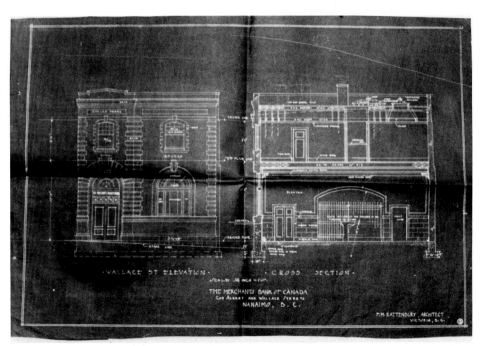

7.10B Elevation of Wallace Street front, Merchant's Bank, Nanaimo.

7.10A Merchant's Bank of Canada (later, Bank of Montreal), Nanaimo, 1911–1912.

7.11 St. Margaret's School, Victoria, 1911.

7.12 Elevation of proposed G.T.P. Hotel Château Miette, 1912.

7.13 Elevation of proposed G.T.P. Hotel Château Mount Robson, 1912.

7.14 Elevation of proposed G.T.P. Hotel, Prince Rupert, 1912.
7.15 Perspective of Rattenbury's proposed G.T.P. steamship terminal, station and hotel at Prince Rupert, drawn by David Myers, 1914.

7.16 Rattenbury as Reeve of Oak Bay.

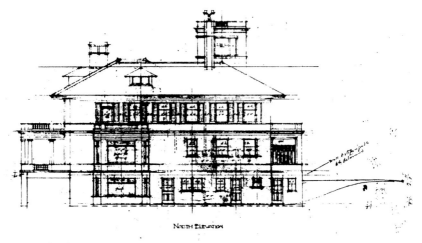

7.17 Sketch elevation of main (north) front of first design for R. W. Gibson House, Victoria, 1914.

7.18 Sketch elevation of rear (south) façade for R. W. Gibson House.

7.19 Sketch elevation of entrance (east) façade of R. W. Gibson House.

7.20 Sketch elevation of revised design for the main (north) front of R. W. Gibson House.

7.21 Rattenbury, and Maclure and Lort, R. W. Gibson house, Victoria, 1918–1919.

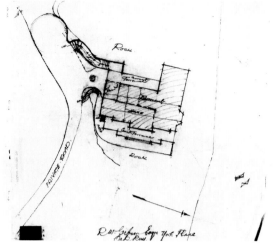

7.22 Sketch plan of site for R. W. Gibson House, 1914.

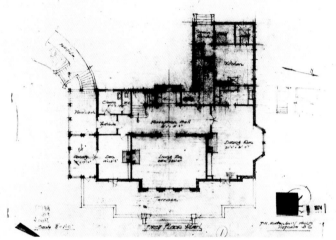

7.23 Sketch plan for main floor, revised design, R. W. Gibson House.

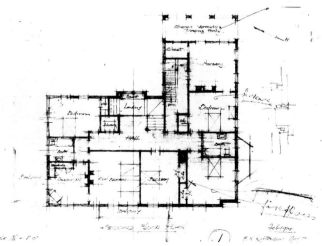

7.24 Sketch plan for upper floor, revised design, R. W. Gibson House.

7.25 Rotunda, Parliamentary Library, 1912–1914.

7.26 Parliamentary Library, Victoria, 1911–1915.

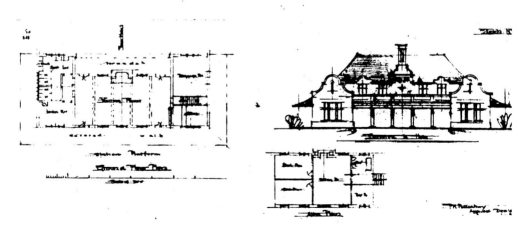

7.27 Elevation and plan for proposed station at Miette Springs, 1914.

7.28 Sketch elevation of a proposed G.T.P. "Mountain Inn," probably to be located at Jasper, 1914.

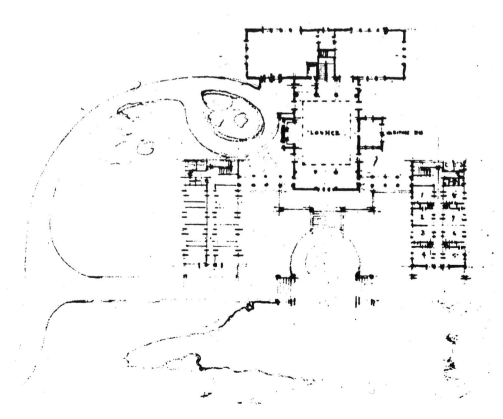

LOUNGE

7.29 Sketch plan of proposed G.T.P. "Mountain Inn," 1914.

Creek, then at Mount Robson a larger establishment is contemplated, and finally, a handsome ten-storey hotel is planned at Prince Rupert, the terminal hotel of the system and designed to accommodate over one thousand guests. The accommodation provided by these hotels should induce many tourists to visit the western mountains of Canada, whose scenery surpasses even that of the Alps."

The Château Miette was intended to house up to 250 guests. At each end of an irregularly composed central building, containing "all the common rooms," and spanned by a Tudor arcade, Rattenbury planned three-storey bedroom wings.[35] He adopted this arrangement "in order to permit the guests to obtain the finest views with the least obstruction from other parts of the building," and, he could have added, to permit the closure of one or more of the wings in the off-season. The "ruggedness of the surrounding country" had decided him to style the hotel in a "modern adaptation of the old Château, with its high pitched roofs and numerous gables." While the roofs in the tall tower to the right of the bay-windowed "lounging room" (60 by 35 feet) and gabled recreation rooms are distinctly French, the low arcade across the front and the stepped and curved gables rising and falling around the façade have an ancestry in English, Scottish, and Dutch architecture of the sixteenth and seventeenth centuries. Yet despite the picturesque profile of the main building, the partitioning of the wings and the even spacing of their gabled projections maintain a symmetry akin to his earlier redefinition of the Château style.

Rattenbury reverted to the symmetrical composition of the Empress, and even imitated its flanking corner towers, on the main building of the larger Château Mount Robson (in May 1913 he had developed but rejected an assymetrical plan also inspired by the Empress [Fig. Appendix C.14]).[36] His final scheme, originally conceived by October 1912, was intended to be "more imposing" and to "accommodate at least 500 guests." The ornamental detailing is simpler, but closer to the French Château, particularly in the pitched roofs of the centrepiece and the circular staircase towers linking the radiating bedroom wings. The reduction of surface ornament, especially on the wings, produces a sense of greater scale and architectural harmony than in the Château Miette drawing. It also gives more prominence to the social hub of the complex, with a tall gabled bay window fronting the lounge that results in a bolder composition. These efforts would have been made more visually dramatic by the intended contrast between the "brick finished rough cast and... terra cotta trimmings." The final plan of the Château Mount Robson (the preparatory studies are examined in Appendix C) called for a dining hall of 65 by 104 feet "with a fine colonnade and six bay windows lighting the hall." Even grander was the "very fine" lounging room, "112 by 64 feet, overlooking the tennis lawns and grounds." About these rooms he placed the "drawing rooms, parlors, writing rooms and verandahs. . . all designed on a commodious scale and to command a fine outlook over the surrounding country."

During these months he was also planning a steamship terminal and station to complement his magnificent hotel in the new "Metropolis of the North," as Hays had been accustomed to describe the fledgling Prince Rupert. The hotel, although reduced in scale from the scheme described in the January 1912 issue of the *Contract Record*, was to be a huge and romantic reinterpretation of the Empress, with some features related to the Château Miette and Mount Robson designs. It was now to contain over 600 rooms, located in a ten-storey central block and "two annexes, six storeys each, which will be connected by corridors." Ever practical, Rattenbury informed the *Contract Record* that the hotel would be "fire-proofed throughout and equipped with all modern conveniences." The plans included a 58 by 62 feet lounging room and a 52 by 62 feet lobby so that the final cost was still estimated at a million dollars.[37] This scheme, however grand, is in fact a simplification of the design depicted in a "birds-eye" view of the proposed G.T.P. buildings at Prince Rupert painted for him by David Myers (Fig.7.15). The grandeur of Rattenbury's planned G.T.P. buildings, perhaps best exemplified by his scheme for Prince Rupert, testifies to his abiding faith in the future of northwestern Canada. He frequently expressed the hope that he could participate in the great challenge of transforming the northern region, with its enormous agricultural and resource promise, into a prosperous and populous region, served by a modern communications network linking thriving cities. This vision was not to be realized, at least by Rattenbury. Nothing was done beyond the digging, in 1913, of the foundation trenches for the Prince Rupert hotel, on what is now part of 2nd Avenue, since the financial and human resources required for its construction were to be sapped by the trench warfare in France and Belgium.[38]

The orderly, though not rigid, layout of well-designed buildings and tree-lined streets in the Myers perspective portray the kind of civic ideal that Rattenbury also sought to implement on his own doorstep in Oak Bay. He showed this in the beneficial influence that he exercised on the Uplands development within the municipality. This comprised some four hundred acres of the former Uplands Farm, which had been laid out by the son of the celebrated American landscape architect, Frederick Law Olmsted, who had been inspired by English theories of Picturesque planning which advocated controlled irregularity to create a harmonious relationship between architecture and nature. The land was placed on the market between 1912 and 1914, and, with Rattenbury as their architectural adviser, the Uplands Company permitted only residential development. While allowing those who purchased plots to select the style of their houses, the company insisted that these be built to high standards and be in keeping with their surroundings.[39] As a member of the Oak Bay Council between 1906 and 1908, Rattenbury had contributed to the conservation of its natural amenities. It was he who had pushed through the establishment of a committee, later dubbed the "Beauty Committee," to keep "watch and ward over the decorative effect of trees planted on boulevards and sidewalks."

In 1913 Rattenbury decided to run for the office of reeve of Oak Bay, spurred on by the attempt of a group led by the less fastidious architect, William Henderson, to have the sea-girt Oak Bay golf course reassessed at the same rate as land scheduled for houses. The true aim of this group, backed by the owners of the golf course, the Gonzales Point Land Company, was the subdivision of the links for housing and, indeed, the reduction of municipal control in that field of speculative investment. Breaking a previous convention, Rattenbury circulated a manifesto among the electors: "I think that the Oak Bay district is one of the most lovely residential areas that I have ever seen, and it is my desire to retain this beauty as far as possible, and the hope that I can do so is my only reason for being a candidate at the coming election for Reeve."[40] He had deplored the erection of "very ugly and cheap looking shacks rented as stores" along Oak Bay Avenue, the main road into the municipality. Regulations should be enacted to reverse such aberrations and, more importantly, to block the subdivision of the golf course. However lucrative the scheme, it would be "a calamity to Oak Bay and Victoria," robbing citizens of a "favourite walk and drive" through "the golf links and along Shoal Bay."

Rattenbury, it must be recognized, owned recreational property along Shoal Bay and was a passionate golfer: "In the meantime I still keep poomfling and slicing and it seems to me that on the whole Golf is going to be the worry of my life," he had commented wryly in a letter written to his sister on 5 January 1908. Yet such personal considerations were undoubtedly secondary to his genuine desire to uphold the public good: "The subdividing of property into comparatively small lots is proceeding so quickly that it is easy to foresee the time when the youngsters will have nowhere to play but the streets," the manifesto continued, "Open spaces where they can play games should, and must, be obtained immediately.... To my mind it would appear that the taxation of gardens or golf links for the support of buildings providing fire protection, police, lighting and schools means that inevitably gardens will disappear and close buildings ensue." These were sound arguments for humanitarian principles of town planning, which have by no means lost their validity. More sectional were his proposals that the working men of Oak Bay, few though they were, should be hired first in the execution of municipal improvements and that the present tarmacadam roads be replaced by permanent paving; he had recommended the adoption of the tarmacadam process as an effective control for dust upon his return from England in August 1905, but without proper grading, this surface was short-lived.[41]

His views were endorsed by other candidates, among them Herrick McGregor, and various local notables, including Oliver and J.J. Shallcross, who announced their support through advertisements in the Victoria newspapers. Rattenbury was elected reeve on 18 January and straightway set about implementing his policies. (Fig.7.16). One of his earliest achievements was the purchase of three and a half acres of land along Willows Beach for public use. But it was the recession of 1913, rather than the passage of planning regulations, that saved the golf course and Oak Bay from the assaults of the speculators. The economic collapse also put an end to his scheme for selling bonds to finance a road-paving programme.

The recession did not, however, diminish his busy schedule of work for the government or the G.T.P. In 1913 the company mounted a concerted effort to complete the western line along the upper reaches of the Fraser and Nechako Rivers, using the supply steamers *Conveyor* and *Operator* and including one of the earliest mechanical tracklayers, appropriately christened "Pioneer."[42] Prince Rupert was progressing quite as fast as Vancouver had done at the same stage in its development. Writing in 1914, Howay was most optimistic about the future of the northern communities, publishing photographs of the bustling wooden terminal town and of the determined first inhabitants of tiny Haysport on the wildly beautiful estuary of the Skeena River. In fact, the G.T.P. opened the line sooner than predicted. The arrival in Prince Rupert of the inaugural transcontinental express on 7 April 1914 boded well for Rattenbury.

In February 1914, as the foundations were being dug for the extensions to the Legislative Buildings, the lumber baron R. W. Gibson asked him to design a large house in Oak Bay. This was to be built on the crest of a spacious plot at 1590 York Place, next to the Lampman property and overlooking the Bay. Responding to a change of fashion in the United States, he shed his former blend of Tudor, Queen Anne, and the Arts and Crafts in favour of the Neo-Renaissance, already popular in Los Angeles and San Francisco (Figs.7.17–19). He conceived a large house in the Italianate style, whose basic symmetry — marked by verandahs at either end — was broken by a large bay window at the front and by a tower at the rear. Subsequently Rattenbury simplified this scheme, giving the house more the appearance of a villa, as recorded in a sketch elevation approximating to the one eventually completed under the direction of Maclure and Lort from July 1919 (Fig.7.20–21).[43] Happily, the complete set of Rattenbury's sketch designs for the house survive.[44] These are valuable for showing his systematic and imaginative approach to design, beginning with a carefully considered site plan (Figs.7.22). In the first, main, series Rattenbury opted for an "L" shaped plan, echoed in the irregular placing of the bay window and tower. (Figs.7.23–24) He placed the main entrance on the left side, reached on the outside by spiral steps that respond to the topography of the site. Beyond the entrance porch (replaced by Maclure and Lort with a library) Rattenbury planned a vestibule leading into the central hall. To create an impression of breadth and light, the staircase climbs in three flights with a half-landing dividing an inglenook below from a tall window above (the windows on the upper floor were to be pivoted for easy cleaning). Off the hall lay the den, drawing room (above a billiard room in the basement), and, opposite the entrance, the dining room, which was separated from the adjacent kitchen by a butler's pantry. On the first floor Rattenbury provided five bedrooms, one dressing room, and two bathrooms, as well as the nursery, each simply decorated. The reception rooms and bedrooms in the body of the house are well served, while being separated from the offices, for on the northwest side stands a wing, initially containing the scullery (including a fitted refrigerator), laundry, and servants' quarters in the basement and a kitchen on the main floor.

Rattenbury might even have been relieved that Gibson decided to delay building operations. Between April and May 1914 he was confronted by the laborious task of finishing the majority of the working drawings for the Provincial Library. As already noted, these were substantially unchanged from the outline plans blueprinted in April 1911, and the interior has been little altered since. The lower floors contain steel book stacks[45] linked by an elevator to the main floor at the level of the Legislative Assembly. The stacks continue into the south projection leading off the octagonal domed rotunda. Almost Baroque in scale, and clothed in white-veined marble, the rotunda is ringed by eight Ionic scagliola columns, each surmounted by carved heraldic animals that frame four arches supporting ornamental balconies. Apart from the arch above the delivery desk on the southern side, another leads into the barrel-vaulted corridor communicating with the Legislative Buildings, while the arches on either side open into lime-wood panelled and beamed reading rooms.[46]

The erection of the simpler office wings proceeded at a brisk pace and was finished by the summer of 1914, some eighteen months after the governor general, the Duke of Connaught, had laid the foundation stone on 28 September 1912.[47] The library, however, could not be completed in time for the official opening planned in August, also to be presided over by the governor general. The order of ceremony had called for Rattenbury to be presented just before the duke unlocked the main door to the Library with a golden key.[48] But the outbreak of war with Germany intervened, causing the cancellation of the ceremony and at the same time trimming the last contracts for fitting up the library and leading to the abandonment of the new museum and printing office.[49] Apart from the interior, the Library was not finished until the summer of 1915 (Fig.7.25). The total expenditure on the extensions reached $1,297,643,[50] and the inflation in costs alarmed a Legislative Assembly anxiously seeking for means of alleviating the loss of tax revenue. Thus in May 1916 the McBride government convened a public enquiry.

The subsequent investigation proved that Rattenbury had kept a careful watch over the accounts, even intervening at one stage to prevent one contract being let at too high a price. "If Mr. Rattenbury had not stepped in," Mr. Brewster, one of the counsel at the enquiry stated, "this higher tender [for the installation of the heating system] would have gone through and the province would have lost $25,000."[51] Rattenbury spoke on his own behalf and insisted that "the new buildings were built very cheaply. The old building, of course, was phenomenally cheap." He admitted that the additions required 20 to 30 per cent more funds to provide a comparable floor space, but he reminded the committee that the differences in costs could be attributed almost entirely to inflation and to the use of more expensive materials. Whereas the roofs, floors, and windows in the older part were of wood, the corresponding members in the additions were of steel, concrete, and copper, and the doors were of steel to increase fire resistance. Once war had been declared, Rattenbury had accepted various economies, including the substitution of artificial for real marble columns in the library.

In company with millions of others, Rattenbury found that his professional activities suffered increasingly as the war intensified. The designs that he sketched for the G.T.P. during the winter of 1914, including an attractive Jacobean-style station for Château Miette (Fig.7.26) and the rustic "Mountain Inn," possibly to be located at Jasper (Figs.7.27–28) were transformed from viable projects to images of a defunct era within a year. The shattering of the world order thus cruelly ended the potentially most creative period of Rattenbury's career.

Eight

FINAL PHASE
1914–1929

The news that Britain had declared war on Germany in 1914 was received with something akin to jubilation by most of the citizens of British Columbia. The conflict was likened to a crusade in defence of the Empire and civilization itself. British Columbians were prepared to fight, "not just for the lust of conquest but because we one and all think that there is grave danger to our Empire, and to the motherland whence the majority of us came," and from every corner of the province men rallied to the colours.[1]

Although Rattenbury was one of the few inhabitants of Victoria, and, indeed, of any part of the Empire, fortunate enough not to lose a close relative, the war years were to prove the unhappiest of his career. By the end of 1914 large numbers of Victoria's able-bodied male citizens had left the city; many actually feared that hostilities would cease before the Victoria contingents could see action. Apart from the completion of the additions to the Legislative Buildings, major architectural projects were suspended and the flow of tourists, essential to the G.T.P. hotel building programme, virtually ceased. Moreover, the enterprising young men of the "Mother Country" who might have emigrated to Canada to settle in the valleys of northern British Columbia were headed in the opposite direction, towards bloodier challenges.

Rattenbury had travelled to Britain in 1914 and took the opportunity to visit Frank, who was then attending an English school.[2] They went together to see the sights of the imperial capital and, while dining in a London restaurant, heard the announcement that war had been declared. Rattenbury, like most residents of Victoria, revered the Empire. But he was no mindless jingoist, and he was to be especially appalled by the carnage of Ypres and Gallipoli, writing to Florrie when again in London in July 1915 that the war seemed to be "slaughter, not fighting."[3] In 1914, however, he had no doubt where his duty lay. He immediately tried to enlist, only to be rejected as too old. Despite keen disappointment, he remained determined to contribute to the Allied cause. In his July letter he informed Florrie that the "war contracts" had "not materialized." Unfortunately, it has not proved possible to discover what form these "contracts" took. He may have planned to supply the British government with timber from his lands. Alternatively, it might have been his intention to provide prefabricated barracks (for which there was considerable demand in Britain in 1915), adapting the scheme he had marketed some years earlier. Whatever the precise nature of the project, Rattenbury must have been dismayed by its failure, which would have reinforced his frustration at being unable to participate in one of the momentous events of history.

These reversals were aggravated by strains in his marriage. His 1915 letter to Florrie (the only one to her that has been traced) begins on a teasing note "Dear Madam" and ends affectionately, with the signature "Daddy," but its content, while not cold, is detached and formal, quite lacking the easy intimacy of the letters to his English relatives or to his daughter. Deprived of the emotional outlet afforded by his correspondence with his mother and lacking the intellectual challenge of work and the lively company of the Union Club, many of whose members were away on active service, he had to remain content with whatever stimulus or pleasure he could find in his home. While Rattenbury would have been unreasonable if he expected qualities from his wife that she had never possessed, her apparent social and intellectual deficiencies do not seem to have been compensated for by much sympathetic kindness or generosity of spirit.[4] Recently acquired correspondence in the Victoria City Archives reveals that Florrie was resented by her own family for her refusal to make any provision whatsoever for Mrs. Dyer, her destitute mother. In 1918 Florrie's sister, Mary Brenner, instituted legal proceedings in the Oregon courts to compel Florrie to provide some support, but she adamantly refused, writing on 7 September that she would under no circumstances help and did not believe in charity. Mrs. Dyer died in poverty in 1919, and even if Florrie could defend her action on the grounds that she had always looked upon Mrs. Howard, who had brought her up and who was still called "Grannie Howard" by her children, as her true mother, this unpleasant episode must have shocked Rattenbury with his strong sense of filial obligations and finally destroyed any lingering affection for his wife. By the middle of 1918 they had begun to occupy separate quarters in Iechinihl. The arrangement seems to have been agreed upon while Mary was away at summer camp, and its significance concealed from her, since she innocently inquired in a letter written on 24 July "How is the new house? I want to come home and see it." These domestic difficulties—progressively compounded by anxiety over his land purchases and his worsening financial situation—undermined Rattenbury's health; he was troubled by poor circulation, fatigue, and deep depression, aggravated by an increasing fondness for drink.[5]

In company with many other landowners, Rattenbury was to suffer great distress as a consequence of the actions of the provincial government over the coming years. Initially, at least, he was in a better position than most, thanks to his association with the G.T.P. It was clearly in the latter's interest that landowners should succeed in attracting settlers to their property, since that would maintain, if not expand, traffic along the railway. Contacts within the company seem to have ensured that Rattenbury's holdings were actively promoted. R.C.W. Lett, for instance, "Tourist and Colonization Agent" for the G.T.P., did not hesitate to answer enquiries from prospective settlers and investors in 1917 by drawing their attention to the excellent location of the lots owned by Rattenbury and the reasonable terms that he was offering.[6]

The prospects for large scale settlement in 1917 would have been bleak enough, but northern landowners were to receive a further setback that year from a government that was under increasing pressure to protect settlers (and in particular returning veterans) from "speculators." Canada, no less than Britain, hoped to provide a "land fit for heroes." Unlike Britain, however, Canada had the asset of undeveloped land that might be the means of fulfilling this pledge. Each province had its own scheme to help returning veterans by settling them in unpopulated areas. John Oliver, minister of agriculture (and, later, premier of British Columbia), favoured three centres, Melville on Vancouver Island, Creston in the Kootenay region, and Telkwa in the Bulkley Valley. In 1917 he introduced "An Act to Promote Increased Agricultural Productivity," the most important clause of which envisaged the creation of a Land Settlement Board with five full-time members entrusted with the purchase of a reserve of land.[7] All those who had served in the Canadian or British Forces were to receive a rebate of $500 on the price of land acquired from the board.

The government approached Rattenbury in November 1917, through the board's chairman, Maxwell Smith, who wrote to him to ask if he would consider making his holdings available.[8] Rattenbury, having already been advised to cease either advertising or selling his property,[9] replied that although his lands had then cost him nearly $9.00 an acre (after allowing for taxes and 6 per cent interest), he was prepared to accept $6.50 an acre, which, after settling outstanding taxes, would result in a little over $6.00. This was well below what he could expect in a private transaction. But he acknowledged the growing opposition in the province to the private ownership of public lands. Smith thereupon invited Rattenbury to meet him personally and to bring along all the relevant documents. Unfortunately, no record of this conference has survived, but it seems that as they poured over the maps and deeds, some of Rattenbury's old enthusiasm was rekindled and that it proved infectious: the chairman was persuaded, the reduction of the price to $6.00 an acre probably acting as the ultimate inducement. Perhaps injudiciously he confirmed their gentleman's agreement in a letter of 16 November and promised to recommend formal acceptance of Rattenbury's offer at the next meeting of the board, to be held on 3 December. Smith appears to have acted in good faith, if precipitously, in giving Rattenbury what could have reasonably been taken as a virtual assurance of an agreement, and in a letter of 17 November to the board he described Rattenbury's holdings as "some of the best land in northern British Columbia."

There is good reason for assuming that at their meeting the board did accept Smith's proposal, since only a decision favourable to Rattenbury could have prompted the letter written on 7 December by Frank C. McKinnon of New Hazelton to Alex M. Manson, member of the provincial legislature for Prince Rupert. McKinnon argued strongly against purchasing land of which he claimed no more than "a small fraction was fit for settlement." Whether McKinnon's communication arose from a genuine desire to protect the public interest or from some personal spite against Rattenbury cannot be determined, but it may be significant that McKinnon wrote to Manson, a politician, and not to Smith, chairman of the relevant board. Furthermore, his criticism of the quality of the land seems excessive. It was not unreasonable to argue that the lands on the Nass River, Stuart Lake and Ootsa Lake were "so awkwardly situated that their settlement for many years would not be practicable" or that the block near Hazelton was "heavily timbered" and would be "costly to clear." Yet to say that these lands were "worth nothing" was unwarranted, and McKinnon's comment that the Bulkley Valley holdings, while somewhat better, were still "not especially desirable" is completely belied by the government's determined efforts to acquire them at a later date. Whatever the merits of the case, the board was ultimately won over by McKinnon's views and an undoubtedly embarrassed Smith was obliged to report to Rattenbury on 8 December that the board had decided to reject his offer. This episode reflects little credit on the board. At worst it could indicate that some members were motivated by personal antagonism towards Rattenbury, at best that they were not competent to perform their task, having rated one and the same area of land as both "worth nothing" and "the best land in B.C."

Rattenbury's indignation would scarcely have subsided when, on 21 January, the board informed him that the question of his holdings had come up again and that his correspondence had been filed. This information, innocent enough, was followed by the ominous phrase, "the actions of the Board in this connection must be largely covered by such legislation as may be passed enabling us to secure adjacent areas so as to facilitate our forming community settlements." This legalistic declaration portended a new round in the battle between the government and private landholders, one that would be waged in an atmosphere of increasing hostility to what the *Colonist* of 18 February called "speculating owners" who were holding on to "thousands of acres of excellent agricultural land in British Columbia producing nothing and lacking the hope of producing anything."

Rattenbury felt impelled to write a stinging rebuke to this charge, which appeared in the *Victoria Times* four days later. He pointed out that the government had promoted land purchase, it being considered "more public spirited to invest our money in the province than to send it out of the province to buy stocks and bonds." He reminded the editor of the difficulties of attracting speculators confronted by excessive taxation, and disclosed his recent attempts to co-operate with the government:

> On enquiry from the Government I have offered them the lands back again at two thirds of their cost to me. I have also offered to join in any scheme to promote settlement, and I believe all other land owners would do the same. What more can we do outside of giving lands back to the province and saying, "You have had our money: now take the lands as well, and leave us with nothing."

Though the letter did continue in a more conciliatory tone, the government was in no mood to compromise. On the contrary, John Oliver, now premier, decided to extend the powers of the board. The *Victoria Times* of 19 April 1918 reported that it would be granted powers of compulsory purchase and that the land would be acquired at an appraised value, with a limited right of appeal. The board was also authorized to instruct owners to improve their holdings within a specified period or to pay a tax of 5 per cent of the assessed value of the undeveloped land (to be pro-rated to make allowance for partial improvements).

During October 1918, as the war in Europe was drawing to a climactic close, these new powers were implemented. "Land Settlement Area No.1" was established in the vicinity of Telkwa, and once again an offer was made to buy Rattenbury's "not especially desirable" holdings. The details of the offer are not known, but the subsequent correspondence suggests that the valuation placed on the land was well below the market price. Not surprisingly Rattenbury declined and undertook to improve his lands during the coming year, as required by the new provisions of the act. He had by now hired a manager, the energetic George Wood, an ex-army officer with experience in selling land for settlement in California. With the aid of Wood and ten other assistants who established trails throughout the area and acted as guides, Rattenbury had already succeeded in selling 4,500 acres by October when the board made its offer. Rattenbury was courteous in his formal dealings with the government but his contempt for them had clearly not diminished, and in December 1918, he circulated the northern landowners, urging them to resist the actions of the board in view of the ridiculous assessments made of the value of their lands. The letter went out under Wood's name, but its tone leaves little doubt of its ultimate authority (and probable authorship): "That the appraisement is a huge joke goes without saying, but it is not much of a joke to the Landowner," ran the text, "the value placed on these lands is, without question, the work of parties who had had no experience of land valuation." It went on to cite land sold at $20 an acre that was rated by the board at $5.50, and ended with the justly sarcastic observation that the "Land Settlement Act was enacted for the purpose of providing a nice salaried job with an ideal expense account." In this confrontation Rattenbury seems to have enjoyed the support of the press in the interior of the province, if not in the lower mainland. In December, for instance, the Smithers *Interior News* reported that Rattenbury's company had shown "liberality in all their dealings with settlers, present and prospective" and mentioned some of its imaginative measures, such as "weekly excursions composed of farmers from various points on the prairies" and a scheme to bring in two hundred head of stock to be handed over to promising settlers under a profit-sharing arrangement.[10]

The board, of course, had the ultimate advantage of legally sanctioned powers. They decided to bide their time for almost six months, then, on 11 June 1919, sent Rattenbury a stern letter listing his holdings in the settlement area (appraising them at an average of about $5.00 an acre) and informing him that unless he carried out improvements as required by the act or disposed of his lands to the board (at the appraised value), these would be subject to an additional 5 per cent tax. Again, Rattenbury stated his intention of ensuring that the land would be settled, informing the board that he was selling at between $4.50 and $12.00 an acre (as opposed to the board's appraisal of $5.00). That Rattenbury at least partly succeeded in making good his claim is confirmed by a letter prepared for the Ontario newspapers by John Kennedy (of the United Grain Growers' Securities Co. Ltd. of Winnipeg) describing a trip through the Bulkley Valley. In the letter, he congratulated Rattenbury for having established a community of English-speaking settlers in the valley and for offering very reasonable terms. Even the board commended Rattenbury's efforts in a letter sent on 19 August 1919, to G. Wellsley Whittaker, president of the Great War Veterans Association. In reply to Mr. Whittaker's expressed concern that so little land had apparently been made available to returning veterans, the board stated that Rattenbury was making strenuous efforts to colonize and that his "activity may be resulting in bringing a number of settlers into that part of the province." Clearly the board was prepared to make use of Rattenbury's reputation when they needed a cover for their own inactivity.[11]

By this time Rattenbury surely lost confidence in the competence, and the fairness, of the land settlement board, and he decided that in order to reduce the risk of personal loss, he should incorporate himself into a company. In December, 1919, he created Rattenbury Lands Limited. Despite its grand title, Rattenbury's last commercial enterprise in the province was launched virtually without capital, the 10,000 shares of $1.00 each being nominal.[12] At the time of incorporation only two shareholders were listed, Rattenbury, as president, and George Wood (who described himself as an engineer) resident in Telkwa, as vice-president and general manager. The records of the company show that at its inception each man began with a single $1.00 share, and, indeed, up to the time of its liquidation, they remained the only shareholders, increasing their holdings on 31 March 1920 to 200 shares at a face value of $200. Rattenbury's pressing concern seems to have remained the need to avoid personal liability, surely remembering the lawsuits brought against him when the B.L.K.N.C. failed. Doubtless, this concern prompted Rattenbury (styling himself as both an architect and an "estate agent" at Telkwa) to sell his interests at Telkwa to Rattenbury Lands for 5,800 shares at a nominal value of $5,800. Though stating his profession as "retired" in the legal documents, he committed himself energetically to the real estate business, becoming the sole agent for a number of companies: The Farm Lands Investment Co., The Ross Sutherland Lands, The North Coast Land Co., The Pemberton Lands and The Spencer Lands.[13]

The revival in Rattenbury's professional activities also seemed to bring about a revived vigour in his private life. On 23 February 1920 Wood wrote to him from the company's Vancouver office, mentioning, among other things, gossip about Rattenbury's close attachment to his nurse. The letter ends, "I know this sounds like tittle-tattle, but as it is spicy I want you to know it. You had better burn this private letter." The topic recurs in later correspondence between the two men, and that Rattenbury may have been involved in more than mere flirtation is indicated by the consideration that he apparently gave to selling Iechinihl and moving to Burnaby, near Vancouver.

Naturally enough, Wood was more concerned with the fate of their company than with Rattenbury's private conduct. In a letter of 25 February 1920 he commented on the absence of news from England adding that "the whole thing is getting on my nerves." By the end of that month, they were doubtless relieved to hear of Rattenbury's appointment as Canadian representative of the Canadian Landowners' Association, an amalgamation of over twenty British companies with land and resource investments in Canada. As a result of this arrangement, Rattenbury travelled to Britain in July 1920, almost certainly in the hope of securing the sale of property and attracting new investments through the association. The visit seems to have received the blessing of John Oliver; on 22 June of that year W. Wilmot, secretary of Rattenbury Lands, wrote to Rattenbury that he had heard that "John Oliver is literally falling on your neck and wishing you God's speed." Despite Oliver's apparent official encouragement, Rattenbury achieved little. On 11 August he wrote despondently to Mary about his lack of progress in London, at the same time expressing concern about her conduct under her mother's supervision.[14] By October his business problems seemed to be almost insurmountable: "This is certainly one hard game I have set myself," he observed to Mary, adding that Wood was confronting problems in British Columbia that would entail a reduction in staff.

Rattenbury was in London until at least January 1921, living in a $4.00-a-week room. While he wrote cheerfully of his social life in the capital, he must have been haunted by his inability to attract large-scale investment. He may even have begun to realize that his great vision of northern development would never materialize. Shortly after his return to Canada, the Land Settlement Board, in June 1921, notified him that certain parts of his land would be purchased compulsorily and settled. In some cases they appraised the land below the figure agreed between Rattenbury Lands and potential settlers who had already agreed to purchase, causing most of them to relinquish their downpayments. In his 1928 appeal, Rattenbury claimed that the board's action deprived him of $520,000, and while this figure might be inflated, Rattenbury Lands had surely suffered a considerable capital loss. Nor was this the last problem. The board imposed a tax of $2.50 an acre of that part of his lands that had not been improved, so that he found himself faced with a staggering assessment of $90,000.

The responsibility for the failure of the settlement scheme did not rest with Rattenbury or his fellow speculators. Bureaucratic incompetence aside, the truth was that, after their experiences in France, many of the returning soldiers preferred to reside in the populated areas where a steady income seemed assured and life less harsh. In fact, Rattenbury was vindicated after his death. When a similar scheme was contemplated in 1942, the federal minister of pensions, Ian MacKenzie, admitted that government efforts to promote settlement after the previous war had been a "dismal failure."[15] One hundred and ten million dollars had been advanced to settlers and nearly $14 million spent on administration while only $66 million had been recovered by the Treasury. Of the approximately 25,000 settlers who had been placed on the land, scarcely a third remained.

Rattenbury's situation by the fall of 1921 hardly justified the letterhead on his contemporary stationery: "RATTENBURY LANDS, THE BEST LANDS IN THE WORLD: AT RIGHT PRICE; ON YOUR OWN TERMS." Yet his residual optimisim was not wholly groundless, since on 29 September he wrote to Kate of having been "as busy as a bee designing a kind of Crystal Palace as an amusement centre for Victoria." Although "everyone seems delighted with it," the proposal would have to be put to a vote before it can be built." It was "practically a huge conservatory, with the centre part large swimming tanks, huge promenade, Dancing, bands, all kinds of things. Flowers, sunshine and games indoors."

The fundamental inspiration for the roof structure of Rattenbury's

Crystal Garden, if not for its size, was the Crystal Palace, Sir Joseph Paxton's famous prefabricated glass and iron building for the Great Exhibition held in London in 1851. However, the Crystal Garden was intended to enclose a mere 100,000 square feet as against the more than 770,000 of the London structure. This famous monument to Victorian British industrial design was reconstructed, in an enlarged form, at Sydenham Hill, south London (which Rattenbury might have visited). It served as a concert and exhibition hall, with a permanent display devoted to the British Empire, until its destruction by fire in 1936. The Crystal Palace established an important tradition of progressive structures erected to house national and international exhibitions, not least in the United States.[16] And, as Rattenbury had told the *Colonist* in August 1905, it was the Americans who had converted such exhibition buildings into "permanent palaces of delight for the people." He particularly admired their social value and especially praised Coney Island, which, "built and rebuilt in a palatial manner, remains as a permanent palace of amusement and fairyland of light and beauty; and not for the original rough population is the metamorphosis achieved, but for the joy and delectation of New York's working thousands generally. The buildings are practically palaces and are as charming."[17] Even in 1905 the beach resort of New York had seemed to provide a model for Victoria, "in view of the proposal for a winter garden etc. now before the city fathers." His suggestion was ignored by the council in 1905, although in 1912 a scheme for a civic swimming pool, backed by the Chamber of Commerce, was put before the taxpayers and rejected. Thus the scheme that Rattenbury described to his sister in 1921 revived those earlier proposals. It was also architecturally related to various smaller-scale iron and glass structures in Victoria, including A. M. Muir's City Market and the conservatory that Painter had added to the rear of the Empress Hotel in 1911. Another conservatory had been built at Hatley Park by the American firm of Lord and Burnham. At their Canadian factory in St. Catharines, Ontario, the same firm were to manufacture the metal roof members for the Crystal Garden, which Rattenbury was to complete from 1923–25, with the assistance of another Englishman, P. L. James.

The dimensions of Rattenbury's "amusement centre," prepared for the Chamber of Commerce in 1921, were of a scale more appropriate to the pre-war boom period, 340 feet long as against the 268 feet eventually executed. In a letter to Alderman George Sangster, written on 21 December, Rattenbury estimated the cost of the foundations alone at $150,000.[18] In it Rattenbury also referred to an "attached sheet," which was presumably one of the drawings from which the blueprints at the

Provincial Archives were taken.[19] These comprise an elevation with two
sections, and floor plans (Figs.8.1-3). At each end of the main front are two
brick towers, square internally but having chamfered edges above round
corner piers.

Just beneath the projecting eave of the roof is a blind arcade, an echo of
the Italianate arched openings of the steel and glazed upper floor. The
Italianate character is intensified by the arched entrance at the centre,
with its framing engaged columns and gable, and by the large window
between the corner towers that blend Venetian and Roman motifs. On
both levels the bays are subdivided into three main sections, continuing the pattern set between the towers. Inside, Rattenbury imagined a
continuous raised promenade sixty feet wide planted with trees and
shrubs. Descending from this level are two tiers of seats overlooking three
swimming pools—he may have decided on three smaller rather than one
large pool because of the poor subsoil on the proposed site between
Douglas, Belleville, and Yates Streets. At one end of the pool area is an
apsidal ended "stage," cutting into the promenade, and two "electric fountains." The promotional literature circulated by the enthusiastic Chamber
of Commerce indicates that the fountains were to have been illuminated
with coloured electric lights and supplemented at night by lights on the
floor of the (heated) pools, which would glisten "in a glorious rainbow
effect."[20] At the street level are a "Banquet Hall" with kitchen, shops,
"Permanent Exhibits of B.C. Sports Industries etc.," two "Special Exhibition Rooms," and an arcade with unspecified "Exhibits."

In making these plans Rattenbury probably consulted James, who had
gained extensive experience in the design and construction of swimming
pools before emigrating from England in 1906.[21] In a letter dated 19 May,
James recalled that he had entered into partnership with Rattenbury
"shortly after" his return from overseas in 1919.[22] They reached an
agreement whereby Rattenbury's name was used to obtain work that was
then designed in detail and supervised by James in return for one-third of
the fees earned on each commission. When compiling notes on their
association in September 1925, James listed a number of such joint under-
takings, the F.H. Bullen house at 924 Esquimalt Road, Victoria, the
"Indian Smoking Room" of one of the *Princess* ferry ships, an unspecified building at Radium Hot Springs, and some unnamed "Apartment
Houses."[23] On 2 February 1922, Rattenbury paid him $30 for enlarging his
"Crystal Palace" plans and perhaps for making certain revisions, since the
James papers include other sketches with a different arrangement of
the accommodation around the pool area.[24]

Rattenbury's optimism about the commission was premature, because the Chamber of Commerce and the Amusement Centre Committee sponsored by City Council failed to raise sufficient funds over the ensuing two years. Equally unfounded was Rattenbury's assertion, in his 29 September 1921 letter to Kate, that "Rattenbury Lands" was "becoming a household name out here," (ironically a phrase he had applied to his ill-fated B.L.K.N.C. venture), and that if only he and Wood were "twenty years younger it would become a huge concern." He was, of course, putting a bold face on the situation, as he went on to do about his severely strained domestic relations. "I still live in my quarters," he noted, which were "delightful," with their "entrance hall, sun room and beautiful den in blue, and old tapestries and old Oak furniture." Nor did he more than hint at the extent to which he had become estranged from his children; "Mary, who seems all at once to be a woman, generally comes in after dinner for an hour or two." He complimented her "naturally fine charac-ter" and commended Frank's aptitude as a life insurance agent, "So far he is very much in earnest and will make good if he will only stick at it. He does not mind tackling anyone. I never could have done it, but appar-ently he has no shyness." An undertone of stoical resignation, though, seeps through his final phrases: "For after all the two great things in life are Health and Friends; one outgrows other things. I seem to have got a whole lot now, just when I really appreciate them. When I was really busy I was too busy to think about them—I mean real friends."

Rattenbury would have needed to draw heavily on those resources over the course of the ensuing year. Before the close of 1922 he had acknowledged not only the final collapse of his marriage to Florrie, but also the inability of Rattenbury Lands to meet the demands of its cre-ditors.[25] One of the "friends" who provided comfort during this difficult period might have been the "nurse" mentioned by Wood. If so, the affair may have petered out through her decision to move to England.[26] Yet he weathered these professional and personal trials, and by the end of the following year fortune seemed to favour him once again. On 23 December 1923 he wrote optimistically to Kate: while he conceded that the government action had caused him losses, through methods that seemed "so unfair," he was more eager to tell her of a recent social event.[27] "Last night I was out to a Dance and danced every dance, until two in the morning," he wrote, "and enjoyed every minute. The Lieutenant-Governor remarked, 'You have simply renewed your youth.'" The renewal owed not a little to an encounter with "a young married" woman "about 26, the belle of the ball and a marvellous musician."[28] She had "knocked me out by saying, 'Do you know that you have a lovely face?'

'Great Scott,' said I, 'Have I? I am going right home to have a look at it. I've never thought it worth looking at yet.' 'I'm not joking,' she said, 'You have almost the kindest face I ever saw.'"

Alma Victoria Pakenham (neé Clarke), the "marvellous musician," belonged to a family that had played a leading role in Victoria's musical life. Her own later success as a musician was largely owing to the encouragement provided by her mother, Frances Wolff, one of twelve children of Ernest Henry Wolff, a German tailor, and Elizabeth Grace, an Englishwoman from Cowley (who claimed a family link with the famous cricketer W. G. Grace). The Wolff family arrived in Victoria in 1891, from which time they organized numerous concerts and became noted for their productions of Gilbert and Sullivan.[29] Alma was born about 1895, possibly in Victoria,[30] and from 1897 she lived for a time in Kamloops. Her mother was the dominating force in Alma's early life;[31] Frances established a school of music in Kamloops with her brother, Ernest Wolff (later to become director of the Pollard Opera Company in California), and devoted herself to furthering her daughter's career (Fig. 8.4).

Eventually Alma was taken east to study at the Toronto College of Music (later absorbed by the Royal Conservatory of Music), whose founder, Dr. F. H. Torrington, was a well-known examiner on the west coast and had already met Alma.[32] She gave piano concerts in Toronto, and a charming "programme" printed there has been preserved. On the cover is her photograph, in which she looks about sixteen or seventeen, and the caption "Alma Victoria Clarke: Concert Pianist." Inside is a "List of Pieces Miss Clarke plays from memory," including works by Beethoven, Chopin, Liszt, Mendelssohn, Rachmaninov, Schubert, Schumann and Verdi. The remainder of the programme is taken up with press notices of previous performances. Typical is the one reprinted from the *Toronto Saturday Night*: "Dr. Torrington has every reason to be gratified with the undoubted success of his talented pupil, Alma Victoria Clarke, of Victoria, B.C. Miss Clarke, although so young a student, has a remarkably good memory and a clear technique, and one is confident that she will make her mark as a pianist."

In 1913 Alma married Caledon Robert John Radcliffe Dolling of Marlin, County Down, who came from a well-known Ulster family; his grandfather had been High Sheriff of Londonderry, and his uncle was the famous "Father Dolling," one of the most distinguished social reformers of the Victorian era. Poor eyesight had prevented Dolling from pursuing a military career, and he was persuaded to try his hand at farming in Saskatchewan. When this proved to be a failure, he moved to Vancouver and took up the real estate business. Although he does not know where they met, Dolling's brother, Harry, who arrived in Vancouver too late for the wedding, still remembers seeing the couple from his brother's office on Granville Street as they returned from their honeymoon. "She was dressed in a white suit and she looked absolutely radiant – a sight I have never forgotten."[33] Upon the outbreak of war the brothers volunteered for service, and Alma travelled with Caledon to London. Eventually commissioned into the 2nd Battalion of the Royal Welch Fusiliers, he was a courageous soldier, being awarded the Military Cross in March 1916, wounded twice, then, on 20 August, during the great Somme offensive, killed by a bursting shell at Mametz Wood.

Devastated by his death, Alma could no longer endure inactivity and joined the Scottish Women's Hospital Organization (Fig.8.5). The British Army declined to make use of the organization because its staff, including the doctors, consisted entirely of women. The French had no such scruples, and the volunteers made an outstanding contribution to the Allied effort under the aegis of the French Red Cross. The records show that "Alina [sic] Dolling" served between January 1917 and January 1918 at the Scottish Women's hospital at Royaumont, a converted abbey, designated as Auxiliary Hospital 301. Much of her work, however, appears to have been at the advance hospital in Villes Coltert, and it was probably from there that she wrote to an aunt on July 24: "There's a fearful French Push on at the moment and can hardly think straight for noise. . . . Am supposed to be asleep now. . . . There's a bally fight going on over head, – they quite intend finishing us this time, – but they've tried before, – and outside of a few casualties and a bit o' damage, – we still remain. But oh! its dreadful this bombarding of the Croix Rouge. – Brought a ripping boy in last night and just as we almost had him in, – he was shot dead, – instantly." She later told her sons of having to hold down men as they had limbs sawn off. Alma herself was wounded, and received a Croix de Guerre from the French government for her services.[34]

While in France Alma met her second husband, Thomas Compton Pakenham, from the family that holds the Earldom of Longford. Born in Japan where his father, Gustavus Pakenham, was a British naval attaché, he was educated in Kobe and at the China Inland Mission School in Chefoo before returning to England to attend the Inns of Court. With the outbreak of war he entered Sandhurst and later received a commission in the Coldstream Guards. Their common interest in music may have brought Pakenham and Alma together, for he was to become the chief music critic of the *New York Times*. He was already married but, in 1920, secured a divorce from his wife and wed Alma. Though their union gave her a son, Christopher Compton, and an entry in *Burke's Peerage* (under the name of Clark), it also caused her considerable distress. She soon discovered that Pakenham was a charming fraud, who told lies with consummate conviction. The couple had little money and departed for America where Pakenham travelled on the lecture circuit, posing as "Dr. Pakenham," an expert on Japanese affairs. His imposture succeeded until his death when the obituary, printed in the *New York Times* on 18 August 1957, also reported that he had attended Harrow and Magdalen College, Oxford. Their relationship so deteriorated that Alma was finally forced to appeal to her mother, who brought her and Compton back to Victoria.

Beautiful and fascinating, but unfortunate and unhappy in her private life, Alma met Rattenbury at the time when his architectural career revived. For after the ecstatic description of their encounter in his December 1923 letter to Kate, he announced the receipt of two major commissions worth nearly $100,000. The first was "the Terminal Building at Victoria for the steamships, next to the Parliament Building," which would be "a handsome little building, as good as anything I have ever done." The second, based upon the "Amusement Centre" he had mentioned previously, was the "Crystal Garden, a kind of Crystal Palace but with a lake of salt water in it, masses of flowers and with Ball-rooms and all kinds of amusements" and "electrical effects." After "quitting for ten years," the commissions gave him "a supreme amount of pleasure, especially in doing better work than I have ever done."

The C.P.R. Terminal was truly one of Rattenbury's best designs. Built to replace his frame structure of 1905, it forms a worthy complement to the Legislative Buildings and the Empress Hotel. The colonnaded harbour front lends dignity and variety to the Inner Harbour and, with those other monuments, remains a testimony to the liberal eclecticism and high standard of his work. A revised version of his second design for the G.T.P. station at Prince Rupert, the new Victoria Terminal is a further Beaux-Arts interpretation of the Classical temple. The result is as urbane, despite its smaller scale, as the Classically styled corporate buildings erected during the decade in Eastern Canada, notably Union Station in Toronto (by Ross and MacDonald with John Lyle) and the Sun Life Building in Montreal (by Darling and Pearson) each with engaged colonnades.

The two longer façades of the terminal, one unbroken and facing the harbour and the other with a projected entrance bay of two piers on Belleville Street, have Ionic columns raised on a continuous plinth and framed by thick piers appropriately sporting masks of Neptune (Figs.8.6–7). The design of these façades is also reminiscent of the pavilions on his scheme for the Saskatchewan Parliament Building. On the shorter sides the outer piers are left unornamented, only the decorative Neptune motif reappearing on the projected inner piers which frame the subsidiary entrances. That arrangement creates a centralizing movement which is reinforced by the continuation of the inner piers above the cornice level and by the attic storey that spans the middle of the building. This contained accommodation for the company records, the engineer, and a draughting room, as shown in blueprints of the working drawings preserved at the Provincial Archives (Figs.8.8–10).[35] Below, on the second floor, were further offices. These floors were reached by a staircase situated on the left of the entrance from Belleville Street. The main floor also provided a large general waiting room, a ladies' waiting room, smoking room, lavatories, a ticket office, parcel room and an office for the company's agent.

This building also was a co-operative effort. The blueprints are signed by Rattenbury and James, addressed from James's office (332 Sayward Building, Victoria) and dated July–September 1923. The drawings were executed by James, who also supervised the contractors: Luney Brothers of Vancouver and the Trussed Concrete Steel Company of Walkerville, Ontario, the suppliers of the "Truscon System of Reinforced Concrete" adopted for the structure. Two years later, in a letter to Rattenbury dated 1 June 1925, James stated that he had consented to work as draughtsman for the terminal provided that he be allowed to "run the job."[36] He also asserted that he had proposed the adoption of "cast stone" for the exterior, which had enabled them "to carry out your idea of a monumental building within cost." James had defined the composition of this material (a mixture of cement, Monterey white sand, fan-shell sand and local washed sand) in an earlier letter to Rattenbury, written in February 1924, in which he had also listed the major amendments made to the working drawings by him during the construction of the terminal: the addition of two feet to the width and of one foot to the heights of the two lower floors.[37] The building was finished by the summer of 1924,[38] and its success led Rattenbury to join the Royal Architectural Institute of Canada that year (remaining a member until 1930) (Fig.8.11). Rattenbury also seems to have succeeded in bringing off his last major land transaction in that year, presumably acting in a private capacity. The *Colonist* of 15 December 1924 reported that negotiations for the sale of 15,000 acres in the Bulkley Valley to a group of Swiss dairymen had been completed with a Herr O.B.

Laser of Zurich, who hoped to bring out the new settlers in March. In fact, only a few arrived, but they did provide a nucleus of Swiss farmers in the area, which was to grow into a thriving Swiss-Canadian community. "Telkwa practically yodels with Swiss," quipped the contributor of an article about the Bulkley Valley published in the *British Columbia Magazine* on 13 October 1951.

Earlier in 1924 the C.P.R. had also revived the amusement centre concept as the Crystal Garden. They undertook to build it for not less than $200,000 and to operate it for an initial period of twenty years, on the condition that the City Council would lease the site for $1.00 per annum, grant exemption from taxation for twenty years, maintain the taxation and water charges on the Empress Hotel at the current figures ($15,000 and $5,000), supply water free for the centre for twenty years, and help to secure foreshore rights associated with the installation of a sea-water pumping station on Beacon Hill.[39] Rattenbury and Basil Gardom, superintendent of construction and repairs for the C.P.R. western hotels, were engaged to speak to various local groups to explain the civic and economic advantages that would result from the centre. Their efforts, and a massive advertising campaign in the press and even in the local cinemas, helped to win the support of the taxpayers who, in the referendum held on 29 December 1923, voted 2,909 to 352 in favour of the agreement negotiated between the city and the C.P.R.

At that time the project, as illustrated in the *Victoria Times* of 29 December, was largely the conception of Rattenbury (Fig.8.12). The illustration depicts a building that would, if anything, be larger than the 1921 version, having a brick façade on the ground floor, with two rows of three square windows set between piers supporting urns, a broad entrance between two Doric columns flanked by pilasters, a curved metal and glass second storey with an ornamental ridge, and a high glazed roof above the swimming area, now confined to a single pool. The actual drawing upon which the *Times* illustration is based, however, was executed by James, and Rattenbury left his partner to complete the detailed working drawings and, apparently, also the extensive revisions that had to be made so as to bring the costs within the $200,000 budget stipulated by the company.

On 26 August 1924, James wrote to Gardom, stating that he wished to begin construction because he had "put in a tremendous amount of time in the preparation of the preliminary and working plans, specifications, etc. since last November" and expressing surprise that he, Gardom, required a full list of the estimated expenditures. But he had been unable to contact Rattenbury who, he believed, was "somewhere near Bellingham," and so he wanted to be paid extra for reckoning the quantities of materials needed for the building. This was the seed of the dispute that arose between Rattenbury and James in 1925 over the division of fees earned on the commission. In the dispute Gardom took James's side, perhaps in the expectation that James would obtain an increased share of the fees from Rattenbury rather than from the company. At any rate, Gardom's attitude could not have been determined by Rattenbury's supposed neglect of the commission since he was in Victoria for part of the time when the scheme was substantially reduced in scale during the summer and fall of 1924.[40] Rattenbury had returned to Victoria by 5 September at the latest. That day he wrote to Gardom explaining his recent absence in America on the ground that he (perhaps accompanied by Alma) had seized the opportunity of looking at various buildings of a somewhat similar nature."[41] With this same letter he submitted a bill of $4,800 for the preliminary work.

Nevertheless, there can be no doubt that James continued to be responsible for the new, detailed, working drawings that were finished by the end of November (Fig.8.13). In these the structure measures 268 by 98 feet, with three (not two) porticoes each 35 by 20 feet. The main portico and ground floor brick walls have been least altered, being merely stripped of decoration. The metal and glass roofs are simpler, while the interior has been considerably changed, especially on the ground floor. The dressing rooms, hot baths, and lavatories have been moved from the basement to the north side, next to the Yates Street entrance, and the exhibition rooms much reduced. The banqueting room or gymnasium (subsequently changed to the lower ballroom) is now entered on the south side from Belleville Street, and the promenades above given over to sets of tea rooms and "ballrooms."

However laborious the task of altering the design may have been, James did not complain about his part in the bargain until 22 May 1925 when the building was nearly finished. The company had refused to pay more than 4 per cent of the cost of the commission (the usual minimum fee was then 6 per cent), so that the half share of the fees would not represent adequate compensation for his work. Accordingly, he asked Rattenbury, not ungraciously, for at least a three-quarter share. Six days later Rattenbury sent a reply, expressing annoyance and surprise.[42] He reminded James that he had waived his one-third share of the fees on some of the commissions that he had passed on to him and, incidentally, claimed that he, and not James, had drawn the plans for the Bullen house,

PROPOSED AMUSEMENT CENTRE
VICTORIA·B.C.

· FRONT ELEVATION ·

· SECTION ON LINE B·B ·

8.1 Elevation and
sections for proposed
Amusement Centre,
Victoria, 1921.

· SECTION ON LINE A·A ·

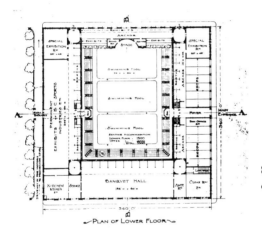

~PLAN OF LOWER FLOOR~

8.2 Plan of lower level
of Amusement Centre.

~PROPOSED AMUSEMENT CENTRE~
& WINTER GARDEN · VICTORIA.

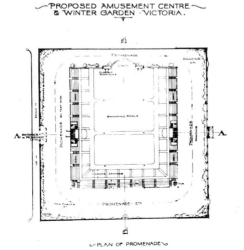

~PLAN OF PROMENADE~

8.3 Plan of promenade
level of Amusement
Centre.

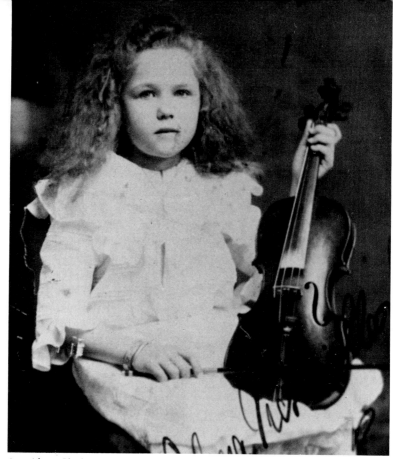

8.4 Alma Clarke, photographed as a child in Kamloops.

8.5 Alma Dolling with nursing friends in France during World War I.

8.6 Rattenbury and James, second C.P.R. Steamship Terminal, Victoria, B.C., 1923–1924.

8.7 Second C.P.R. Steamship Terminal, Victoria, 1923–1924.

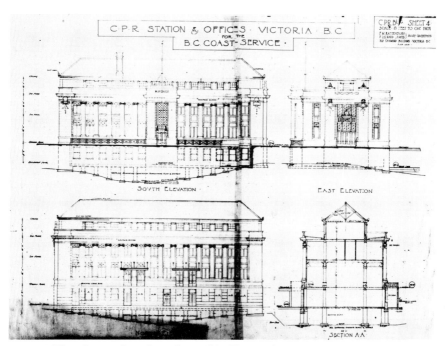

8.8 Elevations and sections, Steamship Terminal, 1923.

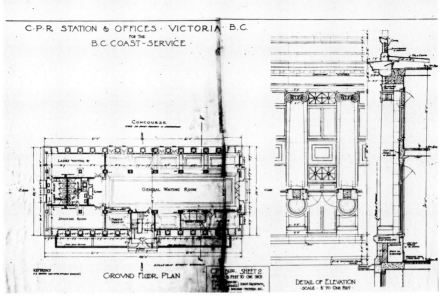

8.9 Ground floor plan and details, Steamship Terminal, 1923.

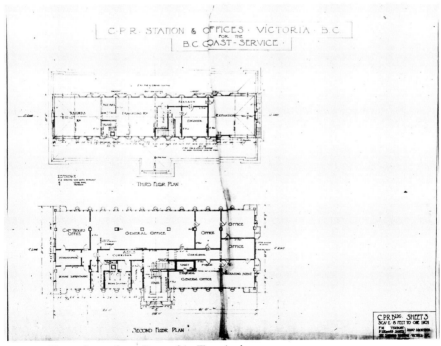

8.10 Upper floor plans, Steamship Terminal, 1923.

8.11 Rattenbury in the early 1920's.

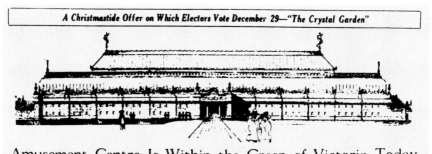

A Christmastide Offer on Which Electors Vote December 29—"The Crystal Garden"

Amusement Centre Is Within the Grasp of Victoria Today

8.12 Sketch of Crystal Garden, Victoria, 1924.

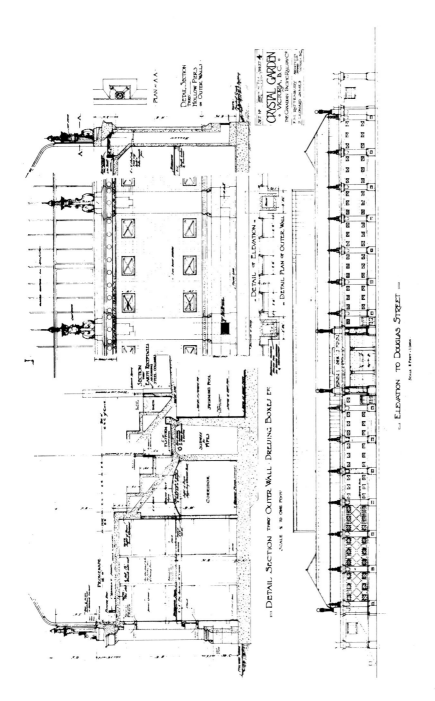

8.13 Rattenbury and James, elevations and details for Crystal Garden, Victoria, as built 1924–1925.

8.14 Postcard of Crystal Garden, 1926.

8.15 Postcard of interior, Crystal Garden, c.1930.

8.16 Francis and Alma Rattenbury after their wedding, 1925.

8.17 The Empress Hotel, showing Rattenbury's original main block, 1904–1908.

8.18 The Empress Hotel, showing W. S. Painter's additions, 1929–1931.

8.19 Rattenbury family photograph before departure for England, 1931.

8.20 John Rattenbury's christening, Okehampton, Devon, 1930; the tall figure is Keith Miller Jones.

although the latter had received the lion's share of the remuneration. He further reminded James that he had been paid more than $1,000 for the draughting work on the C.P.R. Terminal, adding, "You may recall that I allowed you to put your name on the Plan as Associate Architect. At the time you expressed appreciation." He then maintained that he was responsible for both the conception and elaboration of the Crystal Garden, "which has been adhered to except in minor details and in designing the Exterior, also in attending various Public meetings and later in negotiating with the C.P.R. All this work was done before I asked you if you would care to do the draughting work etc., all as you had done on the C.P.R. Depot. But in this case I agreed to give ½ of the fees – viz about $4,000, and you were quite satisfied. Now that the Building is completed, you ask me if I will give you $6,500 and content myself with the balance of $1,500." He regarded James's request as unreasonable, since, as he justly declared, "You were quite at liberty to decline the work & I could have either done it myself or engaged a Draughtsman at much less cost to myself. But you were not only satisfied with the terms but very pleased to get the work or so you said."

Where Rattenbury was unfair to James was in the implication that he had acted merely as a draughtsman rather than as an assistant. James, however, was no less at fault in wishing to change their agreement at so late a date. Perhaps it was a vindictive James who either wrote, or caused to be written, an anonymous letter printed in the *Colonist* on 9 June claiming that Rattenbury had only made sketches for the Crystal Garden. Misguidedly, Rattenbury submitted an irascible reply, published in the same newspaper on 11 June, in which he, too, ignored the facts by claiming that he had not brought James into the commission until after the contract with the company had been signed in the previous November. Confronted by James's exhaustive list of his undeniably important contributions, and opposed by Gardom, Rattenbury ultimately had the sense to increase his associate's share of the commission.[43]

Yet, to propose that the Crystal Garden was not the creation of Rattenbury, or that it is the "magnum opus" of James, would be to overstate the case.[44] The complex is not so far removed from the sketches of 1921 as to suggest a total reinterpretation by James. The substitution of brick walls articulated with pilasters is wholly in character with Rattenbury's work as, for example, in the British Columbia Electric Company Offices. The chief innovation in the final scheme – the decision to erect the structure on a reinforced concrete foundation raft – could well have been proposed by the consulting engineer, David Hardy of Vancouver. James was not an

innovator. Before he returned to England in 1914 to enlist in the British
Army, his designs had followed the blend of regular Tudor and Arts and
Crafts styles popularized by Rattenbury and Maclure. His post-war architecture was no less conventional, and his largest commission, the Federal
Building and Post Office on Government Street, begun in 1947, is a conservative version of the "International Style" which had its first expression
in Europe in the late 1920's. What he did supply, and what Rattenbury
did not wish to give, was the concentrated application to the details of the
complex and its erection. James probably redesigned the pool (the C.P.R.
later engaged him to install a pool in their new hotel at Lake Louise) as
well as the specific layout of the associated facilities and the roof structure.
Here Rattenbury and James both erred, for inadequate provision was
made for the problem of condensation. As a consequence, the pillars and
girders became eroded, a contributory factor to the closure of the Crystal
Garden in 1967. Another weakness in the scheme did not become apparent until 1955. By then the salt water had corroded the pipes and heating
system to the extent that fresh water had to be substituted and a chlorin-
ation plant installed.

Nevertheless, when opened formally on 26 June 1925, the Crystal Garden was hailed as the "Largest swimming pool in Canada" and described
by D.C. Coleman, vice-president of the C.P.R., as an "earnest" of the
company's determination "to make Victoria, Vancouver and British
Columbia in general, the playground of the Western World."[45] For at
least two generations it was the centre of civic social life, and even likened
to a "fairyland."[46] Thus Rattenbury's long-cherished dream was realized
in the last of his commissions to be completed in Victoria, one which
again left an indelible mark upon the city and province (Figs.8.14-15).
Happily, although his "palace of pleasure" languished in a state of dis-
repair for some years, it has been restored as a conservatory and aviary
with a tea-room, dance floor, and restaurant.

"L'Affaire Rattenbury," as James dubbed their disagreement, had serious consequences for Rattenbury's professional standing. It may have reminded the C.P.R. of their problems over the Empress and prompted
the company not to employ him, despite his undoubted qualifications, in
the ambitious programme of hotel-building implemented in the mid-
1920's under the presidency of Sir Edward Beatty, which embraced the reconstruction of the Château Lake Louise, 1925, the Banff Springs, 1926,
and the lavish station hotel at Calgary, 1927. Another factor in their decision, and even in Gardom's attitude towards him, could have been the
scandal aroused by Rattenbury's open courtship of Alma. Compounding

rather than removing the social stigma, both obtained their divorces in 1925. In Rattenbury's case it was granted in January 1925, Florrie having finally agreed to take legal action at the urging of Frank and Mary. Within two months Rattenbury married Alma (Fig.8.16).[47] He agreed to pay Florrie an annual allowance of $225 and to build her a house, designed by Maclure, on a site overlooking Iechinihl.[48] There she died in 1929.[49]

Rattenbury was too infatuated with Alma to care about the shocked reaction of most Victorians. "I got married again, over two months ago," he jubilantly wrote to Kate on 2 June 1925. "I've hesitated writing until I saw how it was going to work out, altho' I have known Alma for over two years. She is the niece of a great friend of mine." He felt that he "had struck oil" and hastened to supply a description. Aged thirty, she looked "like a fragile Madonna, rather sad" yet was "really full of fun, ready for any prank" and "intensely in earnest." She was "full of sympathy and keen to see the nice side of everyone and flares up with rage over any meanness. Talented in literature and poetry and gets a world of amusement out of any living thing, from bugs upwards; butterflies eat out of her hands." She had been "a musical prodigy at 5, practised under the best masters, 'de Packmann etc.' some ten hours a day for nearly 15 years, won every diploma and prize. Gave a piano recital, one after the other, with Samaroff at 25. Musicians say that she is a divine player, that there is none who can surpass her." There follows an equally effusive account of her war service and "awful life" with Pakenham, by whom she had "one young son who will be Lord Longford."[50] Alma was, in short, "a very entertaining, most loveable human soul. And best of all, simply adored by all her girl friends, including those who lived with her in France and by all the elderly people as well." He could not "tell why she has linked up with me—at her age it seems unreasonable, for she had the world at her feet. Perhaps the restful life appealed, and she seems to find all kinds of qualities in me that she likes that I never knew of." As a consequence, it looked "like some years of happiness and interest instead of the loneliness that I see so much around."

Despite his happiness, Rattenbury was very deeply hurt by the hostility of his family in Victoria and their constant efforts to malign Alma in public. "After a good many years of vulgarity," he wrote in an uncharacteristically bitter letter to Mary on 16 October 1925, "you began and for five years have not even tried to be pleasant and the last two years you have done every blessed thing that you could think of to be as unpleasant and vindictive as you know how. . . . I am glad to inform you that I have a delightful home full of kindness, merriment, music and everything that is delightful in life. There is no happier home in the Universe — I don't want even to be reminded of the rotten past life."[51]

The mutual affection between Rattenbury and Alma deepened over the ensuing year. "We are very happy," he wrote to Kate on 1 September 1926, "Alma is a brick and a wonderfully bright and loveable companion. I can't imagine life without her and fortunately she seems as contented with me. With the disparity in years, it seems astonishing to me. We seem to enter into everything together, as if we were the same age." He nursed her devotedly when her health deteriorated alarmingly in 1927. To some hostile Victorians her condition was the consequence of alcoholism or even drug addiction. In fact, as Rattenbury wrote to Kate on 10 February 1928, she had "an abscess on the brain and at least a pint of evil smelling clotted blood and mucus passed out of her nose and ears — lost 12 lbs in weight — but today has just gone out motoring feeling as happy and light-headed as a sand-boy. It is unbelievable, and how most of the time she kept going is beyond me." Then, in May, came joyous news. "Just as she had beautifully recovered she slipped and has a badly sprained ankle; kept her a month in bed and it will bother her for months but she does not seem to mind it a bit, getting rid of her nightmare has been a wonderful thing. And now all the poison is out of her system, lo and behold, her great wish of years is coming true and she is going to be a mother. She is delighted beyond measure and that child will certainly get lots of love — he ought to be some child."

The relentless hostility of Victorian society towards the Rattenburys was, no doubt, a factor in their decision to leave British Columbia. However, the main cause seems to have been the final collapse of his northern investments. On 19 September 1927, five years after it had been ordered into liquidation, Rattenbury Lands was wound up and its name erased from the list of registered companies.[52] In that month Rattenbury decided to seek redress by bringing a suit against the government, which was heard before Mr. Justice Morrison of the British Columbia Supreme Court (in British Columbia the provincial court of first resort, below the Appeal Court). His plea was based on a decision of the Privy Council of Canada which prescribed that where a tax was imposed in such a way as to embrace people known and unknown, and the court was unable to distinguish between them, the imposition was to be viewed as indirect taxation and hence *ultra vires* (beyond the powers of the province). Rattenbury claimed that the imposition of a penalty tax for failure to improve undeveloped lands within a district which had been declared a settlement area constituted an "indirect tax" within the terms of the Privy Council decision. He further argued that the low valuations assigned to land by the board had undermined his development schemes and forced settlers to abandon property on which they had paid deposits. Hence he was suing the board for his loss of $500,000. The provincial government responded that the board, as an agency of the government, could not be sued.

Rattenbury won a minor victory at a preliminary hearing when Mr. Justice Morrison decreed that the board could in fact be sued. But this was only the first round, since the case was then considered by the Court of Appeal. "The law case has been before the Court of Appeal," he wrote in a letter to Kate of 10 February, "and we are awaiting their decision next month. The technical and legal points did not appear in the paper or I would have sent one—it would have interested Frank [Kate's solicitor husband]. It all resolved itself into whether the taxation is 'Direct' or 'Indirect.' We claim 'Indirect,' which is beyond the powers of a Provincial Government. If we win the case we shall this fall take a steamer direct from here through the Panama canal to England, thus obviating the tedious railway journey, so you bet I'm hoping the decision will be in my favour."

On 28 March 1928, the Court of Appeal overturned Morrison's ruling. The taxation powers of the board were also pronounced *intra vires*, and Rattenbury was informed that he had no right of action against the board. With a characteristic refusal to accept defeat and hoping, as he implied in his May letter, to circumvent the fact that in British Columbia "the local judges are political appointees," he decided to take the case to the Supreme Court of Canada. The optimism of that May letter—"I'm feeling top hole, and full of luck"—must have been confounded when, on 26 November, the Supreme Court of Canada upheld the decision of the British Columbia Court of Appeal.

It would be an exaggeration to claim that the loss of his landholdings and the subsequent legal costs impoverished Rattenbury. He still owned stocks in a number of firms (such as the Melrose Paint Company) and, despite his public protestations, had the good sense not to commit all of his assets to his land investments. Nevertheless, his losses were considerable. Over a quarter of a century earlier he had suffered a similar, if less serious, financial blow as a result of his speculations in the North; on that occasion his thriving architectural practice had sustained him. By the end of 1928, however, there did not seem any likelihood of his being able to recoup these losses through architectural commissions. Symptomatic of his declining fame, none of his homes was mentioned in an article on domestic design published in the November 1928 issue of the *Journal of the Royal Architectural Institute of Canada.*[53] He was surely cheered by the birth of his second son, John, in December, but his only prospective work, the "Campanile Hotel," was still, as he had noted in a postscript of his February letter to Kate, "not yet a certainty." By May 1929 the "big Hotel" was "hanging fire." Little can be ascertained about the project beyond the family tradition that it was to be erected on Douglas Garden for a rival company to the C.P.R. This could only have been the C.N.R., which had acquired the G.T.P.'s title to the property but eventually built the Château Victoria Hotel on a different site.[54] Evidently inspired by the celebrated campanile in Venice, the "Campanile" form may have been chosen by Rattenbury to rival the tower W.S. Painter had designed for the "New Wing" he was then adding to the Empress Hotel – almost certainly not to Rattenbury's liking, since it spoiled the symmetry of the original structure (Figs.8.17–18). The motif was currently enjoying a renewed popularity in American architecture, initiated by the triumph of Raymond Hood's Neo-Gothic tower design in the much heralded *Chicago Tribune* competition of 1922 and reflected in contemporary eastern Canadian commercial design.[55] Rattenbury's hope that the commission would "probably come off one of these days," proved to be false; the collapse of the North American economy in the wake of the "Great Crash" of October 1929 decided the company to shelve the project.

That month his old friend Maclure died, honoured by an obituary in the October issue of the *Journal of the Royal Architectural Institute of Canada*, written, ironically, by P.L. James.[56] Maclure's death perhaps symbolized the close of an era to Rattenbury and hastened a desire to seek a new beginning. He resolved to quit the province and the city in which he no longer felt welcome and to return to England permanently. That his son could be baptised in the ancestral parish church at Okehampton must have been a consolation (Fig.19–20). A last act before departing was a generous one: Rattenbury arranged that his Chinese houseman, Foy, should receive an allowance for the remainder of his life.[57]

Nine

ENGLAND
1930–1935

The journey from Victoria to England took over six months. Accompanied by a nursemaid, the Rattenburys sailed through the Panama Canal and from there to Havana. On the voyage from Havana to New York, Rattenbury joined a marathon card session, not realizing that he was dealing with professional card-sharps. By the time they reached New York, he owed a considerable sum and was threatened with violence if he failed to settle. Compton recalls how the whole family was roused in the middle of the night. They escaped from New York by train and headed for Montreal, where they took ship for Europe. Eventually they reached the Mediterranean, spending some time in Venice and in Northern France, where Compton attended school.

When the Rattenburys finally reached England in the summer of 1930, they decided to settle in Bournemouth, a city often likened to Victoria. From a Mrs. Price they rented a pleasant house called the "Villa Madeira," at 5 Manor Road, just opposite St. Swithin's Church (Fig.9.1). The house, though modest by the very comfortable standards to which Rattenbury had become accustomed, was delightfully situated on a quiet street shaded by pines and only a few minutes walk from the magnificent cliffs and beach. Initially, they seem to have been very content, although Rattenbury apparently had no architectural work, the apartment block that he was designing at the time of his death being perhaps his only commission. However, he still retained his zest for commercial enterprises.

With a friend he rented a laboratory close to Trafalgar Square, where they developed and produced a successful antiseptic and mouthwash.

Above all, Rattenbury found pleasure in Alma's musical career. Her grand piano had been shipped over from Canada, and in addition, she resumed playing her violin. On family outings to the New Forest they would sit in quiet clearings among the trees and Alma would play. Her ambitions had now, however, turned from the classical to the popular field, and she began to write romantic songs, with simple melodies and rather trite lyrics.

Rattenbury zealously promoted her career, describing his efforts in a letter to his sister on 12 December 1931. He had approached the music publisher Boosey, with no luck. Undaunted, he went to see the conductor Sir Dan Godfrey, who arranged an introduction to Van Lier, the head of Keith Prowse and Co.:

> Van Lier was a nice fellow (he is a great musician himself). We talked for a time, then he said, indifferently, "Well, play over one of the numbers, the one you think best." Alma in 2 minutes had him enthralled. At the end of ten minutes I said to him, "Well, what do you think?" He said, "I am greatly impressed," and said he would publish one number, have it orchestrated and broadcast all over, and two other numbers for the piano. . . . At present he is at Alma's feet. He told me "she is marvellous. I have travelled all over the world and into all kinds of places for tunes—there are few of them, it is one of the scarcest gifts of humanity, and here is your wife, her mind teeming with exquisite tunes."

"The greatest Publisher in London is absolutely at Alma's feet, acclaiming her as a genius," he repeated later in that fulsome letter, and while Alma was "almost dizzy with it all," she remained "still as simple as ever." He thought her prospects to be unlimited. "Of course it means coming to London to live, it is inevitable: She will be called upon to write music for the Theatres and for Elstree [film studios]."

Alma's success was real, although not as outstanding as Rattenbury had convinced himself, for he had resumed, in many ways, the enthusiasm of his great Yukon venture. It brought in its train a full social life, and the house at Bournemouth became the centre for lively parties, with guests of the stature of Richard Tauber. For quieter relaxation the Rattenburys took holidays in seaside resorts with relatives (Fig.9.2) and were often in London, where they would entertain his nephew, Keith Miller Jones, by then a well-established solicitor; even in the late 1970's Miller Jones could still vividly recall his uncle's happiness during the early years after his return to England.

Increasingly, however, Rattenbury's well-being was marred by a preoccupation with his financial situation. In the 1930's Britain was suffering the effects of the worldwide depression that followed the 1929 crash. Rattenbury, still smarting from the enormous financial loss he suffered as a result of the adverse court decision on his northern lands, endured further losses on the stock market after arriving in England, although by the general standards of the day he was comfortably situated, even wealthy, with a domestic staff and a Fiat car (acquired on the continent in 1930); on his death he left an estate of over $45,000.[1] Nevertheless, he could not escape the conviction that he was headed for financial doom. At first, his parsimony could be treated, as it always had been, as something of a family joke. His stepson Compton recalls Rattenbury asking Sir Edward Lockton to post some letters in town for him after a visit to Bournemouth, then chuckling as he told Compton that they had no stamps on them. But he soon lost the ability to laugh at his failings; indeed, his anxiety was to grow so obsessive that by 1934 he was openly talking about suicide. The situation was aggravated by Alma's extravagence. Rattenbury paid her an annual allowance of £1,000, a considerable sum in those days, even though it had to cover the wages of their staff and the school fees for the boys. He did not require her to account for her expenditures, which not infrequently exceeded the allowance. "Expenses were never brought up in my life with Mr. Rattenbury," she later remarked.[2] If she needed extra money for something that he might consider frivolous she found it expedient to concoct plausible excuses. Thus, on one occasion she wheedled £250 out of him for a trip to London, pretending that she needed an operation (she was, indeed, suffering from pulmonary tuberculosis). Rattenbury had commented that it would involve him in considerable expense, and when later reminded of his protestations, she replied, "Yes, but he always all his life talked like that, so that no-one ever took him seriously on the point of money." When asked why she had recourse to subterfuges to get money, her answer was equally simple, "It saved rows." Alma was irresponsibly generous, giving money and possessions away on impulse: "If anyone sees a cigarette holder and likes it, I always say 'Take it.' It is my disposition."

As Rattenbury's depressions deepened (Fig.9.3), Alma's career flourished. She produced several records with Frank Titterton, the popular tenor: "Zanita," "By Naples Water," "By Some Mistake," "Avalette," "Sheldermene," "You Brought My Heart the Sunshine." The B.B.C. broadcast special performances of her music.[3] With her lively, extrovert personality, she found it easy to make friends in the sophisticated musical circles that were now open to her. She became the object of much com-

9.1 The 'Villa Madeira' Bournemouth, photographed in the 1950's (the adjacent buildings are recent).

9.2 Family holidays in the 1930's. The hatted figure is Rattenbury.

9.3 Rattenbury in the 1930's.

ment from her neighbours in Bournemouth. Her fine clothes and trips to London aroused envy, and it was considered a mark of decadence that she would hold all-night parties in her garden with the lights blazing and the gramophone playing loudly.

In September 1934 the Rattenburys decided to hire a chauffeur to drive John to a local prep school (Compton was attending "Cliff House," a boarding school in nearby Southborne). They advertised in the Bournemouth *Daily Echo* and hired a local lad, George Percy Stoner. The son of a bricklayer, Stoner, had, as a child, moved around the country while his father sought work. As a consequence he had little formal education and a very limited experience of life. It is perhaps difficult to understand why Alma, in her late thirties, talented, well-travelled, and thrice married, was attracted by a dull, rather gauche, teenager. Be that as it may, they became lovers in about November 1934. Whether Rattenbury suspected her infidelity or condoned the liaison has never been established. By all accounts the household remained a fairly congenial one; Alma and her husband seem to have retained a great deal of affection if not passion for each other, and Rattenbury and Stoner were on relaxed and friendly terms, often spending their evenings playing cards and conversing pleasantly on trivial, everyday matters. By the beginning of the following year, 1935, Alma was having qualms about her affair and tried to end it. But Stoner had begun to enjoy his new status and proof of his manliness. He refused to be put aside and even threatened Alma's life. He assumed a posture of bravado, carrying a dagger with a four-inch blade and keeping an air pistol in a box in his room. Then, in March, Stoner and Alma went on a trip to London, where they stayed in some style at the Royal Palace Hotel, Kensington, spending lavishly on clothes and jewellery.[4]

The experience seems to have unhinged Stoner's weak and impressionable mind and to have affected his behaviour on the night of 23 March, shortly after their return to Bournemouth. The Rattenburys were planning to visit a Mr. Jenks, a solicitor and entrepreneur who lived in nearby Bridport, the following day. Rattenbury had designed an apartment block and hoped to persuade Jenks, a close friend, to invest in it. Evidently Rattenbury was still aware of Alma's magnetic personality and asked her to exert her charms on Jenks. Stoner overheard the conversation and put the worst possible complexion on it.[5] Later that evening he entered the living room where Rattenbury sat reading and struck him about the head three times with a heavy mallet. He then confessed to Alma, who made a vain attempt to revive her husband. A local surgeon was summoned to the house, and after Rattenbury had been taken to the nearby

Strathallen Nursing Home, an emergency operation was attempted. It was in vain; Rattenbury hovered between life and death until the morning of 28 March, when he died without regaining consciousness.

At first, both Alma and Stoner claimed responsibility for the murder, each trying to protect the other. Alma was persuaded to change her plea only after she had been visited in Holloway Jail by Compton. Stoner never denied that he had struck Rattenbury, and his counsel pleaded temporary insanity. They were jointly charged and their trial began at the Old Bailey on 28 May 1935.[6] The trial was one of the most sensational of the 1930's, reported widely in the international press. Partisan crowds lined the streets outside the court as 31 May, the day of the verdict, approached. Stoner was found guilty (his sentence was later commuted), Alma acquitted. But she was hounded by journalists, and Keith Miller Jones, who had assumed general responsibility for his uncle's family, arranged for her to stay at the Cleveland Nursing Home in Bayswater. Alma's thoughts were constantly on her children; after only two days she left the nursing home in a state of mental turmoil and took a train for Bournemouth, apparently with a hazy notion of going to see them.[7] On the journey she seems to have realized that crowds would be waiting for her at the house, and she left the train at the nearby village of Christchurch. She walked to the River Avon, stabbed herself with a knife and jumped into the river. Her desperate actions were seen by a passer-by, but she died of her wounds before she could be pulled out of the water.

Alma thus died some two months after her husband, in circumstances equally tragic. She was buried close by him in the Wimborne Road Cemetery. Both graves remain unmarked, mute evidence, in Rattenbury's case, that the monuments to his achievements stand in scenes far distant, in the young towns and rugged landscape of British Columbia.

Appendix A

LIST OF ARCHITECTURAL WORKS AND DESIGNS

The location of original drawings and documentation appears in parentheses at the end of each entry. The symbol A before an entry signifies an unverified attribution. The dimensions and media of the drawings have not been included in this list since most are located in public collections and hence catalogued.

1890 "Design for a Public Day School." This admirably conceived scheme won the prestigious Soane Medallion, awarded under the auspices of the Royal Institute of British Architects. "On the type of the old Elizabethan Grammar Schools," the design is also notable for a well-considered and functional plan. Figs.1.11–12.

1891 Town Hall, Cleckheaton, Yorkshire. While apprenticed in his uncles'
–92 firm, Rattenbury was responsible, either wholly or in part, for the design of this Queen Anne style building, which anticipates many features of his work in British Columbia. Exhibited (entry no. 1750) at the Royal Academy of Arts, London, 1891, under the name of Mawson and Hudson. Fig.1.13.

1892 Roursay Brothers and Company Building, Hastings Street, Vancouver. *The Contract Record and Engineering Review* (hereafter *Contract Record*) for 20 August reported that Rattenbury was preparing plans for this building. There is no documentary evidence to confirm whether this commission materialized, as is the case with the other minor schemes cited in this journal and listed below.

—   Davis Block, intersection of Oppenheimer Street and Westminster Avenue, Vancouver; designs for a three-storey brick and stone building are noted in the *Contract Record* for 26 November.

— A   Roedde House, 1415 Barclay Street, Vancouver. A frame house that combines elements of the British and North American Queen Anne Styles formerly attributed to Rattenbury.

1893   Commercial building, intersection of Cambie and Water Streets, Vancouver; a three-storey block with basement commissioned by "an English client" to replace the Cabinet Hotel, announced in the *Contract Record* for 23 February.

—   Commercial building, Chapel Lane, Bradford. This attractive eclectic design, combining elements of the British Queen Anne and Canadian Château styles, was probably drawn by Rattenbury after settling at Vancouver. Illustrated in the March issue of *The Canadian Architect and Builder*. Fig.2.1.

—   House for C. J. Holtanz, M.R.C.S., Undercliffe, near Bradford. Also published in the March *Canadian Architect and Builder*, the design is typical of contemporary affluent suburban architecture, combining Queen Anne ornamental features with the simpler composition of the Arts and Crafts style. Fig.2.2.

—   Legislative Buildings, Victoria. Rattenbury won the international competition for the new Legislative Assembly of British Columbia in November 1893 with a scheme that synthesizes the British High Victorian Gothic and mid-nineteenth-century Italianate with the American Richardsonian Romanesque styles. Completed by 1898, after a change of contractor and a number of disputes between Rattenbury and his employers, for almost $900,000, more than double the original appropriation (P.A.B.C). Figs.2.3–6, 7–12, 15–16, 22–23, 27.

1894   Courthouse, Chilliwack, B.C. A small frame structure that blends the American vernacular with the Queen Anne style. Burned down, 1951. Fig.2.17.

—   Two unidentified houses in Vancouver, noted in a letter to his uncle, dated 25 August 1894; it is possible that neither was erected.

—   Courthouse, Nanaimo, B.C. Commissioned in 1894 but built between 1895 and 1896, this is a simplified version of the central section of the Victoria Legislative Buildings with Château-style pitched roofs on the corner towers. Fig.2.17.

1895   Victoria Canoe Club, Victoria. Rattenbury was said to be preparing plans for a clubhouse in the 21 March *Contract Record.*

1896   Bank of Montreal, Government Street, Victoria. Rattenbury won an open competition for the bank's main branch with a Château design, responding to the rising popularity in Canada of this synthesis of early

Renaissance English and French architecture. Completed in 1897, the façade on Government Street has been extended, and the original interior unsympathetically modernized. Fig.2.22.

1897 British Columbia Electric Railway Company, first office and car shed, Carrall and Hastings Streets, Vancouver. The plain Renaissance style anticipates his later commercial buildings, and the unifying arches and corner entrance recall the Victoria Bank. Opened 2 September 1898. Fig. 2.26.

c.1897A House for A. S. Dumbleton, 1648 Rockland Avenue, Victoria. Called "Newholme" and erected on a site immediately below the E. V. Bodwell House (see 1899), it was built in a simplified Queen Anne-cum-Arts and Crafts style with Tudor detailing akin to Rattenbury's current domestic work. The date of the house, but not the attribution, is in Gregson, *Victoria*, p.109.

1898 Iechinihl, 1701 Beach Drive, Oak Bay, Victoria. For his personal use Rattenbury designed a small house from the Queen Anne mode of R. N. Shaw and the British and American Arts and Crafts styles. The house was extended on the west side in 1902 and a garage added in 1912. An earlier preliminary study for the house may be represented in a sketch dated May, 1897, discovered in London among his personal letters. Now Glenlyon School. (See also 1904.) Figs.3.2;5.15

— Hotel, Glenora (Telegraph Creek), B.C. Rattenbury called for tenders for a sixty-room hotel in the *Contract Record* for 11 May.

— Bank of Montreal, Rossland, B.C. A photograph of a sketch elevation for this branch, signed and dated "1898," remains in the Provincial Archives. The executed building represents a chastened version of Lockwood and Mawson's Italianate style. The interior has been remodelled (P.A.B.C.). Fig.3.6.

— Bank of Montreal, Church and Columbia Streets, New Westminster. Faced with brick, but with fire-proof concrete banking hall and vault, the façade echoes the Sullivanesque design of Maclure's Temple Building, Victoria (1893), while retaining the domical corner motifs of the Parliament Buildings. Since demolished. Fig.3.8.

1899 Bank of Montreal, 286–291 Baker Street, Nelson, B.C. Estimated at $35,000 in the *Colonist*, 24 December 1899, this is the most elegant of the bank's three branches located in the interior. The symmetrical composition and crisp Classical detailing represent a move away from the Italianate to the academic Classicism of the Beaux-Arts style, by then popular in both the United States and Europe. Fig.3.7.

— Hotel, Greenwood, B.C. Of frame construction, in the American vernacular, this three-storey hotel, 50 by 80 feet, was commissioned by Messrs. Graham and Perry, according to the *Contract Record* for 27 September. Since demolished. Fig.3.5.

– Two commercial buildings, New Westminster, B.C. These are listed with other contemporary commissions in an article printed in the *Colonist*, 24 December 1899. One may have been the Brown Block. Both later demolished.

– Hotel, Rossland, B.C. Estimated at $75,000 in the *Colonist*. This may have been built as the Hotel Strathcona, a large four-storey structure illustrated in Henderson's *Gazetteer* for 1904. Since demolished.

– House (probably for Patrick Burns), Deer Park, B.C. Estimated at $10,000 in the *Colonist*. There is no documentary evidence of its erection.

– Cold Storage Depots at Vancouver and Nelson, and possibly also at New Westminster and Greenwood, for P. Burns and Company Ltd. The Vancouver depot was estimated at $20,000 in the *Colonist*; noted in the *Contract Record* for 27 September. All since demolished.

– "Block of Stores," Vancouver, estimated at $15,000 in the *Colonist*, but not identified.

– Office Block, Calgary, Alberta, for P. Burns. Since demolished, its site has not been located.

– House for E. V. Bodwell, 1626 Rockland (formerly Belcher) Avenue, Victoria. In the current American vernacular of wood frame houses, estimated in the *Colonist* at $15,000 (the *Contract Record* for 27 September stated that the contract was let at $4,000). Fig.3.12.

– Courthouse, Bastion Square, Victoria. Rattenbury renovated the interior of H. O. Tiedemann's building (1889), adding new courtrooms, providing larger fireproof accommodation for the Land Registry Office and installing an elevator. He also introduced a new entrance on Bastion Street. Completed in January 1901 at a cost in excess of $50,000. Altered on various occasions, and now housing the Provincial Maritime Museum (P.A.B.C.). Fig.3. 14–15.

– House for P. Burns, 4th Street South West, Calgary. Commissioned in 1899 (Rattenbury was said to be "preparing plans" in the *Contract Record* for 5 August 1900), this mansion was built of stone between 1901 and 1903 in a Neo-Gothic style but with both Arts and Crafts and Château motifs. Demolished in 1956. Fig.3.16.

1900 Hotel Vancouver, Granville, Georgia and Howe Streets, Vancouver. In the fall of 1900 Rattenbury entered a Château design (which anticipated the Empress in Victoria) in the competition organized by the C.P.R. to replace T. Sorby's enlarged hotel. He was awarded the commission in January 1901, and then estimated the cost of the new structure, to hold 250 bedrooms, at between $400,000 and $500,000; Rattenbury called for tenders, giving the estimated cost as $400,000 and announcing that work would begin in the new wing along Georgia Street (*Contract Record*, 1 May 1901). However, he changed the design, if not the "H" plan into a sophisticated Renaissance style; the second design was published in *The Railway and Shipping World*, April 1902. Only the west wing, on Georgia and Howe Streets, was built (1903–1905), the interiors of the existing structures being remodelled. Of steel frame construction and fireproofed, Rattenbury's wing was enlarged 1910–13 and demolished 1946 (C.P.R. Archives). Figs. 4.2, 13–14.

– Office Block, Bastion and Langley Streets, Victoria. In a letter to his mother, dated 18 December 1900, Rattenbury reported that he had received tenders for an office block in the city. The *Contract Record* for 19 December noted that he was calling for tenders for a pressed brick and terra cotta building at this location.

– House for Resident Medical Officer, Jubilee (later, Royal Jubilee) Hospital. Designed without fee; the award for its construction was listed in the *Contract Record* for 10 October 1900.

– Hospital, B.C. The only reference to this unidentified design for a hospital "up country" appears in a letter of 18 December 1900, where he describes it as a "fairly large building, though not costly at all."

1901 House for Lyman P. Duff, Q.C., 1745 Rockland Avenue, Victoria. An attractive Queen Anne-cum-Arts and Crafts style frame house, notable for a large shingled gable and a fine hand-carved fir staircase. It survives with some alterations. Fig.4.6.

– Hotel Field, or Mount Stephen House, Field, B.C. On 18 February 1901, Rattenbury told the Vancouver *Province* that he was preparing plans for a $20,000 hotel in the Swiss Chalet style to contain fifty rooms. The style of this wood frame addition to Sorby's existing small hotel was actually closer to the Queen Anne with some Tudor details. Designed in March 1901 and completed by March 1902, when the enlarged building was illustrated in *The Railway and Shipping World*. Demolished in the early 1950's (C.P.R. Archives, C.P. Hotels Ltd., Toronto). Fig.4.5.

– B.C. Electric Company Car Depot, Pembroke Street, Victoria. Mentioned in a letter of 20 August 1901 to his mother, this plain brick structure survives. He probably designed an addition measuring 120 feet by 60 feet built along Discovery Street.

– Jubilee Hospital, Victoria. Rattenbury provided, without fee, a design for a children's ward, pay ward, diet kitchen and nurses' home for this hospital, estimated in his 20 August letter at $20,000. The commission was listed in the *Contract Record* for 4 December 1901. Executed, but since altered.

– Victoria High School, Yates, Fernwood and Fort Streets, Victoria. Rattenbury won the open competition for the third High School with, in his opinion, the inferior of two designs. Estimated on 20 August at $30,000, it was built of brick with stone facings in a spare Neo-Gothic style. The *Contract Record* for 15 January 1902 called for tenders for the hot water heating system. Fig.4.11.

–   Scholefield Block, Victoria. In his letter of 20 August Rattenbury also mentioned the award of this commission and estimated the cost at $20,000. There is no conclusive evidence of its location in the Victoria City Archives, nor whether it was in fact built.

–   Paardeburg Gate Memorial, Belleville Street, Victoria, The *Contract Record* for 2 January announced that Rattenbury was preparing plans for this memorial, presumably to commemorate soldiers from Canadian regiments who had died in the Boer War; the Royal Canadian Regiment had performed particularly well in the battle. It was to have been erected opposite the main entrance to the Legislative Building at an estimated cost of $25,000. The project was abandoned.

–   Cable Station, Bamfield, Vancouver Island. Rattenbury designed a large Queen Anne style accommodation block, also containing the telegraphic equipment, linked to a house for the chief telegraphist and a small structure for the cable terminal. Officially opened on 1 November 1902, subsequently extended before being closed in 1959, and largely demolished in 1965. Fig.4.12.

–   Government House, "Cary Castle," Rockland Avenue, Victoria. Following the destruction of the old Cary Castle in May 1899, Rattenbury offered to provide a design on 27 August 1900, but refused to submit an entry to the competition subsequently organized by the government. This was won in January 1901 by a Vancouver firm, whose estimates Rattenbury was asked to verify in August. He claimed that these were too low, and after suggesting that he could provide a cheaper design, estimated at $60,000, and requesting that Maclure be appointed executive architect, he was awarded the commission. While Maclure (who was ill during the construction) probably planned the interior, the asymmetrical Neo-Gothic and Neo-Tudor exterior was surely the work of Rattenbury. His conduct of the commission was lax; the final costs exceeded the budget by nearly $30,000 and became the subject of a parliamentary committee of enquiry which, nonetheless, quashed all accusations of fraud. Completed in 1903, but destroyed by fire in 1957 (P.A.B.C.). Figs.4.7–9.

1902   House for James Herrick McGregor, 1447 Mount Baker Avenue (later St. David), Victoria. This was the first of Rattenbury's more symmetrical Neo-Tudor houses, which anticipated the style Maclure was to adopt in his domestic work from about 1905. Fig.4.10

–   Union Club, 805 Gordon St., Victoria. He added a new wing to the existing structure, demolished in 1914 to make way for a new clubhouse.

–   Hotel Dallas, Victoria. Rattenbury renovated the hotel in the spring of 1902.

–   Hotel Field, Field, B.C. Rattenbury added a separate large wood frame wing behind the enlarged hotel in a more Tudor version of the Queen Anne style. This seems to have been finished by October at a cost of approximately $24,000, as noted in the C.P.R.'s *Contracts and Proposals* book, 1903–10. Demolished in the early 1950's (C.P.R. Archives). Fig.5.4.

— Lake Louise Hotel, Lake Louise, Alberta. In 1902 Rattenbury designed the first of at least one wood-frame extension to the second chalet hotel by Sorby, in a picturesque Arts and Crafts style. This wing cost $31,288 and was further improved in 1903 for about $5,000; C.P.R. *Contracts and Proposals* book, 1903–10. Altered by W. S. Painter after 1906, Rattenbury's additions burned down in 1924 (C.P.R. Archives). Fig.5.5–6.

— C.P.R. Hotel, Summerland, B.C. The *Contract Record* for 4 June 1902 stated that Rattenbury would draw plans for a "first class hotel" estimated to cost $50,000. The hotel was presumably to be situated on the shore of Okanagan Lake. Not executed.

— Electric Street Car Depot, Vancouver. Rattenbury referred to enquiries about a depot in a letter to his mother dated 12 June 1902, possibly either for a new building for the B.C. Electric Company or for additions to his earlier structure (1897).

— Glacier Hotel, Glacier, B.C. The commission for a new addition to Sorby's hotel appears to have been awarded by the C.P.R. during the summer of 1902. Finished by December at a cost of $32,660. The company's index of hotel drawings lists designs for Glacier by Rattenbury for the period 1902–1904, probably detailing other additions. These were all demolished in the 1920's (C.P.R. Archives, C.P. Hotels Ltd., Toronto). Fig.5.8–10.

—A Banff Springs Hotel, Banff Springs, Alberta. In 1902 Rattenbury apparently supervised the construction of a new wing on a site some sixty feet west of Price's original hotel; this could be the "$100,000 building" that Rattenbury, in a letter to his mother dated 2 October 1903, claimed Van Horne had given him to build. The wing, in an Arts and Crafts style, was reported to have been designed by Hutchinson and Wood of Montreal in *The Railway and Shipping World*, June 1902. It was completed in 1903 and cost some $100,500, providing an additional ninety-four bedrooms, which soon proved to be insufficient; a tower block was therefore erected on the west end, possibly to Rattenbury's designs. Demolished in 1926 to make way for the present hotel (C.P.R. Archives). Fig.5.2.

—A Revelstoke Hotel, Revelstoke, B.C. Rattenbury may have designed this structure, with a distinctive gambrel roof, for the C.P.R. (C.P.R. Archives).

1903? Courthouse, Ward and Vernon Streets, Nelson. The competition for a new courthouse had been announced in the winter of 1902. Rattenbury won it with a Château-style design. Erected with some changes between 1906 and 1909, following a delay caused by the poor economic state of the province during the intervening years (P.A.B.C.). Figs.5.13; 6.13–15.

—   Empress Hotel, Victoria (1). Rattenbury's first design, estimated at $300,000 and to house 175 bedrooms, was published in the *Colonist* on 23 May, 1903. It may, however, have been conceived earlier, and even at the time when the C.P.R. directors decided to extend rather than rebuild the Hotel Vancouver. The *Colonist* scheme shows an aggrandized version of the 1900 Hotel Vancouver design, occupying the present site on the reclaimed mud flats at the head of James Bay. (C.P.R. Archives). Fig.5.11. (See also 1904.)

—   Commercial building, Granville Street, Vancouver. The *Contract Record* for 21 January announced that Rattenbury was preparing plans for a four-storey structure to cost $60,000 for Sir William Van Horne; there is no documentary evidence to indicate that this commission was executed.

—   B.C. Land and Investment Agency building, Yates Street, Victoria. Rattenbury called for tenders on a three-storey brick building in the 18 March issue of the *Contract Record*. This was probably the office block "with 12 suites of offices and vaults" he mentioned working upon in his letter of 30 August 1903 to his mother. The Victoria directories suggest that this commission was abandoned.

—   "An addition to a hospital" noted in a letter to his mother dated 4 August 1903 and almost certainly the design for a further extension to the Jubilee Hospital the *Contract Record* for 5 August announced that Rattenbury was preparing. Not executed.

—   House for A. T. Howard, Oak Bay, Victoria. Rattenbury invited tenders in the 21 October issue of the *Contract Record*, but the Victoria directories do not confirm that the house was actually built.

1904 Emerald Lake Chalet Hotel, Emerald Lake, B.C. The C.P.R. Archives record that in January 1904 Rattenbury drew a design for the "Guides Cottage, Kitchen and Cool Room," since destroyed. This may have formed part of a general improvement of Sorby's original building (C.P.R. Archives). Fig.5.3.

—   Empress Hotel, Victoria (2). Rattenbury submitted "Working Plans" (dated March 1904) for the Empress Hotel in May 1904, which were revised on the advice of Hayter Reed by September and further refined by November; specifications for the revised drawings were made contemporaneously. The $465,000 contract for the steel-frame main block of the present hotel was signed in May 1905, and building began in August. The hotel, containing 163 bedrooms, pioneered a more regular type of Château design, adopted by later Canadian practitioners of the style. Following a request to undertake two relatively minor alterations in the internal plan, Rattenbury resigned from the commission in December 1906. Opened on 22 January 1908, the north and south wings, planned in outline by Rattenbury, were built between 1909 and 1914 under the supervision of W. S. Painter, who also added the ballroom at the rear in 1912. A larger extension designed by Painter was built from 1929 on the north side, introducing a picturesque irregularity at odds with Rattenbury's original conception; the interior has survived subsequent remodelling. (C.P.R. Archives. C.P. Hotels Ltd., Toronto, and Empress Hotel Archives). Figs.5.14, 16–22; 6.20A & B; 8.17–18.

—   B.C. Electric Railway Company building, 1016 Langley Street, Victoria. Although he referred to working on the designs in a letter to his mother dated 22 October 1904, actual construction was delayed until 1906, Rattenbury calling for tenders in the 28 March issue of the *Contract Record*. Besides altering the external fabric from stone to brick with stone facings, he appears to have retained his original design. A simplified version of the Nelson Bank of Montreal, it was completed by 1907. Rattenbury might also have designed the extension built on the west side in about 1912. Fig. 5.28.

—   The Oak Bay Hotel (later the Old Charming Inn), 1420 Beach Drive, Oak Bay. The irregular plan, shingled gables, and columned verandah represent a blend of the American Queen Anne and Arts and Crafts styles. Completed in 1905 and demolished in 1962 to make way for the Rudyard Kipling Apartment block. Fig.5.26.

—   C.P.R. Steamship Terminal, 468 Belleville Street, Victoria. Erected at a cost of $8,900 in a Neo-Tudor style but demolished in 1923 to make way for a second Rattenbury terminal. (See 1923.) (C.P.R. Archives). Figs.5.23A & B.

—   House for G. A. Kirk, "Riffham," 582 St. Charles Street, Victoria. A large frame house designed in an orderly and dignified Neo-Tudor style, with excellent interiors. Fig.5.27.

—   House for Mrs. Henry Clay, 810 Linden Avenue, Victoria. A smaller frame house blending Tudor half-timbering with the varied gables and projections of the Queen Anne style. Fig.5.25.

—   Conservatory, Iechinihl. Mentioned in a letter dated 14 November 1904, written to his sister Kate.

1905 A House for Doctor C. N. Cobbett, 1040 Pemberton Road, Victoria. The attribution of this frame house combining Queen Anne and Tudor features, since demolished, depends upon family tradition as related by Geoffrey Castle. Fig.5.24.

—   Glacier Hotel, Glacier, B.C. On 16 August 1905, Rattenbury wrote to Sir Thomas Shaughnessy about the creation of a "centre wing" and "wing A," both of which might have been executed. Demolished in the 1920's (C.P.R. Archives).

—   Lake Louise Chalet Hotel, Lake Louise, Alberta. In his letter of 16 August, Rattenbury also referred to an "addition on the hill" and a further extension at Lake Louise, implying that the former at least was about to be built. Altered 1906–11 by Painter and burned down in 1924 (C.P.R. Archives).

–   Two house designs. On 31 August, Rattenbury informed his mother that
       he had received commissions for one house to be built in Philadelphia and
       another in Manitoba, both presumably comparable in style to Iechinihl,
       as the prospective patrons had sought his services after "passing our
       house." No further evidence for these commissions has come to light.

–A   Humber's Furniture Store (now Law Chambers Building), 45 Bastion
       Square, Victoria. The eclectic Classical style of this building, its
       composition, and certain details of its articulation lend weight to its
       attribution to Rattenbury. Fig.5.29.

–   Warehouse building, mentioned in the 31 August letter. Unidentified,
       unless it is a reference to Humber's Furniture Store.

–   Second house for Judge Lampman, 1630 York Place, Victoria. In this
       house he combined elements of the Queen Anne style with the type of
       Arts and Crafts developed by F. L. Wright. Not begun until February
       1907, as reported in the *Colonist* on 3 January, giving the cost at about
       $6,200. The house was later enlarged and altered by Maclure. Fig.5.30

–   Internal decorations, C.P.R. Steamer, *Princess Victoria*.

1906   "Large Hospital," Edmonton. Mentioned in a letter to his mother dated 28
       January 1906. Unidentified.

–   Courthouse, Georgia Street, Vancouver. Rattenbury won the 1906
       competition with an impressive and noticeably chaste Beaux-Arts design
       that was well planned to fulfil the functions of a courthouse, land registry
       office and police station. Although the foundations were begun in
       November 1906, building was delayed until December 1907, and the work
       supervised by the Vancouver architects Dalton and Eveleigh. The popula-
       tion growth in Vancouver and the province rendered the accommodation
       too small when it was completed in 1911, necessitating the addition of a
       wing along Hornby Street, designed by Thomas Hooper. Reconstructed
       1981–83 as the City Art Gallery, to the designs of Arthur Erickson
       (P.A.B.C. and Vancouver City Archives). Figs.6.1–12.

–   House for J. O. Grahame, 534 St. Charles Street, Victoria. Of frame
       construction, the Grahame house represented a further evolution in
       Rattenbury's regular Tudor style. The *Contract Record* printed a call for
       tenders on 8 August 1906. Figs.6.18–20.

–   Porte-cochère, "Gisburn," Rockland Avenue, Victoria. Rattenbury was
       commisioned by J. B. Hobson to build a porte-cochère on to the front of
       this large San Francisco Bay style house.

–   Grand Trunk Pacific Railway Hotel, Prince Rupert, B.C. Awarded in
       December 1906 (*Colonist*, 21 December) and completed by the spring of
       1907 at a cost of some $50,000, this four-storey gabled frame building was
       intended to be replaced by the magnificent Château-style hotel
       Rattenbury designed in 1912. (See 1912). Demolished. Fig.6.21.

—   Extension to the third Victoria High School. Rattenbury's plans for this
      commission, since lost, but presumably in a Gothic style, were abandoned
      in January 1907 following his acrimonious dispute with one of the school
      trustees.

1907 House for A. M. Coles, 851 Wollaston Street (formerly Stanley Street),
      Victoria. This commission was announced in the *Colonist* on 3 January
      1907. The house, which remains virtually unaltered, is perhaps Ratten-
      bury's most attractive interpretation of the Arts and Crafts style. The
      internal layout is as convenient and commodious as the exterior is varied
      and yet harmonious. The main entrance faces the Dunsmuir Road and
      was formerly set in a large garden with tennis courts, since built over.
      Figs.6.22–23.

—   Departmental and Justice Buildings, Ottawa. Rattenbury unsuccessfully
      entered Tudor Gothic designs in the national competition for these two
      buildings. His drawings, not included among the four prize-winners, are
      lost.

—   Commercial building for the Brackman-Ker Milling Company, Broad
      and Pandora Streets, Victoria. The *Contract Record* of 13 March 1907 re-
      ported that Rattenbury was preparing drawings for this two-storey
      structure with pressed brick walls and a flat roof. Still standing and now
      occupied by a furniture store.

—   Merchants' Bank of Canada, Douglas and Yates Streets, Victoria. A more
      severe Neo-Classical version of the Nelson Bank of Montreal, constructed
      of reinforced concrete faced with Newcastle Island limestone at a cost of
      over $70,000. Subsequently acquired by the Bank of Montreal, it has
      been extended along Yates Street and the exterior and interior altered.
      Fig.6.24–25.

—   Victoria Apartments, Carr Street, Victoria. An unexecuted design, blend-
      ing Tudor and Château motifs, for the Victoria Apartments Limited,
      which failed to survive the 1907 recession. Fig.6.26.

—   Store for W. Wilson, Victoria. Rattenbury called for tenders in the *Con-
      tract Record* for 19 June 1907; its location and subsequent history are not
      documented.

—   House for H. W. Husband, Vernon, B.C. The only reference to this
      frame house comes in the call for tenders printed in the *Contract Record* for
      10 July 1907.

—   Saskatchewan Legislative Assembly, Regina, Saskatchewan. Rattenbury
      originally hoped to be awarded the commission unopposed in 1906. He
      was unsuccessful in the 1907 international competition, for which he pre-
      pared a monumental adaptation of the Vancouver Courthouse in a simi-
      larly Neo-Classical Beaux-Arts style. (Saskatchewan Archives, Regina).
      Figs.6.27–34.

1908 Restaurant and Machinery Hall, B.C. Agricultural Association Fairground, Victoria. Rattenbury invited tenders in the *Contract Record* for 20 May 1908.

— School for the Chinese Consolidated Benevolent Association, Chinese Quarter, Victoria. The *Contract Record* for 2 December invited tenders for "a substantial" three-storey brick building according to plans available at Rattenbury's office.

1909 Commercial Building for D. R. Ker, Fort Street, Victoria. The *Contract Record*, 27 January, announced that tenders were "closed recently" with Rattenbury "for the erection of a brick office"; on 21 April the journal further stated that a contract for its construction had been agreed with Messrs. Dinsdale and Malcolm for an estimated $8,500.

1910A House for Dr. O. M. Jones, 599 Island Road, Oak Bay, Victoria. Unusual since it is built of stone, the house is square in plan and basically Tudor in style. The commission seems to have been shared with Maclure and was brought to our attention by Geoffrey Castle.

1911 Parliamentary Library and Government Offices, Victoria. Rattenbury was commissioned to add the library and new offices behind the Legislative Assembly. At that time he was also asked to prepare designs for a new Government Printing Office and Provincial Museum, to be accommodated in separate blocks on either side of the library. His first design for the library was in the Château style, while the structure erected between 1912 and 1915 was a Classicized version of the Legislative Buildings. The offices were completed by the spring of 1914 and the library by 1916. The allocation for furnishing the library was reduced on the outbreak of World War I, which caused the printing office and museum to be abandoned. The total expenditure amounted to nearly $1,300,000; this figure compares well with the estimates of $750,000 and $1,000,000 respectively ($1,250,000 including the landscaping) printed in the *Contract Record* for 2 August and 4 October 1911. Associated with these works was the diminutive Tudor-style garage for the Legislative Assembly, entered from Belleville Street (P.A.B.C.). Figs.7.2–9, 25–26.

— St. Margaret's School, Fort and Fern Streets, Victoria. An "E" plan frame structure, in a plain style seemingly influenced by F. L. Wright's early domestic architecture, it was demolished in 1970. Fig.7.11.

1912 Merchants' Bank of Canada, 499 Wallace, Nanaimo. Built of concrete faced with brick in a "free Renaissance" style, the diagonal corner entrance linked the single bay front on Wallace with the three bay façade along Albert Street. Later acquired by the Bank of Montreal and altered. The original blueprints are not dated, but the *Contract Record* for 15 January 1912 stated "Plans are being prepared for a bank, cost $15,000" by Rattenbury to be erected in brick alone (Nanaimo City Hall). Figs. 7.10A–B.

– G.T.P. Hotel, Prince Rupert, 2nd Avenue, Prince Rupert, B.C. The *Contract Record*, 17 January, announced that Rattenbury had completed plans for the hotel "cost 1,000,000," comprising "Main building, 12 storeys; two wings, 9 storeys, steel, . . . fireproof construction." The design, now reduced to a ten-storey main block with six-storey wings but still estimated at one million dollars, was published in the *Contract Record*, 30 July 1913, and depicted in a perspective of the Railway's projected buildings signed by David Myers and dated 1913. Designed in the Château style, it was a stupendous interpretation of the Empress Hotel with a proposed accommodation of over 600 rooms. The foundation trenches for the hotel were reported as being finished in the November 1913 issue of the *Canadian Railway and Marine World*, but no further work was undertaken (P.A.B.C.). Figs.7.14–15.

– G.T.P. Hotel, Victoria. Under the listing for Victoria, the *Contract Record*, 17 January, reported "Plans are about completed for G.T.P. Hotel for Grand Trunk Pacific Railway, Montreal. Architect, F.M. Rattenbury, Sayward Building, Victoria. Site in possession of company." (The 21 September 1910 issue of the journal had given the site as between Government, Belleville and Elliott Streets, the former Douglas Gardens, purchased for $291,000.) The entry for 17 January ended with unwarranted optimism, "It is stated work will start early in spring." In fact this project was abandoned, together with all the other G.T.P. hotels, although it seems to have been resuscitated, using a different design, in 1928 under the auspices of the Canadian National Railway. (See 1928.) Studies for or based on the original 1912 design could be among the sketch designs for the other G.T.P. hotels discussed in Appendix C. Figs.C.22–23.

– Château Miette, Miette Springs, Alberta, and Château Mount Robson, B.C. Rattenbury seems to have prepared these two Château-style designs for the G.T.P. between 1912 and 1913, though the Château Miette was to be built first. In both designs the bedroom wings radiated diagonally from the main building containing the public rooms. The Château Miette was conceived as a "hydropathic establishment" to accommodate about 250 guests, while the larger Château Mount Robson was planned as a resort hotel for 500. He also submitted an alternate plan for the Château Mount Robson, dated 1913 and marked "Design B" in which the bedrooms are integrated in a taller single block. Both published in the *Contract Record*, 30 July 1913. Unexecuted (P.A.B.C.). Figs.7.12–13; C.1–23.

1913 G.T.P. Station and Log Depot, Mount Robson. Various designs, some in the Chalet style, for stone and log buildings. Unexecuted (P.A.B.C). Figs. c.24–27.

– G.T.P. Steamship Terminal and Station, Prince Rupert. Two schemes for these facilities remain, dated 5 and 17 April. While the design of the terminal is the same, the station in the former is smaller in scale, and in the Château rather than the Beaux-Arts style; the station is grander in the Myers view. Unexecuted (P.A.B.C.). Figs. 7.15; C.30–33.

—   G.T.P. "Mountain Inn,"? Jasper, Alberta. Rattenbury's scheme comprised
    two gabled log chalets joined to a central block by a covered walk. Unex-
    ecuted (P.A.B.C.). Figs. 7.28–29.

1914 G.T.P. "Station Château Miette," Miette Springs, Alberta. A symmetrical
    Queen Anne style building with Dutch gables. Unexecuted (P.A.B.C.).
    Fig.7.27.

—   G.T.P. Lodge, Miette Springs. A frame building with diagonally placed
    wings, possibly intended as a cheaper alternative for his larger Château
    Miette Hotel scheme. Unexecuted (P.A.B.C.). Figs.C.28–29.

—   House for R. W. Gibson, 1590 York Place, Victoria. The Italianate style
    of the two designs he drew in February 1914 marked a significant change
    in Rattenbury's domestic architecture. The underlying symmetry of
    Rattenbury's first scheme was broken by a broad bay window on the main
    front and a tower on the rear. In the second scheme, as represented in a
    small sketch elevation, he omitted the irregular elements to create a villa
    form approximating the house as built 1918–19 under the supervision of
    Maclure and Lort (P.A.B.C.). Figs.7.17–24.

1921 Amusement Centre, Victoria. Writing to his sister Kate on 29 September
    1921, Rattenbury described this project for the Victoria Chamber of
    Commerce as "a kind of Crystal Palace... practically a huge conservatory,
    with the centre part large swimming tanks, huge promenade, dancing,
    bands, all kinds of things." This scheme, published in the *Victoria Times*,
    the foundations for which Rattenbury estimated at $150,000 in December
    1921, formed the basis of the Crystal Garden he later built with
    P. L. James. (See 1923.) (P.A.B.C.) Figs.8.1–3.

1923 Second C.P.R. Steamship Terminal, 468 Belleville Street, Victoria (in
    partnership with P. L. James, with whom he had already collaborated on
    the Bullen House, 924 Esquimalt Road, Victoria, a smoking room aboard
    one of the C.P.R. *Princess* ferries, an unspecified building at Radium Hot
    Springs, and an unidentified apartment building, presumably in Victoria).
    A revised version of the later Beaux-Arts design for the G.T.P. Station at
    Prince Rupert, the terminal was a worthy addition to Rattenbury's
    architectural contributions to the Inner Harbour. Constructed in rein-
    forced concrete, with an imitation stone facing, as suggested by James,
    who executed the working drawings and supervised the building, it was
    completed in 1924. Now houses the London Wax Museum (P.A.B.C.).
    Figs.8.6–10.

—   Crystal Garden, Douglas Street, Victoria. A smaller version of Ratten-
    bury's 1921 scheme, with only one salt-water pool, this was financed by the
    C.P.R. with tax concessions from City Council. The design of the single
    salt-water pool, constructed on a concrete raft, was by James, who again
    undertook most of the actual work on the commission. The overall con-
    ception, however, remained that of Rattenbury. A dispute over the divi-
    sion of the fees caused the dissolution of the partnership. Completed in

1925, the Garden operated until 1967, although the pool had been converted to chlorinated water in 1955. Restoration of the structure was completed in 1980; the pool area is now occupied by a botanical garden. Figs. 8.12–15.

1928   Hotel Project, Douglas Gardens, Victoria. Rattenbury stated that he had finished a design for the "Campanile Hotel" in a letter to his sister, written in February 1928. Almost certainly commissioned by the Canadian National Railway, which had assumed the assets of the G.T.P. The land had been acquired in 1910 with the intention of erecting a rival hotel to the Empress. The scheme apparently fell victim to the 1929 recession and was not executed.

1931   Rattenbury is reported to have engaged in minor architectural work after
-35   his return to England. No trace of these commissions, if indeed any were executed, has been discovered. Just before his death he had completed a design for an apartment block (in Bournemouth?), possibly to be financed by W. R. Jenks, of Bridport, Dorset.

Appendix B

THE RATTENBURY LETTERS

A. Catalogue of the private letters written by Rattenbury to relatives in England. The collection remained unknown until 1978, when it was discovered in London. John Rattenbury, second son of the architect, writes as follows on the background and circumstances of their discovery:

> I really never knew my parents, since they died when I was five. However, i still retain some keen, but disconnected, memories of family life, a great sense of love for mother and some awe of father. One of my strongest memories of father is looking at a sketch he did for a building. The drawing was the elevation of a house, with trees on either side of the door and was mounted vertically on a board in the drawing room of our house in Bournemouth. This must have been when I was about four years old. I fell in love with the beauty of the pencil lines on the white paper, and that moment probably started me off on my career in architecture.
>
> In later years I learned little more about my parents, due to a natural reluctance of the family to stir up my feelings. In 1950 I moved to the U.S. to study architecture with Frank Lloyd Wright. When his home Taliesin was destroyed by fire in 1951 the documentary material that I had retained, except for some family photographs, was destroyed also. Thus when I was contacted by the authors and learned of their plan to write the present book, I was able to offer encouragement but little factual material beyond the photographs. However, in 1978, I visited my godfather, Keith Miller Jones, a nephew of my father, shortly before he died in London. He recited some interesting stories of father, and revealed a large number of letters that he had written from British Columbia to his family in England (mainly to Keith

Miller Jones's mother and grandmother). This was the first time that I learned of their existence. I read them with much interest, and recognized that they were potentially important for the history of my father's career and for early British Columbia.

Almost all the letters contain, to a greater or lesser degree, details of daily life in Victoria, family news, weather and descriptions of the countryside and the changes in the seasons.

1. 25 August 1894: to uncle (Richard Mawson), from Victoria. 4 pages. Letterhead: Rattenbury elevation of Legislative Buildings. Description of life in Victoria; various commissions; construction of dome of Legislative Buildings (sketches included).

2. 24 August 1898: to mother, from Victoria. 4 pages. Letterhead: "Bennett Lake & Klondyke Navigation Company Limited." Rattenbury's shipping company; account of honeymoon; list of wedding gifts, with donors.

3. 4 November 1899: to sister (Kate), from Victoria. 2 pages. Quiet life in Iechinihl; concern over South African War; reflections on Yukon enterprise.

4. 26 March 1900: to mother, from Nelson. 2 pages. Letterhead: "Hotel Phair." Bank commission in Nelson; Ladysmith celebrations in Victoria; reassurances about brother Jack.

5. 13 April 1900: to mother, from Victoria. 2 pages. Thoughts of living on Continent; pressure of commissions.

6. 4 May 1900: to mother, from Victoria. 2 pages. Dinner with Colonel Perry; planned visit by Pat Burns.

7. 30 May 1900: to mother, from Victoria. 2 pages. Mafeking and Queen's Birthday celebrations; origin of name "Iechinihl"; Florrie's preparations for a bazaar.

8. 22 June 1900: to sister and husband (Frank Jones), from Victoria. 4 pages. Dissatisfaction with life in Victoria; Snooka growing older; conservation problems in Yorkshire cities.

9. 10 July [1900]: to mother, from Victoria. 2 pages. Work for Pat Burns; thoughts on the Boxer uprising in China; father's artistic career.

10. 26 July 1900: to mother, from Calgary. 1 page. Letterhead: "The Alberta, Calgary." Beginning of work on the Burns house; reflections on crossing the Rockies; general lack of enthusiasm.

11. 8 October 1900: to mother, from Victoria. 2 pages. Absence of business; asked to build Cary Castle; onset of middle age.

12. 14 November 1900: to mother, from Victoria. 3 pages. Reminiscences about childhood; lawsuit over Yukon enterprise; Hotel Vancouver competition; pressure to compete for Cary Castle; jocular remarks about father's paintings.

13. 18 December 1900: to mother, from Victoria. 2 pages. Vancouver Hotel competition still undecided; comments on other commissions; decision not to compete for Cary Castle; law case continues; fierce storm while crossing from Vancouver.

14. 1 January 1901: to mother, from Victoria. 2 pages. Christmas celebrations; arrival of father's pictures; anxiety about Hotel Vancouver competition; social life at Union Club.

15. 3 January 1901: to sister, from Victoria. 2 pages. Family gossip; concern over redevelopment of Headingly.

16. 11 February 1901: to mother, from Montreal. 1 page. Letterhead: "Windsor Hotel," with engraving of hotel and inscribed "W. S. Weldon, Manager." Confirmation of C.P.R. hotels at Field and Vancouver; visit to a hockey match.

17A. [February 1901: to mother, from Montreal]. Scrap, 2 half sides. Letterhead: [partially missing, similar to no. 16]. Appointment as architect to the C.P.R.; promise of further commissions.

17B. [February 1901: to mother, from Quebec City, posted with another letter (perhaps no. 17A)]. 4 pages. Letterhead: "Chateau Frontenac, Quebec" and crest. Description of Citadel and Hotel; admiration for architect Bruce Price.

18. 25 February 1901: to mother, from Victoria. 3 pages. Return to Victoria, including avalanche in Rockies; work on hotels at Field and Vancouver.

19. 13 April 1901: to mother, from Victoria, 2 pages. Suffering from a cold; Hotel Vancouver plans completed; brother Jack's marriage.

20. 1 July 1901: to mother, from Victoria. 1 page (incomplete). Trip to Vancouver to discuss hotel commission; Yukon lawsuit successfully terminated.

21. 9 July 1901: to mother, from Victoria. 2 pages. Advice about investments; asked to prepare ornamental arches and illuminations for Duke of York's visit.

22. 16 August 1901: to mother, from Victoria. 2 pages. Competition for Victoria High School; Cary Castle offered; fire on Mary Tod island; Uncle's design for Triumphal Arch.

23. 20 August 1901: to mother, from Victoria. 2 pages. Cary Castle commission to be built with another architect; list of current commissions (together with fees); reminiscences about joining uncles' firm.

24. 24 February 1902: to mother, from San Francisco. 4 pages. Letterhead: "The Pacific Union Club, San Francisco." Impressions of the city and its architecture; professional advantages and disadvantages of moving to U.S.

25. 12 June [1902]: to mother, from Victoria. 1 page. Hotel Vancouver compared with Leeds "Grand"; approached to design streetcar depot in Vancouver.

26. 2 October 1902: to mother, from Victoria. 2 pages. Completion of mountain

hotels before winter; meeting with Van Horne; Florrie's purchase of jewellery with housekeeping money.

27. 7 December, 1902: to mother, from Victoria. 2 pages. Death of brother; Frank taken by Florrie to San Francisco for treatment of club-feet.

28. 26 January 1903: to mother, from Victoria. 2 pages. Encouraging news from San Francisco; designing marble courthouse (Nelson); aggregate of buildings in hand worth $1,250,000.

29. 5 February 1903: to mother, from Victoria. 1 page. News from San Francisco; Rattenbury's problems with dentist.

30. 12 March 1903: to mother, from Victoria. 1 page. Working hard to complete contracts before the summer; rigorous course of physical exercise.

31. 25 April 1903: to mother, from Victoria. 2 pages. Florrie and Snooka return to Victoria; arrival of Cary Castle furnishings and fittings.

32. 13 May 1903: to mother, from Victoria. 2 pages. Furniture not yet installed in Cary Castle; labour troubles in Victoria; visit from F. Morton Rattenbury of Prince Edward Island.

33. 1 June 1903: to mother, from Field. 4 pages. Letterhead: "Mount Stephen House, Field, B.C." Visit to Calgary and to mountain hotels (then almost finished); first mention of C.P.R. project for (Empress) hotel in Victoria and its importance; book received from F. Morton Rattenbury of Prince Edward Island.

34. 14 June 1903: to mother, from Victoria. 4 pages. Letterhead: "Union Club, Victoria, B.C." Visit to circus; plan to visit Montreal to discuss Empress.

35. 24 June 1903: to uncle, from Victoria. 2 pages. Anxiety about mother's health; further plans to go to Montreal about the Empress; additions to Glacier Hotel ordered; socialist tendencies in England; lack of architectural opportunities in Victoria.

36. 25 June 1903: to mother, from Victoria. 2 pages (with a caricature of the family). Additions to Glacier; work on the preliminary drawings of the Empress; planned business visits to Montreal and Vancouver; cheque enclosed as result of successful land investment; worries about incipient baldness.

37. 6 July 1903: to mother, from Victoria. 2 pages. Several house commissions; plans for a camping trip.

38. 4 August [1903]: to mother, from Victoria. Photographs of Swiss hotels received from uncle; discussion between city and C.P.R. concerning the Empress; further work on C.P.R. mountain hotels; Cary Castle attractively furnished.

39. 19 August 1903: to mother, from Victoria. 2 pages. Frank seriously ill; additions to the Hotel Vancouver.

40. 4 September 1903: to mother, from Victoria. 4 pages. Letterhead: "Union Club, Victoria, B.C." Another trip to the mountain hotels; Empress question coming to a head.

41. 15 November 1903: to mother, from Montreal. 2 pages. Letterhead: similar to nos. 16 and 17A (at least three varieties exist). Waiting in Montreal to see Shaughnessy; visit to hotels in the eastern United States.

42. 27 December 1903: to mother, from Victoria. 1 page. Reminiscences about English Lake District; work on Empress plans; Florrie pregnant.

43. 30 January 1904: to mother, from Victoria. 2 pages. Wreck of the *Chatham* off Oak Bay; frequent business visits to Vancouver.

44. 15 February 1904: to mother, from Victoria. 2 pages. Exonerated by the Cary Castle Enquiry; "Certificate of Character" dinner at Union Club, with guest list.

45. 29 February 1904: to mother, from Victoria. 2 pages. Plans for visit by mother; problems and costs of Empress foundations.

46. 9 March 1904: to mother, from Victoria. 2 pages. Negotiations for a car from England; commissions for new houses and a business block; Empress plans almost completed.

47. 13 May 1904: to mother, from Victoria. 2 pages. Birth of daughter Mary; acquisition of property on projected site of the Empress.

48. 1 June 1904: to mother, from Victoria. 1 page. Tenders received for Empress and instructions given to revise plans.

49. 10 June 1904: to mother, from Victoria. 2 pages. Business visit to Montreal postponed; assistant sent in place.

50. 4 July 1904: to mother, from Victoria. 2 pages. Description of daily work routine; revising Empress drawings.

51. 27 July 1904: to mother, from Victoria. 2 pages. Design of interior rooms of the Empress; plans to buy parcel of land in country.

52. 29 August [1904]: to mother, from Victoria. 1 page. Trip to Cowichan Lake.

53. 22 October 1904: to mother, from Victoria. 1 page. Pressure of commissions; list of buildings already in hand.

54. 29 October 1904: to mother, from Victoria. 1 page. Letter is written on a pamphlet of "The Tourist Association of Victoria, B.C." with, on the front, a panorama of the Legislative Buildings and of the Inner Harbour, as well as a list of the officials of the Association, and, on the verso, pictures of prominent Victoria homes. Promotion of Victoria as a pleasure resort; Snooka's progress at school; retirement of Uncle Richard.

55. 14 November 1904: to sister, from Victoria. 1 page. Beauty of Iechinihl's gardens; plans to add conservatory; tremendous pressure of work.

56. 14 November 1904: to mother, from Victoria. 1 page. Working at office in evenings; repeated requests that mother accept additional financial help.

57. 6 December 1904: to mother, from Victoria. 1 page. Preparations for Christmas; reminiscences of childhood; description of daughter.

58. 29 January 1905: to mother, from Victoria. 4 pages. Death of uncle (Richard Mawson); tenders received for Empress; higher tenders than expected.

59. 2 March 1905: to mother, from Montreal. 2 pages. Letterhead identical to no. 41. At Windsor Hotel to see Shaughnessy about the Empress; previous stays at the Windsor during crucial periods in career.

60. 17 March 1905, to mother, from Victoria. 1 page. Bout of flu; contract for Empress let; Florrie having weight problems.

61. 31 August 1905: to mother, from Victoria. 1 page. Commissions for houses in Philadephia and Manitoba; luggage from recent trip to England missing.

62. 10 September 1905: to mother, from Victoria. 2 pages. Reminiscences of visits to England; uncharacteristically demonstrative statement of admiration for mother.

63. 12 October 1905: to mother, from Victoria. 1 page. Greenhouse built at Iechinihl; hiring of gamekeeper to shoot game.

64. 24 October 1905: to mother, from Victoria. 1 page. Arrival of furniture from England; description of rooms in Iechinihl.

65. 31 October 1905: to mother, from Victoria. 1 page. Second house commissioned by Judge Lampman; office decorated with old books and pictures from uncles' firm.

66. 30 November 1905: to mother, from Victoria. 1 page. Designing a house; a new cook at Iechinihl.

67. 9 December 1905: to mother, from Victoria. Decoration of house with holly from "estate"; arrangement of family portraits in dining room.

68. 26 December 1905: to mother, from Victoria. 1 page. Arrival of presents from England.

69. 9 January 1906: to mother, from Victoria. 1 page. Christmas celebrations; wild party given by W. S. Oliver; Rattenbury's coat torn to shreds.

70. 28 January 1906: to mother from Edmonton. 2 pages. Letterhead: "Alberta Hotel, E. D. Gierson, prop.," with engraving of hotel. Enthusiastic description of Edmonton; offer of Alberta Legislative Buildings; trip to Fort Saskatchewan; meeting with William Mackenzie of the Canadian Northern Railway.

71. 21 February 1906: to mother, from Victoria. 1 page (with sketch of Vancouver Courthouse). Trips to Mary Tod Island; embarrassment over Oliver party; Vancouver Courthouse commission.

72. 14 March 1906: to mother, from Victoria. 1 page. Car ordered from England; Frank to have a pony.

73. 16 April 1906: to mother, from Victoria. 2 pages. Indifference to the visit of the Duke of Connaught; thoughts on the San Francisco earthquake; large children's party at Iechinihl.

74. 27 July, 1906: to mother, from Victoria. 1 page, written on pamphlet of "The Tourist Association of Victoria, B.C." Front: as no.54; verso: pictures of prominent Victoria homes (in a different format from no.54), each being identified with comments added in Rattenbury's hand. Visit to dentist; Empress roofed.

75. 5 January 1908: to sister and husband, from Victoria. 2 pages. Accident on Mary Tod Island; debt for land purchases paid off.

76. 1 November [1910]: to mother, from Victoria. 2 pages. Return to Victoria from England; office block burnt down, personal papers and mementoes destroyed.

77. 16 November 1910: to mother, from Victoria. 2 pages. A new tutor for Frank; a successful land deal; concern over mother's health.

78. 1 January 1911: to mother, from Victoria. 2 pages. Christmas news; a football match between Victoria and California.

79. 10 January 1911: to mother, from Victoria. 1 page. Selection of plan for the new Union Club; the rapid development of Victoria.

80. 10 August [1911]: to mother, from Victoria. 1 page. Return to Victoria from England.

81. 29 September 1921: to sister, from Victoria. 2 pages. Letterhead: "Rattenbury Lands," with various slogans and a list of agencies; apologies for delay in writing; work on an "Amusement Centre" in Victoria; description of quarters in Iechinihl; relations with son and daughter.

82. 10 December 1923: to sister, from Victoria. 2 pages. Rattenbury in good health; commissions for Steamship office and Crystal Garden; first meeting with Alma.

83. 21 June 1925: to sister, from Victoria. 3 pages. Announcement of marriage; description of Alma.

84. 1 September 1926: to sister, from Victoria. 3 pages, with original envelope. Happiness of life with Alma.

85. 10 February 1928: to sister, from Victoria. 2 pages. Alma seriously ill; report on legal dispute with government; "Campanile" Hotel for Victoria.

86. 17 May 1928: to sister, from Victoria. 4 pages. Alma pregnant; legal reverses and decision to take case to Supreme Court of Canada.

87. 12 December 1931: to sister [from Bournemouth]. 4 typed pages, incomplete. Efforts to promote Alma's career; her success in London musical society.

B. Private letters of Francis Rattenbury previously in the possession of Mrs. Mary Burton (née Rattenbury) and recently passed on to the Victoria City Archives.

1. 30 July 1915: to Florrie, from London. 4 pages. Letterhead: "Royal Automobile Club, Pall Mall, London." With envelope (unposted, hand delivered by Frank). Frank to return to Canada; scarcity of money; failure of war contracts; reflections on the fighting.

2. 10 May [no year]: to Mary, from Victoria (?). 1 page. Letterhead: "Rattenbury Lands." With unposted envelope. Birthday greetings; gift and candies left in car.

3. 20 May 1919: to Mary, from Victoria. 2 pages. Letterhead: "Union Club." Mary's holiday in Vancouver; small gift of money; arrival of Wood expected.

4. 2 December 1919: to Mary, from London. 2 pages. Letterhead: as no.1. With envelope. Lengthy stay in London anticipated; difficulties with business.

5. 24 July 1920: to Mary, from London. 2 pages. Letterhead: as no.1. Visits to English relatives; concern about Mary's lessons.

6. 11 August 1920: to Mary, from London. 3 pages. Letterhead: as no.1. With envelope. Concern about Mary; busy in London, but many problems.

7. 6 October [1920]: to Mary, from Folkestone, England. 2 pages. Letterhead: "Hotel Metropole." With envelope. Frank to become a farm labourer; difficult time in England; problems faced by Wood.

8. 10 January 1921: to Mary, from London, 2 pages. Letterhead: as no. 1. With envelope. Receipt of Christmas gift; London sales; Wood ill.

9. 16 October 1925: to Mary, [from Victoria]. 1 page (incomplete). Mary's unpleasant behaviour; happiness of Rattenbury's present home.

Appendix C

DRAWINGS FOR THE
GRAND TRUNK PACIFIC HOTELS
AND STATIONS IN THE PROVINCIAL
ARCHIVES OF BRITISH COLUMBIA

The drawings discussed below may not represent all those made by Rattenbury for the G.T.P., since others, especially working drawings for the Prince Rupert buildings, could exist in the Canadian National collection at Montreal, as yet uncatalogued and unavailable for research.

The various references to Rattenbury's work for the G.T.P. in the *Contract Record* between 1910 and 1913 suggest that the earliest designs were for the company's hotels at Prince Rupert and Victoria, followed by those for Mount Robson, Miette, and Jasper. The journal announced the completion of the plans for the Prince Rupert and Victoria hotels on 17 January 1912 and published an article, probably written by Rattenbury, illustrating the Prince Rupert, Mount Robson and Miette hotels on 30 July 1913. The great majority of the detailed drawings and sketches for these and associated G.T.P. schemes remaining in the Provincial Archives are for the Château Mount Robson and Château Miette. Those for the Prince Rupert Hotel date from 1912 but are best studied with drawings made in April 1913 for the G.T.P. steamship terminal and station at Prince Rupert. It should also be noted that some of the sketches, here discussed in the context of the Château Mount Robson schemes, may either represent or reflect Rattenbury's proposal for the G.T.P. hotel in Victoria, to be built on a site adjacent to the C.P.R.'s Empress Hotel and thus probably intended to be in the Château style.

Among the material at the Provincial Archives relating to the Château Mount Robson are photographs and surveys of its proposed site in the awesome valley beneath Mount Robson and the headwaters of the Fraser River. From these, as likely for the other hotels, he sketched a pen and wash landscape depicting the chief topographical features of the area (Fig.C.1: R.P. [7]4). Associated with it is a map showing the railway track, proposed hotel site, and surrounding mountains. The ground plan of the hotel is inked in and envisages a central block with four radiating wings. These were increased to six by October 1912 when he drew the ground plan that forms the basis of the 30 July 1913 *Contract Record* perspective (Fig.7.13). This shows the "T" shaped central building with two short wings on the longer axis, from the circular terminations of which radiate three rectangular blocks (Fig.C.4:R.P.[7]3). Only one of the bedroom wings on either side is drawn in detail, the remainder being described as "Future Bed Rooms." Each was to contain sixty-nine rooms with attached bathrooms, to have a second entrance from the ornamental garden fronting the hotel, and to end in a verandah. The two upper floors are served by circular staircases leading from the broad corridor which runs across the main building. This corridor communicates with the entrance and lobby on the right side, the central lounge, and the raised and bay windowed dining room at the rear. Also, branching off the corridors are four large alcoves, the washrooms, and, on the left, ancillary public rooms. In a second, undated plan, (Fig C.3:R.P.[8]9 sheet 1) two of the bedroom wings have been deleted, while those that have been retained are served by a larger single flight staircase at their junction with the cross-axial corridor. In the hotel proper, all the space abutting the lounge is reserved for a billiard room, and the plan of the kitchen and boiler house simplified. Two interesting details are supplied by the notations which appear on this plan. Firstly, the main front was to be aligned towards the northeast, presumably to face Mount Robson, and secondly, the dining room was to be raised to accommodate a grill room and barber's shop below.

Both plans correspond with the pencil "Sketch Elevation. Hotel Mount Robson," signed and dated December 1912 (Fig.C.2:R.P.[8]40). The main building in this drawing is, in some respects, a contracted version of his first scheme for the Hotel Vancouver, to which have been added features from the Empress Hotel. Two square towers with steeply pitched roofs flank the central block, which also has a pitched roof. But the towers are recessed behind a Neo-Tudor arcade and the centrepiece, the chief decoration of which is a tall bay window and sharply raked gable. The profile of the main building is stepped down to the lower wings, but ascends again via the circular staircase towers with their candle-snuffer roofs, to the buttressed radiating bedroom blocks. The curved gables, set between turrets on the end façades of the radiating blocks, recall the Dutch type originally conceived for the Hotel Vancouver and employed on the Nelson Courthouse.

The 1912 Château Mount Robson scheme may stem from a preliminary design for the Château Miette as represented by a pencil sketch illustrating an asymmetrical central building with gabled blocks, entered from a curved driveway with a fountain in the middle (Fig.C.5:R.P.[8] 13 sheet 4.1). In this study, the main building, fronted by a continuous Neo-Tudor arcade, ascends from left to right. A gabled and turreted projection with a tall bay window holds an uneasy balance between the two differently scaled and ornamented staircase towers that link it to the bedroom blocks. The tower on the right side extends into the courtyard and, having a battlement, is more Château-like in character. The façades of the two bedroom blocks, already of three storeys as in the scheme published by the *Contract Record* in 1913 (Fig.7.12), differ from each other and exhibit a more complicated arrangement of gables, windows, and wall planes than planned for the Château Mount Robson.

The first stage of the Château Mount Robson proper might be the less careful pencil sketch in which Rattenbury has concentrated upon the design of the main building (Fig.C.6:R.P.[8]9 sheet 5). It is also lower on the left side, but it has a shorter verandah, a taller symmetrical central block with a gable, and a pitched roof with high chimneys either side and topped by a lantern. On the left is a circular tower with a candle-snuffer roof joining at least two bedroom blocks. The bedroom blocks on the right are omitted, their space being occupied by an alternative study for the main building which has a lower pitched roof, central bay window, and corner turret. Two more sketch elevations depict bedroom blocks linked by circular staircase towers to intermediate versions of the main building (Figs.C.7.R.P.[8]11 sheets 9 and 8). In one, more precisely drawn, the main building is close to the symmetrical form described above, that is, with a central gable and lantern, and chimneys framing the roof (Fig.C.7. sheet 9). But it now has a large three-sided projection at the centre, with a Neo-Tudor porte-cochère on the left. In the other elevation, the projection is transformed into a full bay window surmounted by a bigger gable, while the Tudor arcade is carried on along the bedroom block to the left (Fig.C.8:R.P.[8]11 sheet 8). A further stage is reached in another sketch elevation that places the porte-cochère on the left and has two square towers with steeply pitched roofs standing at either side and just behind the main building (Fig.C.9:R.P.[8]9 sheet 4). Finally, there are a number of alternative elevations for the bedroom blocks, two with interesting variations on the gable and turret theme (Figs.C.10 and 11:R.P.[8] 11 sheets 13 and 14), and a more detailed pencil sketch for the main building upon which the final scheme was based (Fig.C.12:R.P.[8]11 sheet 7a).

Then, in the spring of 1913, Rattenbury developed a new scheme for the hotel which both reverts to the Empress Hotel and compares with the 1912 design for the Prince Rupert Hotel, only to abandon it before July in favour of his original proposal. The Provincial Archives have four pencil drawings for this, one in pencil on tracing paper marked "MT ROBSON HOTEL Bedroom plan" (Fig.C.15:R.P.[8] 11, sheet 7) and three others, each signed and dated May 2, 1913 and inscribed "Mount Robson Hotel. Design B" (Figs.C.13, 14, 16:R.P.[8]14, sheets 2, 6 and 9). The first of the 1913 drawings, an elevation of the main façade, is further inscribed, "Fireproof. Concrete Walls. Finished White Roughcast," the second, a ground floor plan, "6 Storey Fireproof Hotel," and the third, an upper floor plan, "Total 210 Bedrooms or Building only Blocks 2x3=150 Bedrooms. The Helps Quarters to be in a separate Building." Evidently, he either volunteered, or the company requested, a grander edifice, more akin to the celebrated Empress Hotel. Nevertheless, the number of bedrooms was considerably below the total of 414 projected for the first scheme, unless he contemplated the addition of radiating bedroom blocks. This seems unlikely, although one sheet dated "Sept 20" with a rough sketch for an elevation comparable with design "B" has two equally hurried plans, both with wings extending diagonally backwards from the main building (Fig.C.17:Msc[9]8). This sheet is stapled to four others on which the idea of a large main building is explored, one ink plan and elevation having two large circular projections at either side, similar to those of "Design B" but with candle-snuffer roofs (Fig.C.18). The latter form is taken further in two other sheets of the group (Figs.C.19&20:R.P.[8]14 sheets 3 and 4). Both show a five-storey central block, with a sixth floor represented by dormer windows in the high pitched roof, and single-storied arcaded wings leading to two taller circular pavilions capped by candle-snuffer roofs. But in one, the compacted Empress-like building is flanked by longer two-storey blocks ornamented with smaller versions of the pavilions. From these drawings, and another showing a wide central bay window and curved Dutch gable that commands the centre (Fig.C.21:R.P.[8] 14sheet 1), Rattenbury probably evolved "Design B."

In "Design B" the circular pavilions are attached to the main building and house a palm room on the left and a reading room on the right. The tripartite division of the centre section is more complex. The lower middle bays, distinguished on the ground floor by a three-sided projection, are enclosed by two towers with oriel windows rising through its upper floors. At each corner are two single bays with curved edges, which are linked to the recessed side blocks. These front the two wings that extend back from the main building to form an "L" shape plan, again not unlike the Empress Hotel. The longer wing on the left does not have the tower that rises above the shorter one on the right. Between the cornice and pitched roof of this tower, Rattenbury seems to have envisaged the creation of an observation gallery, which would have afforded marvellous views of Mount Robson, the highest peak in the Canadian Rockies. It is retained in different forms in two further elevations either associated with "Design B" or representing his scheme for the G.T.P. Hotel at Victoria (Figs.C.22&23:R.P.[8]14 sheets 5 and 8). In both these pencil sketches the central block is stripped of the towers and in one (sheet 5), the most monumental, given an additional floor and a broader front. Nevertheless, the internal layout is probably similar to the "Design B" plan, with the reading room in the right hand pavilion, the hall in the right wing, the lounge (replete with an "ingle") and billiard room in the centre, and the palm room in the left pavilion, with the dining room in the left wing served by a single-storey kitchen block behind.

One of the equally long series of pencil sketches on tracing paper for the Mount Robson station and log depot indicates that Rattenbury began work on these ancillary buildings about the time he initiated "Design B" (Msc[9]8). Underneath a plan and elevation for a single-storey five-bay log building is one of a hotel with a large central block flanked by lower wings leading to two circular pavilions capped by the ubiquitous candle-snuffer roofs. Filed under the same heading is a sheet with three more clearly drawn variant elevations and one plan which can be identified from the inscriptions as being for the station (Fig.C.24:Msc[9]8 sheet 3). All these elevations, however, show a gabled projection which reappears in a pencil elevation and plan signed and dated 3 May 1913 and inscribed "Log Depot Mount Robson" (Fig.C.25:R.P.[8]15 sheet 2). The low log walls, deep eaves, and pitched roof are thoroughly North American in character despite the obvious Swiss ancestry — a blend of the C.P.R. and United States rural railway architecture. There is another more finished drawing signed and inscribed "Grand Trunk Pacific Ry. Station at Mt. Robson," which is somewhat closer to the first sketch, being of one storey with a diminutive central gable (Fig.C.26:R.P.[8]8 sheet 7). Whether it was intended as an alternative design for the "Log Depot" or as a separate building cannot be determined. Under the same reference are preserved seven more pencil sketches of elevations and plans for smaller structures. Each is of log construction and has gables of one sort or another. Perhaps the most attractive is the one having a broad gabled projection joined to an octagonal battlemented tower, for which Rattenbury drew two tops, one with a low dome and the other with the dome and a turret (Fig.C.27:R.P. [8]8 sheet 1). Both are influenced by the Arts and Crafts style and the work of H. H. Richardson.

Akin to the Mount Robson station designs are a number of sketches, among which only those for the Miette station can be definitely identified and dated, one being inscribed "Station Chateau Miette" and "Dec. 1914" (R.P.[8]3). Though these succeeded his work on the Prince Rupert hotel and terminal, they are best considered at this point since another of the three pencil sketches inscribed "Chateau Miette" has a tripartite façade comparable with one of the rough drawings for the Mount Robson station. Moreover, the two side pavilions of this elevation have curved Dutch gables that recall various of the Mount Robson Hotel projects. Those gables flank a colonnade with, above, a balustraded terrace and a recessed centre having small Dutch gabled windows on either side of an ornamental Dutch gabled chimney. This composition was worked up in a more finished pencil drawing, signed and dated 14 December but inscribed only "Sketch No. 2" (Fig.7.26).

Three previously unidentified and undated pencil drawings could represent either a proposal for a simple frame hotel at Miette Springs as a cheaper alternative to the Château Miette or a project for a chalet-style lodge at Jasper (Msc[9]42). Two floor plans show a rectangular building having a verandah linked by octagonal blocks with two diagonally placed wings (Fig.C.28). The narrow entrance leads into a cross-axial corridor and faces a staircase. This arrangement conforms with the third drawing, an elevation for a two-storey building flanked by octagonal towers and single-storey wings (Fig.C.29). Raised on a fieldstone basement, the main floor is shaded by a verandah, intended, like the loggias atop the towers, to provide sheltered vistas of the sublime scenery. In the right margin of this elevation is a hurried sketch for the façade and plan of a different building. The plan, two pavilions joined by a passage to a "T"-shaped block, and the elevation, incomplete but with two gabled fronts, are remarkably similar to three other sketches and a blueprint of an elevation inscribed "Sketch of Mountain Inn for the Grand Trunk Pacific Railway" (Fig.7.28R.P.[8]19, sheet 1, blueprint, and sheet 2, elevation; Msc[9]42, plan). The sketch elevation, from which the inscribed blueprint was taken, depicts three gabled log chalets each linked by a covered walk with unfinished timber supports. These face a lake across which sweeps a small yacht, while the drawing is backed by the outline of a mountain range. This surely records his idea for the Jasper resort. The associated plans show that the pavilions were to contain two floors of bedrooms with intervening bathrooms and that the main block would house the public rooms with more bedroom accommodation above (Fig.7.29:R.P.[8]9 2c). The Provincial Archives have a ground plan for the central block with a different

1. Sketch of site of proposed Château Mount Robson, c.1912.

2. Elevation of proposed Château Mount Robson, 1912.

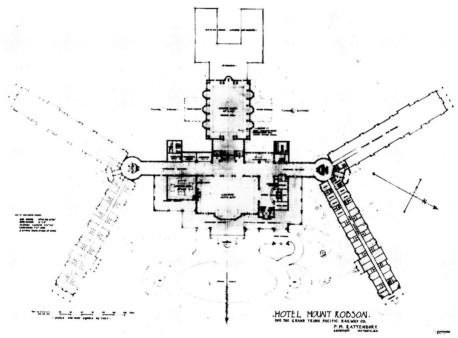

3. Plan of proposed Château Mount Robson, 1912.

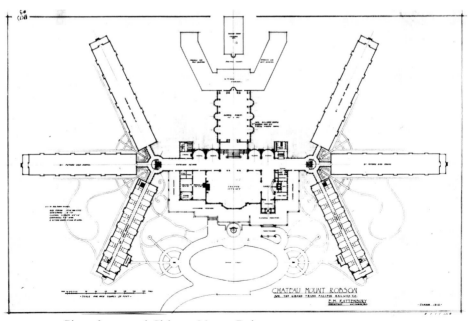

4. Plan of proposed Château Mount Robson, 1912.

5. Preliminary design for Château Miette, c.1912.

6. Sketch design for Château Mount Robson, c.1912.

7. Sketch design for Château Mount Robson, c.1912.

8. Sketch design for Château Mount Robson, c.1912.

9. Sketch design for Château Mount Robson, c.1912.

10. Sketch design for bedroom wing, Château Mount Robson, c.1912.

11. Sketch design for bedroom wing, Château Mount Robson, c.1912.

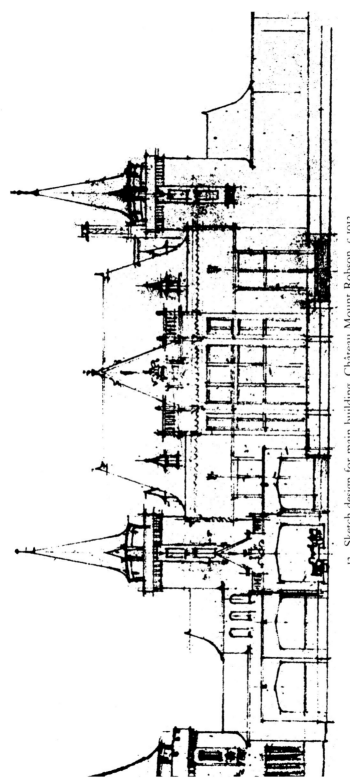

12. Sketch design for main building, Château Mount Robson, c.1912.

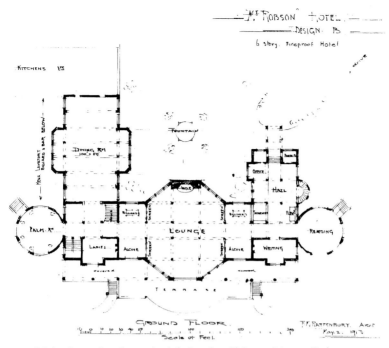

KITCHENS ES

MEN LAVATORY BILLIARD BAR BELOW

DINING RM
100 × 50

FOUNTAIN

OFFICE

HALL

PALM RM

BILLIARD

HALL

READING

LADIES

ALCOVE

LOUNGE

ALCOVE

WRITING

COVERED

TERRACE

GROUND FLOOR

F. K. RATTENBURY. ARCT
May. 2. 1913

Scale of Feet.

13. Main floor plan for revised design for Château Mount Robson, 1913.

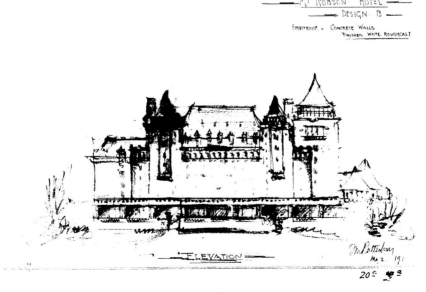

ELEVATION

M[?]. Rattenbury
May 2. 191[?]

20 S

14. Sketch elevation for revised design for Château Mount Robson, 1913.

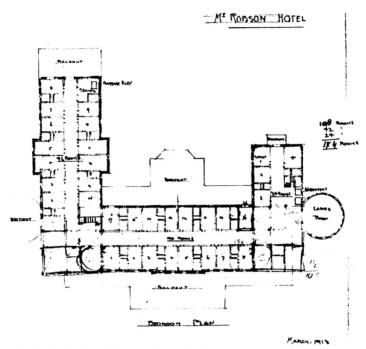

15. Revised plan for Château Mount Robson, 1913.

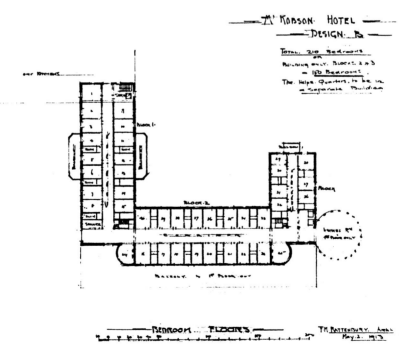

16. Bedroom floor plan for revised design for Château Mount Robson, 1913.

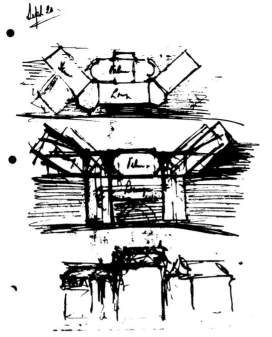

17. Sketch plan and elevation for revised design for Château Mount Robson, c.1913.

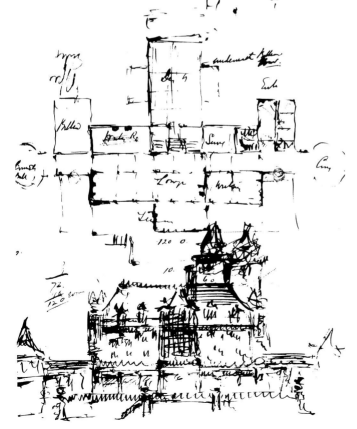

18. Sketch elevation and plan for Château Mount Robson, c.1913.

19. Sketch elevation for revised design for Château Mount Robson, c.1913.

20. Sketch elevation for revised design for Château Mount Robson, c.1913.

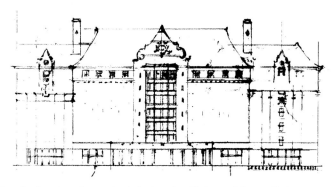

21. Sketch elevation for revised design for Château Mount Robson, c.1913.

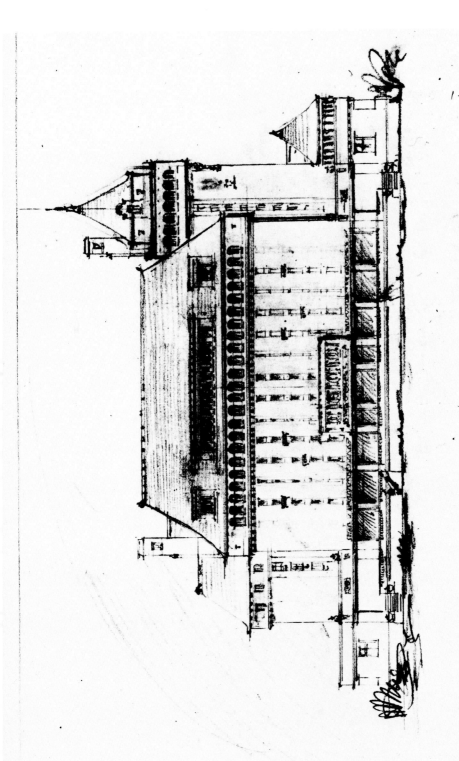

22. Sketch elevation either for revised design for Château Mount Robson, or G.T.P. Hotel at Victoria, c.1913.

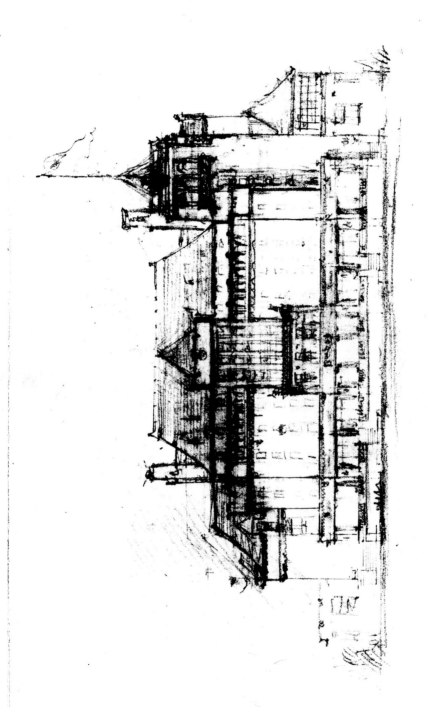

23. Sketch elevation for revised design for Château Mount Robson, or for G.T.P. Hotel at Victoria, c.1913.

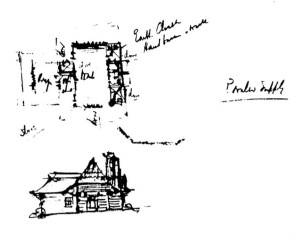

24. Sketch designs for Mount Robson Station, c.1913.

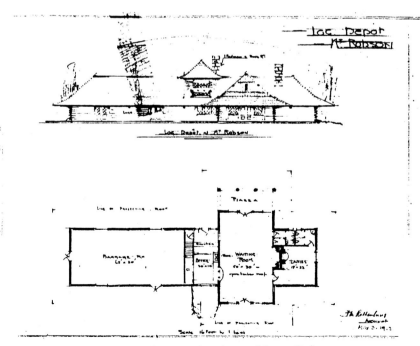

25. Elevation and plan of proposed station at Mount Robson, 1913.

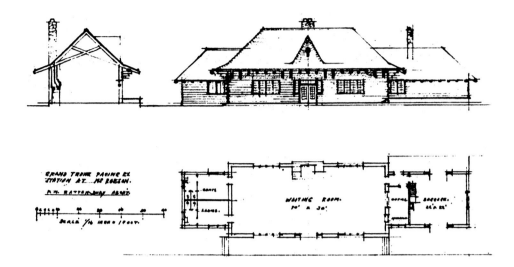

GRAND TRUNK PACIFIC RY
STATION AT Mt ROBSON.

F.M. RATTENBURY ARCHT.

SCALE 1/16 INCH = 1 FOOT.

WAITING ROOM.
70' x 30'

OFFICE.

BAGGAGE.
20' x 22'

COATS
LADIES.

26. Elevation and plan of proposed station at Mount Robson, c.1913.

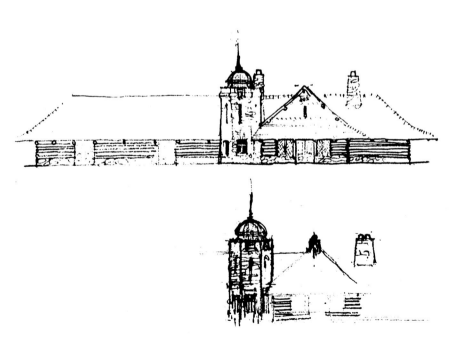

27. Sketch elevation for proposed station for Mount Robson, c.1913.

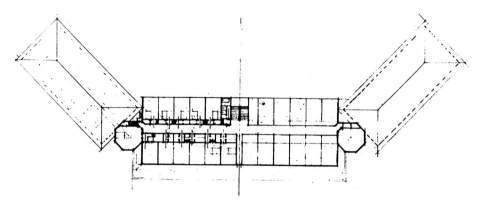

28. Plan of proposed hotel at Miette Springs or Jasper, c.1913.

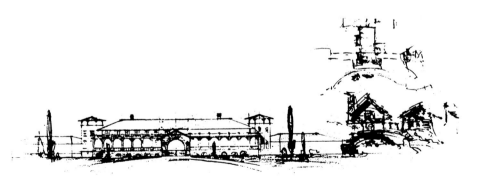

29. Elevation for proposed hotel at Miette Springs or Jasper (left) and sketch elevation and plan for inn at Jasper, c.1913.

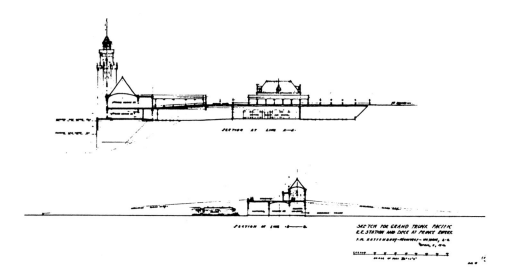

30. Elevation and section of proposed design for G.T.P. station and steamship terminal at Prince Rupert, 1913.

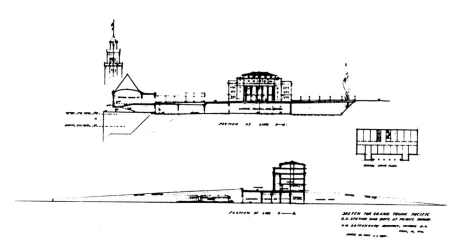

31. Elevation and section of revised design for G.T.P. station and steamship terminal at Prince Rupert, 1913.

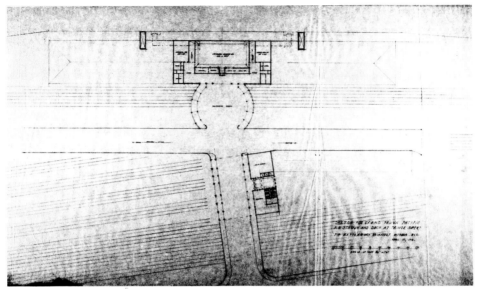

32. Upper level plan of revised design for G.T.P. station and steamship terminal at Prince Rupert, 1913.

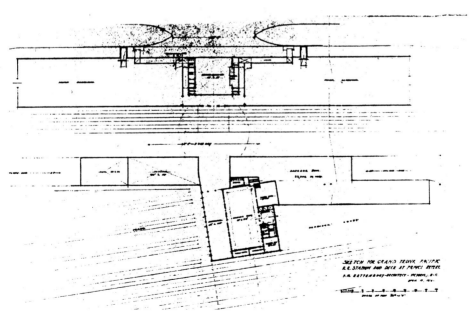

33. Lower level plan of revised design for G.T.P. station and steamship terminal at Prince Rupert, 1913.

layout (R.P.[8]9 2c). The chalet resort eventually constructed at Jasper by the Canadian National Railway in the 1920's bears some relation to these sketches.

Six drawings for the Prince Rupert complex (excluding a series detailing the hotel) remain at the Provincial Archives: two pencil sections through the steamship terminal and railway station, one showing a Classically styled station and the other of a small gabled and pitched roof structure; three associated pencil plans from which at least one blueprint was taken; and one wash elevation of all the proposed buildings in a park-like setting (as promised in the company literature), which is of particular importance as illustrating his final designs for the complex (respectively R.P. [8]4,37,1,38 and 39; and R.P.[8]5). The former group are signed and dated 5 and 7 April 1913 (with the larger station design) and inscribed "Sketch for the Grand Trunk Pacific R.R. Station and Dock Prince while the wash perspective, evidently worked up from Rattenbury's drawings, is signed "David Myers 1913" (R.P.[8]5). It would seem logical to assume that the wash perspective illustrates the architect's final scheme and was commissioned as part of an impending advertising campaign (Fig.7.15).

The more lavish design for the station in Myers's perspective confirms the pattern of increased projected budgeting already indicated by the contrast between the elevations drawn on 5 and 17 April. The 5 April design (Fig. C.30:R.P.[8]37) has a two-storey structure comparable in style with the Mount Robson station designs, fronted by a colonnaded porte-cochère, whereas the 17 April version (Fig.C.31: R.P.[8]4) shows a five-storey edifice with a portico of the so-called Giant Order (columns of two or more storeys in height) recessed between two wings and surmounted by an attic; the extra accommodation could have been intended for company offices. In both designs the platforms, waiting rooms, and associated facilities are situated beneath the station concourse and are reached by internal stairs and elevators. By this arrangement, the platforms are on the same level as the dock and are served by roadways that also communicate with the concourse. In the drawings the terminal has two semicircular colonnaded carriageways on the town side, perhaps in imitation of G. L. Bernini's greatly more glorious piazza before St. Peter's in Rome, which Rattenbury could have visited in 1908 (Figs.C.32,33: R.P. [8]39 sheets 1 and 2). The colonnades lead into a capacious hall and first-class waiting room bounded by lesser accommodation. Once again, access to the dock level was to have been provided by stairs and elevators. The elevators mark the position of the two towers which in the Myers perspective divide the Beaux-Arts style arched centerpiece from the more utilitarian wings. Rattenbury obviously based the design of the towers upon the celebrated Campanile of Venice, the likely inspiration for his unexecuted Campanile Hotel at Victoria dating from about 1929 (interestingly, the G.T.P. pier at Seattle, burned down in 1914, had a single tower, also in the Beaux-Arts style, illustrated in Stevens, *Canadian National*, p. 267).

More significant is the considerable enlargement and realignment of the station in the Myers perspective (Fig.7.15). The main elevation now faces the harbour and comprises three wide, arched openings interspersed with coupled Giant Order Roman Doric columns framed by two three-and-a-half-storey wings, which appear to continue around the corners to enclose colonnades probably similar to those in the 17 April elevations. The main façade is capped by a pedimented eliptical arch and a tall lantern. This façade now spans the intersection of the roadways to the platforms, and when viewed from the harbour, it would have appeared between the towers of the terminal and as a counterpoint to the splendid bulk of the hotel, more massive even than in the *Contract Record* elevation (Fig.7.14). That the Myers perspective represents the final development of Rattenbury's concept for the G.T.P. complex at Prince Rupert is indicated by his visual interrelation of the three buildings. The elliptical arch of the terminal is repeated on a small scale in the attic of the station, the lantern of which echoes those on the terminal towers and sets off the tall gables of the hotel.

Dramatizing this typical Beaux-Arts ensemble is the hotel. In both the Myers perspective and the *Contract Record* elevation, it rises as a grandiloquent reinterpretation of the Empress, adding ideas tried during the course of the planning of the Château Mount Robson. The main block, with its towering steep-sided pitched roof and chimneys, is greatly more impressive than the Mount Robson "Design B," just as its central gabled dormer windows exceed the scale of those on the Empress. Similarly, the corner towers of the Empress reappear in more powerful form, as do the wings proposed in the first scheme for that hotel. Some sense of the magnitude of the Prince Rupert hotel can be gleaned from the number of bays and storeys Rattenbury envisaged: twenty-four bays wide and twelve storeys high, with a further three storeys in the centre.

Recently, Hamish Simpson, headmaster of Glenlyon School, discovered a cache of Rattenbury's drawings for the hotel in the attic of the school (formerly Iechinihl) and presented the collection to the Provincial Archives. The largest group comprises twenty-nine sheets of working drawings, some, as that numbered 44, inscribed, "Full-Size Details G.T.P. Prince Rupert Hotel. F. M. Rattenbury, Architect, Victoria, B.C."; this drawing shows part of the reinforced concrete construction intended for the hotel. The majority of the remainder are marked 37–58 and delineate details of the interior, in the Renaissance style. There are also two blueprints. The first is inscribed on the front, "Prince Rupert Hotel 1st Working Plans and Sketches (1912)" and on the verso, "F. M. Rattenbury (Victoria) B.C., from Brett and Hall-Boston," and "Exhibit 2." (This, together with the three "Design B" drawings for the Mount Robson Hotel, also inscribed with numerals, could have been among the drawings cited in the "Rattenbury vs. G.T.P." file (see Chapter 7, no. 29).) It illustrates most of the ground plan which, minus internal details, is close to the form indicated in the *Contract Record* elevation (Fig. 7.14), but omitting the separate side pavilions. It also shows that the large semi-circular projection at the centre of the hotel in that perspective was intended to be a "Palm Room" and to overlook a broad terrace with formal gardens on either side; at this stage, tennis courts occupy the space assigned to the adjacent pavilions shown in the *Contract Record* elevation and in the Myers perspective. The second blueprint is inscribed, "Truss for Grand Trunk Pacific. Bittman, Engineer, Aug. 5. 13." This was possibly for the roof of the steamship terminal and proves that the G.T.P. projects were proceeding during this period.

NOTES

ABBREVIATIONS

A.E.C.   Arctic Express Company
B.C.S.P.   *British Columbia Sessional Papers*
B.L.K.N.C.   Bennett Lake and Klondyke Navigation Company
C.M.   Cartographic Material
C.P.R.   Canadian Pacific Railway
G.R.   Government Records
G.T.P.   Grand Trunk Pacific
K.M.T.T.C.   Klondyke Mining Trading and Transportation Company
P.A.B.C.   Provincial Archives of British Columbia
R.P.   Reference Plan

NOTES TO THE INTRODUCTION

1. 3: p. 705; this appears at the beginning of a biographical sketch that continues to p.707.

2. *Journal of the Royal Architectural Institute of Canada* 1 (1924): 92ff; for Nobbs, see S. Wagg, *Percy Erskine Nobbs* (Montreal: McCord Museum, McGill-Queen's University Press, 1980). More recently, Martin Segger (*Victoria*, 1974) described Rattenbury as a "brilliant architect," who "understood what corporate or public architecture was all about." Segger does, however, express reservations about his domestic commissions.

3. Replying to the charge that he had ordered foreign oak for the Legislative Buildings, Rattenbury informed the editor of the *Canadian Architect and Builder*, September 1895 (letter dated 24 August 1895), that most of the interior would be furnished with wood from the British Columbia forests and declared, "It has been the earnest desire of everyone concerned with our new Parliament Buildings to utilize as far as possible local and native materials, and we have done so to an extent rarely equalled, I should think, in any building of similar importance."

4. *Canadian Architect and Builder*, September 1906, p. 133, noting that this "suggests the influence of the English architects who have settled there."

5. For the development of the Canadian economy in this period, see K. McNaught, *The Pelican History of Canada*, rev. ed. (Harmondsworth: Penguin, 1975) and R.C. Brown and R. Cook, *Canada 1896-1921: A Nation Transformed* (Toronto: McClelland and Stewart, 1974). Indicative of the growth of the Vancouver economy, which continued at a slower rate after the 1918 Armistice, in the month of January 1913 the city awarded more building permits than any other in Canada, totalling $1,950,000; the total for 1912 had been $26,232,968: *The Contract Record and Engineering Review* 27, no. 4 (22 January, 1913): 63. The *R.A.I.C. Journal* contains further statistics about expenditure on architecture: in 1916, $463,000,000 and in 1922, $331,800,000 (3, no. 2 [1926]: 72), and in 1927, $419,000,000 (5, no. 3 [1928]: 76). See G.W. Taylor, *Builders of British Columbia.* (Victoria: Morriss, 1982).

6. Howay and Scholefield, 3: p. 707.

7. Letter to Sir Thomas Shaughnessy, 25 May 1904, C.P.R. Corporate Archives, R.G.2, Letterbook 84, #460.

8. Quoted from the 1912 C.P.R. pamphlet, *The Empress Hotel.*

NOTES TO CHAPTER ONE

1 The information on Johannes von Ratenburg was provided by Katharine Beauman, niece of the architect, and is based on documents acquired by Mrs. Beauman in Germany before World War II. The documents have since been destroyed.

2. Visitations (which ended towards the close of the seventeenth century) were conducted by representatives of the College of Arms to examine pedigrees and claims to bear arms; their findings were entered into visitation books. Information relative to the Rattenbury family assembled during the Visitation of Devon was collected by Mrs. Beauman in 1956.

3. Reported by his grandson, Harold B. Rattenbury, *China-Burma Vagabond* (London: G.G. Harrap, 1946), p. 12. For a general account of the career of John Rattenbury, see H. Owen Rattenbury, ed. *The John Rattenbury Memorials* (London: T. Woolmer, 1884).

4. John Owen Rattenbury was the second child of John and Mary Rattenbury; The first child was Mary Owen (1835-1912). John's birth-date of 1837, as

opposed to the previously published 1836, is based on an entry in the Rattenbury family bible.

5. It seems likely, though it can not be established, that the Mawson brothers would have been related to Thomas H. Mawson (1861–1933), the famous North Country landscape architect and town planner. Mawson was consulted in the planning schemes of a number of cities throughout the world, including Calgary, Banff, and Vancouver (where, among other projects, he was involved in the layout of the University of British Columbia). On Thomas Mawson, see E. Joyce Morrow, "*Calgary, Many Years Hence*": *the Mawson Report in Perspective* (Calgary: University of Calgary, 1979).

6. Rattenbury to mother, 6 December 1904.

7. Ibid., 27 December 1903 and 14 November 1900.

8. Ibid., 20 August 1901.

9. An account of the firm can be found in A. H. Robinson, "Lockwood and Mawson. The Story of a Great Partnership," *Bradford Bystander*, November 1971, summarized by Reksten, pp. 8–11. See also N. Pevsner and E. R. Radcliffe, *The Buildings of England. Yorkshire. The West Riding*, 2d ed. (Harmondsworth: Penguin, 1967), pp. 60, 63, 122, 124, 134, 164, 248, 249, 282, 318, 427–28; and D. Linstrum, *West Yorkshire. Architects and Architecture* (London: Lund Humphries, 1978), pp. 380–81, with various references to individual works.

10. N. Pevsner and L. Harris, *Lincolnshire* (Harmondsworth: Penguin, 1974), p. 471.

11. Lockwood's pre-eminence notwithstanding, a number of the firm's most important commissions postdated his departure, including the Bradford Markets and Bradford Club. Mawson and Mawson became Mawson and Hudson in 1887, when William retired and his place was taken by Robert Hudson.

12. Rattenbury to mother, 24 October 1905.

13. For the Victorian fascination with cultural history, C. Dellheim, *The Face of the Past. The Preservation of the Medieval Inheritance in Victorian England* (Cambridge: Cambridge University Press, 1982), especially chapter 2 with reference to the Yorkshire Archaeological and Topographical Society and the Bradford Historical and Antiquarian Society.

14. An eastern reviewer, writing in *The Canadian Architect and Builder* of September 1906, p.133, would remark on Rattenbury's recently completed Oak Bay Hotel: "The conjunction of tower and gable... is one of the privileges in composition which flourish in English work but are denied to us who have to look out for snow." For the Queen Anne style, see P. Davey, *Arts and Crafts Architecture. The Search for Earthly Paradise* (London: Architectural Press, 1980); M. Girouard, *Sweetness and Light: The Queen Anne Movement, 1860–1900* (Oxford: Oxford University Press, 1977); for the British background, A. Service, *Edwardian Architecture and Its Origins*

(London: Architectural Press, 1975), p.5; and for the international scene, H. R. Hitchcock, *Architecture. Nineteenth and Twentieth Centuries*, 4th ed. (Harmondsworth: Penguin, 1977).

15. Richardson was praised in R. Kerr's celebrated edition of J. Fergusson, *History of the Modern Styles* (1891), and his Austin Hall, Harvard, illustrated in *The Builder*, 19 December 1885, pls. 860, 861, 864 and 865, and p.858. On Richardson, see H. R. Hitchcock, *The Architecture of H. H. Richardson. His Times* (Hamden, CN.: Archon Books, 1961), and J. O'Gorman, *H. H. Richardson and His Office* (Cambridge, MA: Harvard University Press, 1974).

16. Vol. 33, 28 March 1890 following p. 224; 4 April, pp. 242–43; and 18 April, following p. 278.

17. Exhibited as no. 1750, "Town Hall, Cleckheaton" under the names of Mawson and Hudson, of the Exchange, Bradford (A. Graves, *The Royal Academy of Arts. A Complete Dictionary of Contributors* [London: S. R. Publishers, vol. 3, reprint 1970], p. 216).

18. In a letter dated 13 May, 1903, Rattenbury informed his mother that he had been visited by F. Morton Rattenbury and that the latter's grandfather had originally emigrated to Prince Edward Island from Devon. Rattenbury was amused by the fact that his distant relative bore a striking resemblance to himself. F. Morton Rattenbury, "pork packer," is probably the son of Nelson Rattenbury, a wholesale grocer born in 1851 (see *Prominent Men of Canada* [Montreal: National Publishing Co., 1931–32], p. 413). Nelson was the son of William and Martha Rattenbury.

19. The Windsor Hotel, the scene of a number of dramatic turning points in Rattenbury's career, stood on Peel St. It was designed (1876–78) by W. W. Boyington. See C. Cameron and J. Wright, *Second Empire Style in Canadian Architecture* (Ottawa: Parks Canada, 1980), plate 60.

20. The most comprehensive illustrated histories of Vancouver are A. Kloppenborg ed., *Vancouver's First Century* (Vancouver: J. J. Douglas, 1977), and P. E. Roy, *Vancouver. An Illustrated History* (Toronto: National Museum of Man, 1980).

NOTES TO CHAPTER TWO

1. *Henderson's Gazeteer* for 1899–1900 lists only seven architects in Vancouver and ten (including Rattenbury) in Victoria.

2. Respectively 3 and 20 August 1892, p.1 and 3, and 26 November 1892, p. 2.

3. The attribution was proposed by D. Bodnar in a script for "Then and Now," produced on Vancouver Community Television network, 15 May 1975. But there is no documentary corroboration, and Hilda Weeks, a contemporary resident of the street, recalls, however, that the Roedde House was definitely not designed by Rattenbury (information kindly supplied by J. Watts). The house measured some 36 by 54 feet, excluding the kitchen

wing, and contained a hall, parlour, dining room, and one bedroom on the main floor, with five bedrooms and a bathroom and lavatory above.

4. 6, no.3, n.p.

5. The superior attitude of the eastern judges is evident in the announcement of their decision, published in the November issue of the same journal (p.110). They congratulated J. Francis Brown of Toronto, as he had just recently begun to practice, but did not pay the same compliment to Rattenbury, whom they called "W. J. Rattenbury."

6. P.A.B.C., CM/C677; this reference also applies to the nineteen remaining working drawings, numbered 2–21. The preservation of these and other drawings and documents now at the P.A.B.C. is due to Alan Hodgson, architect of the restoration of the Legislative Buildings. The perspective and other of Rattenbury's drawings are reproduced in M. Segger, *The Parliament Buildings*, who also illustrates some of the rejected entries. A larger version of the elevation and plan that Rattenbury entered in the competition were published in the *Canadian Architect and Builder*, May 1893 (Fig.2.4); the succeeding issues illustrated the submissions by Sorby (placed second) in a weak Château style, and Dick and Wickson (placed third) in the Romanesque mode.

7. The report of the Public Works Department in the 1894 *British Columbia Sessional Papers (B.C.S.P.)*, pp. 785–87 described Rattenbury's design as a "free rendering of Classic, many Romanesque features being introduced. Bold outlines and careful grouping have been more considered than small and costly detail, which would be unsuitable for the stone of the quarries of the province." The report praised Rattenbury's use of local materials and of such functional features as the fireproof concrete for the door and window lintels, corridors, and the covering of the steel members. In addition, it stated that the contract for the foundations of the central block had been let to J. E. Philips and Co. at $54,791. For the United States capitols, see H. R. Hitchcock and W. R. Seale, *Temples of Democracy* (New York: Harcourt Brace Jovanavich, 1976).

8. Respectively illustrated and discussed by J. Physyck, *Marble Halls* (London: H.M.S.O., 1978), and Service, *Edwardian Architecture*.

9. The Treasury was situated on the left (east), the Ministry of Education on the right, of the rotunda. The commissioners of Lands and Works, the Record Office, and the Department of Immigration were located around the Assembly. Abutting the rotunda are staircases to the gallery of the Assembly, the offices of the attorney-general, provincial secretary, minister of agriculture, speaker, and the council room, library, and rooms for the committees of Parliament, each identified by various local woods. The lieutenant-governor's apartments were placed above the entrance on the third floor (called the second by Rattenbury on the working drawings, following the English practice of describing the main level as the ground floor). To facilitate the entertainment of his guests, a kitchen was introduced behind the southern gallery, adjacent to the press reporters' room. Most of the remaining accommodation in the wings, served by the corridors, remained

unallocated. This surplus in office space must have pleased the cabinet, no less than such functional features as the inclusion of secondary staircases giving access to the outer blocks of the main building, the contiguous lavatories on each floor, an elevator, and a heating system.

10. See Reksten, p. 36.

11. The rumour takes a variety of forms. One version, reported privately by Frank Rattenbury, Jr., is that Richard Mawson still considered his nephew an apprentice at the time of the commission and took offence because an appropriate portion of the fee was not remitted to him.

12. Illustrated by J. M. Crook, *Victorian Architecture: A Visual Anthology* (London: Johnson Reprint Co., 1971) p. 259.

13. The newspaper reported: "They [Lockwood and Mawson] built the whole of the model town of Saltaire, churches, mills, universities and markets. On many of these Mr. Rattenbury worked, after having served his articles for six years, gaining great practical experience from them." The journalist had clearly sought to enliven his copy with some imaginative exaggeration. Obviously Rattenbury was too young to have participated in the design and construction of Saltaire, although he doubtless tried to enhance his public image by stressing that he had learned his profession in a firm that had been responsible for such an important project. There were no "universities and markets" at Saltaire; "universities" is a misnomer for the Saltaire Institute while the word "markets" implies that he mentioned the Bradford Covered Market.

14. The nineteen sheets remaining in the Provincial Archives (C.M./C677) are signed "F. M. Rattenbury, Architect, Victoria and Vancouver B.C.," and dated May 1893. Sheet number 2, the plan of the basement of the main building, is further inscribed, "This is one of the drawings referred to in my contract on December 6, 1893."; G.R. 54, box 23, file 395, is the contract for the installation of the press gallery, dated 2 May 1899.

15. P.A.B.C., C/C/30.7R18. This reference includes other correspondence relative to the commission up to 1897.

16. The total cost, based on the figures printed in the *B.C.S.P.*, 1893–99, not including the foundations, amounted to $865,110.01.

17. The report of the Public Works Department, *B.C.S.P.*, 1894, lists the contractors as Messrs. F. Adams, masonry; Bishop and Sherborne, carpentry; Albion Iron Works, metal work; H. T. Flett, plasterwork; W. H. Perry, copperwork; and E. Spillman, painting. They agreed to finish the central building by 30 November 1895 (though this section was not completed until 1896).

18. The fees paid to Rattenbury are listed in the Public Accounts, 1892–99, *B.C.S.P.*; over the ensuing years his fees were as follows: 1893–94, $12,702.85; 1894–95, $5,147.50; 1895–96, $8,148.00; 1896–97, $5,108.74; 1897–98, $6,539.82, and 1898–99, $1,728.44.

19. Reksten, pp. 24–27, supplies a fuller review of the correspondence relating to the affair.

20. P.A.B.C., C/C/30.7/P23.1.

21. *The Contract Record* 6 (21 March 1895): 1, states that Rattenbury was making designs for a clubhouse for the Victoria Canoe Club in the city; as yet no documentary evidence has been discovered to confirm this commission.

22. In the 1894 provincial elections the Theodore Davie administration was returned with a slightly reduced majority.

23. Rattenbury's proficiency could not, however, lengthen the life of the wooden beams supporting the roof; their deterioration prompted the government to initiate the renovation and restoration of the Legislative Buildings in 1972. For the restoration, see D. Bogdanski, "The Restoration of British Columbia's Parliament Buildings," *Canadian Collector* 2 (1976): 56–58.

24. *Province*, 31 December 1951, p.5. The 1894–95 Public Accounts, *B.C.S.P.*, record the cost as $3,476.25 (the contract with the builder A. C. Henderson amounting to $2,985.00 and the remainder included Rattenbury's fee of $149.25).

25. The Public Accounts, *B.C.S.P.*, 1896, state that the contract figure was $32,550.39, but that the tenders amounted to $27,808.00; the final cost listed in the 1877 Public Accounts was $29,093.14. Rattenbury was paid $1,852.65 in fees, the last installment of $236.00 being paid in 1900. A useful review of the building, constructed by Bradbury and Hurst, appears in E. Mills, "The Early Court Houses of British Columbia," Parks Canada, Ms. Report No.2881 (Ottawa, 1977). P.A.B.C. has a specification for the heating system, G.R. 70, vol. 2, file 45, and tenders for the building dated 1895, G.R. 81; the maps and library division also has photocopies of a shingle style design for a wooden courthouse by another, unidentified architect.

26. From the central corridor extending the length of the building behind the entrance, branched offices for the government agent, assessor, collector, inspector of mines, court registrar, sheriff, police, and two cells. The first floor was reserved for the courtroom, 43 by 30 feet, flanked by one room for the judges in each of the towers and others for the jury, barristers, prosecutors, witnesses, library, and two waiting rooms. The court was lit by a clerestory window above the gallery and by the stained glass opening above the entrance; this glass was made by Henry Blomfield and Sons, who were to decorate Government House in 1903: R. Watt, "Henry Blomfield and Sons," *Heritage West* 6 (1982): 28. The walls were panelled with alder to the height of the thick ceiling trusses. Besides the gallery, on the second floor was a grand jury room and ante-chamber, all served by a separate granite staircase at the rear.

27. For this phenomenon and its significance in the history of Canadian architecture, see H. Kalman, *The Railway Hotels and the Development of the Château Style in Canada* (Victoria: University of Victoria, 1968), and A. Rogatnick, "Canadian Castles: Phenomenon of the Railway Hotel," *Architectural Review* 141 (1967): pp. 365–72.

28. Quoted in a retrospective article by the *Vancouver Sun*, 12 April 1972.

29. P.A.B.C., C/C/30.7/R18.

30. Ibid.

31. P.A.B.C., C/C/30.7/H11.

32. Rattenbury to Gore, 5 October 1897: P.A.B.C., C/C/30.7/H11.

33. P.A.B.C., C/C/30.7/R18.

34. See Liscombe and Barrett, pp. 113–16.

35. Illustrated in C. Malden, *Lighted Journey* (Vancouver: B.C. Electric Company, 1948). Information on the building was kindly supplied by Brian Kelly, archivist of B.C. Hydro, successor of the original company. Rattenbury may possibly have revised this design for the somewhat more ornate brick building at 426–430 Homer Street, Vancouver, occupied by the Wrigley Printing Company before 1903; illustrated in *Henderson's B.C. Directory*, 1925, p.1240. This commission is not included in the list of Rattenbury's buildings for lack of documentary evidence.

36. The *Victoria Times* described the Legislative Assembly as a "veritable Triumph of Art and Architecture," and noted that the throne had been made by Messrs. Muirhead and Mann. Among other factual information on the building, the report stated that the wrought-iron gates at the entrance were manufactured in London, the Heine safety furnace in the basement by Bennett and Wright of Toronto, and the kitchen equipment in the lieutenant-governor's apartment by the Albion Iron Works; in the matter of materials it recorded that the rotunda was lined with Tennessee marble and the Legislative Assembly with Indiana oak. The *Colonist* for the same date added that the fresco artist and decorator was Victor Moretti.

37. The Duke of York's statement is recorded in Howay and Scholefield, 3:706.

NOTES TO CHAPTER THREE

1. T. Adney, *The Klondike Stampede of 1897–98* (New York and London: Harper, 1900), pp. 11–12.

2. The description of the *Amur* is taken from Edward E. P. Morgan and Henry F. Woods, *God's Loaded Dice – Alaska 1897–1930* (Caldwell, ID.: Caxton, 1948), p.22.

3. S. Steele, *Forty Years in Canada* (Toronto: McGraw Hill-Ryerson, reprint, 1972), p. 310.

4. Reported in the *Colonist*, 15 May 1898.

5. The notices begin to appear on 22 June. Advertisements in the press indicate that when gold was discovered in 1898 near Lake Tagish (the Atlin fields), the *Nora* was diverted to transport passengers to that area.

6. In a list of donors of wedding gifts that Rattenbury included in the 1898 letter to his mother, he noted that Mrs. Hall gave a "silver bound pocket book – carved."

7. As the later letter to his mother indicates, Rattenbury did not in fact manage to go all the way to Dawson.

8. This letter, and the following one by Partridge, were made available by the Yukon Archives; Department of Information Resources.

9. The *Colonist* of 9 July 1898, reported that Flora Shaw, the "most distinguished lady journalist in the world," was on her way to Skagway, "after which she will go over the White Pass to Bennett, there taking the steamer to Dawson, which she expects to reach by July 20."

10. The announcement appears to conceal what was, in effect, an internal reorganization of one and the same company, since *Henderson's Gazetteer* indicates that both the B.L.K.N.C. and the K.M.T.T.C. had the same Head Office at 23 Leadenhall St., London.

11. W. R. Hamilton, *The Yukon Story* (Vancouver: Mitchell Press, 1964), p.238, lists the names of the steamboats operating between Whitehorse and Dawson in 1899.

12. Information kindly supplied by A. C. Retallack, Public Relations Officer, White Pass and Yukon Route.

13. *Henderson's Gazetteer* indicates that the company stayed in existence, with Rattenbury as its Victoria agent, until at least 1904.

14. p. 325, n. 3.

15. See, for example, the report in the *Colonist* on 31 August 1898: "Miss Flora Shaw's trip from London to Dawson in 31 days... will show our friends in the Old Country that we are not so very far off after all."

16. The letter also records that he had become an uncle, with the birth of Keith, the first of Kate's three children. A good-natured rivalry between brother and sister over the merits of their respective children afforded much scope in the correspondence for gentle and whimsical humour.

17. On Maclure, see L. K. Eaton, *The Architecture of Samuel Maclure* (Victoria: The Art Gallery of Greater Victoria, 1971); J. D. Freeman, "The Other Victoria," *RACAR* 1(1974): 37–46; L. D. Mazer and M. Segger, *City of Victoria Central Area Conservation Report* (Victoria: Heritage Advisory Committee, 1975); and M. Segger, "In Search of Appropriate Form," *Canadian Collector* 11(1976):51–55 and "Variety and Decorum: Style and Form in the Work of Samuel Maclure 1869–1920," *Bulletin of the Society for the Study of Architecture in Canada* 7 (1981): 4–12, especially useful for its review of American and British influences in Canada. Rattenbury also differed from Maclure in not belonging to the Island Arts Club; see C. Johnson-Deane, "The Formation of the Island Arts Club in Victoria, British Columbia," unpublished paper, read at the 1981 B.C. Studies Conference.

18. Merrist Wood is illustrated by A. Saint, *Richard Norman Shaw* (London and New Haven: Yale University Press, 1976), plates 65, 68. For the American style, see V. Scully, *The Stick and Shingle Style* (New Haven: Yale University Press, 1974); and for the suburban Arts and Crafts in Britain, P. Davey, *Arts and Crafts*.

19. Howay and Scholefield, 2:448–51, 467–81.

20. Remittance men were sons of respectable British families who, lacking good prospects, were despatched to the Dominions on a small allowance. *Henderson's Gazetteer* for 1904, p.341, includes the following appraisal of Greenwood: "It stands 2,200 feet above the sea level, and in summer is climatically a delightful spot to live in."

21. Rattenbury's use of steel "I" beams in the structure of the Nelson bank is noted in *Nelson: A Proposal for Urban Heritage Conservation* (Victoria: B.C. Heritage Conservation Report, 1980), p.115, with illustration. McKim was the chief architect in the firm of McKim, Mead and White; see L. Roth, "McKim, Mead and White Reappraised" in *A Monograph of the Works of McKim, Mead and White, 1879–1915* (New York: Arno Press, reprint, 1977).

22. See A. Drexler, R. Chafee, N. Levine, and D. van Zanten, *The Architecture of the Ecole des Beaux-Arts* (New York: Metropolitan Museum, 1978).

23. See T. W. Paterson, *British Columbia: The Pioneer Years* (Langley, B.C.: Stagecoach Press, 1977), pp.125–29.

24. Roy, p.56, illustrates what is almost certainly the depot designed for Vancouver. It shows a simple interior, with refrigerating equipment and cutting tables standing on a concrete floor. The ceiling has exposed steel beams; the walls are white tile, with large three-light windows.

25. *Henderson's Gazetteer* for 1899–1900 shows that Bodwell, a successful Q.C., was then residing at Wilson's Hotel.

26. Margaret Ormsby, *British Columbia: A History* (Toronto: Macmillan, 1958), p.327, notes that, "The outbreak of the South African War in 1899 found British Columbia standing loyally at the side of the Mother Country: in no other section of Canada was there greater martial ardour or more enthusiastic endorsement of the British cause."

27. Rattenbury's restlessness may have been intensified after learning in mid-June that "Pat Burns cannot get away as soon as he expected, in fact cannot tell when he can get away; even his marriage has to be put off."

28. P.A.B.C., CM/A 9511–9512, dated April and May 1899; G.R. box 23, file 403 contains a specification for the alterations, including a draft in Rattenbury's hand, dated May, 1899, and a contract for the alterations signed between the government and W. Ridgway-Wilson on 4 August 1898, presumably invalidated by the subsequent appointment of Rattenbury. The contractor was Richard Drake and the steelwork was supplied by the Carnegie Company.

29. Mazer and Segger, *Victoria Conservation Report*, p.19.

30. P.A.B.C., C/C/30.7/R.18. The 1899–1901 Public Accounts, *B.C.S.P.*, give the total cost as $54,636.41, including Rattenbury's fees of $1,926.40.

NOTES TO CHAPTER FOUR

1. This is based on 5 per cent of the cost of building up to February 1899: $898,537, as given in the Public Accounts, *B.C.S.P.* In fact, as shown by a letter dated 28 December 1904, addressed to the Hon. R. F. Green, chief commissioner of lands and works, by Rattenbury's lawyers, Barnard and Rogers, Rattenbury claimed at least $3,211.89. The letter, incidentally, is endorsed: "Have O[rder] in C[ouncil] prepared making it as explanatory as possible for $2,500 in full settlement" (P.A.B.C., C/C/30.7/R18); payment noted 1904–1905 Public Accounts, *B.C.S.P.*, 1906.

2. Howay and Scolefield, 2:497. For the commission, Cotton, *Mansions*, pp.70–75. The total cost of the work is given as $111,394.21.

3. P.A.B.C., C/C/30.7/R18.

4. Ibid.

5. Sorby's building was an early and classicized version of the Château style, developed on the basis of the Queen Anne mode as reflected in the gables and chimneys that rose above its steeply pitched roofs. More American were the elegant elliptical arched two-storey verandahs that ran along the Georgia Street elevation. The addition was also of masonry construction but in an Italianate style; the identity of the architect remains uncertain.

6. The Union Club, notoriously rowdy, stood at the corner of Douglas and Courtney Streets, opposite the Strathcona Hotel, until 1912; H. Gregson, *A History of Victoria, 1842–1970* (Victoria: Observer Publishing Co., 1970), pp.157–58.

7. The name of the company (provided by the *B.C.S.P.*) was mistakenly given as Byrens and Tait in the press. The other competitors were R. M. Fripp, T. Hooper, Parr and Fee, and C. J. Soule. John M. Byrens and Edwin G. W. Sait each practised at New Westminister. Byrens invented a "storm latch" described in the January 1900 issue of the *Canadian Architect and Builder*. Sait's other work included the H. T. Kirk house and three isolation blocks for the Royal Columbian Hospital, both New Westminister, 1908.

8. In fact, Wolfe landed his troops at Anse au Foulon (Wolfe's Cove) below the Plains of Abraham, situated some two miles west along the St. Lawrence from the site of the hotel in the former French Upper Town (C. P. Stacey, *Quebec 1759*, 2d ed. (London: Pan Books, 1973]).

9. See Kalman, *Railway Hotels*, pp. 26–27. Maxwell had produced a more symmetrical and frankly French interpretation of the Frontenac and of Price's other pioneering C.P.R. buildings, Windsor Station, Montreal (1888–89) and the Place Viger Hotel and Station, also in Montreal. Another influence may have been the Portland House Hotel, in Portland, Oregon, designed for the Northern Pacific by McKim, Mead and White, being of a simplified Château style with polygonal staircase towers linking the flat front to the side pavilions; illustrated, W. C. Shopsin and M. G. Broderick, *The Villard Houses* (New York: Viking Press, 1980), p.39.

10. W. Kaye Lamb, *History of the Canadian Pacific Railway* (New York: Macmillan, 1977), p. 223.

11. The contractor was John Coughlan (who owned brick yards in New Westminster); the final cost was $19,000. Additions to the buildings in 1907 at a cost of $8,000 added 60 by 120 feet, containing storage tanks, paint shops, and so forth.

12. O. Lavallée, *Van Horne's Road* (Montreal: Railfare Enterprises, 1974), p. 290. Field was named after a friend of Van Horne, the Chicago industrialist Cyrus W. Field, who donated $1,000 to its construction.

13. Quoted by Rogatnick, "Canadian Castles," p. 365.

14. "A Winter Journey to Japan," quoted in J. M. Gibbon, *Steel of Empire* (Toronto: McClelland and Stewart, 1935), p. 337.

15. Ibid., p. 99.

16. The photograph also shows a small gabled building to the west, which was probably designed by Rattenbury.

17. C.P.R. Corporate Archives, p.84; C.P. Hotels Ltd., Toronto, hold "Plans and details original Drawing Station [and] Additions," 30715 (1–10) and 30716 (1–12), signed and dated March 1901 and October 1902.

18. P.A.B.C.,C/C/30.7/R18.

19. On 3 January 1901, he wrote: "What a rotten place Headingly will be if they begin building over all the large grounds rows of terrace houses."

20. P.A.B.C.,C/C/30.7/R18.

21. The plan, further signed "F. M. Rattenbury, Supervising Architect," is R.P. (8) #2; this reference includes 1 roof and 2 floor plans, all drawn in ink on tracing paper; a blueprint of the plan is catalogued as R.P. (8) #4, and a blueprint for the kitchens, signed by Rattenbury, R.P. (8) #6. The 1901–1902 Public Accounts, *B.C.S.P.*, 1903, record that Maclure alone was paid as "Architect" (the fee was $1,342.90, Rattenbury first receiving a fee [of $600] also as "Architect" in 1902–1903, and Maclure receiving $560 in the same period). In 1903–1904 Rattenbury was paid $1,131.47 for advising the government on office furnishings, in all likelihood mainly for his work on the by then notorious Government House commission. The total costs of the new buildings listed in the Accounts, 1901–1904, were $120,672.29.

22. The house was called "Fairview" and established the fashion, followed by Maclure, for Tudor detailing on houses. *Henderson's Gazetteer* for 1903 indicates that the McGregor family were in residence before the summer of that year.

23. P.A.B.C., G.R.54, box 22, file 378 contains the order to add the porte-cochère, dated October, 1908, and a blueprint signed "F. M. Rattenbury, Victoria B.C. 1908." The 1908–1910 Public Accounts give the costs as $3,614.75, including Rattenbury's fee of $185; the contractor was A. Wood.

24. He had been entitled to a fee of $127.57. Later, however, in May 1905, he made a claim for these fees, in all $348, when not invited on the grounds of

his busy schedule by the hospital authorities to complete a further extension for a children's ward, a commission eventually carried out by Thomas Hooper. Rattenbury might actually have drawn the plans for this addition in 1903 since the 5 August issue of the *Contract Record* stated that he was preparing designs for an extension to the hospital. There are references in the *Colonist*, 19 and 20 May and 17 November 1905.

25. Rattenbury's description of his uncle's submission suggests a temporary arch, but it is possible that the design was for a permanent triumphal arch, to be dedicated as a memorial to the Boer War. One of the duties performed by the Duke of York on his imperial tour was the distribution of medals to those who had served in the South African War.

26. G. N. Savory, "Colonial Business Initiatives and the Pacific Cable: A Study in the Role of Private Enterprise in the Development of Imperial Commun- ications" (M.A. Thesis, University of Washington, 1972), shows that the cable was chiefly a C.P.R. scheme pushed by Sir Sanford Fleming and backed by Lord Strathcona and the Canadian government. He notes that the origins lay "in the desire of the Canadian Pacific Railway to funnel trans- Pacific trade across its railway lines to the rest of North America and to Great Britain" and that it was considered "an essential complement to steam- ship traffic" (p.190). The cable did not make a profit until 1916.

27. For the buildings and the history of the station, see B. Scott, "Bamfield Bachelor Quarters," *Colonist*, 5 November 1978. On 1 November 1902, the *Colonist* had carried a report of the public meeting held in Victoria to celebrate the opening of the "All Red" line, attended by Mayor Hayward.

28. Illustrated in *Here Today. San Francisco's Architectural Heritage*, 8th ed. (San Francisco: Chronicle Books, 1975), p. 83.

29. Respectively, p.99 (March), p. 123 (April), and p. 65 (February), predicting that "the new hotel will be a magnificent structure, up-to-date in every particular." The drawing from which the illustration was made has not sur- vived. The hotel before Rattenbury's addition is illustrated in a lithograph on p. 43 of the C.P.R. brochure, *The New Highway to the Orient* for July 1900. Rattenbury's Renaissance design anticipated not only Swales and Painter's Vancouver Hotel but also the unexecuted projects for hotels in the city by Braunton and Leibert and by Somervell and Putnam, illustrated in the *Year Book of the British Columbia Society of Architects* (Vancouver: News Advertiser for the Society, 1913); Rattenbury, incidentally, is not listed as a member of the society.

30. A private dining room and a dining room for the servants of guests were linked to the bedroom floors by a private staircase. The top floor seems to have been reserved for the staff and guests' servants.

31. *Province*, 17 December 1901. The best illustrations of Rattenbury's wing are in the Vancouver City Archives, HOT, pp. 33, 37; and the illustrations of the exterior and interior respectively on pp. 48 and 71 of *Greater Vancouver Illustrated* (1906).

32. C.P.R. Corporate Archives, *Contracts and Proposals* book, 1903–10. p.84, lists the following payments for 1903: 31 October, $14,314 to Robertson and Hackert for the laundry; 25 November, $7,500 to Canadian General Electric for the electric generator; 7 December, $3,400 to Baynes and Howe for the "Gas House": for 1904: 21 July, $1,025 to W. O'Neil for fire escapes: for 1905 (among smaller payments on p. 92): 31 May, $590 to Carruthers Manufacturing Co. for showcases for the newstand; 6 June, $350 to C.J. Cummins for decorating; 20 June, $1,099 to J.D. Ross for bar fixtures; and 7 November, $317 to Hinton Electric Co. for "rewiring" the new wing. In the summer of 1905 the company also paid for repairs to the roof of, and the replacement of the screen in, the contiguous Vancouver Opera House.

33. The Vancouver economy had recovered from the depression and was, by then, positively booming, in consequence of the exploitation of the natural resources of the province. *Greater Vancouver Illustrated* described the city as "Canada's most progressive Twentieth Century Metropolis" and the "Liverpool of the Pacific." Sir Thomas Shaughnessy's correspondence includes two letters, dated 1 and 10 May 1906, concerning the projected construction on Kitsilano Beach (then barely part of Vancouver) of a wooden hotel, costing about $65,000, to accommodate guests should the old parts of the Hotel Vancouver be demolished.

34. According to *Greater Vancouver Illustrated*, p.71, it was "furnished to accommodate three hundred guests [and] is known far and wide for its splendid decorations, and the table service is conceded to be the finest of any hotel in the northwest."

35. For the new wing of the Union Club, see Segger, *Victoria*, p.141.

36. Howay and Scholefield, 3: 519. Lotbinière had been appointed in 1900 by the federal Liberal Prime Minister, Sir Wilfrid Laurier, following the questionable support Lotbinière's predecessor, T.R. McInnes, had afforded Joseph Martin when briefly premier of British Columbia.

37. There are references in the letters to the arrival of the furnishings for Cary Castle. On 13 May 1903, he informed his mother: "A young Mr. Thornton Smith from Staynes and Wolfe had been here the last week. He seems a smart young chap and I think has been doing very well for his firm. I was able to throw a few things his way. He came to dinner one night also. He was rather disappointed though that the furniture is not yet in Cary Castle. He was a month too soon." On 25 June he could report, "I have just started unpacking the furniture for Cary Castle; we shall have it all completed and furnished this day month I expect," and on 4 August, "The Staynes and Wolfe Cary Castle fittings are on whole very good. Some of the rooms are very charming. Have you seen Thornton Smith since his return, I wonder."

38. Reksten, p.69.

39. Rattenbury to Hon. R. Green, chief commissioner of lands and works, 13 December 1903.

40. On 8 January 1901, he reported to his mother: "I have just had two plaster casts of Snook's feet made and am sending them to London to get proper

boots made; the ones I got here are no good. One foot is alright but the other twists inwards yet considerably. He can walk and run but, if not attended to, it will not look well when he grows up. I think proper boots will make it alright, though." On 25 February of the same year, he wrote, "I am anxiously awaiting the new boots I ordered from England as it does his feet no good having badly fitting ones, and I don't want any more operations if it can be avoided."

41. Rattenbury to mother, 12 June 1901: "We had a letter the other day from Jack and his wife – all well – he does not say anything to me about leaving the sea."

NOTES TO CHAPTER FIVE

1. On these developments and the earlier plans of George Stephen to recreate a steamship run between Vancouver, Victoria, and San Francisco, see W. Kaye Lamb, *Canadian Pacific*, pp.241–50. The Van Horne Letterbooks in the C.P.R. Corporate Archives cease in 1899.

2. Rattenbury wrote his 14 June letter in a cheerful mood, " I have just been to a circus with Snooks and his mother. There were thousands of children – and the Victoria children are really a beautiful lot, dozens of clear skinned healthy tots, all simply delighted at the monkeys, dogs, clowns, etc., Snookie one of them."

3. This attribution was made by Omer Lavallée, archivist to the C.P.R.

4. p.202.

5. B. Robinson, *Banff Springs. The Story of a Hotel* (Banff: Summerthought, 1973), pp. 38–41, with illustrations 39 and 40, not attributing the work to Rattenbury, but without reference to *The Railway and Shipping World* article and giving the cost as $500,000. The commission for the actual design may not have gone to Rattenbury, as Banff came under the jurisdiction of the Western, rather than the Pacific, division of the C.P.R. The *Contracts and Proposals* book, 1903–10, p.72, notes that $1,076 was paid to Meyer Bros. for installing machinery on 3 April 1903, and $423 to John Watson for iron fire escapes on 13 July 1903.

6 The drawings were numbered H 17–16 (1–3), but have since been destroyed.

7. The index of hotel drawings includes "plans and details of original Dining Station and Additions," respectively 30715 (1–10) and 30716 (1–12), signed by Rattenbury and dated March 1901 and October 1902, probably mainly for the first addition; and "Architectural Plans," "Mechanical Plans," and "Electrical Plans," respectively 14470-1-10, 14470 –1–14 and 14472-1-6, signed by Rattenbury and drawn between 1902 and 1904. (These drawings are now stored with C.P. Hotels Ltd., Toronto.) Two brief references to other work probably overseen by Rattenbury appear in Shaughnessy's Letterbooks: Shaughnessy to I. G. Ogden, 3d vice-president, on 9 November 1903,

approving the expenditure of $880 for "fire protection" and on 17 August 1904, endorsing payment of $625 to Spillman and Todd for painting the Mount Stephen House and Emerald Lake Chalet, respectively RG 2, Letterbooks 83 and 85. The *Contracts and Proposals* book, 1903–10, p.91, records that $381.95 was paid to J. Henderson on 17 April 1905 for an addition to the laundry.

8. C.P.R. Corporate Archives, p.84.

9. The index of hotel drawings lists designs for altering and enlarging the hotel signed by Painter in 1906, 34649 (1–18); from 1906–11 Painter lengthened Rattenbury's wing, refaced its lake front, and added a large half-timbered and gabled wing at right angles.

10. C.P.R. Corporate Archives, RG2, file 78966; the letter was written from Victoria.

11. Rattenbury proposed that the "Centre Wing be completed and should the additional 21 rooms not be deemed sufficient, I would recommend Wing 'A,' on the site of the present Annex, be first built; this would give 30 more additional rooms, subtracting the rooms in the present Annex. The advantage would be in the appearance, and in concentrating the rooms towards the same end of the building [presumably towards the lower, station, end of his wing], and the present annex has not a very much longer life, I suppose – getting rid of the exposed heating plant under the Annex would also effect an economy in service." Aspects of the history of the hotel, though not of its construction, together with illustrations, appear in the C.P.R. pamphlet *Glacier. British Columbia. Canadian Pacific Rockies*, text mainly by M. Macbeth, undated but c.1922; and W. L. Putnam, *The Great Glacier and Its House* (New York: American Alpine Club, 1982).

12. Quoted by Kalman, *Railway Hotels*, p.6. Rattenbury's Glacier House is illustrated, though not attributed to him by H. Kalman and D. Richardson, "Building for Transportation in the Nineteenth Century," *Journal of Canadian Art History* 3 (1976), fig.30.

13. A photograph of the Glacier Hotel in a C.P.R. brochure on the Banff Springs Hotel in their Archives, believed to date to 1897, shows a somewhat shorter version of this annex with a smaller central gabled projection.

14. C.P.R. Corporate Archives, *Contracts and Proposals* book, 1903–10, p. 84.

15. Illustrated in *Here Today. San Francisco Architectural Heritage*, p. 50.

16. C.P.R. Corporate Records, RG2, Letterbook 83; the *Contracts and Proposals* book, 1903–10, p. 84, noted the payment of $2,150 to R.J. Holt on 16 December 1903 for installing a steam-heating plant.

17. Segger, "In Search of Appropriate Form," p. 52, first identified the Neo-Gothic structure as a college.

18. Reksten, p. 81, has proposed that Rattenbury had conceived the scheme well before May 1903 since his sketch in the *Colonist* included, on the left, Hooper's projected Carnegie Library at the corner of Government and Humboldt Streets, despite the fact that almost two months before, on 3

April, the council had decided to erect it on Yates Street. It may be, however, that Rattenbury simply preferred the original site chosen for the library.

19. Victoria City Council Minutes, Volume 10, 1901–1905. Further sparse references to the negotiations appear on pp. 385–86, 402, 408–9, 450, 460, 465, and 558. These references are of particular importance in establishing that Rattenbury's sketch printed on 23 May, and the accompanying interview with Shaughnessy, preceded the formation of the Victoria "hotel" committee.

20. G. Holloway, *The Empress of Victoria*, 2d ed. (Victoria: Empress Publications, 1976), p. 7. The city council minutes (see n. 19 above), pp. 408–9 record the receipt on 8 June 1903 of copies of Bill No. 63 about the "Tourist Hotel" as "finally passed and assented to by the Lieutenant-Governor."

21. In general, Rattenbury seems to have been more concerned with the problem of dealing with individual politicians than with the broader issue of political principles. Only one other overt political statement has survived. British Columbia suffered a constitutional crisis in 1900, resolved with the victory of the Conservatives under James Dunsmuir in the elections held in June of that year. In a letter dated 22 June 1900, Rattenbury referred to "a most exciting general election to finish off with. Fortunately the right side came out on top." In 1903 the Conservative party under Balfour was in power in Britain. The burning issue was Chamberlain's proposed tariff reform, and it is difficult to identify the "socialist tendencies" that seem to have troubled Richard Mawson.

22. Rattenbury appends an amusing sketch of the family, complete with dog, to this letter. He is depicted in a Panama hat and a rather plump Florrie is subtitled, "Florrie – getting stout."

23. What the reporter most appreciated about this forthcoming "enduring monument to the taste and skill of the architect" was the "handsome, medieval wrought iron electroliers" intended to be installed over the entrance and corner tower "not unlike the ancient cressets [and these are surely Rattenbury's words] which aforetime flamed ruddily down the narrow causeways in the quaint towns of the Middle Ages." Blueprints of the original designs, dated January 1903, and of those "corrected" in August 1906, after the commission was revived, remain in P.A.B.C., G.R. 54, box 24, file 406; this also includes the specification, dated August 1906, and blueprints for the external wall and railing, and the internal fittings, dated 1908. A drawing of the main floor plan is catalogued as C.M./A9517. The 1903–1904 Public Accounts, *B.C.S.P.*, 1905, record the payment of $1,050 to Rattenbury for "Architect's services." Rattenbury's courthouse replaced one built 1893–94 to the designs of A. M. Muir.

24. C.P.R. Corporate Archives, RG2 file 73093, the reference for the other telegrams quoted in this paragraph.

25. Ibid.; Jennings's letterhead consisted of an illustration of the Hotel Denny.

26. Ibid., file 73728; this also contains a letter from the chief engineer to

McNicoll dated 23 November relating a discussion with Rattenbury, who had blamed the failure upon insufficient piling below the infilling. The engineer recommended that Rattenbury consult C. S. Bihler of Tacoma, former divisional engineer of the Northern Pacific Railroad. The causeway itself had been designed by the city engineer, Charles H. Topp.

27. In a letter dated 3 June 1904 Rattenbury referred to "Mr. Reed's suggestions of last November"; for the text of this letter see page 157.

28. Kalman, *Railway Hotels* p. 18.

29. Published in V. Petit, *Châteaux de la vallée de la Loire* (Paris: C. Boivin, 1861).

30. The bays are divided by two *antae* in imitation of the Choragic Monument of Thrasyllus at Athens.

31. Kalman, *Railway Hotels*, p. 25, fig. 24. Interestingly, Cormier imitated Rattenbury's façade composition, but inverted the arrangement of the pitched roofs, so that the roof over the central block of the court rose above those on the flanking towers.

32. C.P.R. Corporate Archives, RG2, file 73728.

33. On 21 November 1903 Rattenbury confirmed a conversation he had held with Shaughnessy that afternoon, in which he was authorized to "engage expert assistance and to spend to the extent of $500 with regard to the foundation"; C.P.R. Corporate Archives, RG2, file 73093; Shaughnessy telegraphed next day, noting that Rattenbury should have written "an amount *not exceeding $500* in securing expert advice about the foundation"; RG2, Letterbook 83,#268.

34. Cited in L. B. Crawford and J. G. Sutherland, "The Empress Hotel, Victoria. Sixty-five Years of Foundation Settlements," *Canadian Geotechnical Journal* 8 (1971): 77–93.

35. Shaughnessy decided to engage the Shankland Co. in July 1904; they presented their report on the 29th of that month. The contract, signed on 7 September 1904, called for 22,000 cubic yards of excavation, 2,853 Eucalyptus timber piles, 50 feet long, 500 at 20 feet long, 60,500 f.b.m. planking, and 9,000 cubic yards of concrete. The hotel has settled approximately 30 inches from north to south.

36. Rattenbury was later to acquire an American Cadillac.

37. C.P.R. Corporate Archives, RG2, file 74993, the source for all the references in this paragraph.

38. Ibid.; Reed proposed meeting Shaughnessy at the Place Viger Hotel in Montreal to discuss his memorandum, which the president clearly thought unnecessary, given his telegram of 26 May.

39. Ibid., Letterbook 84,#460.

40. Ibid., file 74993.

41. The 1904 drawings are preserved at C. P. Hotels Ltd., Toronto, 31507 (1–11), incorrectly dated November in the index; further elevations and details are indexed under 31506 and 31509.

42. The 163 bedrooms consisted of 27 on the first floor, 38 on the second to

fourth floors, 31 on the fifth, and 21 on the sixth. The majority had attached bathrooms, except the bedrooms on the top floor, which were fitted in beneath the pitched roofs. At this level, the guests shared bathroom and washroom facilities, which, as on the lower floors, were placed behind the staircases at either end of the main corridor across the hotel, gentlemen on the left (north) side and ladies on the right. Each floor was also served by two elevators, one for the staff ascending from the kitchen on the north side, and the other for the guests ascending from the lobby abutting the porte-cochère on the south side.

43. For the original interior, see the *Colonist* report of 1 December 1903; and for a description of the hotel after its opening, see G. Holloway, *Empress*, n. 10. Further information on the construction of the hotel appears in Segger, *Victoria*, pp. 137–39.

44. The C.P.R. *Contracts and Proposals* book, 1903–10, p. 85, states that the contractors, Smith and Sherborne, were paid $8,900 ($8,300 is pencilled below) for the office on 2 November 1904.

45. Gregson, *Victoria*, p. 223, states that the hotel was built in nineteen days.

46. *Colonist*, 28 April 1968.

47. The ground was broken on 15 March 1906, and the structure completed by 26 July, at a cost of some $15,000. The contractor was T. Catrall. Information kindly supplied by B. Kelly, archivist of B. C. Hydro.

48. C.P.R. Corporate Archives, S. P. 204 (September) including an alternative scheme for fireproofing the basement, ground, and first floors only, and S. P. 189 (November). Rattenbury selected the "Roebling" system, which comprised steel-ribbed wire cloth centring and cinder concrete arches for the floors; the partition walls were of fireproof brick. The September specification included instructions on the cutting and cost of Haddington Island stone, noting that the quarries were then owned by W. A. Huson of Victoria.

49. C.P.R. Corporate Archives, RG2, Letterbook 84,#398½, confirmed in a letter signed by Shaughnessy on 13 February 1904.

50. C.P.R. Corporate Archives, *Contracts and Proposals* book, 1903–10, p.91, recording the payment of $675 to John Haggerty for clearing the site on 10 July 1904. Earlier on 22 March Haggerty had received a contract for gravel infilling around the site, amounting to 25,000 cubic yards at the rate of 60¢ a cubic yard, p. 85.

51. *Colonist*, 8 August 1905.

52. Ibid., 9 August 1905.

53. This building is attributed to Rattenbury in the *City of Victoria Heritage Conservation Report*, p. 53.

54. The scheme was evidently a success, since on 31 October he reported to his mother: "We are pretty well living on game just now. My gamekeeper has been very busy. He brought in a bag today of 8 pheasant, 8 grouse and 15 quail for 3 days shooting."

55. It is possible that he refers to this earlier house in a letter written to his

mother on 4 August 1903: "This month I have been rather busy letting contracts for some homes." The second house was not begun until February 1907, the *Colonist* on 3 January announcing the award of the contract to Noble Bros. for "approximately $6,200."

56. In the *Colonist*, 1 December 1903, Rattenbury is quoted as saying he would "follow" the *Princess Beatrice.*

57. Rattenbury, so decisive in his professional career, displayed an amusing indecision over his daughter's name. On 13 May 1904 he reported that "May arrived safely" and added, "I suppose the question now is the name. You say 'May,' Florrie suggests 'Stephanie.' I hold up my hands for 'Mary Katherine' – when you have some good names in the family why not stick to them? I did suggest 'Martha' from the Okehampton book, but the suggestion did not meet with the approval that it deserved." On 12 June he noted, "just a month since "Hester" arrived. . . . How do you like Hester for a name? one of the old Rattenbury Okehampton names." (It will be recalled that Hester was the lady who came very close to being buried alive.) On 4 July he had changed his mind yet again, "I think we shall call her Hester Mary or Mary Hester." Finally, on 27 July he informed his mother, "For your definite information MARY, plain Mary is to be the name. When one has tired of thinking of the fancy names the old familiar names always seem the best."

58. A reference to this celebration is found in a letter from William Oliver in the Public Archives; Oliver wrote that he was missed at the annual party: "Irving broke one of my wife's best drawing room chairs, and Rattenbury's dress coat which was bought for the occasion was hanging in rags as he left. It was a very successful celebration and as my wife and family are still in the old country no one was disturbed" (4 January 1906, Newcombe Collection, P.A.B.C.).

NOTES TO CHAPTER SIX

1. *Colonist*, 23 May 1903.

2. *Victoria Times,* 3 February 1906

3. D. Bodnar, "The Prairie Legislative Assemblies"(M.A. Thesis, University of British Columbia, 1979), pp. 24–72.

4. The Canadian Northern Line had an enormous impact on the Prairie region. From 1903 the company sited standard townsites along their lines: North Battleford, for example, had been ushered into existence in June 1905 with only one house, but six months later it had a population of 500 (farm property at $6 an acre had become city lots at $10 a frontage foot); see J. W. Davidson, "The Canadian Northern Railway," *Queen's Quarterly* 14 (1906): 108.

5. G. R. Stevens, *History of the Canadian National Railways* (New York: Macmillan, 1973), provides an excellent biography of Mackenzie, including a full review of his friendship with Mann; see also R. Black, "Mackenzie and Mann—Builders of a Transcontinental Railway," *Contract Record* 27(1912):58–60.

6. In the same letter he also refers to the progress of the Empress: "The big Hotel is looming up. I wish there was a chance of my engaging a suite for you, I would have it decorated in rose brocade."

7. See Liscombe and Barrett. It may be noted that the Canadian National Railway Station by Pratt and Ross, Vancouver, 1917–19, has a somewhat similar configuration to the Vancouver Courthouse, with raised engaged columns on either side of the main entrance.

8. P.A.B.C., G.R.77, file 1, contains a telegram dated 10 May 1906 from Edmund Burke of Toronto, president of the Ontario Association of Architects, who was paid $300 to judge the competition, sent to F.C. Gamble, stating that only design "four" was acceptable, which implies that none of the other entries was, despite Rattenbury's cautiousness, "swaggerer" than his own. Tenders for, and correspondence relating to, various of the contracts for the courthouse (all in excess of $400,000, and not including the heating, plumbing, and furnishings), from May 1908, handled by Dalton and Eveleigh as supervising architects: P.A.B.C., 54, vols. 21 and 24 (files 404, 405, and 409) and G.R.77 (files 2–4).

9. Apart from the extension to the Vancouver Courthouse, 1912, by Hooper, who had, admittedly, worked in the Beaux-Arts style before (as in his 1903 design for the Carnegie Library, Victoria), J. J. Honeyman and G. D. Curtis built Classically styled courthouses at Revelstoke and Vernon, both 1911, the latter with an *in antis* Ionic portico; for these buildings, see Mills, *Courthouses*. Somervell and Putnam incorporated Rattenbury's courthouse in a grandiose plan for a "Proposed Park," occupying the blocks to the north and south, published in the 1913 *Year Book* of the B.C. Society of Architects.

10. This occupied block 51 and was purchased by the B.C. government for $35,000; 1906–1907 Public Accounts, *B.C.S.P.*, 1908.

11. *Province*, 14 March 1907.

12. CM/B9513. Signed and dated April 1907, and numbered 2–12.

13. Vancouver City Archives, Add. Ms. no. 83, dated May 1907.

14. The excavations were dug by Messrs. Smith and Sherborne and the steel supplied by John Coughlan and Sons, both of Vancouver. The steel beams of the staircase in the rotunda were manufactured by W. MacFarlane and Co. of Glasgow. The granite basement came from Nelson Island. The remodelling of the courthouse for the Vancouver Art Gallery has revealed a number of faults in the construction, attributable to the contractors, not to Rattenbury. The 1906–1910 Public Accounts, *B.C.S.P.*, give the costs, omitting the purchase of the site, as $460,887.74; the final total was considerably greater, since the 1910–1911 Accounts state that the completion of

the courthouse and the plans for the addition amounted to $199,093.89. Rattenbury's fees were $20,410.47; Dalton and Eveleigh were first paid for supervising the work in 1907. The new wing cost over $250,000, according to the Public Works Department report in the 1915 *B.C.S.P.*

15. *Province*, 30 August 1906.

16. One reason for Rattenbury's being passed over might have been the complaint by the judges that the courts were poorly lit (*Province*, 10 April 1909).

17. On the remodelling process, see B. Shapiro, "The Three Block Project: Classicism and Modernism Combined," *Trace* 15 (1981): 10–18.

18. Public Accounts 1906–1909, *B.C.S.P.*; Rattenbury's fees, paid in 1906–1907, were $1,852.39. The contract price was $74,990: P.A.B.C., G.R.54. vol.24, file 406, also containing the extant drawings, blueprints, and documentation. See also, *Nelson: A Proposal for Urban Heritage Conservation* (1980), p.134, with illustration, but incorrectly stated to have opened in 1905.

19. It had arrived by 17 July 1906, since he refers to it in a letter to his mother.

20. A similar tone of flippancy is revealed in a letter written on 10 July 1900 to his mother: "The Governor-General of Canada, Lord Minto, is coming to stay in Victoria, and has taken a house close by us. I hope he is a neighbourly cuss."

21. Rattenbury mistakenly dated his letter 16 April, although it must have been written (or completed) a few days later, since the great earthquake occurred on 18 April 1906.

22. The residences are identified in Rattenbury's hand: "Our shack, Crow-Baker's house, Bryden's house, Fred Pemberton's gardens, Cary Castle, Arbuthnot's house, [Hooper] the architect who tried to down me."

23. See Eaton, *Maclure*, intro.

24. The *Colonist*, 29 July 1906, announced that Rattenbury was calling for tenders on the Grahame house (to be received by 4 August), and stated that the contractor for the porte-cochère would be T. Catrall.

25. Reksten, p.86, suggests that his resignation from the Empress commission came about because of a quarrel with Mrs. Hayter Reed, wife of the superintendent of western hotels. But apart from the fact that he had informed the *Colonist* in December 1903 that "Much assistance will be given in the matter of decoration and arrangement by Mrs. Hayter Reed," he must have known how highly she was regarded by Van Horne. It was Van Horne who had persuaded Hayter Reed to relinquish the post of Indian superintendent in the Northwest Territories and join the C.P.R., and he had invited his wife to furnish the Château Frontenac, which Rattenbury had earlier praised.

26. Professor Robert Todd writes: "The theatre in question was a wooden structure originally built in 1899, and opened as the Alhambra. Subsequently it was known as the Royal Theatre (1903), and People's Theatre (1903–1905). In late 1905 it was taken over by Sullivan and Considine's Seattle-based

vaudeville circuit. They undertook extensive renovations, described in the *Province*, 30 January 1906. The *Province*, 20 September 1906, reported that the theatre was declared unsafe by Vancouver Building Inspector McSpadden. See also, "The Organization of Professional Theatre in Vancouver, 1886–1914," *B.C. Studies* 44 (1978–1980): 8–9.

27. The opening was reported in the The *Railway and Shipping* (later, *[Canadian] Railway and Marine) World* for February 1908, p. 119; an illustration of the completed hotel appeared in the April 1907 issue, p. 255.

28. *Colonist*, 21 January 1908. Such flowery lyricism was not unique to Phillips-Wooley, as is evidenced by the 1912 C.P.R. pamphlet, *The Empress Hotel*, which asks, "What fairy lore transcends the tale of this latest in the Canadian Pacific Hotel chain, an architectural monument to progress, where was, but a decade since, a dreary tidal flat?"

29. Howay and Scholefield, 3: 549–50. Howay's optimism would have been fed by the construction of the G.T.P. Marine Terminal, including a drydock, ship repair and shipbuilding plant, begun in 1912, for which the federal government had granted a subsidy of $2,200,000 in 1911 (*The Railway and Marine World*, respectively February 1912, pp. 92–96 and November 1911, p. 1037); the complex was finished before November 1915 (ibid., p.424).

30. The design was described as a "handsome frame structure" in the *Province* of 6 November 1906, where the cost was estimated at $40,000–$50,000 and the projected completion date given as May 1907. The *Canadian Architect and Builder* for February 1908, p. 14, under the heading "A Model City" announced that the Boston landscape architects Brett and Hall had been engaged by the G.T.P. to lay out Prince Rupert.

31. Saskatchewan Archives Board, Regina, Records of the Department of Public Works, Legislative Building Competition, file no. 118.

32. For this episode, and the history of the school, see P. L. Smith, *Come Give a Cheer* (Victoria: Victoria High School Centennial Celebrations Committee, 1976), esp. p.62.

33. The vote of censure was proposed by trustee McKeown and seconded by trustee Lewis, though the superintendent was authorized to confer with Rattenbury; his drawings and estimates (the figure is not given in the minutes) were presented on the 23rd, but not discussed again.

34. *Colonist*, 24 January, 1907. The conditions of the competition are recorded in Appendix A – Part III, 6–7 Edward VII, Sessional Paper No. 19, A1907.

35. The judges were Edmund Burke, Alcide Chausse, president of the Quebec Association, and D. Ewart, chief architect of the Department of Public Works. An article on the competition, entitled "Architects in Competition," appeared in the *Ottawa Evening Journal*, 4 September 1907; the first prize was awarded to E. S. Maxwell. Another report, in the *Canadian Architect and Builder*, October 1907, pp.210–11, reviewing the first twenty-one designs in the competition, did not mention Rattenbury's entry; pp. 201–2 have a further account of the competition, while the second-prize design by Darling and Pearson is illustrated, pp. 204–9.

36. See Segger, *Victoria*, p. 83.

37. The advertisement listed the "Preliminary Board of Directors" as "Joshua Kingham, of Kingham and Co., Coal Merchants, William H. Parsons of Parsons and Co., Real Estate, Henry A. Bulwer, gentleman, John A. Hinton, of Hinton Electrical Co., and Samuel Johns, of Johns Brothers, general merchants."

38. Rattenbury told the newspaper that the Saskatchewan Parliament was to be larger than the Victoria Legislature, being estimated to cost at least half as much again, and that each competitor would be paid a fee of $1,500.

39. This phase of British architecture is reviewed in Service, *Edwardian Architecture*.

40. See Hitchcock and Seale, *Temples of Democracy*; they were designed, respectively, by M. Butler and R. Clark, and G. R. Mann and Cass Gilbert.

41. There is no reason to assume that Rattenbury ceased to correspond with his mother during this period. The one surviving letter was found separately from the main body of correspondence and is presumably the only one to have survived.

42. The engineers faced a daunting task: twelve million tons of earth had to be moved and four million tons of rock blasted to complete the first 100 miles from the coast. The completion of this section was reported by Hays at the 1911 meeting of the G.T.P. shareholders. Hays at that time predicted that the track would reach Aldermere, 240 miles east of Prince Rupert, in 1912: *The Railway and Marine World*, November 1911, p. 1037. He also reported that "the large areas of arable land situated in the valleys" adjacent to the line, and the "tide of immigrants and settlers" would create "a large traffic available for transportation as soon as the railway can be completed." In 1912, after one of the most impressive feats in the history of railway construction, the crews reached Finnemore, 416 miles east of Prince Rupert, where the link-up with the eastern section from Winnipeg was to take place. The laying of that section was slower than envisaged, so that the first through-train did not steam into Prince Rupert until 14 April 1914.

43. Recorded in a press cutting in the Provincial Archives, "Fifty Years Ago," from the *Colonist*, 1908 (month and day not indicated).

44. Reksten, p. 88, suggests that Rattenbury was provided with prior information by the company's lawyer, Ernest Bodwell, for whom he had designed a house some years before.

45. On 13 September 1906, for instance, the *Colonist* reported that Colonel Topping had organized an exhibition of local produce from the Bulkley Valley at the Nelson Fair.

46. This comment was made in a letter to the *Victoria Times* of 19 April 1918; for the amounts involved, see chapter 2, n.16. Rattenbury's holdings are marked in detail on four maps held by P.A.B.C. (C.M.C.1006–9).

47. 2 (1911), pp. 602–12; Talbot had crossed the country in 1910 by pack-horse and canoe.

48. For example, the *Colonist*, 31 January 1903, 7 June 1903, 2 August 1903, *Province*, 30 October 1903. On the mineral deposits near Telkwa, see the *Province*, 5 October 1906, *Times*, 15 December 1906, *Colonist*, 31 July 1907.

49. See n.43.

50. The B.C. government gazetted a pre-emption reserve in the Nass Valley on 25 February 1909. The P.A.B.C. holds a letter dated 30 July 1909 from the B.C. Land Investment Agency to Rattenbury (A/E/Or 3/R181). The letter is accompanied by a cheque in part payment for a section of the land for which Rattenbury had applied to the government. The section is described as 640 acres and is one of twenty applications.

51. Writing to his mother on 1 November 1910, Rattenbury was still optimistic, reporting that on his return from England he had found that his "various properties were much more valuable. . . . So I actually was making money and not spending it whilst away. So all round I have been very lucky."

NOTES TO CHAPTER SEVEN

1. On 27 February 1908 his mother wrote to him of her serious problems with gallstones, and of being visited by the mayoress. The letter is held by the Victoria City Archives (see chapter 8, n.3).

2. *Victoria Times*, 10 June 1908.

3. In the *Colonist* of 6 December 1906, Rattenbury, commenting on the criticisms expressed by a resident of Winnipeg, T. Blackwood, about the cramped streets of Victoria, agreed only that Fort Street should be widened.

4. *Contract Record* 22 (9 September, 2 December 1908).

5. *Contract Record* 23 (27 January 1909); on 21 April the *Contract Record* announced that the contract had been let to Dinsdale and Malcolm for $8,500. Earlier on 20 May 1908 the magazine had carried Rattenbury's call for tenders on a Restaurant and Machinery Hall to be erected on the B.C. Agricultural Association Fairgrounds at Victoria, but no further information on this commission has been discovered thus far.

6. *Contract Record* 23 (29 December 1909). In the 13 April 1910 issue it was announced that "negotiations are in progress between the G.T.P. and the Hudson Bay Company for the acquisition of property on Wharf Street, on which the former may erect a new hotel." On 3 August the company reported that it had "secured options on property to be used as the site for their hotel." The 7 September issue of the journal recorded the visit to Victoria of C. M. Hays in connection with the letting of the "contract for the office building to face Wharf Street." Then on 21 September the journal stated that the company had "acquired over two acres of land on Government, Relleville [Belleville] and Elliott Streets, Victoria, facing the Parliament Buildings, on which will be erected a first class hotel as part of the transcontinental system" at an estimated cost of $291,000. This last

information was noted also in *The Railway and Marine World*, October 1910, p.845.

7. D. Pethick. *British Columbia Disasters* (Langley, B.C.: Stagecoach Press, 1979), pp. 155–59, provides an account of the fire; Maclure's office was destroyed at the same time. Rattenbury's office was in Room 3; the 1914 Victoria directory records the address of his office as 621 Sayward Building.

8. Correspondence from Scholefield, the provincial librarian, proves that he had moved to an office on Langley Street by April 1911: P.A.B.C., for instance, G.R. 146, vol. 3, p. 85 (Scholefield to Rattenbury, 11 April 1911).

9. *Contract Record* (30 November 1910), estimated at $120,000.

10. A number of tall buildings, echoing the commercial style of Chicago via Seattle and Portland, had already been erected in Vancouver, notably W. T. Whiteway's seventeen-storey *World* Building, 1911–1912, for which see Kalman, *Vancouver*. The increasing scale of Vancouver commercial architecture is further indicated by the designs for the proposed office buildings, published in the 1913 *Year Book* of the B.C. Society of Architects.

11. In ink on tracing paper, the plan, signed "F. M. Rattenbury Architect," is C.M./C17618, and the elevation is Plan 3 616. 9 FC B862 n.p.

12. When drawing this elevation, Rattenbury had made a bold pencil sketch of one of the globes, on which the Atlas figures are placed at the centres of a differently designed tower, reproduced Segger, *The Parliament Buildings*.

13. The letters written by Scholefield to Rattenbury are preserved in Scholefield's correspondence at the P.A.B.C., G.R. 146, vol. 3, pp. 85ff. and G.R. 726, box 1; these references apply to all the letters cited in this section of the text. Scholefield was tardy as well as cautious; for example, he did not send Rattenbury the schedule of required accommodation he had compiled on 1 March 1910 for the government until 18 April 1911, nor did he send information on the best suppliers of library stacks until 13 July 1911.

14. R.P.(8) 18, sheets 1–4; blueprints based on drawings, R.P. (8) 46. The elevation, preserved only in a photograph, is in P.A.B.C., Visual Records.

15. On R.P. (8) 18 there is a note referring to these statues "4 statues south Kensington," presumably a reference to Aston Webb's academic Classical design for the Victoria and Albert Museum, 1891, executed 1899–1909.

16. The floor plans of the museum are included in the April 1911 plans for the library and Legislative Building extension, R.P. (8) 46.

17. P.A.B.C., G.R. 726, box 1. Scholefield was then attending the annual meeting of the American Library Association at the Maryland Hotel in Pasadena, California.

18. Noted in Scholefield's letter of 21 June to Rattenbury: P.A.B.C., G.R. 146, vol. 3, pp.527–32. Scholefield wanted the reading and reference rooms enlarged to 30 by 40 feet and asked, among other alterations, that stairs be introduced next to the lift in the stacks. The letter, however, also contained a full list of required accommodation for the library.

19. Typical of the letters that Scholefield addressed to Rattenbury, was the one written on 28 June (G.R. 146, vol 3, p. 375): "I have just received a letter from Mr. Jennings, a friend of mine who happens to be in Victoria for the Coronation celebrations, and I have pleasure in sending to you, herewith, a copy of it [absent from the archives]. . . . Mr. Jennings looked over the plans which I carried to you the other day and he was kind enough to say that, considering our limitations, the arrangement is in every way excellent. How splendid it were, had it been possible to connect the new east and west wings with one fine façade facing south on Superior Street. Then the library would indeed have been one of the finest on the continent."

20. For example the *Contract Record* 25 (2 August 1911) announced that tenders were being called for the extensions and library block, then estimated at $750,000. By 4 October the same journal gave the estimated cost as $1,000,000 or $1,250,000.

21. R.P.(8) 20–45, dated from October 1913 to 18 May 1916; blueprints of the second and third floor as built, signed "Mr. Whittaker Acting Supervising Architect" and dated "28.9.'17" detail the final furnishing of the interior of the library.

22. *Contract Record* 25 (4 October 1911) announcing that work would begin on 22 November.

23. Fraser's contracts, together with those with all the other tradesmen, are listed in the Public Accounts, 1911–13, *B.C.S.P;* the accounts for the period 1911–13 record the expenditure of $1,297,643.03 on the commission, including $64,914.34 paid in fees to Rattenbury. The main contractors were Messrs. McDonald and Wilson, and his clerk of works was A. Wood. A report of the parliamentary enquiry into the cost of the commission printed in the *Victoria Times*, 1 May 1916, states that the contractors were chosen by the chief commissioner of public works, W. S. McDonald, and not by Rattenbury. Fraser had been a "druggist" some nine months before, and the firm of McDonald and Wilson (with Snider) had performed poorly in the Vancouver Courthouse commission. The steel frame for the wings and library was supplied by J. Coughlan and Sons of Vancouver: G.R. 929, box 13, containing letters of confirmation of the contract, dated 23 November 1911 and 19 September 1913, sent by the company to McDonald and Wilson. In November 1911 Coughlan agreed a figure of $49,000.00, noting that "this price includes for the self-contained steel frame in accordance with all [the] steel plans, as prepared by Mr. Rattenbury, and the entire work subject to his approval." By September 1913 the figure, presumably now for the library alone, in accordance with "specifications and Steel Plan 'B,'" had risen to $57,000.00; alternatively, they also offered to "furnish the steel in accordance with wall bearing plans" for $42,000. G.R.54, box 39, has a specification for the library furniture, dated 1914.

24. Noted in the press cutting, "Right Wing of the Buildings," Vancouver City Archives, Rattenbury File, dated 6 September 1947.

25. P.A.B.C., Maps Msc. (9) 11, three blueprints; the cost of this commission seems to have been included with the accounts for the extensions to the Legislative Building and Parliamentary Library.

26. It is interesting to note that F. L. Wright's tradition is represented in the work of Rattenbury's second son John, a pupil of Wright and now working at Taliesin West; for illustrations of John Rattenbury's architecture, see B.A. Spencer, ed., *The Prairie School Tradition* (New York: Watson-Guptill Publications, 1979), pp. 252–53, 256.

27. The best review of Muthesius's ideas and those of Adolf Loos, within the context of contemporary architecture, is R. Banham, *Theory and Design in the First Machine Age* (New York: Praeger, 1970).

28. The *Contract Record* of 17 January 1912 stated that plans "were being prepared" for a bank to "cost $15,000" of "two storeys, brick." The building first appears in the 1909–11 underwriters' map of Nanaimo; the full set of blueprints, numbered 1–6 and inscribed "Merchants Bank of Canada. F. M. Rattenbury Architect," are preserved at the City Hall, Plan A181: information kindly supplied by J.D. and N.E. Oliver of Insight Consultants and Alison Habkirk of the Nanaimo Planning Department.

29. *The* (later *Canadian) Railway and Marine World*, November 1911, p.1037; the Winnipeg Hotel, or "Fort Garry," was designed at a contract price of $1,500,000 by Ross and MacFarlane of Montreal. The same partnership was awarded the commissions for the G.T.P. hotels, the "Macdonald" in Edmonton and the "Qu'Appelle" in Regina, both at $1,000,000: *The Canadian Railway and Marine World*, October 1913, p. 531.

30. The *Contract Record* 26 (3 January 1912) reported that: "competitive plans will be called for University Building at Point Grey. Owner, Provincial Government; provincial architect, F. M. Rattenbury, Victoria."

31. According to the *Contract Record* 25 (1 November 1911), Rattenbury had recently reported to the Victoria City Council that the G.T.P. had "under consideration the erection of a large hotel," on the condition that they be granted a tax exemption, and that "it is likely that 10 years exemption will be made."

32. There are no references to Rattenbury's work in the G.T.P. records, the Sir Robert Borden papers, the Justice Department records, or the Grand Trunk Arbitration Hearings (all preserved at the Public Archives).

33. *The Canadian Railway and Marine World*, October 1913, p. 513; by that date only 236 miles of track remained to be laid between Prince Rupert and Winnipeg, and construction was underway on the hotels at Winnipeg, Regina, and Edmonton.

34. The drawings are preserved in the Provincial Archives under reference numbers indicated in the following notes and in Appendices B and C.

35. The Provincial Archives have a pencil sketch on tracing paper closely corresponding to the published perspective, R.P. (8)13. A precedent for the angled form of the wings existed in such American hotels as the El Tovar,

Grand Canyon, Arizona, built twelve years earlier in 1901; J. Limerick, N. Ferguson and R. Oliver, *America's Grand Resort Hotels* (New York: Pantheon Books, 1979), p. 129. For contemporary hotel design, especially in Britain, see also P. Boniface, *Hotels & Restaurants 1830 to the Present Day* (London: Royal Commission on Historical Monuments, 1981).

36. The drawings, inscribed "Mount Robson Hotel Design B" and dated 2 May 1913, indicate that Rattenbury developed and then dropped a scheme in which all the accommodation was compressed into a massive Château-style building having an "L" plan. The pitched roof turrets and oriels inflate the motifs of the hotel as published in the *Contract Record*. It was to be on a larger scale than the Empress, though less symmetrical.

37. Since the Prince Rupert hotel did not progress beyond the digging of the foundation trenches, it is not clear what, if any, fees Rattenbury would have received. It is possible that a dispute over unpaid fees might have led to threatened or actual legal proceedings, implied by the reference to a "Rattenbury vs GTP" file (apparently lost) in the company records for the hotel (Public Archives of Canada, RG30, vol. 3431, G.T.P. 2748).

38. The November 1913 issue of *The Canadian Railway and Marine World*, p. 531, reported that the "excavation for a large hotel at the terminal at Prince Rupert was recently completed." Apart from the working drawings referred to in the Appendix, the Maps Division of the P.A.B.C., files E and F, has two undated specifications for the hotel, respectively headed "General Buildings Specifications" and "Specification. Power, Heating & Ventilating," and also a general specification, including a list of materials and the respective responsibilities of the architect and contractors.

39. Olmsted's plan was illustrated in the 1913 *Year Book* of the B.C. Society of Architects. A useful summary of the development appears in Segger, *Victoria*, pp.309-11; only nine plots had been sold by 1914, and forty by 1930. See also Gregson, *Victoria*, pp.202-3, stating that the development was financed by the Credit Foncier Company; Gregson also notes that the 1912-13 land boom was spurred partly by the anticipated opening of the Panama Canal, scheduled for 1914 (pp. 189-90 and 208-9).

40. *Colonist*, 14 January 1913.

41. Ibid., 8 August 1905.

42. Howay and Scholefield, 3:548.

43. Blueprints for the house as built, signed by Maclure and Lort, dated July 1919, remain in the Oak Bay Municipal Hall.

44. P.A.B.C., R.P. (7) 2 sheets 1-13, some dated February 1914, R.P. (9) 2B, and R.P. (7) 16 sheets 1-17.

45. Manufactured by the Snead Company Ironworks, Toronto, who received a blueprint dated 20 May 1913. The Provincial Archives also has three sheets of plans for the stacks, of which one is inscribed "Library Bureau, 146 Franklin Street, Boston, Mass.," R.P. (8) 16.

46. To the left of the corridor is a staircase and to its right offices for the staff.

The latter are duplicated on the third floor, where the three arms formerly contained, from east to west, the parliamentary archives, the northwest Canadiana section, and a map and exhibition room. These spaces are lit by windows framed on the exterior by coupled columns. The natural lighting is supplemented by an electrical system originally installed, as other blueprints indicate, by the local firm of H. C. Moss.

47. There is little remaining documentary material in the Provincial Archives on the actual building of the library, except G.R. 54, box 39, a specification for the library furniture, dated 1914.

48. The proposed order of ceremony is set out in a letter from Scholefield to the premier, Richard McBride, dated 10 July 1914. An exhibition of fine arts and rare books was to have been arranged for Princess Patricia, the duke's popular daughter: P.A.B.C., G.R.726, box 1.

49. P.A.B.C., G.R. 726, box 1, Scholefield to McBride, 11 November 1914, with the revised contents for furnishings representing a reduction of about $5,000; fortunately the main structural contracts, having already been signed, could not be cut.

50. Public Accounts, 1911–15, *B.C.S.P.*; $500,000 was spent on the library.

51. *Victoria Times.* 11 May 1916.

NOTES TO CHAPTER EIGHT

1. C.L. Flick, *"Just What Happened:" A Diary of the Mobilization of the Canadian Militia* (London: Chiswick Press, 1917), cited by Ormsby, *British Columbia*, p. 521.

2. Probably as a result of his father's overindulgence, Frank had developed into an unruly adolescent. In 1910 Rattenbury was obliged to find a private tutor for him, and reported to his mother on 16 November that he had engaged "an Oxford man, young, and, I should think, a born teacher." Less than two months later, however, the young Oxford man had diplomatically informed him that he had "obtained a good position" and asked to be discharged. Frank was then sent to a private school in England to receive the discipline that his father had failed to instill. Keith Miller Jones recalled that Frank caused something of a scandal in his English school by turning up for class wearing a real gun.

3. This letter to Florrie is part of a collection of material relating to Rattenbury formerly in the possession of his daughter Mary and recently handed on to the Victoria City Archives. It has not yet been catalogued but was made available through the kindness of the city archivist, Ainslie Helmcken. A number of the letters from the collection are referred to in this chapter, namely: all those written from Rattenbury to Mary, written by or to Florrie, written by Wood and Wilmot (of Rattenbury lands). The letter written to Rattenbury from his mother, alluded to in chapter 7, n.1, comes from the same source.

4. These impressions of Florrie were conveyed by Ainslie Helmcken, who adds that she had great difficulty in gaining acceptance by Oak Bay society.

5. Rattenbury is usually depicted as an excessive drinker in his later years. Compton Pakenham, his stepson, has pointed out, however, that although Rattenbury was fond of drink, his consumption was not excessive and he was rarely, if ever, drunk.

6. For example, he wrote to L. W. Shiebel of the Nebraska National Bank on 19 June 1917 and to F. J. Lange of Saskatchewan on 6 November 1917. These letters are held by the P.A.B.C. (see n.8).

7. *Colonist*, 28 April 1917.

8. A considerable body of correspondence relating to the dealings of the Land Settlement Board with Rattenbury appears in the files of the board, now deposited with the P.A.B.C. (G.R. 929, vol. 13, folder 12).

9. This claim was made by Rattenbury in his later court case; it was denied by the government.

10. The newspaper clippings are held in the Land Settlement Board File (n.8) and can be dated approximately by a covering letter of 23 December 1918.

11. Rattenbury seems to have disposed of at least one of his pieces of property to the board during this year. The list of 11 June 1919 includes "Lot 788, Rge.5 C.D. 160 acres, app. val. $5.00 acre." This was sold to the board on 28 October 1919.

12. While the main office of Rattenbury Lands was situated in Telkwa, the company also maintained a branch office in the Metropolitan Building, Vancouver. The records of the company have been transferred from the Office of the Registrar of Companies and are now stored on microfilm at the Provincial Archives, ref: 3948.

13. These agencies are known from the letterhead on his business notepaper. In all, as advertisements in the contemporary press indicate, Rattenbury Lands could offer over two million acres for sale.

14. Rattenbury advised Mary to stick to her lessons, not to go to dances or parties, and to avoid being lightheaded and frivolous.

15. *Province*, 21 April 1942, p. 8.

16. For the history of iron and glass design in the nineteenth century and its influence upon mainstream architecture, see Hitchcock, *Architecture*, chapter 7, and with specific reference to the Crystal Garden, see Segger, *Crystal Gardens*, pp. 101–7.

17. 8 August 1905, in an interview on his return from England. Rattenbury was referring to "Lunar Park" and "Dreamland," opened respectively in 1903 and 1904; illustrated, pls. 344–46 in R. Whitehouse, *New York. Sunshine and Shadow* (New York: Harper and Row, 1974).

18. P.A.B.C. Add. MSS. 502 (James), 8/16. Rattenbury also enclosed a bill for his drawings, amounting to $2,306.

19. R.P. (7) A-C, each headed, "Proposed Amusement Centre, Victoria," although B adds the phrase "Winter Garden."

20. Noted in *Crystal Gardens*, p. 77.

21. James's career is reviewed by A. Kerr in *Crystal Gardens*, pp. 79–89.

22. P.A.B.C., Add. MSS. 502 (James), 8/20.

23. Ibid., 8/18.

24. Ibid., respectively 8/16 and 8/15 (sketches).

25. That the final break between Rattenbury and Florrie came in this period is indicated in a letter written by Kate to Florrie on 13 December 1922, expressing sadness at what had happened. While the collapse of Rattenbury Lands was caused mainly by global economic factors and by government action, the efficiency of the company cannot have been helped by the constant internal friction between Wood, as general manager, and Wilmot, as secretary. They seemed to have nursed a hatred for one another, revealed in their correspondence to Rattenbury. Wilmot, in a subordinate and more vulnerable position, was particularly malicious and tried to damage Wood's reputation by recounting his sexual escapades.

26. This reconstruction is based on a letter written to Rattenbury from London by his old friend (and participant in the Cary Castle "Certificate of Character" dinner) Cuyler Holland, on 6 December 1923. "O yes, tell me about your love affair," Holland requested. "I heard something about it a year or so ago—and now I hear that she is coming to England." It is tempting to assume that Holland was referring to Alma, Rattenbury's second wife. But Holland implied that the affair had been going on since at least 1922. This seems to rule out Alma whom, according to Rattenbury's 10 December 1923 letter to Kate, he had met only immediately prior to his writing. That Alma had but recently arrived in the city at that date is suggested by the report of a concert that appeared in the *Colonist* of 6 December 1923. The report notes that she "was a stranger to the majority of the audience" when she first came on the platform.

27. Rattenbury was pleased also to be able to report on a great improvement in his health and that he had played 36 holes of golf the previous week without any fatigue.

28. Rattenbury prefaced the description of the first meeting with his second wife with the thought: "The funny thing is that whilst I have had very little to do with women in my lifetime, the whole blessed lot, married and single, from 25 years old up, made a chum of me, and it is jolly nice whenever I go out to have them all making themselves as agreeable and pleasant and even affectionate as they possibly can, paying *me* compliments." According to family tradition, their first meeting was engineered by Alma's mother and aunt, Florence Criddle. Florence was married to Percy Criddle, a Victoria merchant and member of the Union Club, who would have known of Rattenbury's marital problems and consequent loneliness. In interviews with the popular press in 1935, Frank Titterton, the well-known singer who became a close friend of Alma in England, created the impression that her first meeting with Rattenbury followed the dinner held on 29 December 1923 to celebrate the passing of the by-law necessary for the building of the Crystal Garden.

29. Information on the early history of the Wolff family was kindly provided by
    Bert Harbottle and Betty Brown, descendants of Ernest and Elizabeth
    Wolff. Material on the Wolffs' contribution to the musical life of Victoria
    was generously made available to the authors by Professor R. Dale
    McIntosh of the University of Victoria from the research conducted for his
    forthcoming book on the history of music in British Columbia.

30. The Department of Vital Statistics, Victoria, has been unable to trace any
    record of Alma's birth. Her death certificate states that when she died in 1935
    she was 38. However, her first son, Compton Pakenham recalls that in about
    1935 his mother was distressed because she had passed her fortieth birthday.
    Victoria is entered as her birthplace on the birth certificate of her second son
    John. The problem of the absence of birth records is compounded by a fam-
    ily tradition that W. W. Clarke was her stepfather and that her natural
    father was a prospector who disappeared in the north.

31. Alma's father, W. W. Clarke, is described by the family as a shy, retiring in-
    dividual, who stayed in the background. Her mother, on the other hand,
    was a noted eccentric. She dyed her hair red and filled her house with stuffed
    animals. She was no doubt instrumental in arranging the interview with
    Alma recorded in *Westward Ho* (later *Beautiful British Columbia*) 6 (1910):
    87–90.

32. Raymond Massey, *When I Was Young* (Toronto: McClelland and Stewart,
    1976), pp. 20–22 (confirmed in correspondence), states that Alma attended
    Havergal College, Toronto, at the same time as he did, that is, in 1902.
    Unfortunately, *Ludemus*, the school yearbook, has no record of her atten-
    dance.

33. Information kindly supplied by Harry Dolling, who lives in retirement in
    County Down, Northern Ireland.

34. Articles published in the British and Canadian press during 1935 stated that
    she was decorated for her services in France. The records of the Scottish
    Women's Hospital Organization indicate that an orderly in Alma's unit, "a
    superb piano player," received the Croix de Guerre. Compton Pakenham
    has confirmed that the Croix de Guerre was awarded to his mother.

35. R.P.(7) 5–14, dated 1923; the Archives have a blueprint of the terminal dated
    July 1924, drawn by James (R.P.[7]) and blueprints of the second and third
    floors with minor alterations signed by both men and dated July 1928.

36. P.A.B.C., Add. MSS. 502 (James), 8/20.

37. Ibid., 8/7.

38. The completion date is confirmed by a letter of 21 July 1924, listing "things to
    be done," after consultation with Rattenbury (ibid., 7/9). His membership in
    the Institute is recorded in the *Journal of the Royal Architectural Institute of
    Canada* for 1925, p. 114; 1926, p. 130; 1927, p. 105; 1928, p. 114; 1929, p. 124; 1930,
    p. 118; however, he was not listed under "Architects" in Henderson's *B.C.
    Directory*.

39. A detailed account of the history of the structure is provided by C. Smyly,
    Crystal Gardens, pp. 15–39.

40. See Kerr, *Crystal Gardens*, p. 85.

41. P.A.B.C., Add. MSS. 502 (James), 8/17.

42. Ibid., 8/20.

43. Gardom's letters are included in the above reference.

44. Kerr, *Crystal Gardens*, p. 89, has so argued.

45. Quoted in ibid., p. 19.

46. By Pierre Berton, ibid., p. 11.

47. The absence of records in British Columbia suggests that they may have sought to avoid public notice by marrying discreetly in the U.S.

48. The Victoria City Archives collection contains a contract of an offer from Florrie to purchase the lot at $1,200; until the house was completed, Florrie lived with her children at 1472 Fort Street.

49. As a letter in the Victoria City Archives collection shows, Mary omitted to pay the organist the customary $5.00 for playing at the funeral.

50. Another example of Rattenbury's enthusiasm leading to self-delusion: Alma's son was in line for the Earldom of Longford, but as *Burke's Peerage* shows, his claim was very remote.

51. The sheet is endorsed, in Mary's handwriting, "My father's letter to me. Alma's influence I would think."

52. On 19 September 1927, M.G. Garat, registrar of companies, gave notice that Rattenbury Lands was to be wound up; it was finally struck off the register and dissolved on 25 October 1928.

53. B. C. Palmer, "Development of Domestic Architecture in British Columbia," pp. 405 ff.

54. Compton Pakenham recalls the Campanile project. He believes that it was to be built for the C.N.R. and was to stand in Douglas Gardens. He notes that the company was very anxious that the scheme be kept secret to prevent the escalation of land prices, but that Rattenbury could not resist inviting friends and neighbours (including the postman) to view his plans, which caused him to be severely reprimanded by his client.

55. This development is reviewed in Hitchcock, *Architecture*, pp. 483–84. The issues of the *Journal of the Royal Architectural Institute of Canada* from 1927 illustrate the major Canadian examples, including Ross and Macdonald's Royal York Hotel, Toronto (June 1928, coloured rendering), dominated by a central tower block. The finest expression of the taste in western Canada was McCarter and Nairne's Art Deco styled Vancouver Marine Building, begun in 1924.

56. 6 (1929), p. 382.

57. Rattenbury's holdings in B.C. were valued at $31,275 in 1935 (*Colonist*, 18 July 1935). After Rattenbury's death, his estate, in accordance with his wishes, was placed in trust for his son John and stepson Compton.

NOTES TO CHAPTER NINE

1. $17,500 was realized from the sale of Iechinihl; $28,500 represented the residue of his other assets after the demands of heavy legal expenses following his death. His estate was divided equally between John and Christopher; his will was contested by Frank and Mary, who received $125 and $25 a month for one year from the assets remaining in British Columbia.

2. This and the following remarks of Alma are taken from the transcript of her trial.

3. For instance, on Saturday, 29 April 1933 at 7 P.M. Sidney Baynes and his orchestra played his arrangement of a number of her pieces. Source: B.B.C. Archives.

4. Characteristically, Alma thought of her children even during this trip with Stoner. Compton possesses a letter written to him by his mother on the notepaper of the "Royal Palace Hotel, Kensington," in an envelope postmarked 22 March 1935. Alma mentioned stories that she had written for him and had enclosed with the letter.

5. Information on Stoner's motive for the murder was kindly supplied by Mrs. Daphne Kingham (sister of Thomas Compton Pakenham), who learned it from Alma during a prison visit before the trial.

6. For the trial, see *inter alios,* Michael Havers, Peter Shankland, and Anthony Barrett, *Tragedy in Three Voices: The Rattenbury Murder* (London: William Kimber, 1980); F. Tennyson Jesse, *Trial of Alma Victoria Rattenbury and George Percy Stoner* (London and Edinburgh: William Hodge & Co., 1935); E. M. Lustgarten, *The Woman in the Case* (London: A. Deutsch, 1955); Reksten, pp. 141ff

7. Alma's thoughts on her last day are revealed in a series of notes that she scribbled just before her death.

BIBLIOGRAPHY

Bibliography of Works on the Career of F. M. Rattenbury

In the text these works are referred to only by the author's name and, if necessary, an appropriate abbreviation of the title.

Barrett, A.A. "The F. M. Rattenbury Letters." *Manuscripts* 33 (1981): 5–9.

Berton, P., et al. *The Crystal Gardens*. Victoria: Crystal Gardens Preservations Committee, 1977.

Cotton, P. "The Stately Capitol." *Journal of the Royal Architectural Institute of Canada* 35 (1958): 116–18.

————. *Vice-Regal Mansions of British Columbia*. Victoria: Elgin Publications, 1981.

Howay, F.W., and E. O. S. Scholefield. *British Columbia from the Earliest Times to the Present*. Vancouver: S. J. Clarke, 1914. Esp. vol. 3, pp. 705–7.

Kalman, H. *Exploring Vancouver*. 2d ed. Vancouver: University of British Columbia Press, 1978.

Liscombe, R.W., and A. A. Barrett. "Two Drawings by F. M. Rattenbury." *RACAR* 6 (1980): 113–15.

Pethick, D. *Men of British Columbia*. Saanichton, B.C.: Hancock House, 1975. pp. 157–61.

[Rattenbury, F.M.]. "Grand Trunk Pacific Hotel Development in the West." *Contract Record*, 30 July 1913.

Reksten, T. *Rattenbury*. Victoria: Sono Nis, 1978.

Segger, M. "The Architecture of Samuel Maclure and Francis Mawson Rattenbury. In Search of Appropriate Form." *Canadian Collector* 11 (1976): 51–55.

————. *Victoria. A Primer for Regional History in Architecture*. New York: Watkins Glen, 1979.

————, ed. *The British Columbia Parliament Buildings*. Vancouver: Associated Resource Consultants, 1979.

Select bibliography of other works cited in the text.

Adney, T. *The Klondike Stampede of 1897–1898.* New York and London: Harper, 1900.

Banham, R. *Theory and Design in the First Machine Age.* New York: Praeger, 1970.

Black, R. "Mackenzie and Mann—Builders of a Transcontinental Railway." *Contract Record* 27 (1912): 58–60.

Blaikie, W.G. *Summer Suns in the Far West.* London and New York: T. Nelson, 1890.

Bodnar, D. "The Prairie Legislative Assemblies." M.A. Thesis, University of British Columbia, 1973.

Bogdanski, D. "The Restoration of British Columbia's Parliament Buildings." *Canadian Collector* 2 (1976): 56–58.

Boniface, P. *Hotels and Restaurants 1830 to the Present Day.* London: Royal Commission on Historical Monuments, 1981.

Bridges, W.B. *Some Account of the Barony and Town of Okehampton.* Rev. and enl. by W. H. K. Wright. Tiverton, 1889.

Brown, R.C., and R. Cook. *Canada 1896–1921. A Nation Transformed.* Toronto: McClelland and Stewart, 1974.

Cameron, C., and J. Wright. *Second Empire Style in Canadian Architecture.* Ottawa: Parks Canada, 1980.

Crawford, L.B., and J. G. Sutherland. "The Empress Hotel, Victoria. Sixty-five Years of Foundation Settlements." *Canadian Geotechnical Journal* 8 (1971): 77–93.

Crook, J.M. *Victorian Architecture: A Visual Anthology.* London: Johnson Reprint Co., 1971.

Davey, P. *Arts and Crafts Architecture. The Search for Earthly Paradise.* London: Architectural Press, 1980.

Davidson, J.W. "The Canadian Northern Railway." *Queen's Quarterly* 14 (1906): 197ff.

Dellheim, C. *The Face of the Past. The Preservation of the Medieval Inheritance in Victorian England.* Cambridge: Cambridge University Press, 1982.

Drexler, A., et al. *The Architecture of the Ecole des Beaux-Arts.* New York: Museum of Modern Art, 1978.

Eaton, L.K. *The Architecture of Samuel Maclure.* Victoria: The Art Gallery of Greater Victoria, 1971.

Flick, C.L. *"Just What Happened": A Diary of the Mobilization of the Canadian Militia.* London: Chiswick Press, 1917.

Freeman, J.D. "The Other Victoria." *RACAR* 1 (1974): 37–46.

Gibbon, J.M. *Steel of Empire.* Toronto: McClelland and Stewart, 1935.

Girouard, M. *Sweetness and Light: The Queen Anne Movement, 1860–1900*. Oxford: Oxford University Press, 1977.

Graves, A. *The Royal Academy of Arts. A Complete Dictionary of Contributors*. London: S.R. Publishers, vol. 3, reprint 1970.

Gregson, H. *A History of Victoria 1842–1970*. Victoria: Observer Publishing Co., 1970.

Hamilton, W.R. *The Yukon Story*. Vancouver: Mitchell Press, 1964.

Here Today. San Francisco's Architectural Heritage. 8th ed. San Francisco: Chronicle Books, 1975.

Havers, M., et al. *Tragedy in Three Voices: The Rattenbury Murder*. London: William Kimber, 1980.

Hitchcock, H.R. *The Architecture of H. H. Richardson. His Times*. Hamden, CN: Archon Books, 1961.

———. *Architecture. Nineteenth and Twentieth Centuries*. 4th ed. Harmondsworth: Penguin, 1977.

———, and W. R. Seale. *Temples of Democracy*. New York: Harcourt Brace Jovanovich, 1976.

Holloway, G. *The Empress of Victoria*. 2d ed. Victoria: Empress Publications, 1976.

Jesse, F. Tennyson. *Trial of Alma Victoria Rattenbury and George Percy Stoner*. London and Edinburgh: William Hodge, 1935.

Kalman, H. *The Railway Hotels and the Development of the Château Style in Canada*. Victoria: University of Victoria, 1968.

———, and D. Richardson. "Building for Transportation in the Nineteenth Century." *Journal of Canadian Art History* 3 (1976).

Kloppenborg, A., ed. *Vancouver's First Century*. Vancouver: J. J. Douglas, 1977.

Lamb, W.K. *History of the Canadian Pacific Railway*. New York: Macmillan, 1977.

Lavallee, O. *Van Horne's Road*. Montreal: Railfare Enterprises, 1974.

Limerick, J., N. Ferguson and R. Oliver. *America's Grand Resort Hotels*. New York: Pantheon Books, 1979.

Linstrum, D. *West Yorkshire. Architects and Architecture*. London: Lund Humphries, 1978.

Lomas, M. "Western Canada's Musical Prodigy." *Westward Ho!* 6 (1910): 87–90.

Lustgarten, E.M. *The Woman in the Case*. London: A. Deutsch, 1955.

Macbeth, M. *Glacier. British Columbia. Canadian Pacific Rockies*. C.P.R. pamphlet [1922].

McLaughlin, M.J. "The Competitive Design at Ottawa." *Canadian Architect and Builder* 20 (1907): 210–11.

McNaught, K. *The Pelican History of Canada*. Rev. ed. Harmondsworth: Penguin, 1975.

Malden, C. *Lighted Journey.* Vancouver: B.C. Electric Co., 1948.

Massey, R. *When I Was Young.* Toronto: McClelland and Stewart, 1976.

Maxwell, E. and W.S. "Legislative Buildings, Regina, Sask." *Canadian Architect and Builder* 21 (1908): 11–14.

Mazer, L.D., and M. Segger. *City of Victoria Central Area Conservation Report.* Victoria: Heritage Advisory Committee, 1975.

Mills, E. "The Early Courthouses of British Columbia." Parks Canada Ms. Report no. 2881 (Ottawa 1977).

Morgan, E.E.P., and H.F. Woods. *God's Loaded Dice – Alaska 1897–1930.* Caldwell, ID: Caxton, 1948.

Morrow, E.J. *"Calgary, Many Years Hence": The Mawson Report in Perspective.* Calgary: University of Calgary Press, 1979.

Nobbs, P.E. "Architecture in Canada." *Journal of the Royal Architectural Institute of Canada* 1 (1924): 91–95.

Nelson: A Proposal for Urban Heritage Conservation. Victoria, B.C. Heritage Conservations Report, 1980.

O'Gorman, J. *H. H. Richardson and His Office.* Cambridge, MA: Harvard University Press, 1974.

Ormsby, M. *British Columbia: A History.* Toronto: Macmillan, 1958.

Palmer, B.C. "Development of Domestic Architecture in British Columbia." *Journal of the Royal Architectural Institute of Canada* 5 (1928): 405–16.

Paterson, T. *British Columbia: The Pioneer Years.* Langley, B.C.: Stagecoach Press, 1977.

Petit, V. *Châteaux de la vallée de la Loire.* Paris: C. Boivin, 1861.

Pethick, D. *British Columbia Disasters.* Langley, B.C.: Stagecoach Press, 1979.

Pevsner, N., and L. Harris. *Lincolnshire.* Harmondsworth: Penguin, 1974.

Pevsner, N., and E. R. Radcliffe. *The Buildings of England. Yorkshire. The West Riding.* 2d ed. Harmondsworth: Penguin, 1967.

Prominent Men of Canada. Montreal: National Publishing Co., 1931–32.

Physyck, J. *Marble Halls.* London: H.M.S.O., 1978.

Putnam, W.L. *The Great Glacier and Its House.* New York: American Alpine Club, 1982.

Rattenbury, H.B. *China-Burma Vagabond.* London: G. G. Harrap, 1946.

Rattenbury, H.O., ed. *The John Rattenbury Memorials.* London: T. Woolmer, 1884.

Rattenbury, J. *Memoirs of a Smuggler.* Newcastle upon Tyne: Frank Graham, 2d reprint ed., 1967.

Robinson, A.H. "Lockwood and Mawson. The Story of a Great Partnership." *Bradford Bystander,* November 1971.

Robinson, B. *Banff Springs. The Story of a Hotel.* Banff: Summerthought, 1973.

Rogatnick, A. "Canadian Castles. Phenomenon of the Railway Hotel." *Architectural Review* 141 (1967): 365–72.

Roth, L. "McKim, Mead and White Reappraised." *A Monograph of the Works of McKim, Mead and White, 1879–1915*. New York: Arno Press, reprint 1977.

Roy, P.E. *Vancouver. An Illustrated History*. Toronto: National Museum of Man, 1980.

Saint, A. *Richard Norman Shaw*. London and New Haven: Yale University Press, 1976.

Savory, G.N. *Colonial Business Initiatives and the Pacific Cable: A Study in the Role of Private Enterprise in the Development of Imperial Communications*. M.A. Thesis, University of Washington, 1972.

Scully, V. *The Stick and Shingle Style*. New Haven: Yale University Press, 1974.

Segger, M. "Variety and Decorum. Style and Form in the Work of Samuel Maclure 1869–1920." *Bulletin of the Society for the Study of Architecture in Canada* 7 (1981): 4–12.

Service, A. *Edwardian Architecture and Its Origins*. London: Architectural Press, 1975.

Shapiro, B. "The Three Block Project – Classicism and Modernism Combined." *Trace* 15 (1981): 10–18.

Shopsin, W.C., and M.G. Broderick. *The Villard Houses*. New York: Viking Press, 1980.

Smith, P.L. *Come Give a Cheer*. Victoria: Victoria High School Centennial Celebrations Committee, 1976.

Spencer, B.A., ed. *The Prairie School Tradition*. New York: Whitney Library of Design, 1979.

Stacey, C.P. *Quebec 1759*. 2d ed. London: Pan Books, 1973.

Steele, S. *Forty Years in Canada*. Toronto: McGraw Hill-Ryerson, reprint, 1972.

Stevens, G.R. *History of the Canadian National Railways*. New York: Macmillan, 1973.

Talbot, F.A. "The Future of New British Columbia." *United Empire* 2 (1911): 602–12.

Taylor, G.W. *Builders of British Columbia. An Industrial History*. Victoria: Morriss Publishing, 1982.

Todd, R.B. "The Organization of Professional Theatre in Vancouver, 1886–1914." *BC Studies* 44 (1979–80): 3-20.

Wagg, S. *Percy Erskine Nobbs*. Montreal: McCord Museum, McGill-Queen's University Press, 1980.

Watt, R. "Henry Bloomfield and Sons." *Heritage West* 6 (1982): 28–29.

Whitehouse, R. *New York. Sunshine and Shadow*. New York: Harper and Row, 1974.

Woods, G.F. *God's Loaded Dice – Alaska 1897–1930*. Caldwell, ID: Caxton, 1948.

PHOTOGRAPHIC CREDITS

The Architectural Review: 3.3; The Bank of Montreal: 3.6–7; A.A. Barrett: 1.2, 2.15, 2.25, 4.1, 6.1, 6.16, 9.1; J. Barrett: 4.7, 8.14–15; Mr. & Mrs. B. Bowes: 6.19A–B; Bradford Metropolitan Libraries: 1.4; *The British Architect:* 1.11–12; B.C.Hydro: 2.26, 5.28; *The Builder:* 2.13–14; *Building News:* 1.9; *Canadian Architect and Builder:* 2.1–2, 2.6, 5.23A; C.P.R. Archives: intro. 3, 2.4, 4.4, 5.1–3, 5.5–8, 5.10, 5.20; C.P.R. Hotels: 5.14, 5.16–18; G. Castle: 5.24; *Colonist* 5.11, 6.26; *Contract Record:* 6.24–25, 7.12–14; K. Gibson: 1.5–8, 1.15, 3.11; Glenbow-Alberta Institute: 3.16; Government of B.C., Heritage Conservation Branch: 6.13; Houghton Library: 3.9; Kirklees Metropolitan Council: 1.13; R.W. Liscombe: 2.21–22, 3.10, 5.25, 5.27, 5.29, 6.18, 6.20, 6.22A–B, 7.26, 8.6–7, 8.17–18; Municipality of Oak Bay: 7.16; Nanaimo Heritage Society: 7.10A; Nanaimo Planning Department: 7.10B; National Monuments Record: 2.5B; Provincial Archives of British Columbia: 2.3, 2.7–12, 2.16–20, 2.23–24, 2.27, 3.1–2, 3.4, 3.13–15, 4.5–6, 4.8–12, 4.15, 5.4, 5.9, 5.13, 5.19, 5.21, 5.22, 5.23B, 5.26, 6.3–12, 6.14, 6.15, 6.17A–B, 6.21, 7.2–9, 7.11, 7.15, 7.17–25, 7.27–29, 8.1–3, 8.8–11, 8.13, App.C 1–33. *Province:* 4.2; The Queen's Printer: 5.15; *The Railway and Shipping World:* 4.13; F.B. Rattenbury: 1.16; J. Rattenbury: 1.3, 8.4–5, 8.16, 8.19–20, 9.2–3; Rhode Island Historical Society: 6.35; The Saskatchewan Archives Board: 6.27–34, 6.36; Vancouver City Archives: intro. 2, 1.14, 4.3, 4.14, 6.2; Vancouver Public Library: 3.8; M. van Rensselaer: 1.10; Victoria and Albert Museum: 2.5A; Victoria City Archives: intro. 1, 3.12, 5.12, 5.30, 7.1; *Victoria Times:* 8.12; *The Wave:* 3.5.

INDEX

Buildings are indexed according to location; **bold type** indicates a Ratten-bury commission (not necessarily executed) or attribution. Figures in brackets refer to illustrations.